INTERNATIONAL BUSINESS 96/97

Fifth Edition

Editor

Dr. Fred Maidment
Park College

Dr. Fred Maidment is associate professor and department chair of the Department of Business Education at Park College. He received his bachelor's degree from New York University in 1970 and his master's degree from Bernard M. Baruch College of the City University of New York. In 1983 he received his doctorate from the University of South Carolina. His research interests include training and development in industry. He resides in Kansas City, Missouri, with his wife and children.

A Library of Information from the Public Press

Cover illustration by Mike Eagle

Distributed in the United States by Richard D. Irwin, Publishers

Dushkin Publishing Group/
Brown & Benchmark Publishers
Sluice Dock, Guilford, Connecticut 06437

The Annual Editions Series

Annual Editions is a series of over 65 volumes designed to provide the reader with convenient, low-cost access to a wide range of current, carefully selected articles from some of the most important magazines, newspapers, and journals published today. Annual Editions are updated on an annual basis through a continuous monitoring of over 300 periodical sources. All Annual Editions have a number of features designed to make them particularly useful, including topic guides, annotated tables of contents, unit overviews, and indexes. For the teacher using Annual Editions in the classroom, an Instructor's Resource Guide with test questions is available for each volume.

Printed on Recycled Paper

VOLUMES AVAILABLE

Abnormal Psychology
Africa
Aging
American Foreign Policy
American Government
American History, Pre-Civil War
American History, Post-Civil War
American Public Policy
Anthropology
Archaeology
Biopsychology
Business Ethics
Child Growth and Development
China
Comparative Politics
Computers in Education
Computers in Society
Criminal Justice
Developing World
Deviant Behavior
Drugs, Society, and Behavior
Dying, Death, and Bereavement
Early Childhood Education
Economics
Educating Exceptional Children
Education
Educational Psychology
Environment
Geography
Global Issues
Health
Human Development
Human Resources
Human Sexuality

India and South Asia
International Business
Japan and the Pacific Rim
Latin America
Life Management
Macroeconomics
Management
Marketing
Marriage and Family
Mass Media
Microeconomics
Middle East and the Islamic World
Multicultural Education
Nutrition
Personal Growth and Behavior
Physical Anthropology
Psychology
Public Administration
Race and Ethnic Relations
Russia, the Eurasian Republics, and
   Central/Eastern Europe
Social Problems
Sociology
State and Local Government
Urban Society
Western Civilization,
   Pre-Reformation
Western Civilization,
   Post-Reformation
Western Europe
World History, Pre-Modern
World History, Modern
World Politics

Cataloging in Publication Data
Main entry under title: Annual Editions: International Business. 1996/97.
     1. International business enterprises—Periodicals. 2. Business—Periodicals. I. Maidment, Fred, *comp*. II. Title: International business.
ISBN 0-697-31088-4   338.88′05

Fifth Edition

Printed in the United States of America

Editors/ Advisory Board

To the Reader

In publishing ANNUAL EDITIONS we recognize the enormous role played by the magazines, newspapers, and journals of the *public press* in providing current, first-rate educational information in a broad spectrum of interest areas. Within the articles, the best scientists, practitioners, researchers, and commentators draw issues into new perspective as accepted theories and viewpoints are called into account by new events, recent discoveries change old facts, and fresh debate breaks out over important controversies.

Many of the articles resulting from this enormous editorial effort are appropriate for students, researchers, and professionals seeking accurate, current material to help bridge the gap between principles and theories and the real world. These articles, however, become more useful for study when those of lasting value are carefully *collected, organized, indexed,* and *reproduced* in a *low-cost format,* which provides easy and permanent access when the material is needed. That is the role played by *Annual Editions.* Under the direction of each volume's *Editor,* who is an expert in the subject area, and with the guidance of an *Advisory Board,* we seek each year to provide in each ANNUAL EDITION a current, well-balanced, carefully selected collection of the best of the public press for your study and enjoyment. We think you'll find this volume useful, and we hope you'll take a moment to let us know what you think.

When the first edition of *Annual Editions: International Business* was being compiled a few years ago, the world was a very unstable place. Power in the then-Soviet Union was very much in question, and there was uncertainty everywhere. The day Boris Yeltsin jumped on a tank outside the Russian Parliament was the day that I was writing the introductory essay for the section that included articles on the Soviet Union. In fact, I was typing part of that essay when the news bulletin reporting Yeltsin's act came over the radio. Needless to say, I had to rewrite the essay.

International business is where the economy of the world is heading. Virtually all countries and all organizations will be engaged in doing business with other organizations outside of their home country. Students of business administration, indeed, all people involved in business, need to be aware of the new international environment; they need to be aware of the opportunities and the problems associated with doing business outside of their home markets; they need to understand that the same type of opportunities await all who engage in business.

Business must respond to this change in the environment by keeping an open mind about the opportunities available to it on a global basis. The articles that have been chosen for *Annual Editions: International Business 96/97* comprise a cross section of the current literature on the subject. The collection addresses the various aspects of international business with emphasis on the foundations of international trade, the environment of international trade, and how corporations respond and deal with this environment. While it is probably impossible to prove in a scientific way, the general tone of the articles seems to be more optimistic than it was a few years ago. This is not to say that all the news is good (because it is not), or that all of the problems have been solved (because they never will be), but there has been a change. The general tone of the literature seems to be more hopeful, more optimistic, and less bleak and foreboding. There is more talk about opportunity and success and less talk about problems and failure. A new era may have begun.

This publication contains a number of features designed to make it useful for people interested in international business. These features include a *topic guide* for locating articles on specific subjects and a *table of contents* with abstracts that summarize each article with key words in bold italics. The volume is organized into four units dealing with specific interrelated topics in international business. Each section begins with an overview that provides the necessary background information to allow the reader to place a selection in the context of the book. Important topics are emphasized, and challenge questions address major themes.

A new era has begun for *Annual Editions: International Business.* The 96/97 edition is completely reorganized and has been designed for greater and more effective use with textbooks that are currently in print in the field. New sections and many new articles have been chosen for *Annual Editions: International Business 96/97,* and I hope that the book will prove to be of even greater use in the future.

We would like to know what you think about our book. Please take a few minutes to complete the article rating form in the back of the volume. Anything can be improved, and we need your help to improve *Annual Editions: International Business.*

Fred Maidment
Editor

Unit 1

The Nature of International Business

Six selections describe the dynamics of today's international business community.

Handwritten: 1-800 376 8515 Psychic

The concepts in bold italics are developed in the article. For further expansion please refer to the Topic Guide and the Index.

Unit 2

The International Environment: Organizations and Monetary Systems

Five articles examine international organizations, the international monetary system, and the finance of international businesses.

Unit 3

Foreign Environment

Sixteen selections discuss how international markets are influenced by the common pressures of financing, the economy, sociocultural dynamics, politics, the legal system, labor relations, and other forces.

The concepts in bold italics are developed in the article. For further expansion please refer to the Topic Guide and the Index.

The concepts in bold italics are developed in the article. For further expansion please refer to the Topic Guide and the Index.

Unit
4

How Management Deals with Environmental Forces

Nineteen articles discuss challenging aspects of managing in the international business community.

The concepts in bold italics are developed in the article. For further expansion please refer to the Topic Guide and the Index.

The concepts in bold italics are developed in the article. For further expansion please refer to the Topic Guide and the Index.

Topic Guide

This topic guide suggests how the selections in this book relate to topics of traditional concern to students and professionals involved with international business. It can be very useful in locating articles that relate to each other for reading and research. The guide is arranged alphabetically according to topic. Articles may, of course, treat topics that do not appear in the topic guide. In turn, entries in the topic guide do not necessarily constitute a comprehensive listing of all the contents of each selection.

TOPIC AREA	TREATED IN:	TOPIC AREA	TREATED IN:
Communications	2. Challenge Grows Thornier 10. Global Financial Markets 16. Asian Infrastructure 17. India 19. Cultural Awareness 22. Group of 7 26. Harmonization of Standards 31. Planning for International Trade Show Participation 32. Forming International Sales Pacts 38. Timberland's New Spin on Global Logistics 44. Transnational Management Systems	European Union (cont'd)	32. Forming International Sales Pacts 40. Global Glance at Work and Family 41. Lessons from HR Overseas 42. Right Way to Go Global 43. Son Also Surprises
Developing Countries	1. Global Growth Is on a Tear 2. Challenge Grows Thornier 3. New Power in Asia 4. Second Thoughts on Going Global 5. Capital and the Division of Production 6. International Trade and Investment 7. From GATT to WTO 8. Hemispheric Prospects 9. Toward Greater International Stability 11. Financing Trade 13. Gradualism and Chinese Financial Reforms 14. Putting Global Logic First 15. Latin America Heats Up 16. Asian Infrastructure 17. India 18. Ethics in the Trenches 19. Cultural Awareness 20. American Involvement 21. Political Risk Analysis 23. What GATT Means 24. High-Tech Jobs 28. New Sexenio 32. Forming International Sales Pacts 33. Export Channel Design 34. Moving Mountains to Market 35. Yes, You *Can* Win 36. Framework for Risk Management 37. Negotiating the Honeyed Knife-Edge 38. Timberland's New Spin on Global Logistics 39. North American Business 40. Global Glance at Work and Family 41. Lessons from HR Overseas 42. Right Way to Go Global 43. Son Also Surprises 46. Off and Running in Vietnam	Finance	1. Global Growth Is on a Tear 3. New Power in Asia 5. Capital and the Division of Production 9. Toward Greater International Stability 10. Global Financial Markets 11. Financing Trade 12. European Monetary Reform 13. Gradualism and Chinese Financial Reforms 14. Putting Global Logic First 15. Latin America Heats Up 16. Asian Infrastructure 18. Ethics in the Trenches 20. American Involvement 21. Political Risk Analysis 23. What GATT Means 27. Industrial Sea Change 28. New Sexenio 34. Moving Mountains to Market 35. Yes, You *Can* Win 36. Framework for Risk Management 37. Negotiating the Honeyed Knife-Edge 42. Right Way to Go Global 44. Transnational Management Systems 46. Off and Running in Vietnam
		Human Rights	4. Second Thoughts on Going Global 5. Capital and the Division of Production 13. Gradualism and Chinese Financial Reforms 14. Putting Global Logic First 17. India 18. Ethics in the Trenches 20. American Involvement 21. Political Risk Analysis 25. Role of Labor 28. New Sexenio 40. Global Glance at Work and Family 41. Lessons from HR Overseas 46. Off and Running in Vietnam
European Union (European Economic Community)	1. Global Growth Is on a Tear 6. International Trade and Investment 7. From GATT to WTO 9. Toward Greater International Stability 10. Global Financial Markets 12. European Monetary Reform 14. Putting Global Logic First 19. Cultural Awareness 22. Group of 7 24. High-Tech Jobs 26. Harmonization of Standards 29. International Market Leaders 30. Global Retailing 2000 31. Planning for International Trade Show Participation	Management	2. Challenge Grows Thornier 4. Second Thoughts on Going Global 5. Capital and the Division of Production 6. International Trade and Investment 7. From GATT to WTO 8. Hemispheric Prospects 14. Putting Global Logic First 15. Latin America Heats Up 16. Asian Infrastructure 17. India 18. Ethics in the Trenches 19. Cultural Awareness 20. American Involvement 22. Group of 7 23. What GATT Means 24. High-Tech Jobs 25. Role of Labor 27. Industrial Sea Change 29. International Market Leaders 32. Forming International Sales Pacts

The Nature of International Business

- Introduction to International Business (Articles 1 and 2)
- International Trade and Foreign Investment (Articles 3 and 4)
- Economic Theories on International Trade, Development, and Investment (Articles 5 and 6)

The world is growing smaller each day. Communication and transportation have made the planet Earth a smaller place for the people that live on it.

Global growth is accelerating, especially in the developing countries of the Pacific Rim, and it is starting to increase in Latin America. In the article "Global Growth Is on a Tear," Louis Richman discusses what this means and why it is important. Industrialized countries, such as the United States, Japan, and Germany, will continue to grow, but at a much slower rate than the emerging "tigers" of the Pacific Rim. China, in particular, with over 1 billion people, is a country with tremendous potential. It is, however, a nation with incredible needs. The infrastructure needs to be built. Railroads, roads, bridges, sewer systems, and electrification are all desperately needed in China, and this is where much of the growth will take place. It will not be easy, and there are risks, especially political risks in China, but the prize is so attractive that many Western organizations will willingly accept those risks.

While international trade continues to grow, it continues to becomes more and more complex. It is a simple equation. The more countries, the more trading blocs, the more people that are involved, the more complicated things become. Rules, such as those associated with the General Agreement on Tariffs and Trade (GATT) and the World Trade Organization (WTO), can be set, but the more rules that exist, the greater the potential for gray areas between those rules. Not only is international trade becoming more complicated, but it is also becoming more competitive. The developing countries of the world are challenging the established countries in a variety of areas. Software is being developed in India; electronics manufacture is leaving Japan and going to other countries in Asia; and textiles, the traditional first step on the road to industrialization, have become major industries in a variety of emerging countries. Indeed, as the second article's title states, "The Challenge Grows Thornier."

When most people think of powerhouse economies in Asia, they tend to think of Japan. However, that may be changing. As with so many things, trying to measure something depends on how and what is counted. For now, Japan may be number one in Asia by most calculations. But is it, really? China is generally rated number two. But when Greater China is calculated, including the mainland, Taiwan, and the Overseas Chinese in places like Hong Kong and Singapore, then, as noted in "The New Power in Asia," Greater China is the leading Asian economic power.

Theories of trade are also changing, and the resources necessary to engage in international trade are reflecting this change. In the past, utilitarians talked about the four factors of production—land, labor, capital, and the entrepreneur, and how each country had certain advantages over other countries in these areas. Today that old analysis does not necessarily work. Transportation and communication have made the relative advantages in the four factors of production less important. In the case of land, or raw materials, the transportation system has made the relative importance of this factor of production less imposing. Japan, for example, has virtually no natural resources, yet few would argue with the success of the Japanese economy.

The entrepreneurial factor can be seen everywhere. It is not just Americans who start new ventures, but Chinese, South Americans, and Europeans. The former Soviet bloc more than demonstrates the ability of even former communists to become entrepreneurs, as do developments in mainland China over the past 10 years. However, these new beehives of entrepreneurial activity may have their problems learning to negotiate the world of business, just as infants have difficulty learning to walk. But eventually, just as a small child, they will be on their feet and running everywhere.

Labor, perhaps the most sedentary of all the factors of production, has even shown signs of movement. Labor has always been willing to move, but historians have tended to view these movements as migrations of peoples, not as the movement of a mundane factor of production. Immigrations from Europe to Australia, South Africa, and North and South America have been made by people seeking a better life for themselves and their families. This same kind of movement goes on today. Australia is still gaining population through immigration; Europe is experiencing waves of new workers from former colonies, whether it is Algerians in France or Indians and Pakistanis in Great Britain; and the United States continues to receive immigrants from all over the world, especially from

Latin America, both legal and illegal. Whatever the reason, these people certainly represent potential labor, at least, and they are all seeking better lives.

Finally, capital, or the means of production, has shown an ability to go global. Ever since the start of the industrial revolution, there have been countries that were "developed," or with the means of production, and countries that were "lesser," or "least" developed (that is to say, generally without the means of production). But that is starting to change. Because of the global transportation and communication system, the location of production facilities is not as important as it once was. In addition, real and potential growth is now to be found in these developing countries. Any organization looking to grow will find it much easier to do so in an economy that is rapidly expanding than in one that is saturated and growing only as fast as the population. Capital and the division of production are global at last and will be even more so in the future.

Looking Ahead: Challenge Questions

The world is growing smaller. How have improvements in transportation and communication affected international trade?

Economies are growing all over the world, but the most rapid growth is in the emerging countries of the Pacific Rim. How would this be important to business people in the strategic planning of their businesses?

How has the mobility of production factors changed the importance of these factors when considering theories of international trade?

GLOBAL GROWTH IS ON A TEAR

Developing economies are driving the expansion. If they're smart, companies in the U.S., Japan, and Europe will climb aboard.

Louis S. Richman

Nearly lost in all the dire headlines—MEXICAN PESO COLLAPSES! ECONOMIC AFTERSHOCKS OF JAPAN QUAKE! U.S.-CHINA TRADE WAR LOOMS!—is 1995's Big Event: the beginnings of a global expansion of breathtaking proportions where developing countries, not the usual elite club of rich nations, head the charge. As the chart shows, the 16 largest such economies will average an estimated 6% annual growth in GDP through 1996, more than double the rate of the mature economies of North America, Japan, and Europe. Says economist Miron Mushkat of Lehman Brothers in Hong Kong: "The developing economies are beginning to assume a leadership role as a driver of global growth."

Even more epochal, this enormous shift is taking place in a post–Cold War world where the players compete in economic contests rather than ideological ones. For mature economies, the big opportunity is in riding these winds of change. By becoming more competitive, they can boost exports, create more jobs for themselves, and assure a prosperous future. The U.S. economic rally, an early arrival at the planetary growth party, could even surpass the record expansion of the 1980s.

Risks abound, of course. International investors are understandably nervous of developing economies, particularly after Mexico. And central bankers dread inflation and have their hand perpetually poised over the lever that hikes interest rates. But for all this, the worldwide boom is likely to prove exceptionally durable. For one thing, previous expansions have seen nations advance—and then tumble—in lock step. This time around, the world's business cycles are more independent of one another. Witness the unilateral timetables that the U.S., Europe, and Japan have followed out of their most recent recessions. Now watch how countries in Asia, East Europe, and Latin America—many of them embracing free markets for the first time—compete as scrappy individuals that can win or lose regardless of other economies.

All this vibrant, self-sustaining growth could keep the more mature economies cooking with increased demand for their products, just as the U.S. benefited from the reconstruction of war-wrecked Europe and Japan in the 1950s and 1960s. But the timing of the 1990s boom catches the traditionally elite waist-deep in sweeping technological and organizational change. The challenge in these countries, says Robert Hormats, vice chairman of Goldman Sachs (International), will be to preserve their competitive edge amid a frenzy unleashed by the worldwide ratcheting up of both supply and demand.

Call it the Restructuring Recovery. New rivals surfacing from every point of the compass are putting heat on manufacturers throughout the U.S., Europe, and Japan to step up investment in their search for efficiencies. In the U.S., for example, gross capital spending on new plant, equipment, and office technologies increased at a near-record rate of 12.5% in 1993 and in 1994. The Organization for Economic Cooperation and Development (OECD), the economic research agency in Paris, forecasts that such investment will continue to increase in 1995 and yet again, for an unprecedented fifth consecutive year, in 1996. In the European Community, capital spending

REPORTER ASSOCIATES *Patty de Llosa and Kimberly Seals McDonald*

LOOK WHOSE GDPs ARE PICKING UP THE MOST SPEED

Percent

Region	Country	1994	1995 proj.	1996 proj.	1996 GDP projections Billions, U.S.
Mature Economies	CANADA	4.3	4.3	2.9	$633
Mature Economies	GERMANY	2.8	3.4	3.7	$2,311
Mature Economies	BRITAIN	3.9	3.1	2.3	$1,150
Mature Economies	U.S.	4.0	2.7	1.8	$7,383
Mature Economies	FRANCE	2.4	3.2	2.9	$1,503
Mature Economies	JAPAN	0.8	3.4	3.9	$5,252
Mature Economies	ITALY	2.5	3.0	2.4	$1,171
Asia	CHINA	11.3	9.9	8.2	$739
Asia	SINGAPORE	10.2	8.6	6.8	$84
Asia	MALAYSIA	8.8	8.5	7.2	$97
Asia	THAILAND	8.1	8.5	6.2	$177
Asia	SOUTH KOREA	7.9	7.4	6.3	$491
Asia	TAIWAN	6.2	6.7	6.2	$287
Asia	INDONESIA	6.3	6.2	5.3	$184
Asia	HONG KONG	5.7	6.0	5.7	$167
Asia	INDIA	4.9	5.0	4.9	$368
Latin America	ARGENTINA	6.3	5.6	6.1	$356
Latin America	CHILE	4.4	5.8	6.2	$58
Latin America	BRAZIL	2.6	4.5	4.6	$949
Latin America	MEXICO	3.2	0.7	2.1	$377
Eastern Europe	POLAND	5.7	6.0	5.8	$100
Eastern Europe	CZECH REPUBLIC	4.3	6.8	6.0	$49
Eastern Europe	HUNGARY	5.1	3.2	5.7	$45

Growth Rates | 1994 | 1995 proj. | 1996 proj. |

FORTUNE CHART / SOURCE:DRI/McGRAW-HILL

will rise some 6% in 1995 and 8% in 1996 as manufacturers try to close a widening competitiveness gap with the U.S. and Japan. The estimated $60 billion repair bill for the Kobe quake is sure to increase Japan's spending over the previously forecast 1.4% in 1995 and 4.1% in 1996.

Soaring investment is already yielding hefty dividends. Flexible automation equipment that improves quality and efficiency in U.S. factories is boosting productivity and helping to fuel profits. Similar benefits are showing up elsewhere. In Germany, for example, labor productivity in manufacturing jumped 7.5% during 1994, while unit labor costs should nudge up this year by a mere 0.1%.

Also paying off bigtime: capital spending for computerized inventory-tracking technology and the just-in-time management techniques it makes possible. Manufacturers around the world are reducing dramatically the costly stockpiling of raw materials and intermediate products. This contrasts with the early phases of past recoveries, when inventory building accounted for as much as half of total GDP growth. In their race to acquire the materials they'd need to fill anticipated orders, producers would bid up prices and thus light the fuse that ignited inflation.

But now that pattern appears to be ending. A recent OECD study has found that inventory accumulation in Germany accounted for about 22% of the total growth that brought the country out of its recession trough last year, compared with some 44% in the recovery of the early 1980s. In Japan's nascent recovery, stock building is adding just over 6% to total growth, vs. 15% in the 1983 upswing. And in the U.S., manufacturers reduced inventories by some 14% in early 1992. This compares with an inventory accumulation that accounted for more than 43% of total growth coming out of the 1982 recession. In the current expansion, these tighter disciplines have partly quelled the war between growth and inflation. Says Woody Brock, who heads the Strategic Economic Decisions consulting firm in Menlo Park, California: "Instead of 2.5% growth and 4% inflation, we're seeing 4% growth and 2.7% inflation."

Continued steady, low-inflation expansion should be all the more sustainable because of the degree to which the global recoveries are out of sync. In the four preceding business cycles, says Victor Zarnowitz, director of the Center for International Business Cycle Research at Columbia University, the economies of all the eight largest industrial nations, including those of the U.S., Germany, and Japan, fell and rose in tandem. But, that lock-step bust-and-boom tradition was shattered in the latest downturn. The U.S. slid into its recession in the summer of 1990. But the economies of Europe and Japan didn't even dip until mid-1992, nearly a year after the U.S. had begun its upswing. The decoupling, says John Lipsky, chief international economist for Salomon Brothers in New York City, should slow the buildup of potential excesses that set off inflation—and that invite central banks to increase interest rates, dousing growth.

An unusual dampener for U.S. inflation last year was its $200 billion trade deficit. Lipsky estimates that this import surplus knocked about half a percentage point off GDP growth, holding it to a less inflationary 4% rate while helping to reignite recoveries abroad among the country's trading partners. Now, as U.S. growth slows and demand for imports cools, the accelerating expansions of Europe and Japan will stimulate demand for American goods.

Meanwhile, the prospect of an extended period of balanced growth in which exports play a more prominent role is giving major cyclical U.S. industries a chance to strut their regained competitiveness. Chemical manufacturers, America's largest exporters, put themselves through a decade of painful downsizing, and the gradual resumption of demand abroad will lift industry profits. Paul Raman, an analyst with the New York investment firm S.G. Warburg, expects that the 20% unit-cost advantage enjoyed by U.S. chemical companies over their European and Japanese competitors should enable the Americans to gain market share.

Raman estimates that U.S. chemical producers will see a 5% increase in net profits for each 1% increase in production volumes. The industry is already looking great. It had an outstanding 1994, when profits jumped between 30% and 40% on a 7% growth in domestic sales. Raman

thinks that an easing of U.S. growth in 1995 and 1996 will be more than offset by the 5% increase in demand he's forecasting from Europe. That, he says, should let chemical manufacturers maintain production capacity through 1996 at a profitably high 90%.

Growing confidence that global growth will extend the life of the current U.S. expansion is encouraging some cycle-sensitive manufacturers to stretch out their planning horizons. Case in point: Detroit's reinvigorated automakers. Steady, moderate growth, points out Chrysler's chief economist W. Van Bussmann, will minimize the dislocations of the industry's typical boom-bust cycle. This will help his company make continued progress in improving product quality while keeping employment high, he says. Ford Motor, flush with near-record profits from buoyant U.S. car and light-truck sales last year, plans to increase capital outlays and new-product development spending by some 20% over the next five years. The company is aiming for heroic leaps in productivity—by more than 100%—as it looks to double export volume from North America by the end of the decade.

THE LIKELIEST KILLER of his global boom is, of course, the usual suspect: interest rate increases, the central bankers' generic cure for inflation. Certainly inflation is an especially sinister felon because it stalks an economy so quietly before striking. The bankers are also aware of inflation's recidivist history, especially now because, with economic growth occurring in every corner of the globe, the pressure to bid up prices for scarce resources is much stronger than in past expansions.

So where do they see inflation threatening? Just about everywhere. Most commodity prices have been moving up at an accelerating rate since the end of 1993; the Commodity Research Bureau's index of spot raw material prices has advanced by nearly 18%. But it could have been worse. Manufacturers have become more sparing in their use of raw materials—they now account for just half a percentage point of GDP—and hot global competition prevents producers from passing on their higher commodity costs to consumers.

Right now potential wage inflation looks like the more serious worry. Though U.S. unemployment edged up to 5.7% in January, it is still below the 6% rate that many, including dyspeptic bond traders, consider compatible with stable inflation. This non-accelerating inflation rate of unemployment (Nairu, as economists call it) has been rising for the past two decades. OECD labor economists say its biggest footprints have been left in Europe, where rigid labor rules and initiative-sapping unemployment benefits have caused the Nairu to soar. It was about 5% in the late 1970s and is some 9% today, the economists say.

Even though U.S. manufacturers are up against their capacity limits, there's still plenty of idle plant around in the decoupled expansions of other countries to hold prices of finished goods in check. Consumer price inflation in Europe, for example, is near a 30-year low, and Brian Mullaney, an economist with Morgan Stanley in London, forecasts that CPI growth in Europe will stay flat at 2.8% through 1995. In Japan, where the strong yen has deflated the cost of most dollar-priced commodities, economist Dick Beason of investment firm James Capel Ltd. in Tokyo estimates that a gradual recovery this year will boost consumer prices just 1%.

Still, central bankers in the mature industrialized economies and in the fast-emerging ones seem determined to err on the side of caution. Says Farid Abolfathi, an international economist at DRI/McGraw-Hill, the economic forecasting firm: "The children of Paul Volcker [the former Fed chairman and renowned inflation warrior] are everywhere. There's an almost perverse competition among them

CANADA'S ENDANGERED BACON

■ What rich irony. Global investors are in a sweat over the potential financial problems of emerging markets in countries where domestic saving rates are high, currency reserves are strong, and government deficits are stable—or even declining—as a percentage of GDP.

The real problem may be lurking in those same investors' back yard if, as is statistically likely, they live in an "advanced" industrial economy where savings are falling, deficits ballooning, and interest rates heading up. The $430 billion increase in public debt in the U.S., Europe, and Japan to $780 billion between 1990 and 1993 clearly dwarfs the $100 billion current account deficits the emerging markets are running.

Europe's governments are counting on the continued strengthening of their economies to help rein in their swollen budget deficits and stabilize debt. But even with moderate growth, most of them find themselves caught in a vise. They are desperate to lower taxes to foster job creation and reduce sky-high unemployment, but they are reluctant to antagonize voters by taking an ax to popular social spending. For example, Sweden's new government, facing one of Europe's highest deficits—it represents 11.2% of GDP—punted until at least 1998 on

making promised spending cuts that would stabilize that social welfare state's debt burden.

The pressure on European interest rates and currencies, warns Columbia University economist Victor Zarnowitz, could bring in an economic slowdown within a year. "Europe's fiscal disorder is very, very destabilizing," he warns. Short-term interest rates in Sweden and other heavily indebted European countries like Italy and Spain are already four percentage points higher than in Germany, and the krona, lira, and peseta all fell sharply in the week following the collapse of the Mexican peso.

Canada is in a similar stew. Its deficit is 6.2% of GDP. (In the U.S., the figure is 2%.) Canada's annual interest payments on federal debt absorb 40% of all government expenditures. Short-term rates have moved up five percentage points in 1994, to 8.2%, but even that hasn't stopped currency speculators from bidding down the Canadian dollar to a near-historic low of 70 cents against the U.S. greenback. Economist Robert Fairholm with DRI in Toronto worries whether the Liberal government will deliver a new budget in February austere enough to save the Canadian bacon. Says he: "If Canada doesn't stabilize its debt, it courts a currency crisis of unprecedented proportions."

Debt as a percent of GDP

FORTUNE CHART / SOURCE: OECD

to be the first to raise rates." Volcker's scions at the Fed, including his successor, current Chairman Alan Greenspan, have led this cautionary pack, hiking short-term U.S. rates seven times in the past year, most recently to 6.5%—or back to where they were in 1991.

Because the slowing effects of rate increases don't show up until six months to a year later, the chances that the Fed's pre-emptive hikes will push the U.S. into a 1995 recession are remote. Even so, a sharp deceleration of U.S. growth, accompanied by rising interest rates in other countries, could stall the global expansion. Countries like Italy, Sweden, and Canada, which operate under enormous debt (see box), look particularly vulnerable.

ALSO HOBBLING global growth, if only temporarily, are the increases in U.S. interest rates, which have narrowed the spread between safe returns domestically and riskier ones overseas, and encourage investors to keep their money close to home. Says David Shulman, chief equity strategist at Salomon Brothers: "The Fed is the world's lawn sprinkler. When U.S. interest rates were low, liquidity spread to the farthest reaches of the global lawn. Now that the Fed is tightening, the capital flowing to the remoter emerging markets is drying up."

Not entirely. Scary as the plunge into Asian and Latin American currencies and bourses may look in the aftermath of Mexico's meltdown, investment in the dynamic growth economies via country funds or particular stocks will likely continue. For one thing, many investors consider the big risk to be more than outweighed by potential gains. Foreign securities still account only for 1.2% of U.S. investors' portfolios despite the fact that they have more than doubled since 1990.

Whatever its immediate problems, even Mexico hardly merits all the hyperventilating one hears. Yes, its mismanaged liquidity problems will reduce the country's short-term growth prospects and will slow demand for U.S. imports. But Christopher Probyn, a DRI economist, estimates that the drop in orders will shave U.S. exports by only 1.5% over the coming two years. After that, he says, Mexico's fundamentally sound long-term economic prospects will begin to reassert themselves.

As for those countries still in the shadow of the clouds sent up by Mexico, Lehman Brothers economist Mushkat sees two silver linings. First, a slower inflow of portfolio capital should prove easier for still immature developing economies to absorb.

Second, Mushkat expects that market regulators in those places will use the cooling of investor ardor to reform their stock and bond exchanges, the better to compete for capital once the passion returns.

Until then, emerging economies will be able to tape their own large reservoirs of domestic savings. Gross saving rates in many countries from Brazil to India exceed 20% of GDP and run as high as 45% in China and Singapore. This puts most of the West to shame. The rate in the U.S., for example, is 12%, and in Britain nearly 13%.

Even as portfolio investors hold back, increasingly open emerging markets should have little problem attracting foreign direct investment (FDI) in everything from pizza restaurants to power stations. Since 1989, worldwide FDI has nearly tripled, to more than $80 billion last year. The lure is irresistible. Among U.S. multinationals, nearly 20% of total pretax profits now come from sales by foreign affiliates. Their profit margins in the dynamic developing economies—9.5%—are more than twice those earned in North America, Europe, or Japan.

Infrastructure spending is the flywheel at the heart of the emerging nation growth engine. By some estimates, investment for power generation, transportation, telecommunications equipment, and the like could add up to $1 trillion by the end of the decade, a potential bonanza for U.S., European, and Japanese manufacturers of capital goods—and a cushion against slower growth in their home markets. This boosted demand is even giving new vitality to some sunset industries. Anticipating weakening domestic sales, for example, restructured U.S. steelmakers are plotting their first significant export push in better than a decade.

BECAUSE infrastructure investments are usually backed by the operating revenues they generate, they are far less vulnerable than portfolio investment to sudden shifts in investor sentiment. Recognizing that this spending helps break through bottlenecks that retard further development, governments of emerging nations are giving these projects top priority. Not surprisingly, foreign companies are eager to seize some of this action. Among them: the Hughes division of General Motors. In late 1994 it was awarded a license by India to install and operate the country's first private earth relay system, transmitting data via satellite for commercial users.

AT&T has reached out and put together a string of like deals. Over the past six years its Network Systems group has created seven joint ventures in China, and it counts Indonesia, Thailand, and the Philippines among its fastest-growing international markets. In January AT&T signed a $150 million contract to provide gateway switches to the telecommunications authority in South China, the first phase of a multiyear, $500 million telephone system upgrade. Richard Brandt, a group vice president, estimates that the project, financed with conventional bank loans, will pay for itself within a year of completion. Brandt expects that the resulting communications improvement will spark additional investment as companies are drawn to the region. Says he: "The multiplier effects are absolutely staggering."

The rate of expansion among the dynamic emerging markets will, of course, eventually slow. In 1995—the Year of the Pig in the lunar calendar, by tradition a year of prosperity—growth will slow in six of 13 Asian economies, including China's, say economists at Jardine Fleming, the Hong Kong bank. But for the foreseeable future, says Keith Ferguson, an economist with Barclays de Zoete Wedd in Hong Kong, probably none of the six will experience the kind of business contractions common in the mature industrial nations. Instead, they will see some rise in unemployment against a backdrop of continued increases in GDP—characteristics of a so-called "growth recession."

This isn't such bad news. Jardine's economists forecast that these "slowing" economies will still be growing, at an average 7.2% a year. We should all celebrate the Year of the Pig with such recessions.

The Challenge Grows Thornier

To compete globally today, business leaders must stand up to calls for protection of narrow self-interests.

Preston Townley

Preston (Pete) Townley is president and CEO of The Conference Board.

n welcoming the attendees to this veritable summit meeting of top executives of the world's leading corporations, I noted that no time was more important for their gathering than the present. Such occasions often call for hyperbole, but I did not feel that I was stretching things in so labeling the present as a challenging time for business leaders.

The 10th convening of the International Industrial Conference (IIC) came at a time of visible achievement for business and broadening acceptance of the market system around the globe. At the same time weak governments—threatened by ever-more-fragmented national, political, and economic interest groups—were stumbling, and international bodies created after World War II to facilitate peace-enhancing prosperity were looking overwhelmed. A dichotomy of great significance to the world's business leaders.

When the IIC convened four years before, the mood was one of optimism about the significant changes under way that most believed augured a bright new world for the business-enterprise system. In the opening plenary in 1989, Peter Drucker sagely forecast the disintegration of the Soviet Union. While few in attendance bought that immediately, there was little doubt that the shift of the world economy to the market system was accelerating. With it the advance of a truly global business environment seemed inexorable. The conference devoted its three days to how corporations worldwide were dealing with that phenomenon. The lessons learned then and expanded in Conference Board research and meetings since remain valid. But the challenge of competing in the global context has gotten thornier and, perhaps, nastier.

The IIC's existence spans five decades of remarkable world growth. The combination of advancing business productivity and retreating trade barriers has resulted in prosperity for the world's people as never before seen in history. And yet it was the clear sense of the attendees at the 1993 IIC that the continuation of this progress was threatened.

From *Across the Board,* January 1994, IIC Supplement, pp. 2-5. © 1994 by the Conference Board, Inc. Reprinted by permission.

This convening of the quadrennial IIC was designed to look at the reality of regionalization within the global framework. The hackneyed phrase, "Think globally, act locally," has always applied, but the driver now is not just more-localized tastes and cultures but the impact of national/political fragmentation and the reactions to economic stagnation.

The developed world has the blahs—and maybe worse. Europe's economic integration is stalled. Japan's economic engine sputters. And we at The Conference Board sound like a broken record every month as we report consumer confidence remaining below the horizon. In these less-than-robust economic times, narrowly defined self-interest intensifies. There are rising national and subnational claims to political independence—threatening economic interdependence. The shrill voice of protectionism was loud as the IIC convened in September. It was all too clear that around the globe, promotion of the general interest was threatened by increasing calls for protection of narrower self-interests.

Thus the challenge to business has taken on a new complexity over the past four years. It is not just how one can be competitive in a world of ever-more-integrated economies and borderless markets. The view I offered in my opening comments to the delegates was that there was an urgency to take a more proactive stance in reinvigorating economic growth; that it was in the interest of all that business leaders from the 58 countries represented at the IIC urge their governments to look beyond short-term political concerns and to resist taking actions to impede progress toward the benefits of economic integration. Moreover, for the business leaders themselves it was not a time to shy away from risk. It was a time for corporations, alone or in alliance, to take on the tough undertakings, be they opening new markets, advancing technology, or investing in developing nations.

It was our extreme good fortune at the conference to have as a keynote speaker President Carlos Salinas de Gortari of Mexico to hammer home the message of taking risk in the interests of improving the welfare of all citizens. As he recounted the achievements of the five years of his presidency in returning economic growth with stability to Mexico, my own thoughts went back to my meeting with him in November 1992, when I invited him to deliver the keynote.

President Salinas asked me then why the conference attendees would want to hear from him. I assured him that recounting his record of success in opening Mexico's mar-

Preston (Pete) Townley

ket economy, restoring investor confidence, and advancing the well-being of the people provided ample material for his speech. I assured him that the highest-impact content that issues from Conference Board platforms always comes from recitation of direct experience. (We leave philosophy and theory to others.) It also escaped neither of us that the timing of the San Francisco meeting in September 1993 likely would be opportune for his interest in the outcome of U.S. action on the North American Free Trade Agreement (NAFTA). He noted in his speech that neither of us had guessed how opportune.

Such was the compelling content of President Salinas' remarks and the powerfully appealing patriotism that he exuded that the hall truly burst with enthusiasm when he finished. This mood carried over for the remainder of the conference. And it built to a significant action.

The International Industrial Conference never has been convened as an action-taking body, nor are positions developed and debated. But the concern of the attendees at this 10th meeting continued to grow in voice as the meeting proceeded. The palpable threats to the world's well-being from the parochial forces standing against the movement to continuously freer trade seemed all too clear to those at the conference. The overwhelming evidence of the contribution to that well-being from the movement to ever-freer trade that has been in force since

The **Conference Board's mission** since its 1916 founding has been to improve the business-enterprise system and enhance the contribution of business to society. A principal vehicle for accomplishing this mission always has been to bring business executives together to learn from the practical reality of each other's experiences and to provide understanding of the environment in which they operate. Nowhere is the perspective obtained of a higher order than at the International Industrial Conference. And nowhere is the scope of learning about successful business practice so extensive.

—P.T.

World War II appeared to matter little to the strident voices of the 150 or so AFL-CIO-organized demonstrators who marched outside at the first day's meeting. Thus, on the final day of the meeting, a resolution was passed to urge the government members of the General Agreement on Tariffs and Trade (GATT) to bring the Uruguay Round to a successful conclusion before the Dec. 15 deadline. And the group also specifically urged the U.S. Congress to ratify NAFTA with all deliberate speed. Both were advanced "recognizing the importance of free trade in furthering the well-being and advancing the long-term interests of . . . all the world's people."

Here were business leaders from 58 countries, of obviously disparate interests, agreeing on the importance of free trade. Although many can personally benefit from protection, they voiced support for continued reduction of barriers. Were the political leaders listening? As this is written, one does not know. As this is read, the answer may be clear.

But for all the intensity of feeling about the issue of free trade, the IIC followed a normal pattern of business leaders capitalizing on the opportunity presented for one of the greatest networking and learning experiences available. During the three days, in addition to the plenary sessions, there were 31 panel sessions, 15 discussion meetings held in boardrooms throughout the Bay Area, and participation of more than one-third of those in attendance as discussion leaders and presenters. Again, the emphasis was on practical experience and perspective, not speculation and theory.

From my own experience, one clear truth is that successful businesspeople are pragmatic folk. Tell them the rules and they will play under them to win, no matter how inhibiting the strictures may be. The best of them adjust as changes occur, and they keep focused on one thing: serving the customer.

The final plenary-session panel, which I had the privilege to chair, brought this home very clearly. Xerox Corp. Chairman and CEO Paul Allaire's characterization of customers as "unreasonable"—they want solutions *now*—gained full concurrence from his fellow panelists: Brian Loton, chairman of Australia-based The Broken Hill Proprietary Company Ltd., and Robert Studer, president of the Group Executive Board, Union Bank of Switzerland.

This panel of a manufacturer, a natural-resource processor, and a financial-service provider developed in breadth the changes in priorities that have occurred in pursuing global opportunities over the past four years. Tailoring for the customer is a much greater

challenge than may have been anticipated in the 1980s. The first identifications of global mass-market opportunities in the early 1980s derived from the apparent universal appeal of new electronics such as the transistor radio and the mass thirst for Coca-Cola. But capturing the opportunity has not proven to be a task of simple execution. The homogenous product or service may exist, but the standard-issue consumer has not been found.

The overriding challenge for the company operating across borders is still to balance the maximizing of production and distribution efficiencies with the optimal targeting of and delivery to differentiated consumer tastes. "Differentiated" is too sterile a word. Brian Loton called them "impatient and demanding customers." And Paul Allaire raised the perspective to a new level of practical complexity when he positioned the challenge as, "how to serve the Japanese customer residing and doing business in New York City as he was used to being served in Tokyo."

And it is clear that this is not a static game. Things are constantly on the move—including that Japanese executive between Tokyo and New York. Recognition of the speed of change, in fact the accelerating speed of change, is a given for heads of major global companies who stay focused on developing and maintaining competitive advantage with this demanding customer. Capital and technology flow across borders easily. Skills are everywhere. Electronic interconnectedness provides real-time access to information and facilitates instant communication that blurs the distinction of day and night, let alone location on the globe.

What becomes obvious as you hear these leaders speak, often challenging each other, is that formerly significant components of competitive advantage such as mass, financial power, proprietary technology, or brand-name reputation—and the list goes on—can no longer be counted on to assure a company's leadership position in an industry or in a market. It appears that even the most stable and longest-lived element of competitive advantage for any leading company is vulnerable. Successful business leaders take this as a given and go on from there. And where they focus their attention most importantly is on the capability of their organizations. Critical words recur in the discussion: *speed, flexibility, openness, environment.*

Organizational capability is critical to business success anywhere, but it may be the

> **Even the longest-lived element of competitive advantage for any leading company is vulnerable.**

fundamental source of competitive advantage for the global corporation. A company's ability to evaluate opportunity, mobilize resources, decide on action, deliver quality, and execute promptly in an ever-shrinking time frame, against what is most likely to be a localized moving target, is, in the long run, going to determine success or failure. Exploitation of opportunity through such things as new products, massive presence, technology, innovation, brand-name reputation, and even large marketing budgets can be dissipated relatively quickly in these fast-moving times. The organization's ability to continuously anticipate change, determine action, and make positive things happen rapidly will be the only real determinant of maintaining market leadership.

In seeking this, Paul Allaire begins by recognizing that the old command-and-control structure of organization management is dead. It probably has been dead for most large companies for a long time, but the best have recognized the passing and buried the body. Many others may be giving the demise lip service, but the reality is that the ghost is alive and well and inhabiting another organizational structure labeled something else. Still others may be hanging tough with singular direction from the top that somehow continues to dissipate as it wends its way to the bottom of the organization.

ut having made this case against command and control, Allaire just as forcefully offered the view that the top is the source of specific strategic direction. Clear communication of strategy enables local management to make decisions in the context of organizational capabilities that reinforce company strengths. It also markedly improves the odds of coherent action across borders and product lines. Note that it *improves the odds* but does not guarantee optimal outcomes. There remains the challenge of coordinating responsibility and authority at the intersection of product and region. The matrix form of organization in international management just does not go away.

Bob Studer's five regions of Union Bank are organized in what he calls the "typical matrix." He accepts that conflict will occur and wants it to surface to be handled. He believes that management at all levels of the organization must recognize this and that there is no substitute for honesty and openness in resolving the conflicts that occur. To assure that these values are shared in the organization, all Union Bank managers, early in their careers, are put through demanding training courses. Top executives are involved in this training and subsequently the training is reinforced regularly to assure that the spread of common values is sustained throughout the organization.

What emerges here is a new reality of managing in the global-regional-local world. It is a realization that there are no magic solutions to the tough job of managing organizations to utilize resources most efficiently and to deliver to customers most competitively. The matrix is not a panacea; it is more likely to be a source of conflict. But it seems to be the organizational form of choice if for no other reason than it is—borrowing from Winston Churchill's description of democracy—the worst form of organizational system for international management except for all the rest. To make it work requires shared values and a clear understanding of direction at all levels and locations in the organization. That takes constant attention and repetition. Or as Bob Studer put it, "explaining it over and over again." Only then can you achieve the flexibility to act locally without losing the leverage of the global power that the company brings to the market in the first place.

Brian Loton fully agrees with the requirement of flexibility and speed, but he puts additional emphasis on sensitivity in operating locally. Broken Hill Proprietary's principal businesses develop and process natural resources. In today's world that extractive activity has to be conducted with extreme local sensitivity. Moreover, the presence and involvement of governments is often more direct and demanding. And yet the customer for the output may well be far away and "unreasonable" about meeting its production schedule. The organization not only has to accommodate this, but to be successful it has to deliver with speed in spite of it. Simplified management procedures are essential and people across the organization have to really know each other and appreciate each other's circumstances. Trust is no small element in a global company's capabilities.

This final plenary panel provided an excellent capstone exposition of the best of business practice in getting from global to local in these challenging times. The fragmentation that has occurred (and continues) since the 1989 IIC meeting has not made the task any easier. But the best performers recognize that just as world politics and local markets are dynamic, so, too, must company organizations and approaches be dynamic. With change a constant, there always will be ample subject matter for discussion when the world's business leaders get together. There certainly was in San Francisco last September.

> **Successful business leaders focus their attention on the capability of their organizations.**

THE NEW POWER IN ASIA

Louis Kraar

The symbolism in the drawing . . . is traditional: The dragons are contending for a pearl, an Oriental emblem of great riches. What's modern is the identity of the players. In the struggle to create and capture wealth in the East Asian side of the Pacific Rim, the role of the smaller dragon these days is being played by Japan. The big dragon is an entity that holds no seat at the U.N. but is emerging as *the* economic power to reckon with in the region, Great China—the 1.3 billion citizens of the People's Republic, plus those dazzling entrepreneurs, the 55 million Overseas Chinese.

As these charts reveal, the three small nations where the Overseas Chinese predominate—Hong Kong, Singapore, and Taiwan—have by themselves eclipsed Japan as the primary source of capital and foreign investment for the region with the world's fastest-growing economy. Toss in the assets controlled by Chinese businessmen in countries where they are a minority, such as Indonesia (3% of the population) and Thailand (10%), and this ethnic group's clout grows even larger. The Overseas Chinese are conservatively estimated to control some $2 trillion in liquid assets. If these enterprising souls lived in one country, its gross national product would tally at least $500 billion—larger than the $410 billion GDP of mainland China.

SOURCES: IMF, SINGAPORE GOVT, TAIWAN GOVT.

HONG KONG $43.0

SINGAPORE $77.9

JAPAN $106.4

TAIWAN $91.0

Overseas Chinese $211.9

Foreign Reserves 1993 $ billions

SINGAPORE $2.5

TAIWAN $4.4

HONG KONG $19.1

Overseas Chinese $26.0
By country of origin

FORTUNE CHART

JAPAN $3.7

Foreign Direct Investment in Asia
1993 $ billions

new mindset. Its giant companies are far and away the region's technology champions and will continue to dominate key industries such as electronics and automobiles. But having long provided the model and much of the capital for other Asian countries to develop export-driven economies, Japan will likely see its role diminish somewhat in the years ahead. Says Robert Lloyd George, a British investment banker in Hong Kong and

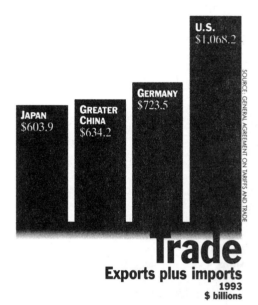

U.S. $1,068.2

GERMANY $723.5

JAPAN $603.9

GREATER CHINA $634.2

SOURCE: GENERAL AGREEMENT ON TARIFFS AND TRADE

Trade
Exports plus imports
1993 $ billions

Now combine the People's Republic exports and imports with those of Hong Kong and Taiwan, and Greater China already accounts for a larger share of world trade than those arch-exporters, the Japanese (see chart).

That edge can only grow. Drawn by China's capable pool of low-cost labor and its growing potential as a market that contains one-fifth of the world's population, foreign investors continue to pour money into the PRC. Some 80% of that capital comes from the Overseas Chinese, refugees from poverty, disorder, and communism, who in one of the era's more piquant ironies are now Beijing's favorite financiers and models for modernization. Even the Japanese often rely on the Overseas Chinese to grease their way into China. Example: Minoru Murofushi, president of the giant trading company Itochu, says that his long-term association with an influential Indonesian Chinese, Oei Hong Leong, has led to a joint venture for Asahai brewing beer in the PRC.

Partially as a result of this, China's economy, which advanced at a torrid 13.4% clip last year, has become a potent tonic for the entire Pacific Rim. Says economist Lawrence B. Krause in a report issued by the Pacific Economic Cooperative Council, an organization of government officials, business people, and academics: "Even Australia and the United States find China the fastest-growing market of any size … With Europe still mired in recession and Japanese imports either stagnant or declining, dependence on China for growth of export markets is unlikely to be reduced very soon."

None of this means, of course, that it's time to treat Japan as an also-ran. After several tough years, that economic colossus seems to be coming back, and with a

author of *The East-West Pendulum*: "Now it is the Overseas Chinese states of Southeast Asia which are taking up the baton. My contention is that the leadership of Asia, in economic and cultural terms, will pass to the Chinese during the next 20 years."

However that struggle plays out, here's the good news for international business: Propelled by both the older Japanese dynamo and the newer Chinese engine, East Asia's economies will continue expanding considerably faster than the 2%- to 3%-a-year global average. Switching analogies, Kenneth Courtis, senior economist for Deutsche Bank Capital Markets in Tokyo, suggests thinking of Chinese and Japanese capitalists as the economic equivalent of oil and vinegar. Says he: "They don't really mix, but they complement each other well. The Overseas Chinese are the oil—the lubricant that makes deals possible—and the Japanese are the vinegar—the technology, capital, and management that really packs a punch."

That potent combination should ensure that this area of some two billion people—stretching from Japan and South Korea through China and southward to Indonesia, Malaysia, and Thailand—keeps getting richer quicker than any other region at any time in history. South Korea's GDP alone has grown as much in a single generation as America's did in the last century. Outside Japan some 75 million Asian households will have incomes roughly equal to those of middle-class Americans by the year 2000.

No wonder this swatch of Asia is the most promising market for aircraft, cars, construction equipment, and much else. The U.S., for instance, exports more goods to Singapore than to Italy, and more to Malaysia than to the entire former Soviet Union. Exciting, big-ticket opportunities gleam behind the boring word *infrastructure*. Over the next six years, Asian countries plan to invest more than $1 trillion in telecommunications roads, ports, power plants, and airports. . . .

BEFORE WE MOVE ON from China, however, it's essential to add a few words of caution. While that country's great leap away from communism toward the market has started with a tremendous boom and its long-run potential looks promising, the short- to medium-term hazards are large. Right now, in fact, the PRC is reeling from the side effects of breathless expansion. Its double-digit growth rates are bumping into the limits of a primitive transportation system, inadequate electric power, and such basic environmental constraints as shortages of clean water. Inflation, raging at over 20% annually, hit 27% in major cities in August. Free-market reforms on the farms have boosted food production but also liberated from communes millions of peasants who are streaming into cities in search of jobs. Mobs of those migrants can be seen camped at every municipal railway station. And according to the bureaucrats in Beijing, a get-rich-quick fever among Chinese has created widespread corruption that could derail their modernization drive.

Well aware of the chaos, the PRC's leaders hope to curb inflation by reducing the country's economic growth rate to 11% this year and perhaps to only 9% to 10% next year. What makes a soft landing difficult to pull off is that the country remains awkwardly poised between fading Marxism and would-be capitalism. As economist Krause puts it, "The old planning system has not been fully dismantled, and the market system has not yet matured." Thus, while Beijing can slam on the monetary brakes, they are only loosely connected to the real economy. For one thing, decision-making has shifted heavily from the capital to local officials, who are in no mood to curb entrepreneurial activities on their turf.

The obvious solution is for China to press ahead with wider pro-market reforms, but that is proving devilishly complicated. Says Sanjoy Chowdhury, chief regional economist for Merrill Lynch in Singapore: "Much of Beijing's legitimacy now comes from its ability to deliver economic gains. With the collapse of communism and the demystification of Mao, economic development has become the prime justification for communist rule."

The biggest drag on China's economy and drain on Beijing's resources is the huge pack of state corporations that are industrial dinosaurs. About half of them—some 50,000 enterprises—are losing money, and their total debt is estimated at nearly $70 billion. True, several profitable state enterprises, such as Shanghai Petrochemical, have gone public in both Hong Kong and the U.S. But rather than close down the clunkers, the government keeps lending them money, which fans inflation and prevents meaningful reforms of the financial system. Chinese leaders talk about letting the losers go bankrupt or cutting off their access to scarce raw materials. But there's no sign of action. The senior citizens in charge—the average age of the Politburo is 64—are evidently paralyzed by fears of causing mass unemployment.

In the meantime, some enterprising Overseas Chinese are doing what they can to ensure that the PRC becomes a more hospitable place for international investors. Perhaps the most ambitious is Lee Kuan Yew, the senior leader in Singapore. At home Lee has created a model for what Beijing admires but has yet to replicate: a well-ordered, prosperous nation led by an incorruptible regime that maintains firm political control. China's supreme leader, Deng Xiaoping, in fact, has urged his countrymen to learn from Singapore.

A WILLING TEACHER, Lee now hopes to further China's evolution toward free enterprise—and in the process provide profitable opportunities for his countrymen—by building what's essentially a miniature version of Singapore in Suzhou, about 50 miles west of Shanghai. The Singapore government will provide the management expertise for what is officially called the Singapore-Suzhou Township, while 19 Singapore companies will help build it on a 27-square-mile site. So far, Singapore has signed up 14 companies from the U.S., Japan, South Korea, and elsewhere to invest a total of nearly $900 million in Suzhou factories.

Despite the extraordinary backing Beijing is giving this deal, Lee's biggest challenge will be assuring those investors that the town will be run with efficiency and honesty, qualities that are rare elsewhere in the People's Republic. To close the gap, 300 Chinese officials will be trained in Singapore, which will station about 100 of its own administrators in Suzhou to coach them. Says one Singapore official: "If multinational corporations feel comfortable investing in Singapore, they should feel comfortable in Suzhou."

In general, however, even China's most enthusiastic foreign backers acknowledge the dangers that lie ahead. Says William Purves, chairman of HSBC Holdings, the London-based company that controls Hongkong & Shanghai Banking Corp. in Hong Kong: "Fundamental problems are still largely being evaded, and this will limit good investment opportunities for some time."

Until those clouds clear, the most active investors in China will remain the Overseas Chinese, particularly those based in Hong Kong, who invest in the PRC not only to make money but also as a form of political insurance. When control of Hong Kong, now a British colony, shifts to Beijing in less than three years, will that capitalist enclave still be allowed to operate unfettered? The communists have said yes, but Hong Kongers figure the best way to ensure that outcome—and protect their immobile assets, such as real estate—-is to continue helping the PRC get rich too. To improve their odds of making money, though, the Overseas Chinese usually steer clear of joint ventures with state corporations, focusing instead on setting up small factories and developing real estate.

In coming years, the other source of capital sure to reshape Asia's economic landscape is Japanese direct investment. To cope with a strong yen, Japan's corporate giants have no choice but to accelerate the migration of their most labor-intensive manufacturing to Asian lands with lower wages and cheaper land.

True, that expected surge of money from Tokyo has not been much in evidence yet. Japanese investment in the rest of Asia rose only 3% in the most recent fiscal year, ended in March. But rest assured it will come, even if pressure on the yen abates somewhat. The reason: Back home, Japan is graying fast. It already boasts the world's highest average life expectancy, over 76 years for men and 85.5 years for women. That great accomplishment in human terms is also a guaranteed economic burden. By the year 2020, more than 20% of Japanese will be over 65 years old. Taking care of this venerable flock will consume an equivalent one-fifth of the country's GDP. To support the elderly, Japan's capital must inevitably flow to fast-growing countries that boast an over-supply of young, energetic workers.

Happily, the Pac Rim offers an abundance of such choices. Though it's the least likely site for Japanese investment, the country that has most closely emulated Tokyo's example of nurturing corporations with government assistance is Korea. This year its economy is soaring along with a growth rate of nearly 8%. Success, however, means that Korea is no longer a low-wage nation. Its simple industries like garment making and assembling consumer electronics are being taken over by the likes of China and Indonesia. Yet in technological know-how, Korea still lags well behind Japan and the U.S.

To stay prosperous, Korea is teaming up with the latest flock of Asian states rising like geese along the development route mapped by Japan. Example: A group of Korean manufacturers led by the conglomerate Samsung is working with a PRC aircraft manufacturer to develop a new 100-passenger jetliner for the Asian market. Likewise, Korea's automakers are tripling their production capacity to six million vehicles annually—much of which will be assembled in Indonesia and other Asian countries.

Among the region's still industrializing economies, the pacesetters flourish mainly in industries handed down from Japan, Korea, the U.S., and Europe. Malaysia, for instance, has become the world's largest exporter of semiconductors by welcoming the leading foreign makers of those chips and providing them with a dependable work force. Thailand and Indonesia, too, are outposts for international manufacturers of Barbie dolls, clothing, running shoes, and ball bearings.

Even the Philippines is showing signs of dynamism and renewed political stability. Its economy, which stalled for the past several years, should expand about 4% this year. Daewoo and Hyundai of Korea are going there to assemble autos. Hitachi plans to make small disk drives for computers, and Federal Express has set up an Asian cargo hub. As President Fidel Ramos puts it, "We're back in business in the heart of Asia."

How do the Asians do it? In a recent study of what it called "The East Asian Miracle," the World Bank turned up no magic formula, no single set of government policies. The key, its experts concluded, is culture: "People in these economies have simply studied harder, worked harder, and saved more than people in other countries." That prevailing attitude, buttressed by the wealth-creating rivalry between Japan and Greater China, guarantees that for the foreseeable future Asia will remain the most dynamic force in the global economy.

Second Thoughts on Going Global

Riskier emerging markets have spooked some players—but many big companies are staying the course

If any country was the model of success in the new world economic order, Mexico was it. The country's U.S.-trained technocrats seemed to be doing everything right. They flung open Mexico's markets to free trade, rolled out the red carpet for foreign investors, privatized lumbering state companies, and beat down inflation. But since the peso's devaluation, this virtuous cycle has turned vicious. Mexico's currency and stock markets have crashed, and unemployment has soared. The North American Free Trade Agreement, the engine of hemispheric growth, has produced a dangerously weak partner for the U.S. The implication is that far from triumphing around the world, the free-market model has hit a wall.

Now, the Mexican crisis is giving rise to second thoughts about the course of the global economy. Overall, the consensus opinion among executives, portfolio managers, academics, and government officials is still encouraging. The structural foundations for free markets, such as open borders and privatization, seem to be as solid as they were before the rupture in Mexico.

NEW DEALS. But the realization is sinking in that as these markets develop, bouts of volatility will cause periodic panics. For the short term, that's bad news for the mutual funds and investment houses that have piled into the immature financial markets of the developing world. More conflicts will erupt between the Finance Ministers in these countries and the investors of this so-called hot money, which seeks out the best returns and shuns the biggest risks. Countries such as Mexico, which despite its progress grew dangerously addicted to short-term borrowings, will be eventually punished by the markets for their profligacy. Governments in Asia are moving to protect themselves by erecting hurdles to curb the flow of hot money. Even in Western Europe, some opponents of the new order may try to blunt the power of bond investors who are assailing the welfare state's costs.

In this turbulent atmosphere, the initiative could pass to the other source of foreign capital in emerging markets—the multinational corporations, which control hundreds of billions in assets and have growing operational expertise in far-flung markets. For now, executives at these companies seem optimistic about global opportunities, peso devaluation or no. To these giants, says Robert E. Donovan, executive vice-president of ABB Asea Brown Boveri Ltd., the giant engineering concern: "[Mexico] is just a bump in the road."

Well, maybe. Some of these companies may have invested so heavily in emerging markets that they are locked into a long term view. Yet as mutual-fund money flees homeward, it's likely multinationals' patient capital will look even more valuable to governments intent on development. China's recent concessions on intellectual-property rights, which favor such companies as Microsoft Corp. and Time Warner Inc., also enhances corporate clout.

So even while the Mexican crisis smolders, chief executives are searching out more deals. In recent days, Anheuser-Busch Cos. signed a pact to buy 80% of a big brewery in Wuhan, China, while Motorola Inc. announced new deals in China, including a $28 million joint venture to make semiconductors in Sichuan province.

To the Germans, who have invested billions in central Europe since the fall of the Berlin Wall, the Mexican crisis seems very far away. "We invest in real factories there, not in bonds," says Gerhard Seufert, head of the Central European division of the Economics Ministry. Companies from Daimler Benz to Siemens to the big utilities are operating in Poland, Hungary, and the Czech Republic.

In Latin America, the region most shaken by Mexico's devaluation, Volkswagen has revealed plans to invest over $2.5 billion in Brazil. And GM Hughes Electronics Corp. decided to expand its satellite-TV service throughout the region.

Even in Mexico, many companies still see the country's value as an exporter now and, later, as a consumer

From *Business Week*, March 13, 1995, pp. 48-49. © 1995 by the McGraw-Hill Companies. Reprinted by special permission.

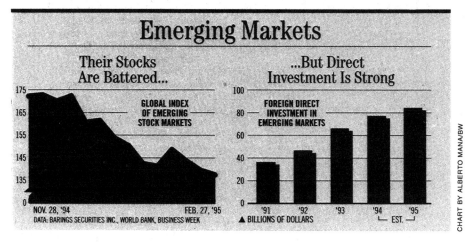

Emerging Markets

Their Stocks Are Battered...

GLOBAL INDEX OF EMERGING STOCK MARKETS

NOV. 28, '94 — FEB. 27, '95

DATA: BARINGS SECURITIES INC., WORLD BANK, BUSINESS WEEK

...But Direct Investment Is Strong

FOREIGN DIRECT INVESTMENT IN EMERGING MARKETS

'91 '92 '93 '94 '95

▲ BILLIONS OF DOLLARS └ EST. ┘

CHART BY ALBERTO MANA/BW

market again. A Matsushita Electric Industrial Co. division is building a cadmium-nickel battery plant in Tijuana. Chrysler Corp., which manufactures both for export and domestic consumption in Mexico, wants to convince more of its suppliers that now is exactly the right time to invest there, according to President Robert A. Lutz.

But Lutz is taking the long view, since conditions in Mexico are getting tougher. Sales of Chrysler vehicles are down 40% in the first two months of the year. Recession is stalking Argentina, too, in the wake of the Mexican crisis. To convince foreign bondholders that a Mexican-style devaluation is not imminent, the Argentine government is searching for major cuts in spending.

In this tense atmosphere, portfolio managers wonder where trouble will strike next. Pakistan and the Philippines, for example, have accumulated large current-account deficits. Thailand, which has issued a lot of short-term debt, had to stop a run on its currency as foreign investors beat a temporary retreat. Declares Alan J. Stoga, managing director of consultants Kissinger Associates Inc: "We know that there will be other Mexicos."

On Western Europe's doorstep, Hungary's festering budget problems illustrate the strain of passing from a communist welfare state to something resembling capitalism. Hungary's current-account deficit of $3.7 billion and overall foreign debt of $28 billion are danger signs in such a small economy. A ministerial crisis over privatization has also caused jitters. Yet here the pressures of outside investors have seemed to prevail: The government has recommitted itself to rapid privatization and more austerity.

NO RUSH. The greatest beneficiaries of the new investment mood for now may be Asia's proponents of the Japanese model of slow, controlled development. Japanese financiers already say that Mexican events have repudiated the go-fast approach of the "Berkeley mafia," the free-market purists who have been advising many Asian governments. "We think a gradual approach is better than rushing," says Schinichiro Kobayashi, a senior manager at Bank of Tokyo who spent 19 years in Latin America. "You have to consider each country's strength and [economic] maturity."

More countries may well adopt versions of the Asian model to avoid Mexico's fate. William Ebsworth of Fidelity Investments in Hong Kong recently visited India to check out equity investments there. But he was surprised to find the Indians now frowning on portfolio investment. Direct foreign investment is fine, but there is talk of India reducing the shares foreigners may hold in a domestic company to 10% from 24%. In China, government officials are concerned that hot money is adding to the country's inflationary woes. So regulators in Beijing have brought to a near halt foreigners' purchase of stock issues.

By exposing the weak underpinnings of global development, the Mexican crisis has given everyone its first look at how risky the new world really is. The next job for the architects of the global financial order is to build in restraints and early-warning systems that will encourage growth without letting it get out of control. It's an urgent mission that nations will ignore at their peril.

By Christopher Power, with Rose Brady in New York, Joyce Barnathan in Hong Kong, Karen Lowry Miller in Bonn, and bureau reports

Capital and the Division of Production: Global At Last?

GEORGE M. VON FURSTENBERG

George M. Von Furstenberg is Rudy Professor of Economics at Indiana University and holder of the Bissell-Hyde Fulbright Professorship in Canadian-American Relations at the University of Toronto for the academic year 1994–95. He is indebted to university colleagues Michele Fratianni, Peter Pedroni, Elyce J. Rotella, and Nicolas Spulber, for a number of useful suggestions and expert advice.

The move to competitive capitalism in the developing countries has started to bring about the long-anticipated worldwide dispersion of capital.

The dispersion of capital is becoming global at last. The consequences of this historic transformation may not be entirely favorable to advanced industrial countries. But we can understand today's reality better in the light of the conditions and attitudes that prevailed before World War I. It may not be that things always stay the same or move in circles, but ideological speculations about the worldwide dispersion of capital and its consequences, common a century ago, have recently acquired startling relevance.

What has happened since 1986 is astonishing. The flow of foreign direct and equity investment to developing countries has grown from a trickle to a midsized stream, if not yet a torrent. Indeed, when the first refreshing wave of international debt relief, privatization, and opening up rushed over the developing countries in the mid-1980s, it buoyed foreign direct investment (FDI) almost instantly. It allowed net FDI in developing countries to double in a couple of years—from a flow of $12 billion in 1986 to $24 billion in 1988. A second surge, that started in 1990 and shows no signs of abating, carried FDI further to a net inflow of $35 billion in 1992.

Next to FDI, portfolio investment in foreign equities contributes most directly to the formation of risky business capital in private hands. In this respect, hardly a business day passed in the year before the Spring 1994 nose dive of global markets without investment houses (from Morgan Stanley on down) launching yet another closed-end country or developing-region fund. Indeed, it is difficult to find a country or city-state of any economic size (one obvious exception being the Islamic Republic of Iran) for which Wall Street has not yet created at least one such fund. Furthermore, U.S. houses are not alone in thinking that an uncommonly low price-earnings ratio anywhere cries out for more capital. Investors from all of the most advanced industrial countries are dispatching capital on its foreign mission of bringing the real discount rates applied to expected profits—i.e., the rates of return required on productive capital—down to civilized levels all over the world.

What is remarkable about this is the uncanny recurrence of developments, of which the essentials were first observed and extrapolated for the near-term around a century ago. History is not so much repeating itself as vaulting over a century. Is it mere coincidence that 1894 was the year in which the English version of the first edition of Marx's *Capital, Volume III* came out?

Subtext of a dead prophecy

Marx on capital, and Hobson and Lenin on imperialism, could all be a big bore in the closing years of this century. Marxism-Leninism has been collapsing as an official ideology of states. At the same time, the last glaring remnants of imperialism (such as Hong Kong)—ceded to Britain in the Opium War of 1841-42—are being liquidated, although not exactly to the "celestial majesty" that once ceded it. Thus, past forms of communism and imperialism are being swept into the dust bin of history. They appear to be suffering the very collapse which Lenin had foretold for capitalism, once it had passed through its "highest" and "final" stage—imperialism. Even international arms races and internal militarism are in remission. Military-industrial rivalry no longer seems fated to engorge the boils of imperialism until they burst into war.

But now that Marxism-Leninism is no longer radioactive politically, and imperialism is no longer an effective cudgel for slamming rich countries, we can take what is suggestive and visionary in the grand polemics and leave the rest. Jewels mounted on rusted rails of mistaken prediction are jewels nonetheless for those who are free to pick and choose where to take them. Some of these jewels are acquiring a riveting sparkle in the dusk of this century. The classic writers of Marxism-Leninism and imperialism are recalled here as speculative political economists who were committed to distinct frameworks of analysis. Within these analyses, they found things to say about capital, international finance, profits, and economic convergence between developed and developing countries that have regained pertinence— after a long eclipse.

1894 to 1994

What is capital mobility supposed to do to nations? A century ago, there was much discussion of rates of return on capital and of international differences between them. Speculations about their fate, and that of capitalism, had played a crucial role in a number of theories and critiques of political economy. The

fathers of ideology heatedly debated the phenomenon of capital chasing profits in developing countries and considered what the dispersion of capital would mean for all workers and consumers. Overaccumulation of capital and falling rates of profit tended to be the agreed-upon historical tendency leading to crises that posed risks of conflict globalization. These crises presaged either system collapse through revolutionary dynamic or preventive reform. Even today, left-leaning writers tend to use the profit rate as their central indicator of the state of the capitalist economy.

In one sense, they are not alone. Growth theorists, including the founder of neoclassical growth theory, Nobel prize winner Robert Solow, focus on "the profit rate" gross of interest paid and depreciation allowances, or on what economists call the marginal product of capital (MPK). They define the "steady state" as a conjuncture in which inputs and outputs grow at such a rate as to hold the MPK constant, in view of whatever factor biases there are in technological progress; they then reason about the best of these possible steady states. In this neoclassical version, a higher saving rate or faster accumulation lowers the MPK gently to a new level, and does not continue to drive it down until the capitalist system crashes. Used politically, it has turned *under*accumulation relative to the optimum level, or "capital shortage" and insufficient investment in human and object capital, into the principal growth issues to worry about.

Now, if politicians say we should invest more at home, do they also mean that we should oppose increased investment abroad? Last year this type of debate became starkly topical. Almost every key argument—pro or con—made over the passage of NAFTA unwittingly and shallowly repeated what Hobson and others had already weighed carefully almost a century ago. These arguments have turned on the emotional question of whether the third world (as represented by Mexico) is to be feared as a low-wage, low-standards competitor that needs to be restrained, or whether it is a "periphery" being preyed upon mercilessly by the "center," unless somehow protected from continued foreign domination. Are the advanced industrial countries sucking out the developing countries? Are the advanced countries driving down the relative price of the products of the developing countries? Or, indeed, are they decapitalizing them, as certain UN agencies were fond of arguing in the 1960s and 1970s? Alternatively, are living standards in industrial countries now being undermined by low-wage countries which have learned to lure away some of their capital and technology and to put both to good use privately instead of waiting for the delivery of foreign aid into wasteful, official hands?

There is also the Panglossian view that *every* country stands to gain from increased capital mobility and freer trade. That glowing diagnosis need not necessarily be wrong. The same reforms that induce increased foreign-owned investment in developing countries may help mobilize their own saving for greater private investment and efficiency. In that case, there could be faster growth of real incomes and markets for both foreign and domestic participants, with economies of scale and ultimately increased national saving and investment for all.

On the flip side, themes such as social dumping and the undercutting of U.S. labor's bargaining position, the withdrawal of capital from American labor, and the exploitation of the imbalance ("surplus value") between Mexican wages and productivity were broached long ago. All the historical adaptation needed was to substitute "British" for "U.S." and "East-Indian" for "Mexican." The debate over whether NAFTA is mostly about an expansion of mutually beneficial trade, or one-sided trade and making Mexico safe for U.S. investment, also has long been foreshadowed. Starting with Marx and his critics, there was a running argument over whether imperialism should be judged, and its dynamic understood, by what it does to the volume and international division of commodity production and exchange, or by what it does to the accumulation and worldwide distribution of capital. In the shorthand of the NAFTA debate, the pitch was 20,000 jobs per $1 billion of added U.S. exports to Mexico on the commodity side against 30,000 jobs lost per $1 billion of U.S. investment diverted to Mexico on the capital side.

Adam Smith

Pitched battles like these have been fought since colonial times. As empire had been the business of Great Britain for centuries, there is always Adam Smith and his 1776 *Inquiry into the Nature and Causes of the Wealth of Nations* for a rich supply of pertinent observations. Smith considered foreign commerce and found it likely to be most profitable with rich neighbors: "As a rich man is likely to be a better customer to the industrious people in his neighbourhood than a poor, so is likewise a rich

nation." He explained the costs of protection and the advantages of free trade and explored the motives for establishing new colonies. Nevertheless, he felt forced to conclude, "To expect, indeed, that the freedom of trade should ever be entirely restored in Great Britain, is as absurd as to expect that an Oceana or Utopea should ever be established in it . . . [M]aster manufacturers set themselves against every law that is likely to increase the number of their rivals in the home market . . . [and] enflame their workmen to attack with violence and outrage the proposers of any such regulation." With regard to the colonies or other regional groupings, such conclusions about political connivance with "the mean rapacity" and "monopolizing spirit" of merchants and manufacturers would point to managed trade.

Smith did not recognize clearly that producers and trading companies, or what are now vast retail organizations, have multiple personalities and frequent personality disorders in this regard. In their capacity as producers, or input and merchandise buyers, they like to be unrestricted and free to engage in global sourcing on the most advantageous terms. As investors, they also want to be free to choose their most profitable location anywhere in the world and resent foreign barriers to entry and establishment. As sellers, on the other hand, they like to restrict competition in the home market and seek market segmentation, while retaining the freedom to challenge such restrictions abroad. Because Smith differentiated too little here, this article will deal with considerably more complete, if acid, interpretations of global tendencies—such as those of Marx and Engels, Hobson, Hilferding, and Lenin instead (see *Finance Capital: A Study of the Latest Phase of Capitalist Development* and *Imperialism, The Highest Stage of Capitalism: A Popular Outline* in For Further Reading). This history sets up the leap to the present.

Marx and Engels

For Marx and his influential interpreter and editor, Engels, "the law of the falling tendency of the rate of profit" played a key role in spurring a variety of counteracting measures or "causes" designed to delay the ultimate collapse of capitalism. In his construction of capitalist development, the composition of "total" capital in use shifts inevitably from "variable" capital—equal to the value of labor contained in work in progress—to "constant" capital. The latter category comprises all inputs other than "living" labor, foremost of these being producer durables and inventories, or other types of "dead" labor used to produce current output. Marx treats all items in this category as inherently incapable of contributing to "surplus value" and, hence, profits. The surplus value that may arise only on variable capital, divided by total capital, is Marx's definition of the rate of profit. Thus, a given rate of surplus on variable capital yields a lower rate of profit on total capital—that is, the greater is the weight of constant relative to variable capital in the progress of capitalism.

To retard the supposed decline in the average rate of profit implicit in this development, monopoly capitalists, interconnected with high finance and government, will resort to actions that afford a partial respite. They will attempt to raise the rate of surplus value on variable capital by increasing the "exploitation" of labor and by reducing the portion of constant capital in total capital. The latter can be done most readily in less-developed areas of the world, where an earlier phase of capitalism can be reconstructed. Increased exploitation of labor, however, can be accomplished, not only by measures that lower the reservation wage to bare subsistence in colonial possessions, but also by raising the productivity of labor without increasing real wages proportionately. In both cases, the amount and rate of surplus value, which are the absolute and relative measures of "exploitation," are bound to rise. Yet, according to Marx, "even a rising rate of surplus value has a tendency to express itself in a falling rate of profit." Foreign investment and the creation of a world market—globalization, in today's jargon—may be able to slow this tendency, but, in Marx's analysis, they cannot prevent it.

How large might the initial international differences in rates of return on capital be, and how would they be affected through the export of capital? Marx presents some illustrative figures that show the average rate of profit rising from 20 percent to 66.67 percent, as the amount of "constant" capital working with a fixed amount of "variable" capital is cut by a factor of eight. He tentatively associates the higher rate with an undeveloped country, and the lower rate with a country at a higher stage of development. He sees "no reason" why, if "capitals" invested in the colonies yield higher rates of profit, "these higher rates . . . should not enter as elements into the average rate of profit and tend to keep it up to that extent."

In 1853, ten years before starting to write Volume III of *Capital,* Marx had already speculated that infrastructure investment in British colonies, such as in railways, would be the forerunner of modern industry in these colonies, even if that was not the intention of the mother country. The equalization of the average rate of profit between countries will then be accomplished "in a more or less perfect degree . . . to the extent that conditions in the respective countries are adapted to the capitalist mode of production."

Marx went on to elaborate: "The incessant equilibration of the continual differences is accomplished so much more quickly, (1) the more movable capital is, the more easily it can be shifted from one sphere and one place to another (under force of competition and with the help of the credit system); (2) the more quickly labor-power can be transferred from one sphere to another and from one local point of production to another. . . . But this equilibration meets great obstacles, whenever numerous and large spheres of production, which are not operated on a capitalistic basis (such as farming by small farmers), are interpolated between capitalist spheres and interrelated with them."

It appears, therefore, that according to Marx-Engels, capital exports from developed to undeveloped countries serve to equalize rates of return on capital only very gradually between them. The tendency toward equalization will take hold only when the latter group of countries becomes more developed by "adapting to the capitalist mode of production." The reason is that their average rate of profit then declines faster, but from a higher level, than in more developed countries. According to condition 2 (see above), mobility of labor would be required to accelerate the process.

Hobson, Hilferding, and Lenin

Even "liberal" writers of a century ago tended to agree that rates of return on capital were destined to decline to crisis levels within the existing system of inequality of income and influence. Reformers among them tried to remedy that system primarily through social legislation that protected and empowered labor to some degree. In *Imperialism: A Study,* written in 1902, Hobson offered such reforms as a socially superior alternative to the international dispersion of capital. As the scramble for colonies intensified and capital exports began to grow rapidly after 1870, he identified "the growing cosmopolitanism of capital" as "the greatest economic change of recent generations."

This change, it turned out, was far from liberal in the European tradition. Rather, "[i]mperialism . . . implies the use of the machinery of government by private interests, mainly capitalists, to secure for them economic gains outside their country." It divides the world into spheres of influence and exclusive rights. This is how Hobson characterized "regionalism" before World War I: "[It] repudiates free trade, and rests upon the economic basis of protection."

These characterizations recur in Lenin's writings on imperialism as the "highest" (1916) or "latest" (1917) stage of capitalism, or as "capitalism of transition or a dying capitalism," but with special emphasis on finance capital. For Hobson, ". . . the motor-power of Imperialism is not chiefly financial: finance is rather the governor of the imperial engine, directing the energy and determining its work: it does not constitute the fuel of the engine, nor does it directly generate the power."

Lenin, however, assigned a more active and initiative role to finance capital. He charged that "monopoly has sprung from the banks" and that "finance capital has led to the actual division of the world." The end result, in either case, is that imperialism violates one of the conditions that Marx had enumerated (under condition 1 as seen on previous page) for the rapid equalization of average rates of profit on capital—freedom of trade and the absence of all but "natural" monopolies.

The organization of international money and finance and its supporting network of institutions became ever more global and efficient in the decades preceding World War I. Competition and arbitrage became particularly keen in the capital-market segment for international loans to official borrowers. Partly because of this increased competition, "counteracting measures" arose once again under imperialism to shore up profits. Lenin provides some concrete indications:

"Finance capital has created the epoch of monopolies, and monopolies introduce everywhere monopolist principles: the utilization of 'connections' for profitable transactions takes the place of competition on the open market. The most usual thing is to stipulate that part of the loan that is granted shall be spent on purchases in the creditor country, particularly on orders for war materials, or for ships, etc. . . . The export of capital abroad thus becomes a means for encouraging the export of commodities. . . . Krupp in Germany, Schneider in France, Armstrong in England are instances of firms which have close con-

nections with powerful banks and governments and cannot easily be 'ignored' when a loan is being arranged."

Hilferding's classic, *Finance Capital*, while first published in 1910, several years after Hobson's *Imperialism* but before Lenin's, elaborates on the conflicting tendencies that increased potential efficiency in financial markets, while also fomenting imperialist attempts to restrict competition. The tension is between greater technical efficiency in the international loan market (due to lower cost and increased speed of transportation, communication, and organizational control), the increase of the perfection of *potential* competition, and the desire of imperial nations to prevent *actual* competition from rival nations and their firms. Thus while first stating that "the export of capital is the means of equalizing national rates of profit," Hilferding hastens to add that the tendency to equalization may be limited to the rates of profit on the foreign and domestic investments of each nation on its own:

"Export capital feels most comfortable, however, when its own state is in complete control of the new territory, for capital exports from other countries are then excluded, it enjoys a privileged position, and its profits are more or less guaranteed by the state. Thus the export of capital also encourages an imperialist policy."

Similarly, in the international loan market, the tendency toward equalization at first appears successful, but then, in colonial banking business, monopoly profits appear to creep right back. On the one hand, Hilferding writes that "[t]he struggle for markets for goods becomes a conflict among national banking groups over spheres of investment for loan capital, and since *rates of interest tend to be equalized on the international market,* economic competition is confined here within relatively narrow limits" (emphasis added).

However, he observed earlier : "So far as the rate of interest is concerned it is much higher in undeveloped capitalist countries, which lack extensive banking and credit facilities, than in advanced capitalist countries. Furthermore, interest in those countries still includes for the most part an element of wages or entrepreneurial profit. The high rate of interest is a direct inducement to the export of loan capital. Entrepreneurial profit is also higher because labour power is exceptionally cheap. . . . In addition, . . . ground rent is very low or purely nominal. . . . Finally profits are swelled by special privileges and monopolies."

Hilferding thus recognizes that, even when some lines of international transmission of capital between the industrial mother countries, or between each of them and their own colonies, are efficient and open or contestable, the loan conditions faced by the ultimate borrowers in undeveloped countries may be less favorable—if, indeed, loans for private borrowers are available at all. As long as the mother country retains effective control of colonial governance with all its rules, licensing requirements, and powers of enforcement, the reason for this differentiation is not that country risk or creditor risk intervenes but that local monopolies and (planned?) lack of financial development exact their toll.

Contemporary recurrence

Until recently, many of these considerations still applied. Prior to 1914, country risk was low in developing countries, because they were firmly in the hands of colonial masters. Country risk was judged low once again, although for quite different reasons, in many developing countries in the second half of the 1970s. During this period, countries such as Mexico and Brazil could, at times, engage in government-guaranteed borrowing at spreads as small as 3/8 of one percentage point above dollar LIBOR (the London interbank borrowing rate). Yet, frittered away to finance unsustainable external and budget deficits associated with excessive consumption and subsidies to government enterprises, those low costs of officially guaranteed borrowing did not "sink in." The real rates of return required by private investors in producer durables in those countries showed no signs of converging to the low U.S. levels observed in comparable risk classes of productive assets. For instance, required gross rates of return on producer durables averaged about 24 percent per annum in Mexico until recent years, compared with 13 percent in the United States.

Lenin had made the observation that "capitalism is growing far more rapidly than before; but this growth is not only becoming more and more uneven in general, its unevenness also manifests itself, in particular, in the decay of the countries which are richest in capital." This observation does not appear to have been historically correct up to World War I, and it certainly did not have the predictive quality Lenin had intended. At least until the late 1980s, there was no systematic convergence of living standards between the industrial countries of Lenin's time and the developing world. Just as the purchasing power of British GDP per capita did not decline relative to that of India during the period of Britain's dominance, the United States maintained its lead over the developing world, once it had become the preeminent economic power. On a purchasing-power parity basis, real GDP per capita in the developing countries was just below 10 percent of U.S. per capita GDP in 1960, and it was still only 10 percent in 1990. Furthermore, the developing countries' share of the world's population will grow from two-thirds in 1960 to four-fifths by the year 2000, according to United Nations estimates.

The fact that, contrary to what Marx, Lenin, and Hilferding had expected of capitalism, capital exports to developing countries did not continue to grow rapidly may have contributed to this lack of convergence. In 1914, almost 50 percent of foreign investments were undertaken outside Europe and North America in what was then the undeveloped world. For Britain alone, the net capital stock held abroad doubled from 1870–75 to 1913–14 by various estimates to at least 30 percent of the total capital stock owned by Britain at home and abroad, and its FDI claims accounted for at least 40 percent of the total FDI assets of all countries. Again, almost half of the capital stock exported from Britain was held in developing countries. By contrast, 75 years later, in 1989, over 80 percent of the foreign investments of Japan and of the countries of Western Europe and North America represented claims on each other and not on the developing world. Even during the period 1986–90, industrial countries attracted 83 percent of all FDI inflows and contributed 97 percent of all FDI outflows. Yet, during this very period, the ideological and institutional conversion to a more open and more privately manageable economic structure with more secure property rights began to take hold in a number of developing countries.

Countries in which this transformation can credibly be made to stick will be able to attract production facilities and other forms of business capital from abroad. After all, their finest talent speaks English and is trained in North America and Europe, just as is everybody else's. Their remoteness from major markets and centers of communication may no longer matter so much, since geographic distances and information gaps have become progressively easier and faster to surmount. Once their laws and dispute-settlement procedures are up to industrial-country standards of suitability and enforcement, little will stand in the way of the international equalization of rates of return on capital.

Such a development would represent a momentous change from earlier decades, in which systematically higher country risk in developing than in industrial countries formed a *cordon insanitaire* around such countries. Until quite recently, much of the postcolonial developing world had succeeded in making itself so inhospitable to foreign investment that the global chase for the highest rate of profit, so vividly described by Marx, Hobson, Hilferding, and Lenin, largely passed them by. The chase thus did not have the "convergence" effects predicted; nor did it lead to average rates of profit—unadjusted for differences in microeconomic and macroeconomic elements of country risk—becoming more nearly equal between countries at different stages of development.

According to the thesis offered here, those times have changed: One developing country after another has started to make itself attractive to foreign capital on its own terms. This tendency started to spread beyond the four Asian "tigers" in the late 1980s. It has since become particularly acute in rapidly liberalizing and privatizing countries (such as Mexico) which are seeking deep economic integration with a vastly more advanced neighboring country (such as the United States).

To be sure, the developing world still contains some countries whose people are brutalized and impoverished by a malign government, warring factions, or general lawlessness. Most of these miserable countries crowd into the list of those officially classified as least developed in UN publications. A sampling of their names shows why what little foreign capital still works there currently is interested only in getting and staying out. Burundi, Cambodia, Ethiopia, Haiti, Liberia, Rwanda, Somalia, Sudan, and Zaire are examples. But the number of these capital-repellent countries is diminishing; they are becoming ever more marginal, now that, not only

yesterday's disappointments (such as Peru and Argentina), but China, India, and Pakistan are bidding fair to do so as well. The result is that corruption, unpredictability, and regulatory nastiness to foreign capital no longer deprive much of the developing world of private-capital transfers from advanced industrial countries. Those center countries, in turn, cannot possibly staunch the outflow, once the periphery has made itself noticeably more competitive, secure, and inviting. Segmentation of international capital markets, which meant hogging capital in the advanced industrial part of the world, is a thing of the past once again, just as it was before World War I.

Thus, the fascinating analyses and predictions concocted in the pre-World War I Age of Ideology, when the globalization of capital markets without allowance for country-risk-differentials was first examined, may yet find a reality in the closing years of this century and beyond. By choosing to open up to competitive capitalism driven by the private sector, rather than by being broken open through the force of imperialism, more and more developing countries are finally starting to bring about that worldwide dispersion of capital that was expected to yield a certain 'leveling' of living standards a century ago. Ironically perhaps, capitalism, by refusing to die and being reborn, is making some Marxist prognostications come true for quite non-Marxist reasons.

For Further Reading

Rudolph Hilferding, Edited by Tom Bottomore from translations by Morris Watnick and Sam Gordon, *Finance Capital: A Study of the Latest Phase of Capitalist Development,* Routledge Kegan Paul, [1910] 1981.

John Atkinson Hobson, *Imperialism: A Study,* The University of Michigan Press, [1902] 1971.

V. I. Lenin, *Imperialism, The Highest Stage of Capitalism: A Popular Outline,* Foreign Languages Press, [1917] 1965.

International Trade and Investment

Robert C. Feenstra

Research activities of the NBER's Program in International Trade and Investment can be grouped into four broad areas: trade patterns (static and dynamic); trade policy; regional and multilateral trade agreements; and foreign direct investment. Much of the research is motivated by the policy experience of the United States and other countries, and one goal of the program is to evaluate the outcome of these international policies. Another goal is to understand the determinants of trade policies and trade patterns. To this end, members of the program are engaged actively in developing models of endogenous growth, economic geography, and political economy, applied to questions of international (or regional) trade.

Trade Patterns

Current research has moved beyond resource endowments as a determinant of static trade patterns, and has introduced monopolostic competition and product diversity as an explanation for trade flows. Elhanan Helpman has shown that when countries are fully specialized in unique product varieties, and tastes are the same across nations, then a relatively simple equation relating trade flows to country sizes can be obtained.[1] This equation fits the data well for the OECD countries. David Hummels and James A. Levinsohn have reconsidered this empirical evidence, and have shown that the same

equation also fits well for a group of non-OECD countries, including various South American and African nations.[2] Since we do not expect that the trade patterns of the latter countries are determined by monopolistic competition, there is a puzzle as to what is being explained by this equation.

Along with Tzu-Han Yang and the sociologist Gary G. Hamilton, I provided further evidence on the link between market structure and trade patterns.[3] Hamilton's firm-level data on business groups in Japan, Korea, and Taiwan show dramatic differences in the type of vertical and horizontal integration within these countries. We argue that these market structures should correspond to different trade patterns, and in particular, that greater vertical integration (and resulting economies of scale) should lead to less product diversity. We confirm this hypothesis by comparing Taiwan and Korea, in that Korea has less diversity in its exports to the United States. Japan has greater product variety than either of these countries, and that is explained by its substantial size. Dani Rodrik, and later we, provided evidence on the composition or "quality" of export from these countries (measured by a comparison of unit-values and price indexes.)[4]

The dynamics of trade have been extensively analyzed in theory by Gene M. Grossman and Helpman,[5] and various researchers have

begun to test these models. David T. Coe and Helpman find that both a country's R and D stock and the R and D stock of its trade partners affect the country's total factor productivity, supporting the idea that knowledge diffuses across borders through trade.[6] James R. Markusen and I have developed empirical measures of product variety that could be applied to growth accounting.[7] In ongoing work, Jonathan Eaton and Sam Kortum test for international technological diffusion using data on patents within the OECD countries. Magnus Blomström, Robert E. Lipsey, and Mario Zejan have examined the determinants of developing country growth, finding that inflows of direct investment, along with secondary education and labor force participation, are major factors.[8] The empirical evidence linking trade and growth will be the topic of an upcoming NBER–CEPR International Seminar on International Trade, organized by Robert E. and Richard E. Baldwin, to be reviewed in a future *NBER Reporter*.

Dynamic patterns of regional trade play a central role in recent models of economic geography, as developed especially by Paul R. Krugman.[9] Kiminori Matsuyama and Takaaki Takahashi have investigated the welfare properties of the equilibrium in which one region dominates, and show that such concentration can reduce welfare.[10] Jonathan Eaton and Zvi Eckstein present evidence that cities in France and Japan have grown in a parallel manner, with little tendency for divergence to the largest centers.[11] James E. Rauch uses data on the growth of industrial parks in the United States to argue that these allowed developers to internalize agglomeration economies; he also has analyzed the impact of bureaucracies on the historical growth of cities in the United States.[12] J. David Richardson is engaged in developing a database and analyzing trade between states within the United States. Finally, Gordon H. Hanson uses data on the garment industry in Mexico to study the impact of trade liberalization on the regional structure of wages and locational choice.[13]

Trade Policy

Research on trade policy can be divided into work on import quotas and export subsidies; on antidumping and countervailing duties; and on the political economy of trade policy. In the first area, Dani Rodrik and Barbara J. Spencer are challenging the conventional wisdom that quotas and subsidies will lead to high inefficiency and rent-seeking costs, by providing examples where these regimes (arguably) seem to have worked.[14] Kala Krishna and Ling Hui Tan have examined in detail the workings of the Hong Kong market for quota licenses in textiles.[15] Recently I have calculated the deadweight loss associated with the quality upgrading that occurred in U.S. imports of Japanese automobiles in the 1980s.[16]

In the second area, Thomas Prusa and Wendy L. Hansen are investigating the impact of the "cumulation provision," introduced into U.S. trade laws in 1984, on the outcome of antidumping determination.[17] Under this provision, the imports from all source countries are summed by the International Trade Commission (ITC) to determine po-

tential injury. Robert W. Staiger and Frank A. Wolak examine the trade impacts of U.S. antidumping law and determinants of suit filing activity from 1980–5, identifying several channels through which a suit can affect trade even if duties are not levied.[18] Robert E. Baldwin and Jeffrey W. Steagall provide a general empirical analysis of the factors influencing ITC decisions in antidumping, countervailing duty, and safeguard cases.[19]

The political economy of trade policy is an area of growing research interest. Grossman and Helpman have been modeling how trade policies are determined as political outcomes in representative democracies.[20] They focus on the interactions between incumbent politicians, who are in a position to set trade policy, and special interest groups, who make political contributions to these politicians. Their solutions for the political equilibrium allow a vector of tariffs to be determined over many industries, balancing the politician's concern for campaign financing and social welfare. The idea that declining industries may experience a collapse of protection has been studied by S. Lael Brainard and Thierry Verdier.[21] The actual experience of various industries was discussed at the conference "Political Economy of Trade Protection," organized by Anne O. Krueger, and summarized in the Spring 1994 *NBER Reporter*.[22]

A final area that has implications for trade policy are the links between exchange rates, international prices, and wages. Michael M. Knetter, Joseph E. Gagnon, and I have explored the extent to which firms pass-through changes in exchange rates to their prices, particularly in the automobile industry.[23] In a quite different context, Sebastian Edwards has examined the link between exchange rates, trade policy, and growth for developing countries.[24] Robert Z. Lawrence and Paul R. Krugman have recently critiqued the popular opinion that

trade competition accounts for the drop in the relative wages of blue collar workers in the United States. They find that this belief is not supported by the evidence, and that the sources of U.S. economic difficulties are overwhelmingly domestic. This is a controversial conclusion that is bound to lead to further research in the near future.[25]

Regional and Multilateral Trade Agreements

The successful conclusion of the North American Free Trade Agreement (NAFTA), as well as the Uruguay Round of GATT negotiations, underscores the importance of these international agreements in reducing barriers to the flow of goods and services across borders. A number of researchers have been actively involved in studying the political determinants of these agreements and their economic impact. Grossman and Helpman have extended their work on the political economy of protection to investigate the viability of free trade agreements.[26] They find that an agreement between two countries is most likely to be politically viable when the potential trade between the members is sufficiently close to being balanced, and when the agreement would generate substantial trade diversion rather than creation. Unfortunately, this result implies that political support for the agreement is likely to be greatest exactly when the agreement would reduce trade efficiency.

Kyle Bagwell and Staiger have focused on the implications of a regional agreement for further multilateral trade liberalization.[27] They find that in the early stages, regional negotiations likely will be associated with less multilateral cooperation, because the expectations of future trade diversion reduces the fear of future trade wars across blocs. However, once a regional agreement is fully implemented and the trade diversion has occurred, then more liberal multilateral trade policies can be restored. Staiger has investigated in more detail how the flow of resources out of import-competing sectors affect the incentives for multilateral cooperation.[28] Further research on regional and multilateral trade agreements has been undertaken by Richard E. Baldwin, and Carsten Kowalczyk with Ronald J. Wonnacott and Tomas Sjostrom.[29]

Because regional free trade agreements do not harmonize the tariffs levied by member countries on imports from outside the bloc, they require extensive "rules of origin" or domestic-content provisions to prevent imports from entering through the lowest tariff country. These rules play an important role in the NAFTA legislation, and have quite dramatic effects on the efficiency of production. These effects are discussed in general by Krueger, and in the context of empirical simulations by Florencio Lopez-de-Silanes, Markusen, and Thomas F. Rutherford.[30] Additional simulation results concerning the incentives for countries of different sizes to enter into regional agreements are provided by Carlo Perroni and John Whalley.[31]

Jeffrey A. Frankel also has been working on the regionalization of world trade. He has investigated the hypothesis that Japan is coming to dominate East Asia.[32] The common view that the countries in the region have been intensifying intraregional trade can be explained by "natural factors," such as distance, transportation costs, country size, and per capita incomes. In work with Shang-Jin Wei and Ernesto Stein, Frankel then addresses what the trend toward regionalization of trade implies for world efficiency.[33] Given the estimated range of intracontinental transportation costs, they find that the formation of regional free trade areas is likely to distort trade and reduce economic welfare. They call such blocs "super-natural," in contrast to the "natural" trade blocs that would arise

from the proximity of countries under free trade. Barry Eichengreen and Douglas A. Irwin apply a similar methodology to analyze the disintegration of world trade in the 1930s.[34] Considerations of distance and transportation costs also are used by Edward E. Leamer to estimate the future structure of trade between Mexico and the United States.[35]

Foreign Direct Investment

Research on the decisions of multinational firms to invest abroad, and resulting implications for trade flows, also is included within the program. Traditional explanations of multinationals emphasize differences in factor proportions or wages across nations as the motivation for overseas expansion. However, in recent years, over 80 percent of foreign direct investment has been between industrialized countries. Accordingly, Brainard has developed and tested a model that explains horizontal integration across borders by considerations of market access.[36] She finds substantial empirical support for the model using bilateral data on U.S. trade and overseas production for 27 countries and 64 industries. In particular, overseas production is found to increase relative to exports when trade barriers, transport costs, or advertising intensity are high, and when plant economies and investment barriers are low. Brainard also finds that the volume of intraindustry affiliate sales increases as countries are more similar in their factor proportion or per capita incomes, contradicting the factor proportions explanation for multinational sales.[37]

In joint work with Keith Head and John Ries, Deborah Swenson proposes an additional explanation for foreign direct investment.[38] They test whether agglomeration economies—whereby benefits are obtained from locating in the same region as other foreign firms in the

same industry—are a factor in the locational choice of firms. Using data on Japanese manufacturing plants built in the United States, they find that firms are more likely to locate in regions where other Japanese firms operate (especially those in the same business group), after controlling for the presence of U.S. firms in that industry. Aizenman examines the implications of foreign direct investment.[39] He argues that overseas investment will reduce the likelihood of managed trade between the countries, but potentially increase the incidence of cyclical dumping; both these outcomes are welfare improving for the countries involved.

Lipsey examines the long-term trends in foreign investment activity within the United States, as well as in outward direct investment.[40] One of his conclusions is that foreign production has been a means by which American firms have retained foreign market shares even as their shares in the U.S. economy have declined, and that foreign direct investment has served the same function for firms from other countries. He finds little support for the idea that direct investment "exports jobs." More evidence points to a shift in the composition of home country employment toward managerial and technical occupations. The implications of foreign investment for the division of labor at home, as well as for domestic investment, also are being considered by Blomström and Ari Kokko, using evidence from Swedish multinationals.[41]

---

[1] E. Helpman, "Imperfect Competition and International Trade: Evidence from Fourteen Industrial Countries," Journal of the Japanese and International Economies 1 (March 1987), pp. 62–81.

[2] D. Hummels and J. A. Levinsohn, "Monopolistic Competition and International Trade: Reconsidering the Evidence," NBER Working Paper No. 4389, June 1993.

[3]R. C. Feenstra, T.-H. Yang, and G. G. Hamilton, "Market Structure and International Trade: Business Groups in East Asia," NBER Working Paper No. 4536, November 1993.

[4]D. Rodrik, "Industrial Organization and Product Quality: Evidence from South Korean and Taiwanese Exports," in Empirical Studies of Strategic Trade Policy, P. R. Krugman and A. M. Smith, eds. Chicago: University of Chicago Press, 1994, pp. 195–210.

[5]G. M. Grossman and E. Helpman, Innovation and Growth in the Global Economy, Cambridge: MIT Press, 1991.

[6]D. T. Coe and E. Helpman, "International R and D Spillovers," NBER Working Paper No. 4444, August 1993.

[7]R. C. Feenstra and J. R. Markusen, "Accounting for Growth with New Inputs," NBER Working Paper No. 4114, July 1992, and International Economic Review 35(2) (May 1994), pp. 429–447.

[8]M. Blomström, R. E. Lipsey, and M. Zejan, "What Explains Developing Country Growth?" in Convergence and Productivity: Cross-National Studies and Historical Evidence, W. Baumel, R. Nelson, and E. Wolff, eds. Oxford: Oxford University Press, 1994, and "Is Fixed Investment the Key to Economic Growth?" NBER Working Paper No. 4436, August 1993.

[9]P. R. Krugman, "A Dynamic Spatial Model," NBER Working Paper No. 4219, November 1992, and "Fluctuations, Instability, and Agglomeration," NBER Working Paper No. 4616, January 1994.

[10]K. Matsuyama and T. Takahashi, "Self-Defeating Regional Concentration," NBER Working Paper No. 4484, October 1993.

[11]J. Eaton and Z. Eckstein, "Cities and Growth: Theory and Evidence from France and Japan," NBER Working Paper No. 4612, January 1994.

[12]J. E. Rauch, "Does History Matter Only When It Matters Little? The Case of City–Industry Location," in The Quarterly Journal of Economics 108(3) (August 1993), pp. 843–867, and "Bureaucracy, Infrastructure, and Economic Growth: Theory and Evidence from U.S. Cities During the Progressive Era," University of California, San Diego, 1993.

[13]G. H. Hanson, "Localization Economies, Vertical Organization, and Trade: Theory and Evidence from Mexico," and "Increasing Returns and the Regional Structure of Wages," Department of Economics, University of Texas, Austin, 1993.

[14]D. Rodrik, "Taking Trade Policy Seri-

ously: Export Subsidization as a Case Study in Policy Effectiveness," in Tax Policy and the Economy, Volume 8, J. M. Poterba, ed. Cambridge: MIT Press, 1994; and B. J. Spencer, "Quota Licenses for Imported Capital Equipment: Could Bureaucratic Allocation Ever Do Better Than the Market?" University of British Columbia, 1994.

[15]K. Krishna and L. H. Tan, "License Price Paths: I. Theory, II. Evidence from Hong Kong," NBER Working Paper No. 4237, December 1992.

[16]R. C. Feenstra, "Measuring the Welfare Effect of Quality Change: Theory and Application to Japanese Autos," NBER Working Paper No. 4401, July 1993.

[17]T. Prusa and W. L. Hansen, "Measuring the Impact of Cumulation on ITC Injury Determinations: Evidence from Antidumping and Countervailing Duty Cases," State University of New York at Stony Brook, 1994.

[18]R. W. Staiger and F. A. Wolak, "Measuring Industry-Specific Protection: Antidumping in the United States," NBER Working Paper No. 4646, April 1994.

[19]R. E. Baldwin and J. W. Steagall, "An Analysis of Factors Influencing ITC Decisions in Antidumping, Countervailing Duty, and Safeguard Cases," NBER Working Paper No. 4282, February 1993.

[20]G. M. Grossman and E. Helpman, "Protection for Sale," NBER Working Paper No. 4149, August 1992, and "Trade Wars and Trade Talks," NBER Working Paper No. 4280, February 1993.

[21]S. L. Brainard and T. Verdier, "The Political Economy of Declining Industries: Senescent Industry Collapse Revisited," NBER Working Paper No. 4606, December 1993.

[22]See also A. O. Krueger, "The Political Economy of Controls: Complexity," in Global Change and Transformation, L. Stetting, K. E. Svendsen, and F. Yndgaard, eds. Copenhagen: Handelskolens Forlag, pp. 193–210.

[23]J. E. Gagnon and M. M. Knetter, "Markup Adjustment and Exchange Rate Fluctuations: Evidence from Panel Data on Automobile Exports," NBER Working Paper No.4123, July 1992; M. M. Knetter, "Exchange Rates and Corporate Pricing Strategies," NBER Working Paper No. 4151, August 1992, and "Is Price Adjustment Asymmetric? Evaluating the Market Share and Marketing Bottlenecks Hypothesis," NBER Working Paper No. 4170, September 1992; and R. C. Feenstra, J. E. Gagnon and M. M.

Knetter, "Market Share and Exchange Rate Pass-Through in World Automobile Trade," NBER Working Paper No. 4399, July 1993.

[24]S. Edwards, "Trade Policy, Exchange Rates, and Growth," NBER Working Paper No. 4511, October 1993.

[25]P. R. Krugman and R. Z. Lawrence, "Trade, Jobs, and Wages," NBER Working Paper No. 4478, September 1993.

[26]G. M. Grossman and E. Helpman, "The Politics of Free Trade Agreements," NBER Working Paper No. 4597, December 1993.

[27]K. Bagwell and R. W. Staiger, "Multilateral Tariff Cooperation During the Formation of Regional Free Trade Areas," NBER Working Paper No. 4364, May 1993, and "Multilateral Tariff Cooperation During the Formation of Customs Unions," NBER Working Paper No. 4543, November 1993.

[28]R. W. Staiger "A Theory of Gradual Trade Liberalization," NBER Working Paper No. 4620, January 1994.

[29]R. E. Baldwin, "A Domino Theory of Regionalism," NBER Working Paper No. 4465, September 1993; C. Kowalczyk and R. J. Wonnacott, "Hubs and Spokes, and Free Trade in the Americas," NBER Working Paper No. 4198, October 1992; and C. Kowalczyk and T. Sjostrom, "Bringing GATT into the Core," NBER Working Paper No. 4343, April 1993.

[30]A. O. Krueger, "Free Trade Agreements as Protectionist Devices: Rules of Origin," NBER Working Paper No. 4352, April 1993; F. Lopez-de-Silanes, J. R. Markusen, and T. F. Rutherford, "Anti-Competitive and Rent-Shifting Aspects of Domestic Content Provisions in Regional Trade Blocs," NBER Working Paper No. 4512, October 1993; J. R. Markusen and T. F. Rutherford, "Discrete Plant-Location Decisions in an Applied General Equilibrium Model of Trade Liberalization," NBER Working Paper No. 4513, October 1993.

[31]C. Perroni and J. Whalley, "The New Regionalism: Trade Liberalization or Insurance?" NBER Working Paper No. 4626, January 1994.

[32]J. A. Frankel, "Is Japan Creating a Yen Bloc in East Asia and the Pacific?" in Regionalism and Rivalry: Japan and the United States in Pacific Asia, J. A. Frankel and M. Kahler, eds., Chicago: University of Chicago Press, 1993, pp. 53–85.

[33]J. A. Frankel and S.-J. Wei, "Trade Blocs and Currency Blocs," NBER Working Paper No. 4335, April 1993; J. A. Frankel, E. Stein, and S.-J. Wei "Continental Trading Blocs: Are They Natural, or Super-Natural?" NBER Working

Paper No. 4588, December 1993, and "Trading Blocs: The Natural, the Unnatural, and the Super-Natural," presented at the NBER Sixth InterAmerican Seminar in Economics, Caracas, Venezuela, May 28–29, 1993, forthcoming in the Journal of Development Economics.

[34]B. Eichengreen and D. A. Irwin, "Trade Blocs, Currency Blocs, and the Disintegration of World Trade in the 1930s," NBER Working Paper No. 4445, August 1993.

[35]E. E. Leamer and C. J. Medberry, "U.S. Manufacturing and an Emerging Mexico," NBER Working Paper No. 4331, April 1993.

[36]S. L. Brainard, "A Simple Theory of Multinational Corporations and Trade with a Trade-Off Between Proximity and Concentration," NBER Working Paper No. 4269, February 1993, and "An Empirical Assessment of the Proximity-Concentration Trade-Off Between Multinational Sales and Trade," NBER Working Paper No. 4580, December 1993.

[37]S. L. Brainard, "An Empirical Assessment of the Factor Proportions Explanation of Multinational Sales," NBER Working Paper No. 4583, December 1993.

[38]K. Head, J. Ries, and D. Swenson, "Agglomeration Benefits and Location Choice: Evidence from Japanese Manufacturing Investments in the United States," University of British Columbia and University of California, Davis.

[39]J. Aizenman, "Foreign Direct Investment as a Commitment Mechanism in the Presence of Managed Trade," NBER Working Paper No. 4102, June 1992, and "Foreign Direct Investment, Employment Volatility, and Cyclical Dumping," NBER Working Paper No. 4683, March 1994.

[40]R. E. Lipsey, "Foreign Direct Investment in the United States: Changes Over Three Decades," NBER Reprint No. 1851, February 1994, and in Foreign Direct Investment, K. A. Froot, ed. Chicago: University of Chicago Press, 1993, pp. 113–170, and "Outward Direct Investment and the U.S. Economy," NBER Working Paper No. 4691, March 1994.

[41]M. Blomström and A. Kokko, "Home Country Effects of Foreign Direct Investment: Evidence from Sweden," NBER Working Paper No. 4639, February 1994.

The International Environment: Organizations and Monetary Systems

- International Organizations (Articles 7 and 8)
- International Monetary System and Balance of Payments (Articles 9–11)

One of the most obvious developments in international trade has been the development of international trade organizations. Some of these organizations have existed for several decades, while others are very new. They all have several things in common. The first is that while there has been some global agreements such as the General Agreements on Tariffs and Trade (GATT) and the World Trade Organization (WTO), most of the trade organizations tend to be regional, the European Union (EU), which was known as the European Economic Community or Common Market until 1994, and the North American Free Trade Agreement (NAFTA) are simply some of the more obvious examples.

The second is that they involve nations in a sort of customs union, which tends to lower and/or remove trade barriers among members of the organization while maintaining, at a somewhat higher level, trade restrictions for products and services from outside of the regional trade association.

A few, such as the EU, have political ambitions of uniting the member countries into a political union. The EU's headquarters is located in Brussels, and one of the problems that it has had over the years has been the struggle over sovereignty among the countries making up the union and the centralized government in Brussels.

One of the most recently developed trade organizations is the North American Free Trade Agreement (NAFTA), which is a trading agreement between the United States, Canada, and Mexico. NAFTA was built on an agreement that was in force for several years between the United States and Canada. This agreement essentially removed the vast majority of trade barriers between these two countries. NAFTA included Mexico into the deal. This was not accomplished without great political struggle in the United States or without second thoughts, especially after the crash of the Mexican economy shortly after the ratification of the agreement.

Indeed, the essay "Hemispheric Prospects: NAFTA Changes the Game" addresses the questions surrounding NAFTA's influence on North America. NAFTA does broaden opportunities for all organizations involved. However, one major problem is going to be the integration of Mexico, a country that for decades has seemed to be on the verge of joining the developed world, into a union with Canada and the United States. Integrating the Canadian and American economies is a relatively simple task: the legal systems are based on the same philosophy of law; the language is the same; the political system is very similar; many American and Canadian firms are already doing substantial business in each other's countries; and the standard of living, while not exactly the same, is certainly comparable. Mexico, however, is a very different story: the legal system is based on a whole different philosophy of law; the language is different; it has one-party rule; the standard of living is very different; and while many American firms are already doing business in Mexico, much of the activity is designed for export to the United States. Economically, geographically, or politically, it does not make sense to exclude Mexico from economic integration with the rest of North America. The difficulty arises in how to do it.

Another recent development in world trade has been the development of the World Trade Organization (WTO). The WTO was created as a result of the Uruguay Round of the GATT talks and in many ways supersedes GATT. Many challenges face the WTO, and one of the first is going to be the trading conflict between the United States and Japan over automobiles. This is a conflict that has been going on for over 25 years, and it is part of a larger balance of trade problem between the United States and

Japan. Much of it is not to be found in official government policy, but in the way individual firms do business, something that has always been difficult to control and will surely prove a very thorny problem for the new World Trade Organization.

Financial markets have always been a major cause of concern for organizations engaged in world trade. This, along with the International Monetary Fund (IMF) and the World Bank, was the major focus of the Bretton Woods Agreement at the end of World War II. But the financial markets aspect of the agreement failed and while the World Bank and the IMF have continued in their missions, the value of currencies have been unhitched and allowed to float. This has led banks and other international financial institutions to seek greater cooperation and stability in the world monetary markets. It also led to the recognition that world trade conditions were fluid, subject to change, and that a mechanism was needed to help deal with the inherent risks associated with that change. That mechanism was found in the international market for currencies and the associated markets, such as derivatives, that have developed over the years. It is difficult to say what will happen in the future concerning the international monetary system, but the article "Global Financial Markets in 2020" has some ideas.

Looking Ahead: Challenge Questions

Describe the role of international trade organizations. Do you think they help or hinder world trade? Why?

Fluctuations between currencies can turn a banner year into a disaster. What are some of the things that can be done to lower potential risks?

GATT to WTO

The Institutionalization of World Trade

Crucial Tarks

SALIL S. PITRODA

Salil S. Pitroda is a Staff Writer for the Harvard International Review.

O VER THE PAST FEW DECADES, a system of relatively open exchange, particularly in merchandise trade, has prevailed in the world under the auspices of the General Agreement on Tariffs and Trade (GATT). Today, most economists acknowledge this trading system as one of the greatest contributors to the world's rapid recovery from the desolation of the second World War, and to the phenomenal growth in world output thereafter. Through all of those years, however, GATT has served its member countries through a loose and informal structure, with all the inevitable problems that accompany a weak and ill-defined authority. With the passage of the Uruguay Round of trade talks, this trading system is poised to take on a new shape in a permanent institution known as the World Trade Organization (WTO). Although much skepticism and controversy have surrounded the birth of WTO, it is the hope of all free-traders that the new WTO will be able to amend what went amiss with GATT.

A Brief History of Trade

At the beginning of the nineteenth century, economists began to make advances in interpreting why human beings had always engaged in economic exchange. The theory of comparative advantage posited that countries specialize in those goods and services that they can produce more efficiently relative to other countries. When nations concentrate their production on commodities in which they have a comparative advantage, consumers as a whole benefit from lower prices and a greater range of consumption possibilities. Because each good is produced by the country that is best at producing it, scarce world resources are allocated efficiently. Like all economic activities, the distribution of the benefits of trade is not uniform; yet in general and in the long run, trade leads to a more optimal economic outcome with greater competition and greater productivity—a rising tide on which all boats float.

In 1947, such a view of the benefits of international cooperation inspired a group of visionaries gathered in Bretton Woods, New Hampshire, to erect a new economic world order from the ravages of the second World War. The Bretton Woods Accords, which celebrated their fiftieth anniversary last year, established the World Bank and the International Monetary Fund and led to the creation of GATT. These structures, albeit not always true to the visionary spirit in which they were founded, have formed the underpinnings of world economic development for the past half century.

GATT has become the framework for international trade in our time. The body was formed as an interim secretariat for trade negotiations after the United States, bowing to protectionist sentiment, refused to ratify the charter of the stillborn International Trade Organization, a full-fledged institution of the stature of the World Bank and the IMF. Based in Geneva and currently encompassing over 120 member nations, GATT has acted as a conduit for multilateral negotiations on a variety of international trade issues, including tariff and quota policy and trading practices. It has sponsored several rounds of protracted, though eventually fruitful, trade talks where members gathered to hammer out the details of the set of rules governing economic exchange. GATT panels make recommendations on changes in trade regulations and review complaints against member countries.

Despite GATT's success in coordinating international trade policy, it must be remembered that GATT is only an interim body without a fully defined institutional structure and with little legal enforcement power. For instance, many loopholes exist in the mechanism dealing with disputes regarding unfair trade practices. If a country complains of unfair trading practices on the part of another country and a GATT panel concurs with the complaint, the accused country can dissent from the finding, effectively vetoing it and preventing the complaining country from retaliation within the GATT framework. Another increasingly popular way of doing business in an extra-GATT environment is through the creation of regional trade blocs, such as the European Union (EU), the North American Free Trade Agreement (NAFTA) and the impending Association of Southeast Asian Nations (ASEAN) free trade agreement. These regional agreements, in effect, set their own rules of trade, encouraging cooperative exchange within a

From *Harvard International Review*, Spring 1995, pp. 46-47, 66-67. © 1995 by the Harvard International Relations Council. Reprinted by permission.

bloc but hinting of protectionism against countries outside the region. Non-tariff trade barriers (NTBs), such as a German requirement that, for health reasons, beer sold in Germany be made with German water, are also another device for bending GATT rules. Another way of eschewing GATT policy through these regional trading arrangements is to manipulate the rules of origin stipulation. By raising the requirement of local content value, aspiring profiteers and vested interests can turn an ostensible reduction in a tariff into an actual increase by subjecting formerly tariff-exempt goods to duties, thus circumventing the GATT guideline that for any free trade agreement the new common external tariff be no higher than the average tariff of the constituent states before the accord. Without any institutional framework or legal authority, the most that GATT can do, when confronted with such adroit legerdemain with its regulations, is to urge and exhort a spirit of cooperation among member states, each of whom has an individual incentive to cater to local interests by eschewing a rule here and raising a protectionist wall there.

Seeking to address some of these problems, the Uruguay Round of negotiations was launched nearly nine years ago. Under the leadership of GATT Director-General Peter Sutherland, this latest round of trade talks has arrived at a consensus on implementing changes to the international framework that will encourage greater openness and trade integration among the world's nations. First and foremost, the Uruguay Round promises a lowering of trade barriers and a slashing of tariffs by an average of one-third. It broadens the scope of liberalization to include traditionally protected industries such as textiles and apparel. Reflecting the changing nature of world trade, the Uruguay Round will open up exchange in the previously closed but rapidly emerging areas of agriculture, services, and intellectual property. It imposes a new discipline on NTBs and government procurement and offers clarification on subsidies, dumping regulations, quota restrictions and voluntary export restraints. It also lays the foundation for further talks dealing with important trade issues including the treatment of foreign direct investment, labor and environmental concerns, and capital and currency market fluctuations. Most importantly, the Uruguay Round of accords has boldly moved the world a step closer to global free trade by calling for the establishment of the WTO to succeed the GATT secretariat.

The Birth of WTO

The WTO will be a new international institution, on par with the World Bank and the IMF, that will outline a framework for all areas of international trade and will have the legal authority to settle trade disputes. In legal terms, it represents the maturation of the GATT secretariat into a full-fledged, permanent international entity. The supreme decision-making body will be a biannual ministerial meeting, affording the organization more political clout and a higher international profile. This WTO council will then have subsidiary working bodies that specialize in areas of trade including goods, services and intellectual property. Unlike GATT, the WTO will have a clearly defined dispute settlement mechanism. Independent panel reports will automatically be adopted by the WTO council unless there is a clear consensus to reject them. Countries who are accused of engaging in unfair trade practices can appeal to a permanent appellate body, but the verdict of this body will be ultimately binding. If an offending nation fails to comply with WTO panel recommendations, its trading partners will be guaranteed the right to compensation as determined by the panel or, as a final resort, be given the right to impose countervailing sanctions. All members of the WTO will have legal access to these multilateral dispute settlement mechanisms, and all stages of WTO deliberation will be time-limited, ensuring efficiency in dispute settlement. The World Trade Organization will be akin to an International Court of Justice for world trade, with the institutional strength and legal mandate to ensure fair trade and global economic integration.

Who will be the pioneering leader of this newly constructed international organization? The ideal candidate must possess a strategic global vision of world trade while being comfortable with technical complexity. He or she must combine the finesse of a diplomat, the organizational acumen of an experienced administrator and the leadership qualities of a seasoned statesman.

Since Peter Sutherland, the incumbent Director-General of GATT has indicated his wish to stand down in favor of fresh leadership, the competition to be the head of the WTO has been opened up to three dynamic candidates. Renato Ruggiero, the favored candidate of the EU, is a former trade minister of Italy and has also been suggested in the past as a possible president of the European Commission. He has emphasized his experience as a capable administrator with international experience in Brussels, the GATT, and world economic summits. Carlos Salinas de Gortari, who during his tenure as the President of Mexico defined the paradigm for economic liberalization in developing countries, is the candidate favored by the Americas. His international stature as a head of state and his commitment to free trade—as evinced by his personal crusade for NAFTA—are Salinas's most important assets. The South Korean trade minister, Kim Chul-Su, has proven international experience and is naturally supported by countries in Asia and Australia, the fastest growing region in the world. In the end, politics will most likely decide who heads the WTO. Similar leadership positions are opening up at the Organization for Economic Cooperation and Development (OECD) and other international organizations, with political horse-trading sure to play an integral role in determining the new leaders of these organizations.

There are various other strategic issues relating to the establishment of the WTO. At least for the initial transition stage, the new organization is expected to grow by expanding on the existing GATT structure. The WTO will most probably be situated in the existing GATT building in Geneva and will require an increase in GATT's present budget and staff. Yet even with this augmentation in resources, the WTO will still remain far smaller in size than either the World Bank or the IMF.

Aside from such logistical matters, however, the precise nature of the transition between GATT and WTO remains more nebulous. Some countries, such as the United States, have already announced that they will terminate their GATT membership within sixty days of joining the WTO. Such a strict view of WTO's successor status to GATT raises interesting questions about US obligations to GATT members who have yet to ratify their entry into WTO.

Other countries envision the two organizations operating in tandem for a period of two years, with GATT still binding, to ease the transition to the WTO. There is also the question of new memberships. Will Slovenia and Croatia, for instance, who have just applied for GATT membership, be granted direct membership in the WTO? If the WTO does not completely supersede GATT immediately, where does that leave a country like the Sudan, which is not a GATT member, but has applied directly for WTO membership?

Of course, there is also the thorny problem of China, which has just been denied the opportunity of being a founding member of WTO, and Taiwan, whose competing applications will surely pose more dilemmas of politics and protocol. Certainly, careful deliberation will be needed to work out the multitude of implementational, organizational and transitional issues.

The Foundation of the New Order

Given these birth pangs, what are the fundamental qualities upon which the WTO must lay its foundation? As Carlos Salinas de Gortari has outlined in a recent article in *The Financial Times*, the WTO must be representative, reliable and responsive. It must embrace all countries, regardless of their level of economic development, and ensure their prompt and satisfactory integration into a multilateral trading system. Reliability is a much tougher criterion to satisfy. The WTO must clarify GATT rules, broaden its mandate and improve its dispute settlement mechanisms to demonstrate to all member nations that they have a stake in abiding by a rules-based trade regime. Finally, flexibility and responsiveness to the evolving changes of the international economy will ensure that the WTO retains the political support necessary to carrying out its work.

As an organization that has ambitions of leading the global economy into the next millennium, the WTO needs to legitimize its standing in the eyes of politicians and economists wearied by decades of trade negotiations by confronting some concrete and difficult problems. One of the first tasks it might have to face is deciding whether or not it should extend the rules regulating conduct in international trade to cover national competition policies. Ideally, countries should have roughly comparable standards on anti-trust legislation so that greater competition from all-comers, whether domestic or foreign, can be welcomed. But by treading on such sensitive territories, the WTO may stray too far from the trade-related issues at the core of its mandate. The animosities which it incurs in those confrontations may permanently impair its ability to unite its membership on other, arguably even more important, issues in the long run.

One of the most crucial tasks of the WTO will be presiding over the economic and political integration of the former socialist economies. It must provide stable and expanding outlets for these countries' products to encourage the liberalization of their economies and to help them attract much needed foreign direct investment. In fact, all the newly open economies in Latin America, Africa and Asia must be nurtured by a transparent, rules-based and mutually beneficial trading system. In particular, the WTO must encourage the reversal of the growing lethargy in North-South cooperation, especially with regard to Sub-Saharan African countries, which desperately need open international markets for their growth. The organization also has a special responsibility to bring the nearly two billion citizens of China and India, 40 percent of the planet's population, into the world trading regime as full and active members.

On a more macroscopic level, the WTO must effectively coordinate regional free trade agreements to ensure that they do not conflict in goals or create islands of protectionism, but are instead regional building blocks toward the eventual realization of global free trade which almost every economic theory praises as the ideal for future world economic relations. Pursuant to this objective of regional coordination, the institution must stiffen its regulations and their enforcement so that less and less protectionism can be veiled behind devices such as NTBs, rules of origins requirements and other technical loopholes. It must convince member nations that their greatest economic interest is to cooperate with the other nations of the world and not bow to vested interests by taking short-sighted unilateral action. The best means for guaranteeing this end is a vigorous and binding dispute settlement mechanism. In planning for the future, the organization must also proactively embrace the changing nature of the global economy from trade in manufactured goods to trade in information-intensive services and intellectual property. The technical complexity of those issues and the administrative difficulty that will inevitably accompany any rules governing them will be a challenge to WTO's energy, resourcefulness and resolve.

Finally, and very importantly, the WTO must acknowledge and deal with some of the local pains that uncompetitive industries in member nations will feel. In order to avoid the image of an elitist other-worldliness to which so many other well-intentioned international organizations have fallen prey, the WTO must ensure that the gains from trade are trickled down to the populace. Without at least some semblance of equity to compensate for the sacrifices that the working poor will be asked to make in any transition, it will be difficult for WTO to maintain the political and moral support that it needs to push through its vision of world-wide free trade. Ideally, some sort of structural adjustment fund and a common program for retraining displaced workers should be a pillar of the WTO, so that humanity and compassion, as well as hard-nosed efficiency, may be integrated into the organization's founding philosophy. There are undoubtedly a host of other important issues the new WTO should consider, but careful deliberation upon the fundamentals outlined here will be a major step toward solidifying and validating a global free trade system.

Positive Sums from Cooperation

The bottom line of the emergence of the new WTO from GATT is that world trade will be institutionalized in the formal legal structure of an international organization. The more formal status of the WTO will allow it to give more focus and publicity to efforts that attempt to create greater global cooperation in international trade. The institutionalization of trade through the WTO will give some bite to the bark of a well-articulated set of trading rules and policies. With its creation, there will exist an independent political entity that can view the world trading system from a holistic perspective and to check and balance competing interests that seek to bend the trading rules in their national or sectoral favor. By paying judicious attention to the fundamental issues in international trade, the WTO has the potential of becoming a visionary organization that outlines a bold path for international trade and leads the world into a new economic renaissance.

Recent studies have released estimates of the global economic effects of the ratification of the GATT Uruguay Round and the creation of the World Trade Organization. A GATT report released in November 1994 prognosticated that implementation of the Uruguay Round will spur an increase of $510 billion a year in world income by the year 2005. This figure is a vast underestimate, for it does not account for the impact of strengthened procedures and rules in the services trade or better dispute settlement mechanisms. Breaking up the gains by region, the report predicted that by 2005 the annual income gain will be $122 billion for the United States, $164 billion for the European Union, $27 billion for Japan and $116 billion for the developing and transitional socialist economies as a group. Figures estimating the increase in volume in the goods trade range from nine to 24 percent once the liberalization of the Uruguay Round comes into effect. In 1992 dollars, this gain represents an increase in trade flows of upwards of $670 billion. The report also suggests that Uruguay Round provisions for developing and transition economies will have the intended result of encouraging rapid growth, as exports and imports from this group are likely to be 50 percent over and beyond the increase for the rest of the world as a whole. The economic impact of a well-structured and credible institutionalization of international trade is likely to be enormous.

What remains to be done is the actual construction of this economic structure. Nowhere has the debate over GATT and the WTO been more pronounced than in the world's economic leader, the United States. As is to be expected before embarking upon any bold new initiative, those who stand to suffer short-term losses are trying to stand in the way of long-term progress. Protectionist concerns and irresponsible exaggeration have been vociferously fed to the press and the deliberative bodies of the government. One example of such red herrings is a concern about a loss of US sovereignty in becoming a member of the WTO. In truth, any changes in the law of the United States or any other nation will have to be ratified by proper legislative bodies in that country, and so the practical encroachment on national sovereignty is little more than negligible. Of course, there is a germ of truth in

> *All nations, the US in particular, must realize that partnerships are more advantageous than going it alone.*

this argument, for when any nation enters into an international treaty, it must lose some "sovereignty" to the extent that it agrees to abide by the terms of the agreement. Some kind of consensus, such as the sensitive balance that needs to be achieved by the WTO, must be reached to preserve a predictable and liberal international trade regime. To carp at the WTO for having the potential to compromise national sovereignty is little different from saying that national sovereignty is compromised because a country has to abide by any international treaty.

All nations, the US in particular, must realize that partnerships are more advantageous than going it alone, and that economic cooperation is not a zero-sum game. Free trade makes each and every nation more prosperous because it makes the entire world more prosperous. Government leaders around the world would do well to hearken to the words of Rufus Yerxa, Deputy US Trade Representative and Ambassador to GATT: "International cooperation will bring about the economic growth of the future. We cannot survive as an island in a sea of change. If we don't embrace this change, it will be our enemy rather than our friend. Cooperation is in our own self-interest."

Hemispheric Prospects

NAFTA CHANGES THE GAME

A U.S. Perspective

Richard L. Thomas

Richard L. Thomas is chairman and chief executive officer of First Chicago Corporation. He presented a U.S.-based view of NAFTA earlier this year before the Bankers' Association for Foreign Trade. This article is based on that presentation.

NAFTA — the North American Free Trade Agreement — clearly suffered from media overkill during the last months of the NAFTA campaign in the United States. Many were put off by the stridency, the distortion of issues, and the loss of perspective as the battle for passage of NAFTA was waged.

However, we owe it to ourselves to continue the discussion, focusing now on what we've done and on the opportunities NAFTA created.

In particular, we need to think very clearly about real risks and realistic returns. And we should have a vision — or at least a sense — of what the principal longer-term opportunities might be for our companies and businesses, while avoiding the euphoria — or the head-in-the-sand attitudes — that enveloped so much of the debate in this country last year.

BUSINESS VIEWS OPPORTUNITIES

A post-NAFTA survey of North American CEOs by the Conference Board is a good indicator of current expectations. The survey's main findings: *(cont. page 41)*

A Canadian Perspective

Edward P. Neufeld

Edward P. Neufeld is executive vice president for economic and corporate affairs for the Royal Bank of Canada in Toronto, Ontario. This article is adapted from his remarks earlier this year at the Bankers' Association for Foreign Trade forum on NAFTA held in Washington, D.C.

The North American Free Trade Agreement integrates Canada into the future evolution of the Western Hemisphere. It does so while protecting and extending the advantages achieved through the Canada-U.S. Free Trade Agreement (FTA), which took effect in January 1989.

If Canada had not been part of NAFTA, businesses seeking to locate or expand in North America and beyond would have been better off to locate in the United States rather than in Canada — an intolerable outcome for the future of the Canadian economy. So Canada undoubtedly will be part of future Western Hemisphere trade liberalization.

Not that NAFTA will have a major immediate impact — either positive or negative. Canada's two-way trade with Mexico is only $3.5 billion annually, compared with the United States' $214.8 billion. But Canada's experience with FTA, combined with intensive national debate surrounding NAFTA, has substantially clarified a number of issues concerning Canada's future trade relations in our hemisphere: *(cont. page 43)*

(continued from page 40)

◆ More than two-thirds of the CEOs in all three participating countries believe that NAFTA will improve business conditions in their respective nations. U.S. — and particularly Mexican — executives are somewhat more optimistic than their counterparts in Canada.

◆ A majority of business leaders in all three nations believe the trade agreement will help reduce business costs and improve profitability.

◆ In assessing NAFTA's likely effect on their own nation's employment growth, five out of six Mexican executives foresee a positive impact, compared with nearly three out of five U.S. respondents and only two out of five Canadians.

◆ A majority of business leaders in all three nations express support for the various provisions of NAFTA. Tariff reform, market access, investment opportunities, and intellectual property provisions receive particularly strong support. Environmental protection and labor provisions are given a somewhat-less-enthusiastic endorsement in Canada and the United States than in Mexico.

No surprises here, particularly with the main message that the passage of NAFTA has enhanced prospects for continued economic progress in Mexico as well as for increased trade and investment among the three current NAFTA partners. This bodes well for the majority of the North American business community.

Accepting the general belief that opportunities abound, let us focus on a few specifics of what NAFTA really does. We all probably believe that "enhanced" is the right word for NAFTA's impact, given the strong positive trends that existed in the fundamentals well before NAFTA was initiated. But the passage of NAFTA, combined with those fundamentals, has an impact greater than the sum of the parts.

Even the recent assassination of presidential candidate Luis Donaldo Colosio hasn't put NAFTA at risk over the long term. The ruling party has named Colosio's campaign manager, Ernesto Zedillo Ponce de Leon, as its candidate.

The message is simple: There is no turning back the clock on the Salinas and de la Madrid reforms. One of President Salinas' motives in negotiating NAFTA was to embed the policy reforms of his administration in an international agreement that could not be abandoned lightly.

The core of the reform program is secure: an open trade and investment regime, market-determined prices, limited government involvement in the economy, and commitment to low inflation and fiscal balance.

RISK/RETURN BASIS IMPROVES

This, in turn, means a better risk/return basis for investments in and into Mexico. More precisely, we see a trend toward:

◆ Longer time horizons in investment decisions;

◆ Lower discount rates; and

◆ An increase in the flow of investments.

In other words, NAFTA symbolically brings Mexico into the investment-grade arena and the "First World."

NAFTA also is an important signal to other Latin American countries of the benefits of economic and social liberalization. The U.S. business community has hoped for decades for steady progress toward development and stability by all major Latin American countries. NAFTA may turn out to be one of the more effective catalysts in this direction.

NAFTA's passage in the United States, and subsequent ratification by Canada, also should help to improve trade relationships between the United States and Canada. Although much of our current discussion is focused on Mexico, because that's the newest element, we should not forget that Canada is our largest trading partner (Mexico is second). NAFTA can be expected to promote even more trade with Canada, and also to help resolve some of the thorny trade issues that have arisen in recent years.

MAJOR U.S. INDUSTRIES UNHURT

Looking at how NAFTA affects various U.S. business sectors, we can say that:

◆ No major industry is materially hurt, although some industries — like household glassware and some clothing manufacturers — will be adversely impacted.

◆ Increased access to Mexican markets will lead to more freedom of decision-making in allocating corporate resources (by providing an alternative to moving to Southeast Asia, for example). Large "winners" in the near term include (1) capital-goods suppliers, (2) manufacturers of consumer durables, (3) grain producers and distributors, (4) construction equipment manufacturers and contractors, and (5) the auto industry (with some limitations).

Economists say we're already beginning to see increased trade flows between the United States and Mexico. A number of U.S. companies likely held off on exports to Mexico until after Jan. 1 in order to take advantage of lower tariff barriers under NAFTA.

My home base, the Midwest, with its concentration of winning industries, is a major beneficiary of NAFTA. We expect trade levels between Mexico and the Midwest to expand dramatically — much as they did with Canada after the U.S.-Canadian agreement in 1988.

IMPACT ON BANKING

For U.S. financial institutions, NAFTA brings privileged access into a previously protected market. In the near to intermediate term, the principal benefit of NAFTA for U.S. banks will likely be through their relationships with U.S. companies that, in turn, will grow and prosper more than they would have without NAFTA. In addition to serving these customers, economic development in border areas and transportation corridors will yield significant opportunities — and risks — for local banks.

The same is true for Mexican banks and their customers.

A select number of U.S. and Canadian banks will become more directly involved in Mexican markets; initially, this probably will be in the areas of corporate finance, trade banking, and capital markets, and possibly in operational services. We'll see growth in the form of *de novo* installations as well as in joint ventures and acquisitions.

I don't see early, widespread U.S. bank involvements in Mexican retail banking but, interestingly, U.S. finance companies may be more aggressive in this area. There is opportunity for assisting in the development of Mexico's credit-information infrastructure, which we think is also a necessary precursor of broad credit-card issuance.

The opening of the Mexican financial markets to new U.S., Canadian, and Mexican players also will create increased competition and some overheating in both debt and equity markets.

In Mexican banking, we are likely to see most of the following:
◆ Narrowing loan spreads and, as revenues decline, some pressure on risk limits.
◆ Better consumer treatment and lower fees; more required expenditure on marketing and customer service.
◆ New products; increased use of technology, with some players achieving significantly lower costs.

These factors are likely to make it more difficult for early purchasers of Mexican banks to achieve desired returns. And, as in any deregulation, there will be survivors and non-survivors.

We hope Mexican regulatory officials stay on top of their markets and ensure prudential standards, reasonably orderly growth, and

sensibly managed failures. We would argue, for example, for adherence to BIS (Bank for International Settlements) capital standards, better reporting, earlier problem-loan recognition, and conservative loan-loss reserving.

This is not to denigrate the generally excellent quality of Mexico's major banks, which likely will only experience a gradual loss of market share. However, many new, less-experienced banks will be created. As Mexican banking evolves, U.S. banks may be able to play a positive role in technology transfers.

Overall, therefore, the banking picture is pretty rosy; there are increased opportunities for most sectors of the North American banking industry.

LONGER-TERM TRENDS

NAFTA should send a crystal-clear message to other Latin American countries: It is symbolic in that its passage was a positive ratification of hemispheric trade liberalization, and of the political and economic behavior that makes this feasible. By signaling that this is how we will reward reform, NAFTA's passage was a crucial step on the way to real economic progress throughout the hemisphere.

Perhaps as important, on a more global scale, is the positive psychological impact and renewed vigor of U.S. leadership in international economic policy. The first result of this surely was in achieving agreement on GATT (the General Agreement on Tariffs and Trade). The second may be seen in the future growth of NAFTA.

The Clinton Administration has already put expanding NAFTA squarely on its political agenda. The 10- to 15-year time frame set out to achieve the end game is judicious in that there is a great deal that must be accomplished in many countries. However, the economic and political realities — both in the United States and in other Latin American countries — combined

with the vested interests embodied in existing Latin trade blocs, suggest that we won't see a straight-line progress toward a wider NAFTA.

We have much to do to make NAFTA succeed and thereby squelch all the doubters in the United States and Canada. On the other hand, U.S. companies are already using Mexico and its other free-trade agreements as a springboard for more sales into Latin America. If the economic fundamentals keep improving — as they have already done in the case of Chile and Argentina — the political reality can change quickly. The "markets" seem to see the entry of Chile, at the least, as a given. And why not? It is certainly in all of our interests to work toward the goal of a set of stable, democratic countries in an expanded free-trade zone.

Some other observations:
◆ The addition of Mexico — as both an expansion of the North American market for U.S. and Canadian companies and a manufacturing platform for North America — certainly will draw some foreign investment that would otherwise have gone to Southeast Asia and other parts of Latin America or elsewhere. This is good news for the region.
◆ North American firms will become more competitive globally as a result of this greater investment and of larger market scale. North American exports should increase more than they otherwise might have.
◆ As, we hope, Canada benefits from NAFTA-related trade improvement, we may see its economy become more open and cooperation increase among its provinces as well as between Canada and its partners. Success breeds success.
◆ There certainly will be considerable pressure on — and development of — both U.S. and Mexican infrastructure, especially on transportation channels as the trade flows increase. Significant im-

provements in North-South links are obvious, as is more general economic growth in the Southwest. Texas and Arizona already are gearing up for vastly increased business with Mexico. California seems more concerned about increased immigration. The transportation and related services corridor between Texas and the Midwest, in particular, is going to see a period of rapid growth. Financing for infrastructure development — particularly in the near term — is going to be an issue.

While these trends hold a great deal of potential new business for the banking industry, we also should be mindful of the problems we've encountered in the past in going too far afield in financing long-term development projects. But this is a minor note of caution in the overall scheme of promising hemispheric prospects.

All in all, we have a much-improved and exciting outlook for North America after NAFTA than we would have had NAFTA been defeated.

Canadian Perspective

(continued from page 40)

◆ First, while some of Canada's labor-intensive industries are affected by NAFTA, these same industries already were being impacted by other factors.

◆ Second, more open trade does indeed lead to more two-way trade.

◆ Third, the restructuring caused by more open trade makes Canadian industry more competitive in all its export markets.

◆ Fourth, Canada has many exports that Latin America needs for economic development — telecommunications, plastics, automotive, machine tools, metal-working and agriculture sectors have demonstrated success in Mexico.

◆ Fifth, and perhaps as significant as anything, experience is showing that mutual benefits emerge from trade between highly developed and less-developed industrial countries — a lesson of great economic and political importance for the future development of the Western Hemisphere.

BENEFITS TO CANADIAN, MEXICAN BANKS

The financial-services section of NAFTA presents a number of important opportunities for Canadian financial-services enterprises.

Under NAFTA, Mexico provides substantial access to its financial sector upon implementation of the agreement and full access after a reasonable transition period. Specifically, Canadian and U.S. banks are permitted under NAFTA to establish a wholly owned subsidiary in Mexico to carry on a banking business or acquire a Mexican bank. Prior to NAFTA, Canadian and U.S. banks were limited to having a representative office in Mexico.

While Canadian and U.S. banks initially will face individual and aggregate caps on their ownership of total Mexican domestic bank capital, the aggregate cap will be raised progressively until its removal in 2000. This represents a significant liberalization of Mexico's market for financial services.

Canadian commitments to Mexico are similar to those that Canada made to U.S. banks under FTA. Under NAFTA, Mexico receives full national treatment in Canada. That is, Mexico no longer is subject to the 12% aggregate limit on non-U.S. Schedule II bank capital, nor will it have to apply to the Canadian Minister of Finance before opening new branches.

In addition, Mexican investors will not be subject to the provision prohibiting foreign investors from owning more than 25% of a Canadian bank. However, they will continue to face the provision preventing any individual investor, domestic or foreign, or groups of related investors, from owning more than 10% of a Schedule I bank.

U.S. STILL RESTRICTS FOREIGN BANKS

Unfortunately, NAFTA did nothing to reduce the considerable restrictions Canadian banks face in the U.S. market. The Glass-Steagall Act prohibits bank subsidiaries from owning securities firms, a practice which is allowed in Canada.

In addition, the McFadden Act limits interstate branch banking. Finally, the Bank Holding Company Act does not allow the U.S. subsidiaries of Canadian bank-owned insurance companies to continue to operate as bank-owned affiliates.

These restrictions impede Canadian banks' ability to compete in the U.S. market.

It is hoped that the United States will seriously consider regulatory reform in the area of financial services, so that Canadian and U.S. financial-services enterprises will be able to compete on a level playing field in the North American market.

Trade liberalization in financial services will be a major challenge in the Western Hemisphere and, indeed, in Asia, in the decade ahead.

NAFTA'S STRATEGIC IMPORTANCE

It would be a mistake to underestimate the strategic importance of NAFTA, and its extension, for the economic future of the Western Hemisphere. This is as true after the assassination of Mexican presidential candidate Luis Donaldo Colosio as it was before.

We may not witness the conclusion of another GATT (General Agreements on Tariffs and Trade) round for a long time, so NAFTA may be, in any effective sense, the only trade negotiating game in town. This observation does not in any way denigrate the accomplishments of the GATT Uruguay Round — particularly the creation of the World Trade Organization (WTO).

However, a number of developments will make a further comprehensive GATT round difficult. They include:
◆ The growing number of participants (now well over a hundred).
◆ The complexity of the issues to be negotiated (e.g., knowledge-intensive services).
◆ The importance of investment as an element of trade.
◆ The political sensitivity of remaining protected areas (e.g., agriculture, culture industries).
◆ And, the very nature of today's protectionism based on non-tariff barriers (e.g., voluntary export restraints; harassment through countervailing and antidumping actions; and regulatory structures, as in financial services).

At the same time, the function of the World Trade Organization may shift multilateral attention away from global negotiations to settling individual issues and disputes.

If the Western Hemisphere wishes to make progress quickly, it likely will have to do it through extension of NAFTA. The incentive to do so is coming from an increasing realization that such regional arrangements (as in the case of FTA) can bring great benefits, that they need not be in disharmony with GATT principles, and that they do not lead to trading blocks or to significant harmful diversion of trade.

The key message conveyed by creation of regional trading arrangements to non-NAFTA Western Hemisphere countries is that a small number of contiguous countries can establish a much deeper and pervasive level of economic cooperation than can be achieved at the global level.

Does this mean that further attempts to open trade outside North America should be set aside? Absolutely not. Trade outside North America — Asia being a prime example — is exceedingly important to Canada. The recent Asia/Pacific Economic Cooperation Conference in Seattle demonstrated early stirrings of new things to come in North American-Asia/Pacific economic relationships. NAFTA countries would be well advised to encourage development of these relationships.

U.S. TRADE STRATEGIES IMPORTANT

The kind of trade strategies the United States will pursue is of particular importance to Canada. The recent news that the Clinton Administration is drafting a plan for a comprehensive Western Hemisphere free-trade zone to be implemented in 10-15 years is encouraging. So is the news that Chile might, before long, be part of NAFTA.

Much less encouraging is the individual commodity approach the United States is taking to enhancing trade with Japan (auto parts, computer chips, etc.). This is an approach to freer trade best left out of the future development of Western Hemisphere trade agreements.

Also disheartening at times is the tendency of the U.S. government to use every last legal avenue to challenge Canada-U.S. trade panel rules, as in the case of softwood lumber. What has become clear is that NAFTA will operate more effectively if the spirit, as well as the letter, of the agreement is respected.

A well-managed NAFTA, building on the concept and experience of the Canada-U.S. FTA, will help create an environment of growth and development that will bring great benefits to the people of the Western Hemisphere and great opportunities to its business communities, including financial services.

Toward Greater International Stability and Cooperation

Lord Kingsdown

Lord Kingsdown, formerly Robin Leigh-Pemberton, served as Governor of the Bank of England from 1982. He retired from the post in June 1993, when he was given a life peerage by Queen Elizabeth.

High priorities must be an assurance of the security of the payment and settlement systems together with joint agreement on market and interest rate risk.

Enormous changes have taken place in the international financial environment during the last 10 years. Most strikingly, the sheer volume of financial transactions has grown exponentially and the world's capital markets have become increasingly integrated. These developments have been reflected in the changing pressures facing international financial institutions (especially banks). They have also required monetary authorities to cooperate ever more closely, both to protect the stability of the financial system and promote a healthy macroeconomic environment.

What lies behind this extraordinary growth? First, of course, has been the continued growth of international trade and investment flows. This, and the global reach of major multinational corporations, have called for a comparable growth in the provision of financial services. Even more important has been the tide of liberalization that has affected the financial services industry. In particular, controls over cross-border transactions among industrial countries have been almost completely eliminated. Also, the evolution in information technology has dramatically reduced the cost of financial transactions and made possible the development of markets in sophisticated derivative instruments. A fourth development with far-reaching implications has been securitization. As the range of financial instruments has grown, so has the share that is marketable as securities.

These developments have made the distinction between the three main areas of financial activity—banking, securities business, and insurance—harder to define. New forms of maturity transformation, and the desire for liquidity on both the liability and asset sides of balance sheets, have created new orders of risk manage-

From *The Bankers Magazine*, January/February 1994, pp. 34-38. © 1994 by Warren, Gorham & Lamont, New York, NY. Reprinted by permission.

ment that cross traditional boundaries between financial institutions.

In one way or another, these trends have dominated my term as Governor of the Bank of England during the past 10 years. No central banker could ignore them—least of all in London, one of the world's most international and innovative financial centers.

Any central bank's basic concern is with stability. This has two aspects. First, of course, to provide the stable macroeconomic framework that is necessary for the long-run growth of output and employment. But second, and more specifically, any central banker will want to ensure that the network of financial institutions and markets for which he or she is responsible is sound and resilient.

Both of these considerations of stability have an international dimension that has grown in importance over the years. Stability of the financial system in any one country depends significantly on the strength of financial institutions and markets throughout the world. It is therefore important to have confidence that other participants in financial markets are soundly capitalized and effectively supervised, wherever they may be located and wherever their business may be done.

The Work of the Basle Committee

In the field of banking supervision, it was clear as early as 1974 that an international approach was needed. Following the failure of Bankhaus Herstatt in that year, the Group of Ten (G10) countries established a committee of banking supervisors—the Basle Committee—to consider how to strengthen the international banking system.

The original objective of the Committee was to improve "early warning" systems. But this was only a beginning. A major goal has been to ensure the adequate supervision of cross-border banking activity. Two principles are involved: to ensure that no international banking establishment can escape supervision; and to ensure that supervision is adequate. This exercise involved the impor-

tant questions of establishing who undertakes the supervision and how is it carried out.

This first point of establishing who undertakes the supervision was addressed in a document that came to be known as

A major goal of the Basle Committee is to ensure the adequate supervision of cross-border banking activity.

the Basle Concordat, which sets out principles for sharing supervisory responsibilities for banks' foreign operations, as between host and parent authorities. As a result, no banking office within the G10 countries can escape the supervisory net. More recently, the Basle Committee has taken steps to ensure in addition, that all internationally active banks are subject to comprehensive consolidated supervision by their home supervisor.

The issue of how to supervise is inherently more complex. Given differences in national situations, traditions and financial structures, it is obviously neither feasible nor desirable to harmonize supervisory practices precisely. Nevertheless, a measure of agreement is clearly necessary.

During the summer of 1986 (when Paul Volcker was chairman of the Federal Reserve Board in the US), the UK and the US created a bilateral joint approach to the measurement of capital—in effect to "jump-start" the process of international cooperation. Agreement was reached in 1988 on the weightings that would apply to different classes of assets and on a minimum risk asset ratio. This system has now been applied not only in all G10 countries, but in most countries with banks with a significant international presence.

Specific elements of these agreements can no doubt be challenged. However, so far no better alternatives appear to have been put forward. For now, two considerations are worth exploring. First, in a highly competitive and international

The scope for accidents in the international payment systems has grown, as have their potential systemic implications.

banking environment, close cooperation among bank supervisors is essential to achieve the goals of systemic stability and a level, competitive playing field. Second, those responsible for international cooperation in this area can never afford to rest on their laurels.

Looking ahead, two tasks should be uppermost on the agenda. One is to reach agreement on other categories of risk (such as market and interest rate risk) that are inherent in financial activity. The other is to ensure the security of payments and settlement systems.

Payment Systems

This issue of security has become more and more important in my term as governor. With the growth of the volume of payments has come a greater interdependence among institutions, both geographically and across market segments. In 1970, for example, it is estimated that payments through the main funds transfer systems in the US were about 10 times the underlying gross national product (GNP). By 1990, they were 75 times GNP. The scope for accidents has grown, and so have their potential systemic implications.

The Bank for International Settlements has made great strides to strengthen payment systems, both by proposing improvements in netting arrangements and assigning responsibilities among the various central banks involved. A more complete solution lies in a move toward the immediate final settlement of large-value transactions.

Developments in technology now make it feasible for large-value transactions to be settled instantaneously through debits and credits over the books of central banks (often referred to as real-time gross settlement). Such systems are very close to being implemented. When this happens, payments risk as a systemic danger will be virtually eliminated, and the necessary foundation will be built to construct systems for similar certainty to the settlement of other financial transactions, for example in the foreign exchange, money, and capital markets.

International Policy Coordination

The health of the financial system is, of course, only one of the areas in which cooperation among national monetary authorities has become increasingly important. A constant theme throughout my last 10 years as governor has been how to strengthen the coordination of economic policies in order to reinforce stability, both in the context of our efforts to promote economic integration in Europe, and in the wider international context.

The UK's economic interdependence has both a European and a global dimension. Within Europe, the UK is cooperating with its partners in the European Community to deepen the economic ties among our countries and strengthen our policy cooperation.

These efforts need to respect certain key standards:

■ Those economic ties must be based on free market principles. To achieve its potential, any move toward economic and monetary union in Europe must aim to remove unnecessary regulations, open markets to competition, and eliminate barriers to trade and the movement of factors of production. This is the essence of the UK's support of the single market legislation.

■ Macroeconomic policies must be based on the pursuit of stability: in other words, the lasting defeat of inflation and the durable consolidation of national budgetary positions. This in turn will provide the most secure basis for the pursuit of exchange rate stability.

■ Finally, member countries must have a mutual respect for each other's national democratic traditions. Cooperation does not mean the elimination of national differences. Each European country has its own customs, traditions, and legal system, which enrich our common heritage. Forging closer economic cooperation need not conflict with the preservation of national practice across a broad range of economic activities.

Many of the same principles can be applied at the global level. However, the issues that arise in economic cooperation in the larger world economy are not the same as those inside a single region, such as Europe. In particular, the question arises of how to manage macroeconomic interactions in the absence of a framework such as the European Monetary System.

Changes in macroeconomic policy mix can have major effects on exchange rate relationships among the three major currency regions. These swings in exchange rates, in turn, can have adverse consequences of three types. They act as an impediment to the wealth-enhancing growth of international trade and investment. In addition, they interfere with the task of national authorities in achieving stable noninflationary growth. And last, and perhaps most seriously, they tend to inflame protectionist sentiment. Not only is protectionism an ugly form of nationalism, but, if allowed to grow unchecked, it could undermine the collective prosperity of nations.

The Plaza Agreement and the G7 Process

It was a recognition of these dangers, particularly that of protectionism, that gave rise to the Plaza agreement in 1985, and the subsequent intensification of what is now called the Group of Seven (G7) process. The combination in the United States of an expansionary fiscal policy and continued monetary restraint led to a sustained appreciation of the dollar in the early 1980s, and a sharp widening of the US payments deficit.

Not only is protectionism an ugly form of nationalism, but, if allowed to grow unchecked, it could undermine the collective prosperity of nations.

The extent of the dollar's appreciation was unwelcome in any country. It undermined the competitiveness of US export industries, and it complicated the task of restoring price stability in Europe. The protectionist pressures it unleashed caused grave concern in Japan. Moreover, because the widening of the US payments deficit could hardly be sustained indefinitely, there was considerable alarm about the possibility of a "hard landing" when markets eventually forced an adjustment.

The Plaza accord and the subsequent Louvre agreement were remarkably successful in correcting a potentially dangerous exchange rate misalignment. More than that, they confirmed the G7 as an "anti-inflationary club," whose goal was to underpin exchange rate stability through the common pursuit of sound macroeconomic policies.

Of late, the G7 has not had such striking successes in the field of economic policy coordination for both substantive and procedural reasons. Substantively, the objectives of countries differ, as they find themselves at different stages of the economic and electoral cycle, and as beliefs about the nature of underlying economic processes diverge. Procedurally, regular meetings of the G7 nations have sometimes been handicapped by the publicity that surrounds them and the expectations that are aroused by newsworthy comuniques.

Lessons for the G7

Having attended every meeting of the ministers and governors of the G7 in the past 10 years, I believe there are at least four lessons to be learned—two involving the process of policy coordination and two involving the substance.

Meetings among financial officials are most effective if they are kept small and informal. Large, highly organized meetings are not a good environment in which to reach understandings on policy coordination. Furthermore, the aim of regular G7 meetings should be to understand each other's objectives and political and economic constraints. The "spillover" effects from one country's policies onto others also need to be understood so that policy options can be found that lead to a better outcome for all. On the other hand, if some countries attempt to pressure others into adopting policies they are reluctant to pursue, the exercise can degenerate into confrontation.

Another consideration on substance is that policies should be aimed at medium-term sustainability, not short-term fine tuning. It is always tempting to try to respond to the political pressures created by the latest economic statistics. But we follow a more reliable compass if we keep our attention focused clearly on the medium-term goals of price stability and budgetary consolidation.

A final point involves exchange rate stability—the result of convergence in underlying economic policies and performance. It cannot be achieved by actions in the exchange markets alone. Attempts to move exchange markets in directions that are not consistent with underlying policies nearly always end in disappointment.

These may appear to be self-evident conclusions. And so they are. But what is surprising is how strong the temptation is to ignore them when political pressures mount. This is perhaps one of the central reasons why regular meetings among finance ministers and central bank governors can be an important force for good. Every country faces similar pressures and an awareness of the constraints imposed by the fact of international interdependence. In the end, we can provide each other with an invaluable sounding board for ideas—and a mutual support society against the slings and arrows of outrageous political fortune.

GLOBAL FINANCIAL MARKETS IN

2020

Charles S. Sanford Jr.

Charles S. Sanford Jr. is chairman and CEO of Bankers Trust Company, New York.

The need to anticipate long-term trends in financial markets is especially compelling today given the speed at which the financial system is changing.

Our thirst for knowledge, which spurs innovation in financial markets and elsewhere, has been whetted by rapid advances in financial theory and technology as exciting and portentous as the 20th century's major developments in physics and biology.

These advances have spurred development of an ocean of new technologies with application in financial services. But the process of implementing these technologies has hardly begun. Thus my concern is with how these technologies will shape the financial markets by 2020.

Why focus on the year 2020? Twenty-six years is distant enough to allow trends to develop, yet near enough to be useful for long-range planning. And, I like the idea that 20/20 stands for perfect vision—maybe that will improve the odds that my perceptions are correct.

I think that by 2020, banks—certainly as we know them now—will cease to exist. So you will find that I'm going to avoid the term

"banks," and also that, instead of referring to "loans," "borrowings," or "securities," I'll discuss "claims on wealth."

But, basic financial functions will remain the same, even though they will be looked at differently and, as advanced applications of existing technologies come onstream, they will affect how the basic functions are performed. These functions include:
- Financing
- Risk Management
- Trading and Positioning
- Advising
- Transaction Processing

UNCHANGING FINANCIAL FUNCTIONS

Financing facilitates the movement of funds from suppliers to users. Usually it starts with the identification of users and suppliers by a financial institution and ends with the creation of products to satisfy both.

Successful products created by a financial intermediary enable each party to meet its needs for timing and location of cash flows and for the amounts of money to be supplied or used. The intermediary also helps clients assess the merits of alternative products, seeking to find the least costly source of money for users and getting the best possible return for suppliers, taking into consideration their appetites for risk.

Risk Management is the process of moving clients closer to their desired risk profiles by helping them shed unwanted risks or acquire new risks that suit their portfolios. At times, this can be done simply by matching a client who wants to shed a risk with one who wants to acquire that risk. More often, it involves unbundling, transforming, and repackaging risks into bundles tailored to fit the particular needs of various clients.

Trading and Positioning is the buying and selling of claims on wealth. It provides liquidity to clients so they can more easily alter their portfolios or raise cash. It also moves market prices of financial claims closer to their fair values and makes market prices more visible and reliable.

Advising is making decisions on behalf of clients or giving them information and advice that help them make better decisions for themselves.

Transaction Processing is the storing, safeguarding, verifying, reporting, and transferring of claims on wealth.

Although some of these functions are taking on new forms and becoming more sophisticated, they will be needed as much in 2020 as they are today.

REVOLUTIONARY TECHNOLOGY

Information technology already is helping us execute the above-men-

From *Bank Management*, March/April 1994, pp. 30-32, 36, 38-39. © 1994 by the Bank Administration Institute (BAI), One North Franklin Street, Chicago, IL 60606. Reprinted by permission.

tioned financial functions better—and faster—by providing improved data collection, calculation, communications, and risk control. By 2020, those tools will be much cheaper and far more powerful.

Some indicators:

◆ A transistor, once costing $5, now costs less than a staple.

◆ Entire reference libraries are now stored on one 5-inch disk.

◆ Computer users have become accustomed to increasing their processing power by a factor of 10 every five to seven years.

And the progress is geometric because each element — computation, availability of data, communications, and algorithms — feeds on the others.

This revolution in information technology is enabling the financial world to operate on a much more complex level than before.

At times, the speed and power at which computation and communications tasks can be accomplished are so much greater than in the past that the change they spur is qualitative, not just quantitative.

For example, the options business could not operate as it does today without high-speed computers to track its intricacies, including the monitoring of risk profiles and valuations. Computer technology has made it possible to disaggregate risk on a broad scale and redistribute it efficiently, enabling management to maintain greater risk control while giving employees more freedom to use their own judgment. In other words, information technology allows a financial organization to decentralize while improving control.

The ability to program computers to digest ever-larger amounts of information more and more quickly enables us to apply sophisticated automated logic — what we call "automated analytics" — to many problems, such as performing elemental arbitrage tasks. Eventually these programs will be embedded on computer chips, which will be able to solve progressively more

A true global marketplace will be established, with everyone—individuals, companies, investors, organizations, and governments—linked through telephone lines, cables, and radio-wave technology.

complex problems — and on a global basis.

Indeed, by 2020, a true global marketplace will be established, with everyone — individuals, companies, investors, organizations, and governments — linked through telephone lines, cables, and radio-wave technology. With the touch of a button, people will have access to other individuals and vast databases around the world. Such access will be readily available through phones, interactive television, workstations, or hand-held "personal digital assistants" that combine all these functions.

Organizations will be "fully wired" so that their computers will capture incoming and internally generated data, analyze the information, and make it instantly available to any authorized person, wherever he or she may be. Armies of clerks and administrators no longer will be needed to serve as messengers, translators, reconcilers, or summarizers of information.

To further increase financial-system efficiency, all financial claims (including claims on volatility) will be in book-entry form, and ownership of all these claims will be transferable instantly anywhere around the globe via 24-hour multicurrency payment systems. Settlement risk will be eliminated and with it a major bottleneck to transaction flows. This has enormous implications for releasing capital and lowering transaction costs.

ALL-ENCOMPASSING "WEALTH ACCOUNTS"

A key to the financial system in 2020 will be "wealth accounts," in

which companies and individuals will hold their assets and liabilities. These accounts will contain today's relatively illiquid assets, such as buildings and vehicles, as well as what we know today as stocks, bonds, other securities, and new types of financial claims. And the accounts will contain all forms of liabilities.

Computers will continuously monitor wealth-account items, and will constantly mark both assets and liabilities to market, making these items effectively liquid. Within an individual wealth account, the arithmetic sum of the items will be the net worth. Yesterday's income and today's wealth will always be known with a high degree of confidence.

The wealth accounts will be the focal point for financial processing and reporting. The integrity of these accounts will be validated by institutions, much the same as checking accounts or mutual funds are today.

Wealth accounts will be instantly tapped via "wealth cards," enabling a consumer to pay for a car, for example, by instantly drawing on part of the wealth inherent in his or her vacation home.

Wealth accounts also will simplify the provision of credit. In the ultimate extension of today's home-equity lines, instant credit will be available to companies and individuals — credit secured by wealth accounts. Leverage constraints will be established by investors and, perhaps, by central banks. Some investors will continue to extend unsecured credit on the basis of an individual's expected income stream—but this would violate this writer's strongly held view that one should never extend unsecured credit to anything that eats.

Owners of wealth accounts will use automated analytics to help them determine their risk/reward appetites and suggest appropriate actions to achieve those targets. If the owner approves, the wealth account automatically would proceed to implement the program. Of course, some people will prefer the advice of another person on more complex or large transactions, for both expert judgment and psychological comfort.

Automated analytics also will provide customized investment management, making the wealth accounts far superior to today's mutual funds. In effect, individuals will have the option to manage their own mutual funds.

All seekers of financial claims will understand that they will be legally responsible for keeping their wealth accounts up to date in order to have full access to financial markets. These accounts will be electronically accessible to any authorized user, directly or through computerized analytics programs. Privacy will be maintained as with today's checking accounts.

ELECTRONIC MARKETS

Global electronic bulletin boards will be the principal medium through which buyers and sellers will post their needs and execute transactions. Many financial claims, including what are known today as loans and securities, will bypass middlemen — commercial and investment banks — and will be bought and sold by electronic auction through these global bulletin boards, with minimal transaction costs.

While today we have only a few recognized rating agencies, in coming years we will have hundreds — perhaps thousands — of specialized providers of news, data, and analysis which will provide interactive electronic bulletins on demand, real-time, and tailored to each subscriber's particular notion of risk.

There will be no special need for retail financial branches because everyone will have direct access to his or her financial suppliers through interactive TV and personal digital assistants. True "global banking" will have arrived, as every household will be a "branch."

A key feature of markets by 2020 will be the ability to tailor

On any given deal, firms may compete with their nominal clients as well as with their natural competitors.

virtually anything to a client's needs or wishes at a reasonable price, including highly personalized service from financial companies. Firms will be selling to market segments of one.

In addition to bulletin boards open to anyone who pays a nominal fee, users and suppliers of financial claims will be networked to each other to exchange real-time data and documents (computer-to-computer), to automatically execute most day-to-day transactions, and maybe to confer via "virtual reality" electronic meetings. On any given deal, firms may compete with their nominal clients as well as with their natural competitors.

In effect, supplying financial assistance will be a free-for-all. It will not be limited to those calling themselves "financial institutions" because any organization or individual will be able to reply to needs posted on the bulletin boards.

Other elements of the financial world in 2020 are especially hard to predict. Voice recognition, DNA fingerprinting, and secure data encryption will verify transactions instantly, likely preventing many of today's scams. But new forms of "information crime" will appear and will need to be confronted.

Geography will be less of a constraint. Many employees could be geographically dispersed, such as those engaged in processing (for cost advantages), in sales and marketing (to be close to the customer), and in handling local problems that require local solutions.

But the people responsible for creating products and overall strategy will likely still live in major cities. These people need the creative stimulation that is found primarily in cities, where they will

thrive on face-to-face contact with people from different backgrounds and cultures and from different disciplines — artists, scientists, businesspeople, and lawyers.

ADVANCES IN "PARTICLE FINANCE"

In fact, a convergence is taking place among these disciplines as finance becomes more like science and the arts. Financial theory is becoming increasingly important and tremendously useful as theoretical advances have emerged in the last few years. These include portfolio theories, asset-pricing theories, option-pricing theories, and market-efficiency theories.

Many of the financial world's most creative people are devoting their time to these theories and are radically improving our comprehension and management of risk. They deal with variables as relatively straightforward as interest rates and as complex as the weather — all of which have an enormous impact on the markets.

This path-breaking work is providing a solid platform for innovation in practice as well as in theory. The rapidly growing acceptance of derivative-based financial solutions is one very important example of such innovation.

At this point, however, the science of markets is at an extraordinarily early stage of development. We are still in a "Newtonian" era of "classical finance," in which we tend to look at financial instruments—such as stocks, bonds, and loans—in static, highly aggregated terms.

Most classical finance models looking at Bankers Trust today would concentrate on the "beta" of its stock—the stock's volatility relative to the market. These models have great difficulty dealing with the multitude of underlying critical risk factors that produce beta, such as changes in financial-market volatility or global product, transaction-processing volumes, an earthquake in Japan or California, consumer confidence in the United Kingdom, or a change in our corporate strategy. Beta ignores these critical factors, which we term "financial attributes," or grossly summarizes them as homogenous packets of white noise.

Researchers have begun to look for a theory — what we call "The Theory of Particle Finance" — that will help us better understand an asset's financial attributes. Finding such a theory is not just around the corner, but we are seeing signs of progress, and in coming decades a much more powerful financial discipline will be in place.

Particle finance is beginning to look beneath beta to identify an asset's financial attributes, including the attributes' individual and collective volatility. Efforts also are being made to integrate these attributes into the desired financial claims.

This work is creating order from apparent disorder, providing building blocks that will allow more effective packaging and management of risk in an economy whose structure is constantly changing.

The purpose of this research is to reach the most efficient balance of risk and return — getting a higher expected return on the same risk or getting the same return with lower risk.

Although the theory of particle finance is in its infancy, it will be aided by an explosion in computing power and financial data. We can't say which early attempts to advance the theory of particle finance will work; but the developments are intriguing.

For example:

◆ Chaos theorists are attempting to find the underlying structure and pattern — if they exist — of the apparent randomness of changes in asset values.

◆ "Fuzzy logic" is a mathematical way of drawing definite conclusions from approximate, vague, or subjective inputs. Because it attempts to embody certain kinds of human perception and decision-making skills, it may help us understand

The purpose of this research is to reach the most efficient balance of risk and return—getting a higher expected return on the same risk or getting the same return with lower risk.

complex interactive systems that involve human intervention, such as financial markets.

Particle finance and the evolution of technology will substantially reduce the amount of unwanted risk borne by individuals, institutions, and the system as a whole. We will find better ways to quantify, price, and manage today's familiar risks. We also will uncover, quantify, price, and manage risks that exist today but are hidden from view. The net benefits will be great — even granting that new and unforeseen risks could be created by this environment.

APPLYING PARTICLE FINANCE

Meanwhile, progress is being made at the front lines as well as in the labs. Pioneers in the derivatives business are successfully identifying, extracting, and pricing some of the more fundamental risks that drive asset values, such as interest rates, currency values, and commodity prices. Even though today these early applications look crude and primitive, they already have created a new and powerful process for solving important and practical financial problems. These range from limiting an airline's exposure to fuel price increases to helping a company hedge the value of a pending acquisition.

And important new applications are already on the runway: credit derivatives and insurance derivatives, for example.

In coming years, credit risks will be disaggregated into discrete attributes that will be readily traded, unbundled, and rebundled. Intermediaries will manage a large book of diversified long and short posi-

tions in credit attributes. They will make markets in credit-risk attributes and in bundles of attributes customized to suit the particular needs of their clients.

Such tailored products will permit each business to price and manage credit risk arising from its activities in a way that is best for that business. Perhaps even residual credit risks left after this process will be covered by a third-party insurance policy.

As the discipline of particle finance evolves, the primary job of financial institutions will be to help clients put theory to practical use. Just as today's man on the street does not practice particle physics, he will not practice particle finance in the next century.

While advances in financial theory and technology will give talented people more powerful tools to apply their human creativity, individuals will not be replaced with robots. Rather, these advances will enable individuals to apply their judgment with more precision and power.

In addition, highly skilled and creative specialists will continue to be needed to define and solve problems that are particularly complex and unique. These financial specialists will be the highest practitioners of particle finance, combining a creative grasp of financial possibilities with a psychoanalyst-like ability to help clients understand the true nature of their preferences for risk and return.

IMPLICATIONS FOR FINANCIAL INSTITUTIONS

Particle finance presents a cornucopia of new business opportunities for financial institutions. Myriad risks are yet to be uncovered, described in "probability of occurrence" terms, and then rebundled to satisfy client needs.

There will always be a need for **new disciplines and technologies to measure and deal with these risk attributes. In addition, all of these attributes and bundled prod-**

ucts must be stored, safeguarded, verified, reported, and transferred.

Financial professionals will constantly be re-educating themselves. We, for example, are creating a "Bankers Trust University," where our people will be encouraged to spend many of their working hours.

Obviously, in the era of particle-finance theory, financial organizations will take on different appearances, and will require a new type of manager.

With virtually no layers of management, financial organizations will attract a variety of highly skilled and creative experts, including a wide array of people from science and mathematics.

Senior managers at major institutions will perform like orchestra conductors, guiding their "artists" and "scientists" through example and influence rather than by "command and control." Top management will need to direct their technical experts and managers to play in the same key. They differ temperamentally but as finance, sci-

> *While advances in financial theory and technology will give talented people more powerful tools to apply their human creativity, individuals will not be replaced with robots.*

ence, and the arts continue to merge, the manager, scientist, and artist will become more alike. The leaders' most important functions will be to inspire through clear articulation of the organization's values and strategies. They will have to know enough about the business to be the risk manager of risk managers.

Superior judgment will always be essential, and will continue to be highly valued because it will not be embedded on silicon. Depth of talent will be critical to success, so recruiting and retaining people will be management's most important job. Technology will never replace the subtlety of the human mind. People will be the most important

factor in 2020, just as they are now. We must learn how to grow wise leaders from the ranks of specialists, a difficult task.

These concepts will not flourish unless society blesses them. Social critics may say that they are nothing more than a financial engineering exercise to enrich a few at the expense of many — a zero-sum game.

Not true. For as risk management becomes ever more precise and customized, the amount of risk that we will all have to bear will be greatly reduced, lowering the need for financial capital. This will have tremendous social value because more financial capital will be available to produce more wealth to address society's needs. In addition, this will liberate *human* capital by the greater leveraging of talent.

And, these concepts will not flourish unless our clients bless them. Their trust must be earned by delivery of objective diagnostic help and solutions of value. We shall earn it.

FINANCING TRADE WITH LATIN AMERICA

Democracy is now firmly rooted throughout the continent; military dictatorships have been superseded; economies are becoming stable; people are hungry to buy goods and services; and, they have money to do so.

Richard D. Willsher

Richard Willsher runs London-based, International Trade and Finance Consulting, specializing in the finance of international sales of equipment and services.

NAFTA is a done deal. And yet it was not so long ago that Mexico was regarded as a political credit risk to be avoided. There are lessons we can draw from Mexico which might be applied to the other major Latin American export markets.

The demographics of these markets are awesome—the 360 million people, about one third of whom are under age 20 and population growth of 12.8 percent for the eight largest countries of the region in the period 1985–91. Annual private spending totals more than $500 billion. There has been a rapid rise in urban populations and substantial increases in personal consumption. This adds up to an area of the world where more people are hungry to buy goods and services and where they have more money to do so with each passing year.

At the same time democracy is now firmly rooted throughout the continent, the military dictatorships having been superseded. Economies are becoming stable, more so since the introduction of debt restructuring and forgiveness arrangements. These very arrangements have enabled banks which have previously been laden-down with bad debts to trade away their mistakes and write back their provisions, paving the way for financing new commercial activity—if a little more cautiously this time around.

It would be a mistake to treat the Latin American continent as one market. There are considerable differences between the countries, but the main markets are open for business as far as the banking world is concerned. And that is good news for companies planning to start or increase sales there following the long aftermath of the debt crisis.

MEXICO

Just as Mexico was the first to default in 1982, it became the first to re-emerge. The Brady plan was the key element. The issuing of 30-year bonds to bank creditors allowed the stasis of Mexican debt to be liquidated. It spawned a huge market in the trading of less developed country (LDC) debt and also new investment in the Mexican market. Thirteen billion dollars in new money bonds have been issued for public and private sector funding. Equity issues, privatizations, and a host of joint ventures and commercial investments followed. Twenty billion dollars in flight capital returned. In 1992 U.S. exports to Mexico totalled $42 billion. Today the combination of increased trade flows and new money means that banks and other financial institutions are prepared to extend credit to support sales of goods and services to Mexico.

> *" . . . the combination of increased trade flows and new money means that banks and other financial institutions are prepared to extend credit to support sales of goods and services to Mexico."*

Trade credit can now be arranged, without export credit guarantees and without recourse, extending to seven years and longer. Guarantees from local Mexican banks are often required. This can unlock low cost credit which is likely to appeal to the customer while U.S. dollar rates are low. Most major banks with an interest in financing trade are now prepared to confirm letters of credit up to 360 days. This has to do with Mexico's creditworthiness but also with recent banking regulations which relieve banks of the need to set aside capital against short term trade-related business. This last point is applicable to trade finance generally from most other markets.

Although Mexico will have a general election this year, and will have to digest the effects of NAFTA and cope with a trade deficit, it is seen by many in the industrialized world and in the LDCs as a template for the emergence of other economies in the region.

ARGENTINA

Argentina is one of the beneficiaries of the "Mexico effect" yet it is in many ways better off than Mexico. It has a trade deficit one third of Mexico's in gross domestic product (GDP) terms and is much less indebted. Like Mexico it has a rich northern neighbor, Brazil, which sucks in a huge proportion of its exports.

Argentina attracts trade credit in the form of letter of credit confirmations and medium term without recourse support up to three years. Certain doubts hang over it such as: Will Brazil keep buying, its own future being far from clear? Can Argentina keep a stable government, get its fiscal arrangements consistently right, and exploit its huge natural resources?

The exporter to Argentina is obliged to review these issues; they do after all pose a threat to future trade. But the ability to lay off risk does facilitate easier payment terms and because this can now be arranged, Argentina is a worthy target territory.

BRAZIL

1995 is election year in Brazil. This year inflation is likely to be in the 500 to 2000 percent range—which is a pretty broad guess. With successive changes in government, finance ministers, Brady plan agreement dates, and privatization strategy, the future looks uncertain.

But look at the fundamentals. Brazil has huge natural resources—it is believed to hold one third of the world's iron ore reserves, for starters—massive productive capacity, and vast wealth even if it is not fully realized and very unevenly distributed. It is a market which cannot be ignored.

Again, the LDC debt and new issue bond markets are a key to the financing possibilities. Brazilian risk has become liquid. Banks which agree to issue bonds can pre-place them into a buoyant secondary market. Likewise trade debt. Letters of credit issued by prime Brazilian banks such as Banco do Brazil, Banco Bradesco, and Banespa can be confirmed by specialist institutions in London and New York and discounted. Medium term bank-guaranteed trade debt of up to three years in duration is being bought by forfaiting houses. No one said dealing with Brazil was easy but it is possible to secure payment which at least removes some of the risks inherent in selling product there.

CHILE

Chile's debt buy-backs have been the hallmark of its economic recovery and have led to it being the best-regarded of the Latin American markets from a credit standpoint. It is still heavily reliant on copper; it is estimated to have one quarter of the world's reserves. World copper prices are low but Chile is expected to balance its budget in 1994—a remarkable achievement for a country once in hock to the international banks. Its import bill is comprised largely of manufactured goods, machinery, vehicles, and other equipment.

Financing trade is relatively easy. One forfeiter commented that he would "do Chile at five years" but he couldn't get his hands on any notes and when he did it was too finely priced. Which means relatively low financing costs for the exporter to this Latin American market.

COLOMBIA

Colombia still suffers from its image as a narcotics capital but this is fading and 1994 is likely to see a further improvement in its economic well-being and credit status. A consistent 5 percent growth rate has been projected which has one signal advantage; it attracts international investment. Emerging market funds, corporate ventures, and equity investment promote new or expanding commercial operations. This has in turn produced the need for manufac-

Table 1				
LATIN AMERICA'S SUPER SEVEN				
	Population (Millions)	Area (Million Km. Sq.)	1992 GDP (U.S.$ Billion)	EST GDP Growth '93 / '94
ARGENTINA	33.10	2.700	160.00	3 / 3
BRAZIL	152.00	8.500	293.00	4 / 2
CHILE	13.20	0.757	34.40	7 / 6
COLOMBIA	32.30	1.100	47.00	5 / 5
MEXICO	86.50	1.970	205.00	2.5 / 2.5
PERU	22.50	1.280	20.40	2 / 7
VENEZUELA	19.25	0.912	55.00	5 / 0

Table 2

Indicative Cost of Discounting U.S. $ Denominated Trade Receivables*

	Term in Years	Size ($M)	Indicative Pricing
ARGENTINA	3	2	9.00%
BRAZIL	3	3	10.00%
CHILE	5	5	7.50%
COLOMBIA	3	2	7.00%
MEXICO	7	7	8.50%
PERU	1	1	9.50%
VENEZUELA	1	1	6.00%

*All prices refer to promissory notes or bills of exchange which are readily available and carry an acceptance bank or government guarantee. Prices are based upon a straight discount for semi-annual payments of principal and interest.

Tips for Sales to the Super Seven

Seek bank guarantees and sovereign risk from your customers which can be placed with trade finance houses as soon as shipment takes place.

Obtain committed purchase offers from trade finance houses in the pre-shipment period.

Use credit as a selling tool only in so far as it can be covered by banks or political risk insurance.

Use local representatives, embassy information, and up-to-date news to keep abreast of new developments—both good and bad.

Follow the LDC and new issue bond markets.

Watch for the "Mexico effect."

Shop around among banks and trade finance houses—one man's poison is another man's meat!

tured goods in an economy which is largely commodity dependent—oil and derivatives, coffee and coal being the biggest hard currency earners.

With 32 million inhabitants, Colombia is not a marginal market. It is one that might figure larger in exporters projections especially as it does attract bank support for credit operations up to three years against prime local bank guarantees. Banco Cafetero is the bank which is the best regarded.

PERU

Peru has a foreign debt greater than its 1992 GDP. It is a country with a long way to go. Of the "Super Seven" in table 1 it is the weakest and even letter-of-credit confirmations are not readily available. Therefore, it is a market where getting in early may still be possible if trade payments can be adequately secured.

But there is a lesson to be drawn from the LDC market. Peruvian debt was, until recently, priced at just a few cents on the dollar. The price has begun to move upwards which implies that a quick buck is probably being made by speculators but also that it is seen as having growth potential. The speed with which international banks can write back their provisions and get the debt off their books will determine the availability of new trade finance lines. Exporters of primary imported products paid for under short-term letters of credit are likely to be the first beneficiaries of a fresh approach to the market by the banks. Subject to what economic progress can be made and if the Mexico model holds good, this should be the beginning of Peru's rehabilitation.

VENEZUELA

On paper Venezuela has excellent coordinates. With a well-developed hydrocarbons sector—one of the largest refinery capacities in OPEC, and relatively small population, Venezuela ought to lead the pack.

The fact that it doesn't has a lot to do with its political uncertainty. While 1993 growth was expected to reach five percent, zero is expected in 1994. The settlement in oil prices has been damaging as budgets were carried out upon assumptions of higher oil revenues. Nevertheless indications are that Venezuelan stocks will continue to be active in 1994. The Caracas exchange may be small when compared with the world's largest, but it has proven to be one of the most bullish in 1992 and 1993. Investment is happening and if the new government manages to gain the confidence of the outside world, it may continue.

While the "Mexico effect" has certainly spread to Venezuela, it has been blunted by the political and economic uncertainties of the past two years. Trade credit should be kept short, no longer than one year, with the risks placed firmly in the hands of financial institutions rather than in the manufacturers' receivables ledgers.

To conclude, here are some suggestions for credit managers which are designed to encourage sales to the "Super Seven" but avoid the credit perils.

Foreign Environment

- Financial Forces (Articles 12 and 13)
- Economic and Socioeconomic Forces (Articles 14 and 15)
- Physical Forces (Articles 16 and 17)
- Sociocultural Forces (Articles 18 and 19)
- Political Forces (Articles 20 and 21)
- Legal Forces (Articles 22 and 23)
- Labor Forces (Articles 24 and 25)
- Competitive and Distributive Forces (Articles 26 and 27)

For centuries most U.S. businesses focused on the domestic markets. There were many reasons for this. The first was that during the 1800s the United States was probably the most rapidly developing country in the world, a huge continental market, limited only by the Atlantic and Pacific Oceans. This was true up until the end of World War I when the United States, for the first time, became a leading industrial nation. But distances were greater than they are today, and communication was not as swift or sure. In addition, most Americans tended to have at least a partially isolationist outlook on the world. There were exceptions—notably in mining, agricultural commodities, and oil. The time between the two world wars was also marked by the great worldwide depression, which was then almost immediately followed by World War II. After World War II, North America stood alone as *the* great industrial power, and it was not until the 1970s that America received the first notice—in the form of the oil crisis—that things had changed.

While many American firms had established extensive holdings outside the United States, in the early 1970s this represented only about 6 percent of total U.S. business. Conversely, by the end of the 1980s, this figure was close to 33 percent. This means that nondomestic business activity is very important to North American companies. What goes on in Europe and the Pacific Rim has a direct impact on what goes on on Wall Street as well as Main Street, U.S.A.

Doing business outside the United States is different from doing business inside the United States. First of all, there is the monetary problem. Every country has a different currency, banking system, and regulations affecting the financial system. Currency fluctuations can play havoc with the assets and profits of a firm.

Economic and socioeconomic forces also play a role. While the cold war is over, it does not mean that doing business in Singapore is just like doing business in Denver. With a few minor exceptions, such as Cuba and North Korea, capitalism either is now or is rapidly becoming the preferred method of organizing an economy. However, within any country that capitalistic system will not necessarily be a clone of the system in North America. There will be Indonesian capitalism, Chilean capitalism, and Hungarian capitalism, just as there is American cap-

italism, British capitalism, and Japanese capitalism. Each system will be based on the same general principles, but each will be different with its own unique twists.

A factor that is going to have a tremendous impact on international trade is the need to develop infrastructure in the developing world and the maintenance of appropriate infrastructure in the developed world. Highways, railroads, airports, and sewer systems will require incredible attention throughout many countries. Asia alone is expected to have over $1 trillion in infrastructure needs over the foreseeable future. Add to this the maintenance and modernization needs of the developed world, plus Latin America and Africa, and there will surely be no shortage of work for contractors and engineers willing to develop these markets.

One of the most fascinating aspects of the global environment is the difference in culture and ideas. Human beings seem to have a wide variety of answers to seemingly mundane, everyday questions. Customs and culture often can play a role in how successful organizations will be when dealing in a foreign market. What may be rude and offensive in one society may be accepted or even expected behavior in another. Understanding these differences and why they are important can often be the key to success in any market.

The political environment also plays an important role in international trade. Some countries are more politically stable than others. Nationalization of foreign assets is not an unknown, and corporations have little or no recourse when their assets are suddenly appropriated by the government. History teaches us that this is a real risk, and learning to analyze and deal with that risk is something that multinationals have to do. This is discussed in the essay "Political Risk Analysis in North American Multinationals: An Empirical Review and Assessment."

When dealing with world trade, the laws of many nations are in the process of developing. Industries are currently international in scope. The world is now the market, and this includes small, as well as large, businesses (as outlined in John DeMott's article "What GATT Means to Small Business"). Agreements are being reached concerning all forms of enterprise. Telecommunications is one case in point. Modern business simply could not be conducted without telecommunications. It is

a key industry. The major industrialized countries have recognized this and have come to an agreement. Nathaniel Nash addresses this issue in "Group of 7 Defines Policies about Telecommunications."

Labor is another important aspect of the environment. Different countries have different attitudes and rules concerning labor and the relative relationship of labor to the economy, government, and corporations. Attitudes and practices differ significantly. For example, in the United States it is common for the relationship between labor and management to be adversarial, while in Germany, representatives from the labor unions often sit on their company's board of directors. The only thing that is certain about labor is that workers now compete in an international environment. No country has a monopoly on highly skilled labor, as shown in "High-Tech Jobs All over the Map," and if workers are going to be competitive in the future, they will need the skills necessary to succeed in the worldwide labor market.

Finally, if nothing else, the environment for international trade will be highly competitive. Global markets mean global competitors. Successful organizations are going to be the ones that can change and adapt to meet the competition. Not being able to change will spell disaster for any organization, but flexibility and adaptability will be the keys to effectiveness in the coming world business environment.

Looking Ahead: Challenge Questions

Doing business outside the United States is different from doing business inside the United States. What are some of the ways that the foreign environment is different from the domestic environment?

Political risk has always been a part of international business. What are some of the approaches that North American multinationals are using to deal with these risks?

One of the challenges in the coming century will be the development and maintenance of infrastructure. What opportunities will these infrastructure needs provide for international firms?

European Monetary Reform:
Pitfalls of Central Planning

The European Community is finding that bureaucrats who have the arrogance to think they can impose their wills on other nations' economies are doomed to failure.

Kevin Dowd

Mr. Dowd is professor of financial economics, Sheffield Hallam University, England, and the author of Laissez-Faire Banking. *This article is based on a Cato Institute Foreign Policy Briefing.*

ONE OF THE IRONIES of recent years is that, while central planning was being thrown out in Eastern Europe, the countries of the European Community (EC) were going in the opposite direction in a misguided effort to establish a centrally controlled superstate. That culminated in the Maastricht Treaty of 1991, which set out a blueprint to increase significantly the powers of the EC government in Brussels, establish a European central bank, and replace the present national currencies with a new common currency.

The authors of the treaty—the would-be Founding Fathers of a United States of Europe—set out to plan the future of 300,000,000 people, regardless of whether they wanted it or not. Not surprisingly, it provoked a storm of controversy, and the process by which member governments sought to ratify the treaty effectively destroyed whatever legitimacy it might have had.

In Great Britain, calls for a referendum were ignored because polls suggested the English did not want the treaty, and the government managed to get the agreement through Parliament only by the narrowest of majorities and by blackmailing skeptical MPs from its own party. The experience in Denmark was even worse. The government put the treaty to a referendum, and the Danes rejected it.

Rather than accept the result of the referendum, the EC heads of government responded by trying to make the Danish people think that the treaty had been altered to take their concerns into account. They did so by producing a "declaration"—a meaningless piece of paper with no legal standing whatsoever—at the Edinburgh summit of December, 1992. That declaration stated that, while the treaty remained unchanged, Denmark would not be bound by the provisions on European monetary union, common citizenship in the European union, and common defense and security issues. The Danish government then took that legally worthless declaration as an excuse to present the same Maastricht Treaty for a second referendum. It managed to persuade enough voters that the treaty had been altered to meet their concerns, and the pact was accepted in the second referendum.

Still, European governments could not deceive the financial markets, which delivered a devastating verdict against the treaty by destroying the platform—the Exchange Rate Mechanism (ERM)—on which European monetary union was to be built. The treaty calls for the ERM to be expanded and "solidified" into a genuinely fixed exchange rate system, and the final transition to a common currency only can take place once that task has been completed. However, the policies of different governments are fundamentally inconsistent, and market operators were not fooled by attempts to disguise those inconsistencies. There were speculative attacks on the ERM, and, by the summer of 1993, it had effectively been destroyed. Whatever European politicians and bureaucrats may say, and despite the fact that the treaty went into effect without the ERM, the Maastricht Treaty essentially is a dead letter.

The roots of the debacle go back a long way. Most European politicians and civil servants see a "strong" state as necessary to protect "their" citizens, whom they regard as unable to look after themselves. That paternalism in domestic policy goes hand in hand with a mercantilistic view wherein the world economy is a group of mutually antagonistic trading blocs in a state of near-ly permanent trade war. That "Fortress Europe" mentality has been associated with the promotion of an artificial sense of European nationalism, the principal characteristic of which is animosity toward the U.S. and Japan.

A second contributing factor is real-politik. The EC originally was built on a bilateral axis between France and Germany, and in recent years the two countries' relationship has become increasingly unbalanced. The French government and the president of the EC Commission, Jacques Delors, became concerned with Germany's renewed assertiveness. If they could not contain Germany indefinitely by themselves, they concluded, they should contain Germany by establishing a federal superstructure above her. They set about to persuade German politicians to accept that superstructure while they still had the influence to do so.

A third factor was dissatisfaction with the German Bundesbank's dominance within the ERM. The ERM had been set up in 1979 to provide a zone of exchange rate stability in Europe, and the Bundesbank's relatively conservative monetary policies had helped reduce inflation in countries such as France and Italy. Despite those benefits, the Bundesbank's dominance within the ERM widely was disliked by politicians in France and, to some extent, the United Kingdom, which saw in it sinister overtones of German hegemony in Europe.

In June, 1988, Delors persuaded the heads of government at their summit in Hanover, Germany, to establish a committee, under his chairmanship, that would put together a program to implement his vision

From *USA Today Magazine*, March 1995, pp. 70-73. © 1995 by the Society for the Advancement of Education, Inc. Reprinted by permission.

12. European Monetary Reform

of Europe. In 1989, the Delors Report set out a detailed plan for a federal European superstate. There was to be a radical centralization of fiscal powers and a massive increase in the resources channeled through the EC itself (*i.e.*, the Brussels bureaucracy). The separate European central banks also were to be merged into a new supranational central bank modeled on the U.S. Federal Reserve System, and the existing European currencies were to be merged into one. As a preliminary step, Britain, Spain, and Portugal were to join the ERM, which they had hitherto not done. Member governments then agreed at their Rome summit in December, 1990, to hold a further intergovernmental conference to agree to a new treaty that would amend the Treaty of Rome of 1957, on which the original European Economic community had been founded.

One might have thought that such an ambitious idea would have merited mature consideration of possible alternatives. Instead, the committee produced their plan with such speed that it is probable that they already knew what they were going to say before they started. According to Charles Goodhart of the London School of Economics, the Delors Report "reads as if its authors were convinced that there is only one currently feasible strategy for the coming phases of European monetary unification: this is a federal strategy, a Hamiltonian strategy, to transfer increasing powers to a federal centre of the United States of Europe. No alternative is even considered."

The scheme was to be accepted in toto and implemented according to a tight and rigid timetable. There was no willingness to engage in debate even after the documents had been produced, and those who criticized the plan were ignored or dismissed as "bad Europeans" who stood in the way of progress. Eleven of the 12 member governments promptly accepted the plan; only the British government rejected it. A lot of pressure was brought to bear on the British government to fall into line, and Prime Minister Margaret Thatcher eventually felt obliged to make concessions, the most significant being sterling's entry into the ERM in October, 1990.

The heads of government met to hammer out the new treaty at their summit in December, 1991. The resulting Maastricht Treaty set out the objectives of the new European Central Bank (ECB), as well as its structure and governance. The ECB was to be a federal central bank modeled on the U.S. Federal Reserve System. Existing national central banks would become branches maintained by the ECB with a status analogous to that of the individual Federal Reserve banks within the Federal Reserve System.

It also laid out a timetable for implementing the reforms, the most important feature of which was that stage 3, covering the irrevocable fixing of exchange rates and transition to the common currency, should begin no later than Jan. 1, 1999. To reduce transition problems before monetary union, the treaty also set out "convergence criteria" that should be met before any currency was to be admitted into the final system of fixed exchange rates before the start of stage 3.

Once the treaty had been agreed to, it had to be ratified by each member state according to that nation's political system. The treaty was not open to further negotiation, and no contingency plan was made for its rejection by any member state. With characteristic hubris, the framers saw the ratification process as little more than a formality, and each government was concerned only with ensuring that the treaty was ratified back home with minimum political inconvenience. Norway's rejection in November, 1994, proved how wrong they were.

The Maastricht Treaty is riddled with problems. Perhaps the most important is that it provides no guarantees about the value of the currency. Admittedly, article 2, which deals with the ECB, does state that the bank's "primary objective . . . shall be to maintain price stability," and any other ends it might pursue have to be consistent with that aim. However, the substance of that clause is undermined by the fact that the treaty does not define what is meant by price stability. That objective thus becomes operationally meaningless, and the central bank always can claim to have to achieved it in its periodic reports.

As Goodhart pointed out in 1992, "Such reports are occasions for the expressions of ex-post justification of whatever, for good or ill, those in authority have chosen to do. Without a clear definition of price stability, and preferably some incentive in the form of bonus payments for achieving that outcome, there is no firm basis for accountability. The ECB's report is bound to state that their actions were consistent, as they saw best, with the achievement of price stability over the appropriate horizon. Most Central Bank reports have made that claim year after year for decades! . . . The failure to define price stability provides . . . a system constructed by, with, and for Central Bankers, to give them an easier life. It is neither necessary nor desirable."

The Maastricht "guarantee" of price stability thus is unconvincing. At the very least, the authors needed to provide a reasonably precise definition of price stability so that people could assess whether or not that objective had been met. Price stability might have been defined in terms of a retail price index showing no trend rate of growth, for instance, with year-to-year deviations that remain within some relatively narrow range. In addition, the treaty should

have included some provisions to encourage the central bank to meet its price stability objective and set penalties if it failed. The governor of the central bank automatically could be fired, for example.

Undermining price stability

The ECB's "commitment" to price stability is undermined in other ways. An important issue in the constitution of any central bank is the extent of its independence from political interference. There are good reasons to expect that the political authorities will be more inclined than central bankers to resort to inflation—they usually have shorter horizons, have an incentive to use short-term monetary policy to engineer pre-election booms, etc.—and the empirical evidence strongly suggests that the more independent central banks deliver lower inflation rates. If the ECB is to be expected to achieve stable prices, it needs to be independent of the political authorities.

Once again, the treaty provides only superficial reassurance. Article 7 of the protocols and article 107 of the treaty explicitly state that the ECB should be independent of the political authorities. That independence is reinforced by article 104 (1) of the treaty prohibiting loans by the ECB or national central banks to EC institutions or member governments, a stipulation that would appear at first sight to protect the bank by prohibiting predatory government demands for cheap credit.

The problem is that the prohibition of loans to governments immediately is qualified in article 104a (1), which states that it applies only to credit that can not be justified by "prudential considerations." Since these have not been defined yet, one can not be sure of the circumstances this exception actually applies to. A more serious loophole is found in article 103a (2), which states that EC institutions can extend financial assistance if a government is "in difficulties or is seriously threatened with severe difficulties caused by exceptional circumstances beyond its control." The treaty makes it clear that the ECB would be regarded as an EC institution. Accordingly, the ECB would be allowed to make loans to member governments despite the prohibition against doing so.

What that means in practice is that, if a national government finds itself faced with fiscal crisis brought on by its own past policies, the EC need only declare that the crisis is an exceptional circumstance beyond the control of the government concerned—the veracity or plausibility of the announcement does not matter—and it can authorize an ECB bailout. Any idea that the ECB would be protected against predatory government demands for credit is an illusion.

Moreover, the same article encourages member governments to pursue irresponsible fiscal policies, since one that does gets a handout that more responsible governments do not. Such an incentive undermines fiscal prudence and creates the very problems supporters of the treaty claim they want to avoid. A rational fiscal federalism would have put the responsibility for fiscal policies firmly where it belongs—on the member governments themselves—and would not have encouraged them to play irresponsible financial games at other people's expense. Europeans can not expect individual member governments to adopt the unpopular policies needed to restore fiscal health if the governments think they can avoid difficult decisions and rely on an EC bailout instead.

The treaty also is very unclear on the regulatory powers of the ECB. Article 2 of the protocols states that the ECB "shall act in accordance with the principle of an open market economy with free competition, favoring an efficient allocation of resources." However, those words are undermined by the fact that the treaty avoids the issue of what an efficient open market economy with free competition actually implies. The article's content is undermined further by the treaty's implication that this type of issue is to be settled in practice by the appropriate authorities as they see fit, meaning, in effect, that they can do whatever they like.

Article 2 also sidesteps various other awkward issues: How can the ECB act in "accordance with the principle of an open market economy with free competition" in an economy that is not open—recall the EC's protectionist policies, does not have free competition, and would have even less under the social chapter of the treaty? Similarly, article 104 (6) allows the bank, under relatively lax conditions, to assume "specific tasks concerning . . . the prudential supervision of credit institutions." The floodgates thus seem to be open to the ECB's acquiring whatever regulatory powers the appropriate authorities feel it should have.

Even when the treaty purports to give some indication of the ECB's future prudential role, it usually does so in a vague and confusing manner. A good example of the muddled thinking that permeates the treaty is its treatment of the normally straightforward question of reserve requirements on commercial banks. Are central banks to be allowed to impose reserve requirements or not? There is much to be said for their elimination, and article 104a of the treaty calls for them to be abolished in stage 2 (the intermediate stage) except as required for "prudential considerations." Leaving aside the fact that such considerations are not defined, article 19 of the protocols then does an about-face and states that the ECB and national central banks will be allowed to impose reserve requirements in stage 3 "in pursuance of [undefined] monetary policy objectives." Having given up their reserve requirements in stage 2, the German and Italian central banks are to be allowed to reimpose them in stage 3.

It is here that the treaty becomes really confusing. The reserve requirements imposed in article 19 are subject to the provisions of article 2 of the protocols, requiring that the ECB "act in accordance with the principle of an open market economy with free competition" and promote economic efficiency. Many economists would argue that reserve requirements are consistent with neither free markets nor efficient resource allocation, so it might be tempting to conclude that reserve requirements are meant to be banned after all. Then again, article 2 of the protocols is itself subject to article 3a of the treaty, which talks vaguely about the policy objectives of the EC and member governments. There is a clear implication that those objectives could override free competition and the efficient allocation of resources if the appropriate authorities were inclined to use them for that purpose. In any case, why include article 19 at all if reserve requirements were meant to be eliminated?

There thus is one article of the protocols that appears to prohibit reserve requirements, subject to the prudential caveat, and another that appears to allow them, subject only to the provisions of a second article of the protocols, a reasonable reading of which would suggest that those conditions could not be met. The latter is itself subject to the provisions of two other articles of the protocols that suggest that reserve requirements might be allowed after all. To make the issue even more confusing, there is the unclear legal question of whether the treaty article prohibiting imprudent reserve requirements overrides, or is overridden by, the two protocols articles that appear to allow them. Where all of this leaves reserve requirements in the end is anyone's guess.

It turned out that ratifying the treaty was not the straightforward formality member governments had anticipated. Denmark and Ireland chose to put it to a popular vote. The Danish vote, which took place in June, 1992, turned down the treaty. Since it had to be ratified by all member governments, this meant that the treaty was legally dead.

Yet, rather than accept that outcome, EC leaders took the line that the Danish government should hold as many referenda as it took for the Danish people to produce the "right" answer, the underlying argument presumably being that the Danes were to be allowed to accept the treaty, but not to reject it. The cracks in the Maastricht ratification process duly were papered over by the meaningless Edinburgh "declaration" of December, 1992, and the Danish government then put the treaty to a second popular vote. Despite the obvious sleight-of-hand and the fact that, a few weeks after Edinburgh, the Danish prime minister was forced to resign for lying to the parliament, the result of the first, legitimate referendum was overturned by the second referendum in May, 1993. European political leaders congratulated themselves on solving the Danish "problem," but, in the process, the treaty had lost whatever legitimacy it otherwise might have had.

Crisis in the ERM

There were other difficulties as well. Financial markets never had been convinced of the merits of the treaty or that individual member governments were prepared to make the sacrifices of their own individual autonomy that the unification process required. Those doubts came to a head with the ERM crisis in September, 1992. The ERM was to play a pivotal role in the unification process, and it was essential that it operate smoothly and build up the credibility with the market that the transition process required. Yet, at the same time, it was clear in the market that certain governments—the British and Italians especially—were reluctant to pay the price that maintaining their exchange rates within the bounds set by the ERM would entail.

The obvious course of action in the marketplace was to bet against the currencies that stood to be devalued. Speculative sales of those currencies soon became unstoppable, and the lira, sterling, and peseta were driven out of the ERM. The macroeconomic policies of the respective governments had been torn to shreds. The British government had seen the "centerpiece" of its macroeconomic policy destroyed and most of its foreign exchange reserves wiped out in a few hours in a futile attempt to defend the pound.

While the English continued to pay lip service to the principle of ERM membership, it was clear that government leaders were in no hurry to return to the system. Moreover, the British government would have found it very difficult to maintain any new set of exchange rate bounds even if it had had the stomach to try. The pressure then intensified on the French franc, which barely managed to survive the attack and stay within ERM bounds. That proved short-lived, and a new attack the next summer forced European monetary authorities to widen allowable exchange rate movements within the ERM and thus, in effect, surrender to market forces. What remained of the ERM was only a ghost of its former self, and any idea that it could somehow "grow" into a unified monetary system had to be dismissed as sheer fantasy. The ERM effectively had been destroyed.

If Maastricht was not the way forward, what else could European political leaders have done? One option would have been to continue with the ERM as it was. Countries such as Britain, France, and Italy would have enjoyed some benefits of the relatively conservative monetary policies of the Bundesbank, much as France and Italy already had done for a number of years. The ERM then would have been regarded as it was in earlier times—as a zone of exchange rate stability whereby other nations benefited from relatively tough German monetary policy. The ERM would have been under less strain and might have survived in reasonable shape.

A better option would have been for individual nations to institute more thorough-going monetary reforms. If the citizens of any given country desire price stability—as they presumably do—the most natural option would be for the government concerned to implement independent monetary reform to achieve it. Such reform would involve, at the very least, the passing of legislation to impose an operational price-level target on the central bank. That target would be stated in terms of a measurable price index, and there would be clearly defined penalties imposed on the central bank or its officials, or both, in the event of failure.

A good example of such an approach is the New Zealand Reserve Bank Act of 1990, which set out a price-level target and gave the central bank incentives to achieve it. A particular advantage of that sort of approach in the European context is that it would have required little or no negotiation with the governments of other EC nations and thus would have circumvented the horse-trading and general compromising that invariably go on when EC heads of government try to agree on anything. If individual European leaders genuinely had wanted monetary reform, they would have been much better off putting their own domestic monetary houses in order—and they easily could have done so.

The Maastricht Treaty is the wrong program implemented by the wrong people for the wrong reasons. It is a classic case of the fatal conceit of central planners, who have the supreme arrogance to think they can impose their will on peoples and markets alike in total disregard of economic rationality or even basic common sense. As economist Adam Smith once noted, allocating capital is too complicated a business to entrust to any government body, especially one presumptuous enough to fancy itself qualified to do the job. Nevertheless, the lessons of Maastricht probably are lost on those who most need to learn them, and one can only wonder what they will dream up next.

Gradualism and Chinese Financial Reforms

Mark Spiegel
Senior Economist

In discussions of the optimal pace of transition from a socialist to a market economy, those favoring a "gradualist" approach often point to the experience of the People's Republic of China. By crossing the river from a centrally planned to a market economy "one stone at a time," as the saying goes, the Chinese appear to have made significant progress towards market reforms without suffering the large output declines faced by countries pursuing more rapid "cold turkey" reforms in Eastern Europe. Indeed, the pace of economic growth in China since Deng Xiaoping's historic 1992 call for deeper economic restructuring and greater experimentation with markets has been staggering. Real GDP grew at a 13 percent annual rate in 1992 and 1993, and double-digit real GDP growth is forecasted again for 1994.

In spite of its dramatic growth performance, the current economic situation in China suffers from the limited control the Chinese central government appears to enjoy over its own monetary policy and the rapid inflation that is emerging as a result. In the first eight months of 1994, prices rose at a 26 percent annual rate nationally.

Policymakers commonly respond to high inflation rates by slowing the pace of reform. Indeed, China reverted back to numerous price controls this fall in an effort to dampen inflation. These price controls are welcomed by the large "state-owned enterprise" sector, half of which is currently estimated to be operating at a loss, since their output prices are already controlled by the government while their input prices often are not. Consequently, by pursuing such inflation-fighting measures as reversion to price controls, Beijing also is effectively pursuing a gradualist path towards reform by aiding firms in the state-owned enterprise sector to avoid bankruptcy.

It might seem, then, that Chinese officials are faced with an undesirable choice between faster reforms and runaway inflation. However, in this *Weekly Letter*, we argue that this is not the case. We examine the problems experienced in the Chinese financial sector during the reform period, and explain why the reforms undertaken in this sector fail to address the fundamental source of China's inflation problems. We argue that a faster pace of reform is compatible with controlling inflation in China.

Problems in China's financial system

China's ongoing need to support the state-owned enterprise sector is a major cause of the nation's inflation problem. State-owned enterprises accounted for 60 percent of the country's total fixed investment in 1993. The state-owned enterprises provide lifetime employment, as well as numerous benefits such as housing and pensions to its workers. It is estimated that shutting down the unprofitable state-owned enterprises alone would result in laying off more than 100 million workers with no benefits. Consequently, political pressure has led both central and local Chinese banks to contribute massively towards maintaining the operation of these state-owned enterprises through the extension of loans of dubious value. The resulting increases in the money supply have generated inflation. This pressure has been exacerbated by the lack of independence of the Chinese banking system, and in particular the People's Bank of China (PBC) from the State Council.

The problem also is aggravated by the structure of the Chinese banking system. Banks are responsible for issuing "policy loans" to finance the deficits of the Ministry of Finance and the losses of the state-owned enterprises. The government dictates both the allocation of capital

Reprinted with permission from the Federal Reserve Bank of San Francisco *Weekly Letter,* December 30, 1994, pp. 1-3. The opinions expressed in this article do not necessarily reflect the views of the management of the Federal Reserve Bank of San Francisco, or of the Board of Governors of the Federal Reserve System.

and the terms of lending to the banking system. The result is that an estimated 40 percent of the loans extended to the state sector are listed as nonperforming.

The process of reform itself also has contributed to inflation. As reform progressed, decentralization diminished the control of the PBC headquarters over the activities of its branch offices. This allowed local governments to pressure local PBC banks to extend credit of dubious quality to local financial institutions.

The situation became critical in 1992 and the first half of 1993. Local branches of the PBC found themselves under heavy pressure to issue loans not included in the central government's investment plan. These funds sometimes were used for highly speculative activities, including real estate ventures and stock market speculation. Indeed, there were reports that branches of the PBC not only failed to regulate this activity, but also were active participants themselves. This forced the PBC to issue additional loans to finance planned investment, further increasing the money supply.

Financial reforms
The government sought to curb many of these problems in its financial sector with a 16-point program for reform of domestic financial policy in July of 1993. The plan restricted credit extension by the banking system, particularly the ability of local financial institutions to engage in speculative activity. In addition, the plan enhanced the ability of the central government to allocate credit towards its priority investments.

The financial system also has been restructured to allow the PBC to function similarly to the central banks in developed countries, such as the Federal Reserve System in the United States, with the mandate to conduct domestic monetary policy through manipulation of bank loan rates, open-market operations, and changes in bank reserve requirements. However, the PBC will not enjoy the independence associated with the central banking systems in many developed nations. The central bank still will be required to implement the policies of the State Council.

In addition, China is converting its four specialized banks—the Bank of China, the Agricultural Bank, the Industrial and Commercial Bank, and the People's Construction Bank of China—into commercial banks. These banks are currently encouraged both to perform as profitable institutions and to offer liberal loans to the unprofitable state-owned enterprises. Under the new system, these banks will be allowed to make their loan decisions independently and will be responsible for their profits and losses. Policy-based lending

activities will be undertaken by three newly created financial institutions: the State Development Bank, the Export–Import Credit Bank, and the Agricultural Banks of China. These banks will be bond-financed and hence will place no direct pressure on the domestic money supply.

Current financial system performance
The reforms of the Chinese financial system appear compatible with a gradualist path of reform. They correct a number of particularly glaring deficiencies from the previous system which led to poor credit allocation decisions and eventual loss of control over the financial system. At the same time, the State Council maintains some control over the PBC and the reforms call for some policy-based credit extension to take place independent of the central bank. However, the Chinese experience subsequent to the July 1993 reforms reveals the pitfalls in this gradualist reform policy.

Initially, the 16-point plan was somewhat successful in tightening credit. However, the tighter credit created problems when farmers harvested a bumper crop. Banks had difficulty paying farmers for their mandated crop production. Combined with the mandate under the plan which forbids banks from issuing IOUs to farmers, as had commonly been done in the past, banks found their working capital constrained. This reduced the magnitude of credit banks were able to issue to the state-owned enterprise sector, which relied on new loans to pay suppliers or to finance outstanding debt. Particularly hard hit were the raw materials sectors; they faced reductions in lenient loans, which threatened to create shortages. This phenomenon has been termed "triangular debt," where unprofitable state-owned enterprises, which are kept in operation through cash infusions from the banking sector, fail to make required payments to other unprofitable firms. The central bank responded to the liquidity shortage largely caused by the 16-point austerity plan by claiming victory over excessive growth and resuming expansion of the money supply. In the November 1993 Central Committee plenary session, calls again were heard to speed up the pace of reform, with references to the 16-point plan notably absent. The backtracking on the austerity plan resulted in a renewed expansion of the money supply and a rapid increase in inflation in the beginning of 1994. In 1994, the government repeatedly switched between austerity policies designed to address the growing inflation problem and expansionary measures designed to avoid unemployment. In March, a State Planning Commission report outlined a plan for lowering the inflation rate to 10 percent through reductions in capital expenditures and bond financing of deficits. This bond financing is possible only through forced sales of government bonds at rates well below urban inflation rates. In addition, political pressures led Prime Minister Li Peng to announce in October of 1994 that local governments would be responsible for maintenance of "acceptably" low food prices. In practice, this implies the reinstatement of price controls and the subsidization of production. These subsidies may yield government deficits requiring monetization, implying further pressure on prices.

Conclusion

While the financial reforms being pursued by China should improve the operation of the financial system, they do not address the problems associated with maintaining the operations of the large unprofitable state-owned enterprise sector. As long as this sector requires continuous infusions of funds to stay afloat, the Chinese government will be required either to forgo other expenditures, such as much needed improvements in infrastructure, or monetize these expenditures by increasing the money supply. Consequently, the reforms of the financial system do not address a fundamental source of inflationary pressure, namely, the policy of maintaining the operation of unprofitable state-owned enterprises. Over the long run, more rapid reform, in the form of closing unprofitable state-owned enterprises, may lead to less inflation rather than more.

However, one should not understate the difficulty associated with closing these enterprises. Under the current system, a large portion of the losses of the state-owned enterprises are policy induced, stemming from price controls and poor management incentives. Consequently, the fact that a state-owned enterprise is currently losing money may not be sufficient evidence to motivate closing it down.

In addition, the government is particularly sensitive to the political difficulties associated with the displacement of 100 million workers. Current estimates suggest that the agricultural sector also is on the verge of releasing a large quantity of labor. Chinese officials estimate that only 200 million of the current 450 million workers in the agricultural labor force can be profitably employed in that sector. It will take time to absorb these laborers into the growing sectors of the Chinese economy, such as the very successful market-oriented township and village enterprises and special economic zones. Therefore, the Chinese government is determined to keep the state-owned enterprises open. Some efforts to improve the productivity of this sector without closing plants have taken place. The government has attempted to merge failing enterprises with healthier ones. There have also been limited movements towards privatization of state-owned enterprises through the issue of equity.

In the meantime, the burden of a gradualist path of reform appears to have fallen on the Chinese financial system in the form of the current rampant inflation. As in most inflationary regimes, the fundamental source of this inflation is unsustainable fiscal policy, in this case, using government funds to bail out failing sectors of the economy. Reform of the structure of the banking sector alone cannot bring inflation down.

**Economics, not politics, defines the landscape
on which all else must operate.**

PUTTING
GLOBAL
LOGIC
FIRST

Kenichi Ohmae

In today's borderless economy, the workings of the "invisible hand" have a reach and strength beyond anything Adam Smith ever could have imagined. In Smith's day, economic activity took place on a landscape largely defined – and circumscribed – by the political borders of nation-states: Ireland with its wool, Portugal with its wines. Now, by contrast, economic activity is what defines the landscape on which all other institutions, including political institutions, must operate. Business and government are just beginning to live with the consequences.

Most visibly, the nation-state itself – that artifact of the eighteenth and nineteenth centuries – has begun to crumble, battered by a pent-up storm of political resentment, ethnic prejudice, tribal hatred, and religious animosity. The most dramatic examples are the former Soviet Union and Czechoslovakia, which both have ceased to exist as nations. But there are many others. In the now unified Germany, the federal government has ceded an unprecedented amount of power to the individual *Länder*. Similarly, Spain's 17 autonomous communities – espe-

cially those with deeply entrenched historical identities, such as Catalonia – are gaining the powers of independent states. In Canada, the French-speaking province of Quebec is actively moving to cut its constitutional ties with the largely English-speaking provinces. Even in dirigiste France, the prefects of President François Mitterrand's government can no longer unilaterally veto decisions made in the country's 22 provinces.

To interpret those events in purely political terms would be a mistake. Of course, nearly half a century of cold war tensions cannot end without dramatic changes on all sides: in the absence of the restraints once imposed by the superpowers, long-repressed political aspirations have burst into the open. But there are three other, more fundamental factors at work. First, the often instantaneous movement of people, ideas, information, and capital across borders means that decisions are

swayed by the threat that needed resources will go elsewhere rather than by cold war allegiances. With the speed and volume of transactions in the global capital market, national governments cannot control exchange rates or protect their currencies, and political leaders increasingly find themselves at the mercy of people and institutions making economic choices over which they have no control. Remember the recent Maastricht-related bout of speculation against the British pound, the French franc, and the Swedish krona? It demonstrated that currency speculators can affect the value of a particular

Kenichi Ohmae, formerly a partner in McKinsey & Company's Tokyo office, is the author of more than 40 books, including Triad Power *(Free Press, 1985) and* The Borderless World *(Harper Business, 1990). He is the founder and director of Heisei Ishin no Kai, a political reform movement in Japan. This article is adapted from a new book,* The End of the Nation-State, *published by the Free Press in 1995. Parts of this article previously appeared in* Foreign Affairs *(Spring 1993, p. 78).*

currency in ways that the government simply cannot counteract, even if it spends billions in an attempt to prop up the exchange rate.

Second, as the flow of information creates a growing awareness among consumers everywhere about how other people live, tastes and preferences begin to converge. Global brands of colas, blue jeans, athletic shoes, and designer ties and handbags are as much on the mind of the

Nation-states are a willing hostage to the past since the future is a constituency that casts no vote.

taxi driver in Shanghai as they are in the home of the schoolteacher in Stockholm. Over time, the accelerating convergence of tastes puts pressure on governments to make sure their people have access to the best and cheapest products from all over the world. When governments refuse – in the name of national interest or market protection or whatever – people will find a way to vote with their pocketbooks.

Third, the nation-state, which was a powerful engine of wealth creation in its mercantilist phase, has become an equally powerful engine of wealth destruction. To stay in office, elected leaders know they must satisfy the often extortionate demands of powerful special-interest groups, such as the unions, farmers, and fishermen in Japan. To maintain legitimacy, they must freely make available to all citizens a common level of public services and support even though they cost vastly different amounts to provide. Their constituents demand the same civil minimum of services – telephone, electricity, postal service, roads, schools, and harbors – regardless of whether they live in Tokyo or on the remote island of Okinawa.

As a result of the effort to provide a civil minimum of services, 44 of Japan's 47 prefectures are now net recipients of government subsidies. The other 3 – all in the Greater

Tokyo area – pay for the rest. The imbalance is striking. The cities of Tokyo, Osaka, Fukuoka, Sapporo, and Nagoya create more than 85% of Japan's wealth. Of those five cities, only Tokyo is a net taxpayer; all the others receive more money from the central government than they pay in taxes. Meanwhile, in the city of Aomori, at the northern end of Japan's main island of Honshu, only $300 million of the annual budget of $1.5 billion comes from local taxes. Everything else comes from the central government.

A government may have understandable political, perhaps even social, reasons to defer to special interests and to observe the civil minimum. Economically, however, it makes no sense. Investing money inefficiently never does. In a borderless world, it is also unsustainable. Sooner or later, usually sooner, the invisible hand of the market will move resources or economic activity elsewhere. During the past several years, for instance, the Japanese government has pumped more than $300 billion into the domestic economy in a Keynesian attempt to jump-start demand after the post-Bubble recession. The strategy worked. But it did not boost local supply or create local jobs. As demand increased, supply came from China, Korea, and the rest of the world. Even in Japan, the instruments of central control are losing their force.

That should come as no surprise. Since nation-states were created to meet the needs of a much earlier historical period, they do not have the will, the incentive, the credibility, the tools, or the political base to play an effective role in the borderless economy of today. By heritage and by experience, nation-states are comfortable with the market's invisible hand only when they can control or regulate it. By orientation and by skill, they cannot help but

make economic choices primarily in terms of their political, not economic, consequences. By electoral logic and by popular expectation, they must always sacrifice general, indirect, long-term benefits in favor of immediate, tangible, focused payoffs. They are a willing hostage to the past because the future is a constituency that casts no vote. The bottom line is that they have become unnatural – even dysfunctional – as actors in a global economy because they are incapable of putting global logic first in their decisions.

Nation-states are no longer meaningful units in which to think about economic activity. In a borderless world, they combine things at the wrong level of aggregation. What sense does it make, for example, to think of Italy as a coherent economic entity within the European Union? There is no "average" Italy. There is no meaningful social or economic group precisely at the midpoint. There is an industrial north and a rural south, which are vastly different in their ability to contribute and their need to receive. For the public official or the private-

By heritage, nation-states are comfortable with the invisible hand of the market only when they can control or regulate it.

sector manager, treating Italy as if it were fairly represented by an average is to mortgage usable insight in return for an economic relic – and a destructive one at that.

Region-States

In a borderless economy, the units that do make sense are what I call region-states – geographical units such as northern Italy; Wales; Baden-Württemberg in Germany; San Diego, California, and Tijuana, Mexico; Hong Kong and southern China; the Growth Triangle of Singapore and its neighboring Indonesian islands; or Osaka and its outlying areas, which are together known as Kañsai. Those are the natural economic zones. They may or may not fall within the boundaries of a particular nation. If they do, it is an accident of history. In practical terms, it does not really matter. What does matter is that

A region-state welcomes whatever will employ its people, give them the best products, and improve their quality of life.

each possesses the key ingredients for successful participation in the global economy – not the least of which is the ability and the determination to put global logic first.

Look, for example, at what is happening in Southeast Asia as the Hong Kong economy reaches out to embrace first Shenzhen and then other parts of the Zhu River Delta, often called the Pearl River Delta, in China. Hong Kong, where per capita gross national product is $12,000, is now the driving economic force in the lives of the people in Shenzhen, and its radiating influence has already boosted per capita GNP there to $5,695. Per capita GNP for all of China is only $317. Even today, those linkages extend beyond Shenzhen to Zhuhai, Xiamen, and Guangzhou as well. By the year 2000, that cross-border region-state could raise the standard of living of some 11 million people to more than the $5,000 level.

Chinese government officials have gotten the message and expanded the "special economic zone" concept, which has worked so well for Shenzhen and Shanghai, to 14 other areas, many of them inland. The concept involves a mix of policies allowing for favorable terms for foreign investment, access to credit, transshipment of goods, and so forth. One such project in Yunnan will become a cross-border region-state encompassing Laos and Vietnam. Within Vietnam, Ho Chi Minh City has launched a similar effort,

called Sepzone, in order to attract foreign capital. Moreover, Indonesia, Malaysia, and Thailand unveiled a plan in 1992, modeled in part on Singapore's Growth Triangle, to link economically their respective cities of Medan, Penang, and Phuket across the Strait of Malacca.

Other such initiatives are in the works. The Tumen Delta Project cuts across China, North Korea, and Russia. In Japan, government and business have expressed interest in a Northeastern Asia Economic Zone, also called the Sea of Japan Economic Zone, which would link the Russian cities of Nakhodka, Khabarovsk, and Vladivostok with the Japanese city of Niigata. There are also proposals to integrate that economic zone with the Tumen Delta Project. Cold war animosities notwithstanding, the signs are favorable: a ferry is already in service across the Sea of Japan.

As of early 1994, the city of Dalian on China's Liaodong Peninsula, in the north, was home to more than 3,500 active corporations – nearly 2,500 of them with foreign affiliations. The mayor of Dalian knows perfectly well that continued economic growth depends on providing an attractive environment for foreign investment. He also knows that the region's leaders cannot responsibly ignore the needs of foreign operations and instead divert resources to protect indigenous state-owned companies, most of which are losing money. Dalian and its people simply cannot afford it. Much the same is true in the three northeastern provinces of China, which have already reached a steeper learning curve than Japan has in the manufacture both of printed circuit boards for laptop computers and of cylinder heads for videocassette recorders – with higher productivity and at only 2% of Japan's wage levels.

That kind of economic progress is possible only when regions are genu-

inely open and responsive – in ways nation-states will not and cannot be – to the real flow of economic activity in today's world. Thomas P. "Tip" O'Neill, former Speaker of the U.S. House of Representatives, liked to say, "All politics is local." But region-states are economic units, not political ones, and they are anything but local in focus. They may lie within the borders of an established nation, but their primary linkage is with the global economy.

Region-states welcome foreign investment. They welcome foreign ownership. They welcome foreign products. In fact, they welcome whatever will employ their people productively, improve their quality of life, and give them access to the best and cheapest products in the world. They have discovered that people often have better access to low-cost, high-quality products when they do not try to produce them at home. Singaporeans, for example, enjoy better and cheaper agricultural products than do the Japanese, although Singapore has no farmers – and no farms – of its own. Furthermore, region-states welcome the chance to use any surplus that accrues from global trade and investment activities to ratchet up the quality of life even more rather than to fund the civil minimum or prop up distressed industries. Their leaders do not go around to other countries trying to attract factories and investment – and then appear on

If economic zones fall within a nation's borders, it is an accident of history.

television back home vowing to protect local jobs and local producers at all costs.

Region-states are the natural economic zones in a borderless world because, by definition, the demands of the global economy shape their contours. They must be large enough to provide an attractive market for leading consumer products but small enough for their citizens to share economic and consumer interests. They must be of sufficient size to justify economies of services – that is, an infrastructure of communications, transportation, and professional services. They must, for example, have at least one international airport and, more than likely, one good harbor with international-class freight-handling facilities. They tend to have between 5 million and 20 million people. The population range is broad, but the extremes are clear: not half a million, not 50 million or 100 million.

When region-states prosper, their prosperity spills over into adjacent areas. Happy economic experiences in and around Bangkok have prompted investors to explore options in other parts of Thailand. The same is true of Kuala Lumpur in Malaysia, Djakarta in Indonesia, and of course, Singapore. It would also be true of the area around São Paulo if the Brazilian government would free it up

When region-states prosper, their prosperity spills into adjacent areas.

to participate as a region-state in the global economy. If it does, São Paulo will probably be ready to join the Organization for Economic Cooperation and Development within ten years. If it does not, Brazil itself may fall off the roster of rapidly developing economies.

The Ladder of Development

What defines region-states is their commitment to being a point of entry to the global economy. But what gives each its special form and shape is its position on the ladder of economic development. Moving up that ladder means being able to put the right policies, institutions, and infrastructure in place at the right time. At about $3,000 per capita GNP, a region-state's desire to get more actively involved with the global economy, both as a market for and as a supplier of basic consumer goods, usually increases steadily. In Japan, for example, the desire took the form of rapidly expanding con-

sumer demand for color televisions, refrigerators, and low-cost automobiles. Below that level – between, say, $1,500 and $3,000 per capita – the emphasis is more on motorbikes, as it is today in Thailand; below $1,500, it is more on bicycles, as it is in Shanghai, China, and throughout Vietnam. At the $3,000 threshold, it makes sense to begin serious construction of modern highway systems, urban rail systems, and the rest of the infrastructure needed to support a higher level of international commerce: drinking water, electric power, communications, and finance.

At the $5,000 threshold, the requirements for economic development change yet again. The strength of the desire to be part of the global economic system escalates rapidly. The demand for quality automobiles takes off, as does the need for up-to-date international airports and a high-speed railway system. At that stage also, the drive for ever greater material prosperity often begins to crowd out, even for local elites, quality-of-life considerations – such as living in a clean environment, running factories that observe Western-style child-labor laws, and structuring work so as to allow for leisure time – which tend not to return in force until GNP moves well beyond the $10,000 level.

Something else happens at $5,000: linkages with the global economy expand, but the softer aspects of the economy – the currency, as well as banking and communications, for example – are not yet fully open to it. The heavy hand of government regulation and control remains firmly in place. The temptation, of course, is to keep it there. After all, why face the disruption and loss of control that a deregulated and open economy would bring?

Most midsize countries in Europe have given in to that temptation, which explains why they have had to struggle so much to get beyond the $5,000 barrier. By contrast, Tai-

Taiwan, Hong Kong, and Singapore deregulated foreign exchange, and their economies shot up.

wan, at a comparable point in its development, aggressively moved to deregulate foreign-exchange and many other markets. As a result, its economy shot up to the $10,000 level in only a few years. Singapore made basically the same kind of leap. So did Hong Kong, which explains why its economy shot by the $5,000 barrier while South Korea's did not, although all four had competed neck and neck until that point.

The evidence, then, is clear: what a government does at $5,000 per capita GNP makes a huge difference in how quickly – and how well – it can join the $10,000 club. If a country genuinely opens itself up to the global system, prosperity will follow. If it does not or if it does so only halfheartedly, relying instead on the heavy, guiding hand of central government, its progress will falter.

Policy Challenges

Policymakers at all levels, public and private, will need to think carefully about how best to avoid government intervention that will stifle the development of region-states. Silicon Valley, the great early jugger-

Hollywood did not turn protectionist just because it faced a capital shortage.

naut of much of the microelectronics industry in the United States, has created industry associations, lobbied the federal government, studied competitiveness as a way to get more federal funding for research and development, and become downright protectionist. The result: Japan has now developed a Silicon Island on Kyushu; Taiwan is trying to create a Silicon Island of its own; and Korea is nurturing a Silicon Peninsula. It is the worst of all possible worlds for Silicon Valley – no new money in California and a host of newly energized and well-funded competitors.

Not that far from Silicon Valley, the story is quite different. When Hollywood recognized that it faced a severe capital shortage, it did not throw up protectionist barriers against foreign money. Instead, it invited Rupert Murdoch into Twentieth Century-Fox, C. Itoh and Toshiba into Time Warner, Sony into Columbia Pictures, and Matsushita into MCA. The result was a $10 billion infusion of new capital – and, equally important, $10 billion less for Japan or anyone else to set up its own Hollywood.

Political leaders around the world are just beginning to pay serious attention to those lessons. But they are – and are likely to remain – the most reluctant of converts. That tendency is, of course, perfectly understandable: their power rests on the traditional nation-state, and its inevitable erosion is not something to be accepted lightly over a cup of tea in the afternoon. But accept it they must. Otherwise, as meaningful economic activity migrates to the region-states that lie within and across their countries' borders, they will be left with hollow political shells and constituents calling for the civil minimum.

Quebec, for example, is not the core economic or even political issue for Canada, although it is of great emotional significance. As the North American Free Trade Agreement takes shape, the relationships between U.S. and Canadian regions –

For political leaders, the erosion of the nation-state is not something to be accepted lightly over a cup of tea in the afternoon.

Seattle and Vancouver (the Pacific Northwest region-state); and Detroit, Cleveland, and Toronto (the Great Lakes region-state) – will become increasingly important. How will Canada's leaders deal with the new entities? How will they guide the confederation? If they are going to be able to run Canada politically, they will have to find workable answers to such questions.

On present evidence, however, it is not even clear they are asking the questions, because they are so preoccupied with the problems of the past. It simply makes no sense, for instance, for the great public issue in British Columbia to be the teaching of both French and English. That is not because educational or language choices no longer matter. It is because the information and investment on which the British Columbian economy depends, now and increasingly in the future, will be linked much more closely with Asia than with its sister provinces.

Much the same is true for China. If it is going to survive economically and politically, it will have to allow the development of multiple autonomous region-states within its territory. In the twenty-first century, even more than today, governing 1.2 billion people with a single, centrally dictated economic policy will prove impossible. To bring its people effectively into the modern industrial world, the government must

educate them. Once they are educated, they will start to think for themselves and to look for information about how the rest of the world behaves. The rest of the world can only hope that plans are in the works for a Commonwealth of China or a Chinese confederation.

What of Taiwan? With the passing of the old Kuomintang generation, Taiwan has to decide where its future lies. If it gets the answer wrong, there is the real possibility of invasion or civil war. If it gets the answer right, Taiwan can readily become a – perhaps even *the* – leading member of a new Commonwealth of China and one of the most important and autonomous economic powers in the world.

The above examples are not isolated ones. Neither are they hypothetical worries based on fictional concerns. Nation-states *are* eroding as economic actors. Region-states *are* taking shape. It is not a question of maybe or perhaps. It *is* happening. No more than Canute's soldiers can we oppose the tides of the borderless world's ebb and flow of economic activity. The only real question, then, for political leaders – the only responsible question – is whether those tides can be harnessed to provide a better life for their people. And that means acknowledging the emergence – and understanding the unique value – of region-states.

LATIN AMERICA HEATS UP

Sure there's political instability, high inflation, and vast pockets of poverty. But that hasn't stopped planners from putting plenty of American dollars on the line.

Bruce E. Beebe and Peter J. Kennedy Jr.

Bruce E. Beebe is an associate consultant with The Futures Group in Glastonbury, Connecticut. Peter J. Kennedy Jr., also with The Futures Group, is director of the firm's Emerging Markets division.

Latin America. Say that to some people and the response is: It's a dirt-poor subcontinent south of Mexico, home to stratospheric inflation, political instability, and a phenomenally inequitable distribution of consumer wealth. That view is an outdated and misleading caricature of a much more complex situation. In truth, South America has a sizable middle class—with a lot of money to spend—starving for "First World" brands and consumer goods. Many Latin governments, also with cash in hand, are just as hungry for industrial technology and partnerships with their Nortéamericanos neighbors; to prove it, they're privatizing more and more industries every year.

While Asia garners much of the attention of the international business press, and NAFTA continues to captivate media in the United States, Latin America is, in some ways, an often overlooked story.

Why are U.S.-based multinational companies (MNCs) giving the area a second chance, after getting burned the last time Latin America "opened up?" For one reason, many of these strategists are betting that Latin America may, in fact, provide profit opportunities in many business sectors that could take up the slack in earnings potential from the comparatively slow-growing U.S. domestic market. Another reason is that today's multi-country trade agreements are different—read firmer—than the ones before. The Treaty of Montevideo, which formed the Latin America Free Trade Association (LAFTA) in 1960, was created in the shadow of alleged foreign-investor exploitation of raw materials (particularly oil, copper, and wood) during the 1950s, and, thus, left so many loopholes for local governmental autonomy that Latin America never was able to speak with one economic voice. LAFTA (whose country members would eventually total 11) estab-

lished sectoral industry groups which met annually to draw up proposals, not contracts, for tariff and nontariff barrier cuts for products. The implementation of these proposals was also left to the discretion of local governments (and sometimes even local producers).

LAFTA's provisions also hinged on a flood of international aid which, at the time, meant creating local, government-supervised economic development. With the governments in control, and, as it turned out, not so successful at money management, LAFTA hardly had a change to create a semblance of a free-market.

Now these faulty underpinnings are removed. LAFTA has dissolved into the much less xenophobic Latin America Integration Association.

Also, the new accords among Central American, Caribbean, and South American countries are being pushed through by the countries and local industries themselves. Last year's hugely successful Venezuela

From the *Journal of Business Strategy*, September/October 1994, pp. 52-55. © 1994 by Faulkner & Gray, Inc., New York, NY. Reprinted by permission.

accord is one example of South America's commitment to free markets, as is the linking of "Mercosul," the so-called Southern Cone Free Market joining Argentina, Brazil, Paraguay, and Uruguay. These accords signal South American governments' overall willingness to loosen their hold on the market's reins. In addition, free trade agreements of the kind recently signed in the region are not easily undone.

Confidence in Latin America is at an all-time high. Even owners of Peruvian securities—the one-time "joke of the bond market"—are having the last laugh. Loans formerly considered worthless now fetch more than 70 cents on the dollar.

The Emerging Middle Class

Traditionally, Latin America is thought to consist of two classes of people: the super-rich minority and the dirt-poor majority. True, Latin America as a whole continues to suffer from an inequitable distribution of wealth. But, economic reform and recovery have brought many middle class Latin American consumers out of hiding. Not surprisingly, as economies have stabilized and inflation has fallen, consumer confidence has returned with a vengeance. Moreover, market-oriented policies, after an often difficult period of adjustment, invariably create jobs and raise incomes.

Today, there are also more precise analytical instruments for measuring wealth. Traditional estimations of gross domestic product (GDP), based on simple conversion of output in local currency to dollars, tend to undervalue national income and thus distort per capita purchasing power. More accurate wealth measures result from using purchasing power parity (PPP) analysis, which takes into account local prices of non-tradable goods such as rent, transportation, and local standards of living, thus providing a more realistic basis for measuring disposable income. PPP has been adopted by the United Nations and World Bank to more accurately estimate developing country income levels.

As the graph on the next page demonstrates, the differences in the two measures are significant. Compared to the traditional exchange rate conversion method, in PPP terms Brazil has double the number of middle income workers (earning the equivalent of $10,000-40,000 yearly). Colombia has three times as many workers in the middle income range.

The middle classes have money to spend on everything from clothes to home furnishings, food to entertainment. In addition to the middle-income level spenders, even the most basic demographic research turns up millions of consumer-goods-hungry teenagers, aging couch potatoes, and, of course, babies.

Of course, members of the middle class do more than just spend money; they also work. In spite of the high rate of illiteracy, the level of entrepreneurial skills and technological know-how in Latin America is quite high. Many American companies have been able to find more than enough skilled workers for their assembly lines as well as plenty of talent to fill management positions.

Mucho Dinero

Several North American companies have recently made sizable commitments to Latin American markets. Long quiet in other international markets, for instance, RJR Nabisco recently bought into a leading Argentine biscuit and chocolate company, Terrabusi. No longer content to play second fiddle to Unilever and Colgate-Palmolive, Procter & Gamble dived into Latin America by buying two major Argentine soap makers.

North American MNCs are everywhere. São Paulo, Brazil, for instance, boasts 38 Pizza Huts as well as numerous Arby's and KFCs. J.C. Penney and Wal-Mart are also both expected to enter this city. It's not hard to see why: São Paulo's metropolitan area has 18 million people—about as many people as Australia.

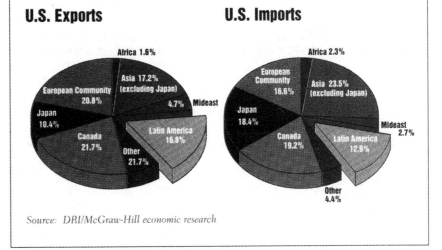

Latin America's Largest Trading Partner is Still El Norte

Latin America's main competition for U.S. trade comes from other emerging countries such as Asia. U.S. exports to developing countries account for 40.7% of an estimated total of $460 billion. Likewise, U.S. imports from developing countries account for 41.5% of and estimated $576 billion.

Of total Latin American exports, of course, the U.S. is the largest market, accounting for an average of 40%, according to Salomon Brothers' research. Another 20% in "exports" really stays home, going to other South American countries (especially Brazil and Argentina) with the last 20% mostly bound for Germany and Japan.

U.S. Exports

- Africa 1.6%
- Asia 17.2% (excluding Japan)
- Mideast 4.7%
- European Community 20.8%
- Japan 10.4%
- Canada 21.7%
- Latin America 16.8%
- Other 21.7%

U.S. Imports

- Africa 2.3%
- European Community 16.6%
- Asia 23.5% (excluding Japan)
- Mideast 2.7%
- Japan 18.4%
- Canada 19.2%
- Latin America 12.9%
- Other 4.4%

Source: DRI/McGraw-Hill economic research

Despite notable successes in certain Latin American cities, nearly all of the new investors in the region are treating Latin America as one big area—targeting a demographic segment (e.g. the middle class) rather than a single city or country. The U.S. printing giant R. R. Donnelley & Sons, for instance, has acquired 90% of Chile's largest printer, whose operations extend to Argentina and Brazil. Information Resources, a U.S. software firm, has merged with Venezuela's leading pollster, Datos Information Resources with plans to cover other Andean countries. Anheuser-Busch, fresh from its investment in Mexico's Corona, is looking for beer partners in Argentina and Brazil.

These investments represent more than just addresses in Latin America for the masthead of a company's letterhead. Planners are putting plenty of American dollars on the line. A 1994 Commerce Department study reports this year's planned capital spending by U.S. overseas affiliates (majority owned) is $7.9 billion in South America (including the Caribbean). It's true that this amount is but half of the $14.5 billion committed to Asia/Pacific—the region most often held out as competing with Latin American for U.S. corporate funds. But a closer look reveals that Latin America is in the lead for manufacturing investment, with almost $5 billion in planned spending on new plant and equipment by existing subsidiaries versus about $4 billion in the Far East (of which almost one third is destined for Japan, a rich developed country).

Mucho to Buy

Looking even deeper, one finds planned affiliate spending this year on transportation equipment seven times greater in Latin America than in Asia. Much of this is in the automotive sector which U.S. firms dominate. In the foods category, also, planned spending in the south is two times that planned for the east.

Still, compared to the '60s, North American companies' strategies are less grand and more cautious. Corporations like Gillette have scaled down production of some products in several Latin American countries because they can more efficiently manufacture and assemble products in larger markets and ship into these markets at low or no duty.

Gillette, Colgate, Kodak, and others are also focusing more on transportation and distribution issues (rather than number of manufacturing locations). This, in turn, means that U.S. multinational strategies are actually driving change in Latin America. As MNCs must reach as many markets as possible from single or at least fewer manufacturing countries, for example, air express and courier services are expanding to meet this need.

In addition, MNCs are pressuring national governments to take regional approaches to their ports and highway programs as well. Latin American countries are responding to the requests. Chile, for example, is hyping the potential of northern port cities Antofagasta and Iquique as gateways to Asia for its own manufacturers, as well as for Brazil's and Argentina's. Experts even predict a major new east-west highway in the Southern Cone, over, around and even under the Andes.

Telephone Tag

In no industry, however, has there been such fervor as telecommunications, arguably the hottest sector for foreign investors worldwide. GTE and AT&T are among the consortium called Venworld that bought into Venezuela's heretofore state-owned telephone company, CANTV. The $1.9 billion acquisition of 40% of CANTV has resulted in new rate struc-

---

Money Goes Far In Developing Economies

Comparing traditional exchange rate calculations with purchasing power parity figures, Latin America's middle class earns more than at first look. And they like to spend money. According to Alfredo Viegas, senior strategist, Emerging Market Research division of New York's Salomon Brothers, Latin American consumer markets are anxious to purchase low end consumer goods: "The food and beverage sector, in particular, has real potential," notes Viegas. Soon, this group will be looking at spending on larger ticket items. "The increasing access to credit will spur demand for more expensive consumer items, such as cars," he says.

As far as what governments and industry are buying, Viegas says Latin America mirrors emerging markets around the globe. "They want infrastructure, energy, and telecommunications," he says adding that in Brazil there are only 7 phone lines per 100 people.

"The difference is that unlike South East Asia, Latin America has a much larger internal market." The fastest growing countries within Latin America, he says, are Chile, Colombia, and Peru.

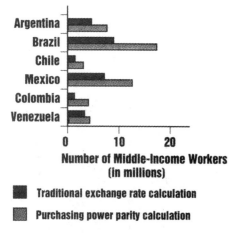

Number of Middle-Income Workers (in millions)

■ Traditional exchange rate calculation
■ Purchasing power parity calculation

Source: The Futures Group

tures, new equipment and much improved service [Although this merger has recently been scaled back this summer due to the banking problems in Venezuela, it is an exception.—Ed.] Reportedly, 100 other foreign companies are also investing in other areas of Venezuela's telecommunications sector.

Since Argentina's telephone company, Entel, was privatized three years ago, U.S. firms have been swarming all over the country selling new services. Investors include Bell-South and GTE, which are developing new cellular service with potential for long distance service. Northern Telecom (NT), the Canadian/U.S. equipment supplier, has also teamed with a Citibank affiliate to invest in NT's Argentine distributor to take part in what are anticipated to be massive sales of switches and transmission equipment.

Telecom privatization is not the only big-ticket sector luring new American capital, however. Argentina privatized all major infrastructure last year with a heavy dose of foreign investment replacing public funding. One notable privatization was Aerolíneas Argentinas, Argentina's passenger airline service.

Chile, too, has moved quickly to get major infrastructure off of government books, as seen by Cyprus-Amax Minerals' new joint venture with Chilean copper giant Codelco.

Brazil even sold off the massive steel company, Cia. Siderúgica Nacional. But it is indicative of telecom's critical role in domestic economic expansion and in linking countries within the region, not to mention the rest of the world, that it has been thrown open to foreign investment so dramatically.

Will History Repeat?

A corollary to this rapid growth in U.S. investment in Latin America is the fear of a backlash to "foreign" (a.k.a. *gringo*) domination. This is unlikely, according to a 1994 study by the Commerce Department indicating that U.S. corporate affiliates account for 3% or less of the gross domestic product (GDP) in Columbia, Chile, Argentina, and Brazil, and less than 2% in Venezuela.

U.S. affiliate output in the region would have to treble to reach the levels of overall GDP share held by U.S. affiliates in Canada and the U.K. In all, there's not much ammunition for anti-foreign hand wringing over outside industrial domination.

Also, this time around, major U.S. corporate players, particularly those in natural resources, are treading very carefully to avoid the colonialist image that led to the nationalization of many industries in the '50s and '60s. One leader in this area is Battle Mountain Gold. Its investment, with a Panamian partner, in Bolivia's Kori

Kollo mines has included supplying materials and architects for local homes; building a new school, a new church, and a hospital; and bringing running water, sewers, and electricity to a previously underserviced area. Battle Mountain also follows U.S. Environmental Protection Agency Standards at Kori Kollo—as demanded by most international lenders and banks.

But it's not just the North American business strategists who benefit from the new, steadier policies—intra-regional exports are up 21%. Profitable economies are, in turn, contributing to a stabilization of the overall political scene as well. The political calmness is, in turn, leading to an explosion of tourists' interests in South America. Tourism is a sector that continues to grow at 13% a year, according to the World Travel and Tourism Council, as reported in the *Wall Street Journal*.

And, while Latin America is clearly benefitting from MNC investment, it is showing that it can still hold its own on the international business scene. Venezuela, Panama, Brazil, and Argentina all boast corporations large enough to make *Fortune's* Global 500. And, when Argentina sold 45% of its oil company YPF for $3 billion—the largest single offering in Latin American history—the buyer was José Estenssoro, a native of Bolivia.

Asian Infrastructure

The Biggest Bet on Earth

Rahul Jacob

Q. Quick, now. In what city has a Baby Bell made a 300% return on money it invested about two years ago?

A. Bangkok.

Bangkok? Thailand? That's right. In 1992, Nynex joined the Thai conglomerate Charoen Pokphand Group to invest $300 million in a venture called TelecomAsia. Looking ahead, Joseph Farina, president of Nynex Network Systems, says with complete confidence: "We'll triple our investment in Asia in the next ten years." What gives? Is the pace in New York too slow for Nynex? By comparison, yes: TelecomAsia did an initial public offering in November 1993, and today Nynex's investment is worth—get this—$1.2 billion. And how do the returns on your newest venture stack up?

In one of the largest privately financed infrastructure projects in the world, TelecomAsia is installing two million digital phone lines in Bangkok. Equipment suppliers include AT&T and Siemens. The project, scheduled to take five years, will probably finish 18 months ahead of plan; TelecomAsia is already accepting applications for telephones 24 hours a day at 7-Eleven outlets.

REPORTER ASSOCIATES *Meenakshi Ganguly and Joe McGowan*

A sweeping new regional economy in the making is history being made. On an unparalleled scale, the countries of Asia are building roads, constructing power plants, and laying telephone lines. Most of this flood of business will be financed the old-fashioned way, and suppliers will continue to bid to win contracts from government utilities. But overwhelmed by the unprecedented sums of money required, governments are also turning to the private sector. Jardine Fleming Securities, the Hong Kong firm, estimates that between now and the year 2000, Asia (excluding Japan) will spend $1.15 trillion on power, transportation, telecommunications, water supplies, and sanitation.

But before you join the throngs of Western business people crowding Asia's airport terminals, examine the risks. Many governments still look on private investors with suspicion and seem philosophically unable to compensate risk (political risk, currency risk—the list goes on) with commensurate reward. For example, the long payback period for infrastructure projects—often as much as 20 years for builders of power plants and toll roads—makes it crucial that investors know they will be able to convert local currency into their own to service debt, say, or to pay their equity investors.

In countries like China, India, and Thailand, a sort of manic, Clintonesque indecisiveness has driven early investors to distraction—will this deal ever get done? Will the terms be as originally agreed to? And cronyism and corruption are as much a part of business in Asia as steam turbines and switching systems.

Many projects will never even make it to the drawing board. Taiwan offers a cautionary tale. In 1991, the government unveiled a grandiose plan to spend $310 billion on infrastructure projects over six years. Today, the investment has been cut in half. Foreign suppliers, stymied by the bureaucracy and by a convoluted bidding process, have found even the pickings that remain hard to get.

Still, the inexorable logic of Asia's demand for services is hard to argue with. E. J. Santos, a director of International Finance Corp., the private lending arm of the World Bank, estimates that two billion people in Asia are without electricity; only 16 in 1,000 have access to a telephone. These numbers are as much the result of money poorly spent as of a paucity of money. Government ownership of utilities in the poorest and most populous Asian countries has been a spectacular failure. More than 20% of electricity generated in Pakistan and India, for example, is lost in transmission and theft.

A conga line of financiers would like to help turn the lights on. A fund sponsored by American International Group and another by George Soros's Quantum Group with GE Capital have each raised some

$500 million or more to invest in Asia's building boom. Suppliers, too, are swaying with anticipation. During U.S. Commerce Secretary Ron Brown's recent visit to China, AT&T announced that it had received a $500 million order over five years to provide equipment for Guangdong province. Alcatel, the French telecommunications company, says Asia will account for 20% of its total sales by the year 2000, up from 10% today. General Electric expects Asia to place 45% of all new power generation equipment orders over the next ten years. And Hong Kong billionaire Gordon Wu is positioning himself to become the Henry Ford of power generation as he churns out Model Ts—standardized electric plants from the Philippines to Pakistan.

Asked to choose the most promising countries for infrastructure development, Andreas Kley, a member of the board of Siemens's power generation group, says without hesitation: China and India. Moments later, he agrees that they are also the most problematic. Adds Kley's colleague, Juergen Oberg, Siemens's executive director for telecommunications in Asia: "If you want to remain a global player, you have to be in China. You will not be able to cut costs in the long run if your market does not include China."

Together China and India have 40% of the world's population. Michel Reveillon, the new chief in Asia for GEC Alsthom, an Anglo-French manufacturer of rail transport and power equipment, suddenly interrupts a discussion of the prospects in China for mass transit systems to ask: "Do you know how many Chinese cities there are with populations of more than one million? Forty." (The U.S. has nine.) General Electric estimates that in the next ten years China will place orders for 168,000 megawatts in additional power generating capacity and India more than 70,000 megawatts; the corresponding figure in the U.S. is 154,000 megawatts. GE expects foreign suppliers to get only a small share of Chinese business in the short term. Says Sheldon Kasowitz, a director with Jardine Fleming in Hong Kong: "Aside from the Four Tigers and Japan, every country in Asia is facing the same issues and making the same choices. They can't continue to fund these projects on sovereign debt."

If Asia is to come close to investing $1 trillion in infrastructure, it needs to construct a reliable regulatory framework.

Observes James Blake, Secretary for Works of Hong Kong, a model for building an enduring public-private partnership: "Governments must recognize that once a franchise has been awarded, they have to facilitate the process so the revenue stream becomes available when the debt needs to be serviced. That's the central role of the government."

Investors can help themselves by creating deals that are fair. Mere moralizing? Maybe not. Says Frederic Rich, a partner with the New York City law firm Sullivan & Cromwell: "Even if a badly advised government is giving up more than it should, don't take it. It puts you at risk because if you're involved in an infrastructure project, you're going to be involved for ten to 20 years. If you look back at the history of infrastructure development in this century, a lot of it was basically on unfair terms between First World developers and Third World takers. Create a business structure that is fair, that is sustainable."

At the same time, protect yourself when you get in bed with the government; the public and private sectors are seldom easily compatible. Vallobh Vimolvanich of TelecomAsia recalls with incredulity that a $5 billion contract the Telephone Organization of Thailand offered his company in 1991 was a mere ten pages long. Says Vallobh: "The TOT is both regulator and operator. There was no clear definition of how it would act." The final contract was much longer and clearly delineated the responsibilities of the TOT. It also allowed for independent consultants to monitor the work being done.

Find ways to put the bureaucracy in a straitjacket, but don't hang your hat on contracts alone. In China, the old joke goes, a contract is a pause in the negotiation. Says Vanessa Chang of KPMG Peat Marwick: "The risk is, you could have a contract torn up or changed. We're just going to have to adjust to that in the West." Adds Robert Broadfoot, who heads the Political & Economic Risk Consultancy in Hong Kong: "Western companies think they can sidestep political risk by putting all the variables in a contract. In Asia there is no shortcut for managing the relationship. Too many Western companies don't have the patience." This doesn't mean graft. It does mean not parachuting in on Monday and flying back Friday. It means not only keeping your avenues open with the Ministry of Posts and Telecommunications in

China but also plugging into the Ministry of Electronics Industry and the People's Liberation Army, since they play large roles in Chinese telecommunications.

Remember that every time you make an alliance, you are just as likely to make an enemy. Going in where monopolies have ruled isn't simply business. Sometimes it can be like war. Embrace the need to build relationships. Put up with all the unctuous backslapping at Chinese government banquets. (Some people find American small talk wearisome too.) Introduce a government official to a business associate he might need to know.

Above all, realize that the biggest business opportunities in a lifetime don't come easy. You have to die a little for them. The main problem is that Asian governments see you, daring investor, as a convenient way of funding an infrastructure project before you turn it back to them to operate.

Unlike governments in Latin America, those in Asia (excepting Malaysia) have shied away from privatization, opting mostly for so-called BOTs, for build-operate-transfer. As the name suggests, a company agrees to build and manage a power plant or a road for, say, 25 years before turning it over to the government. Robert Dewing, a Citicorp managing director in Hong Kong, observes that in reality BOTs are a short sojourn in the quasi-public market before a return to state ownership.

INDONESIA

Mission Energy spent two years talking with the Indonesian government before signing an agreement allowing it to build a $2.5 billion power plant in Paiton. But by the year 2000, a third of Mission's revenues will come from it.

BOTs and other ways of private financing in Asia require a mind-numbing analysis and allocation of risk. That's largely because sponsors raise funds secured only by the revenue and assets of the project; lenders have limited recourse to the assets of the parent company sponsoring the project. Says Sullivan & Cromwell's Rich: "It's not 'I will repay you X amount of money on X date.' It's just not that simple." A contractor, for instance, usually takes on the risk of completion of a project and pays stiff penalties for cost overruns or delays. Because lenders share all the risks with equity investors but none of the upside, it has been relatively difficult to raise debt for such financing. There is, in fact, too much equity chasing too few deals at this point.

Funding will become easier as bond markets in Asia slowly catch up with equity markets. One example: Malaysia's well-developed capital markets enable independent power producers (IPPs) to fund large projects domestically. YTL, a local company, did a $585 million, 15-year, 10% bond offering to partly finance two private power plants. In September, YTL brought one of the plants onstream seven months ahead of schedule. IPPs are likely to take care of Malaysia's power requirements through the turn of the century, even though the economy grew by more than 8% last year and demand for power outpaced that.

In other countries, a heavy dependence on foreign money tends to trip up deals for Westerners because it magnifies the mother of all investor concerns: currency risk. Kevin Files, deputy managing director of Wardley Capital, a Hong Kong investment bank that is part of the HSBC Group, estimates that 50 mainland projects are stalled largely because the Chinese government will no longer guarantee foreign exchange for power plants. "For countries whose currencies are not yet convertible or whose foreign exchange trading systems are not yet mature, governments have to guarantee the availability and convertibility of currency," says Joseph Ferrigno III, managing director of Bechtel Enterprises Asia-Pacific, whose projects include a $400 million tollway in southern China. "A reasonable rate of currency depreciation is a risk the private sector must take."

Getting the final handshake on a deal is at least as harrowing as rounding up the money. Mission Energy, a subsidiary of SCE Corp., spent two years talking with the Indonesian government before it finally signed an agreement that will make it possible to build a $2.5 billion power plant in Paiton. Robert Edgell, Mission's executive vice president, lived for much of 1993 in Indonesia. But there's ample consolation for Edgell and Mission: By the turn of the century one-third of the company's revenues will come from the Paiton project, and beyond that, half of Mission's revenues will be from Southeast Asia. Indonesia, meanwhile, has created a template: It signed a similar contract last month with Gordon Wu after nine months of negotiation. Houston-based Enron raves about the streamlined approval process in the Philippines, which allows companies to get from bidding to construction in under six months.

INDIA

India is likely to make Western investors gray before making them rich. Two years ago it sought bids for cellular franchises in four major cities. Not until 1995 will Bombay businessmen be walking the streets with phones.

Once they shake hands, most business people think a deal is a deal is a deal. But that's not necessarily so with some Asian governments, which have a tendency to meddle. Last year, in a pitched battle with a Japanese-led consortium that was building an expressway in Bangkok, the Thai government quarreled over the level of tolls it had previously agreed to, and then over who had the right to operate the road. University of Illinois economics professor Pablo Spiller observes that, say, lowering the toll that can be charged on a road once it has been built is a subtle form of expropriation. Adds Boris Velic, a rangy Croatian who is a manager with the World Bank's Foreign Investment Advisory Service: "You can't pack up a road or a bridge and leave."

Last year, the FIAS conducted a two-day roundtable on facilitating infrastructure investment—held in, of all places, Bangkok. Says Velic: "We spent 99% of our time discussing how to speed up deals and create a regulatory framework that is transparent and predictable." Successive Thai governments have talked a lot about mass transit systems but made it impossible thus far for companies to build one. Frederic Rich describes the problem this way: "The death from 1,000 cuts is when you haven't been expropriated but it takes ten times longer to do anything. Formal political risk, from ethnic violence, say, or expropriation, is insurable by political-risk insurance agencies. But increasingly investors are understanding that projects can be derailed by little 'p' political risk."

China and India are likely to make Western investors gray before making them rich. In 1992, India sought bids for cellular franchises in its four major cities. The specifications were so vaguely defined and the criteria for evaluation so capricious that the awards were challenged in court. Today there are still no phone-to-the-ear businessmen on the streets of Bombay, but there should be by 1995: The government just recently awarded cellular franchises for India's four major cities. Says Amit Sharma, Motorola's head man in Central and South Asia: "You have to wonder whether some subset of the bureaucracy said, 'If we're going to do this, let's do it on terms that are the least favorable to business.'"

Businessmen grow grayer still when Asian governments, paranoid that private investors might take them for a ride, put an arbitrary cap on rates of return. After watching investors queue up to fund power plants, Beijing recently set a ceiling of 12% to 15% on the return that could be earned from all new power projects. Says Alan Epstein, a partner with the New York City law firm of Kelley Drye & Warren: "It's not an untypical reaction on the part of governments new to privatization. Matching risk and reward is a learning process."

China is not learning fast enough for Gordon Wu, who says a 12% return is a nonstarter. He has seized the opportunity to take his power company into Indonesia, India, and Pakistan, where he plans to build plants and possibly spin them off on the local market. Sitting in his unpretentious office away from the chrome and glass that dominate Hong Kong's posh Central district, Wu outlines his plans to get economies of scale by standardizing plant design across Asia. Having just returned from India in August, Wu, a Princeton graduate, is all praise for the Indian and Pakistani governments. He repeats like a mantra the Indian Power Minister's remark that "there is no power more expensive than no power."

Private participation in the pell-mell rush to build Asia's infrastructure is naturally driven by all the money to be made. But it can be infused with a higher purpose. Companies, after all, are delivering what people desperately need. For all the controversy that surrounded construction of that new tollway in Bangkok, driving it on a good day (traffic jams have not entirely disappeared) can feel like soaring on a rainbow.

In a bold move last month, India laid out telecommunications guidelines that are among the most liberal in Asia. It opened up basic telephone service to competition and allowed foreign firms to take 49% stakes in any joint venture. For confirmation of why this was a popular move with consumers, visit the "Public Grievance Cell" at the oppressive offices of the state telephone monopoly in New Delhi. A government employee sitting closest to the entrance has a sign on his desk saying NO ENQUIRY PLEASE—directed, presumably, at anyone who walks through the door. On a grimy wall across from him is a faded poster of Gandhi with the words: "A customer is the most important voice in our premises . . . He is not an interruption of our work. He is the purpose of it."

Outside, people seem eager to share their grievances. Katayan Mishra opens a dog-eared file that includes an affidavit the government required attesting that he had, in fact, changed residence. He has been trying for two years to have his phone transferred to no avail. The conversation shifts to the government's decision a week earlier to break up its monopoly and allow private competition. "You'll pay a little more to private companies, but at least you'll get the work done efficiently," Mishra says. "Here they just push you around." His face clouds over with resentment as he rushes off to make his complaint yet again before the imperial doors close at 4 P.M. It seems unkind to tell him that 1,813 miles to the east, TelecomAsia was accepting phone applications 24 hours a day in Bangkok.

India Behind the Hype

*Poor phone service and inefficient ports remain problems,
even as investors pour into the subcontinent.*

Eapen Thomas

Bombay-based Eapen Thomas is an Industry Week *contributing editor.*

India's new economic climate has a fan in P. M. Sinha. Three weeks is the most the president of Pepsi Foods Ltd., Delhi, must wait for the Indian government to pass judgment on any investment that PepsiCo Inc. wants to make in the Asian subcontinent's largest country. "I sometimes get a call to [come] have a cup of tea from old friends in the government, because they haven't seen me in a long time," quips Mr. Sinha.

The situation today differs dramatically from Mr. Sinha's 24 years at Hindustan Lever Ltd., a manufacturer of personal-care products and detergents and the Indian subsidiary of Unilever. In his days at the Anglo-Dutch consumer-products multinational, every major decision by a private firm had to be approved by the government.

Purchase, N.Y.-based PepsiCo is part of a foreign-investment boom in India," a country that the U.S. Commerce Dept. regards as one of the world's 10 big emerging markets. Since the early 1990s, India has been opening the trade and investment doors to a once-closed and notoriously difficult market.

PepsiCo is not only selling soft drinks through Pepsi Foods, in which it has invested US$30 million, but also has set up Pepsi India Holdings Ltd., which is capitalized at $95 million. And Pepsi plans to pour in $40 million each when it opens up its Pizza Hut and KFC restaurant chains. "It shows how serious PepsiCo is about India," says Mr. Sinha. "In most countries, [the company has] only franchise operations." And PepsiCo is a good example of a changing Indian economic environment. PepsiCo's initial moves, in 1990, were pilloried by the Indian parliament and press. As a condition of investment, the company was forced to establish joint ventures with Indian companies, to agree to pay for imported ingredients with money generated from export sales, to introduce technology to benefit Indian farmers, and to market its soft drink under a local brand name. Those restrictions no longer exist, and both Pepsi and arch-rival Coca-Cola have, for all practical purposes, 100%-owned subsidiaries in India.

They are not alone among U.S.-based companies looking favorably at India. The roster of firms setting up operations or significantly expanding existing operations includes AT&T Corp., General Electric Co., General Motors Corp., Ford Motor Co., IBM Corp., Kellogg Co., Motorola Corp., Novell Inc., and Whirlpool Corp.

While relatively large companies constitute most of the U.S. investors, opportunities for small and mid-sized companies exist in India. Joint ventures are one approach. Another: the pure technology-licensing agreement, as Indian firms are keen to upgrade.

The American Embassy in New Delhi, India's capital, estimated total U.S. investment in India in 1994 was between $4 billion and $5 billion. In 1993 alone, the Indian government approved more than $1 billion in American investment, making the U.S. the largest single foreign investor in the country of more than 900 million people. Other major foreign investors are Great Britain, Germany, and France.

India is an attractive location. Though millions remain abjectly poor, an estimated 150 million Indians are members of families with relatively large annual incomes of $4,000. However, Asif Adil, a consultant with McKinsey & Co., in Bombay, urges caution. Suggesting that India's middle class numbers no more than 25 million, he says that major foreign automakers planning operations in India will not find the kind of market they expect.

While the size of India's market for big-ticket items is debated, it's clear that the country's workforce is large and well-educated. Many workers speak English. India is rich in professional managers and skilled technicians. Its graduate-engineer population is larger than that of Japan and Germany, and the country has a large pool of scientists. India's legal system is in the Anglo-Saxon tradition. The country is a democracy. Indian accounting systems are similar to those in the U.S. And while the government still pervades much of the economy, India's industrial base is sizable and relatively well-developed.

Nevertheless, India remains a complex, sometimes difficult country for industries to operate in. Scott Bayman, president of GE India, while bullish on India, stresses that business condi-

INDIA AT A GLANCE

	1994	1995	1996
Gross domestic product (billion US$)	296.5	339.4	367.6
GDP (percent change)	4.9	5.0	4.9
Consumer price index	11.2	9.8	7.8
Wholesale price index	11.0	8.6	7.6
Industrial production (percent change)	7.3	7.8	7.5
Population (millions)	916.0	932.4	948.9
Per capita GDP (US$/person)	324	364	387

SOURCE: DRI/MCGRAW-HILL

tions still leave much room for improvement. The government's approval process for foreign investment, for example, needs further streamlining. And elements of India's infrastructure—such as telecommunications, power generation, and roads—need to be improved if businesses are to function smoothly, he says.

India's state-owned department of telecommunications seems unable to properly maintain its network; as a result, dead phones and poor connections are common. Most of India's 22 states lack sufficient generating capacity, and power cuts lasting several hours are not unusual. And India's roads are incapable of handling a rapidly expanding vehicle population.

What's more, Mr. Bayman contends that if companies are to get goods out of the country, especially to meet demands for "just-in-time" delivery, India's ports will have to improve their abysmal performance.

" . . . We got experience which has enabled [us to supply] qualitatively superior maintenance to our customers."

In many instances, foreign companies investing in India just turn the difficulties with faulty phones, power lapses, and goods distribution over to their Indian managers to sort out. Executives from abroad "may not like crawling along for two hours in heavy traffic to get to a plant site. But they know they won't have to do it more than twice," says Alok Bhargava, director of business planning at Emerson Electric Co., liaison office in Bombay.

However, changing government regulations are something that no foreign investor can get away from.

When Digital Equipment Corp., the Andover, Mass., computer manufacturer, decided in 1988 to invest in India, import duties were as high as 250%. But as a condition to operate in India, DEC had to agree to invest in a manufacturing plant and to gradually increase its production activities. The agreement has proved to be impractical. India's computer market is tiny. Yet rates of change in the industry are so fast that one-time investment is inadequate to meet what demand does exist.

As a condition of its investment, DEC was required to enter into a joint venture with the Hinditron Group and to go public—although DEC did not need the money. Now, in addition to all its other duties, DEC must service 30,000 shareholders. With India's import duties on computers now down to 65%—and likely to fall further—DEC's manufacturing investment is redundant. And newer computer-company entrants to India such as Compaq Computer Corp. and Dell Computer Corp. can sell their products without having to invest in production facilities. "Our main advantage in setting up the plant was that we got experience which has enabled [us to supply] qualitatively superior maintenance to our customers," relates Som Mittal, managing director of Digital Equipment India Ltd., in Bangalore.

Apple Computer Inc. has been similarly frustrated. When the Cupertino, Calif., computer firm first looked at India, import duties on computers were as high as 250%. By late 1992, when Apple was contracting with DEC to manufacture its LC-II model in India, tariffs had fallen to 105%. When DEC was ready to manufacture, the government had dropped the tariffs to 85%, which made manufacturing economically foolish. What's more, the LC-II had become obsolete, with consumers looking for a more sophisticated machine. Apple opted out of the manufacturing relationship with DEC.

Apple Computer now has a strong distribution and dealer network in India. And it has launched an aggressive advertising campaign in an effort to woo consumers in a country where *computer* means the IBM PC. "Our prices match those of local Intel-based 486 machines. We have to convince people that an Apple is not necessarily expensive," says Sandeep Bhagi, Apple's Delhi-based country manager.

What's clear is that DEC, Apple, and several other U.S. companies are finding that they have to feel their way into India. And India is a country where no one strategy seems to fit all situations.

Pittsburgh-based H. J. Heinz Inc., for example, set up a 100%-owned subsidiary and bought the food-products division of an Indian company. Coca-Cola acquired Parle, an Indian soft-drink maker with a 60% market share. Whirlpool has taken a stake in Kelvinator (India] Ltd., an Indian refrigerator manufacturer and, like Parle, a market leader.

GE has set up only one wholly owned subsidiary in India, GE Capital India Ltd., and tied it to Stamford, Conn.-based General Electric Capital Services. The rest of GE's Indian investment is in a clutch of joint ventures involving lighting, white goods, medical equipment, machine tools, engineering plastics, and consumer finance. GE has a 51% stake in Wipro-GE Medical Systems Ltd. and virtually runs the joint venture. GE has a 40% share of GE-Godrej Appliances Ltd., a joint venture to manufacture washing machines and refrigerators. GE's equity is 50% in its lighting, engineering-plastics, and consumer-finance joint ventures.

However, having an Indian partner doesn't necessarily assure success. Whirlpool knows. It had to take over control of TVS-Whirlpool Ltd., a manufacturer of washing machines, after years of poor performance.

"We have 40 different product groups, and that means 40 different formulas. It all depends on the market and what a potential partner can offer."

But then there's a list of American firms that report having had excellent experiences with their Indian partners. Emerson Electric, a diversified St. Louis-based manufacturer, entered into its first joint venture in India in 1982. It now has five joint ventures and is setting up a 100%-owned subsidiary. In four of the joint ventures, Emerson Electric is the minority partner.

"If you have partners that add value, there is not much reason to interfere," says Emerson's Mr. Bhargava. At the same time, he recognizes that in introducing some products, Emerson may have to go it alone. "We have 40 different product groups, and that means 40 different formulas. It all depends on the market and what a potential partner can offer."

Infrastructure development in India—improving telecommunications, upgrading roads, improving port facilities, and the like—is one area where the Indian government is likely to be a virtual partner of foreign investors. Strapped for cash, the government has little choice but to turn to the private sector. But the whole process can be torturously slow, because India has little experience in allowing the private sector to undertake infrastructure projects. There's a history of the government doing—or at least trying to do—everything.

Part of the challenge now is to find a way to limit the risks that private entrepreneurs are exposed to without imposing too great a burden on the state. And compounding the challenge, project frameworks must be hammered out by politicians and bureaucrats unused to the concept of the private sector managing infrastructure projects—all while Indian citizens debate the wisdom of this approach and India's press scrutinizes the process.

Enron Corp., a Houston-based gas supplier, knows first-hand about the agonizingly slow pace of the infrastructure-project experience. Two years were required just to get the necessary clearances for the first phase of a $2.5 billion gas-turbine power-generation project at Dhabhol in India's Maharashtra state, a project that also involves Bechtel Enterprises, an American engineering company, and GE Capital.

To attract foreign investors, the government had devised a return of 16% on investment if a powerplant was operated at 68.5% of capacity. The Enron-Bechtel-GE Capital consortium didn't accept the government plan and instead advanced a power-purchase agreement of its own design. It called for a return on investment only if the project was built to cost and if it operated at 90% capacity.

In addition, the consortium had to negotiate with the government to work out a complex package to ensure it would be paid by the Mararashtra State Electricity Board, the state-owned utility to which the project would supply power. The reason for seeking the guarantee: Although the Mararashtra Board is relatively well-managed, most state-owned utilities, which control the largest share of power generation and distribution, are credit risks. And most of the international banks that help finance projects such as the consortium's like to have guarantees from both state and central governments.

Huge amounts of time also were consumed in getting the so-called counter-guarantee, as members of the Enron-Bechtel-GE Capital consortium tried to cover their own concerns and the Indian government tried to limit its risk. "Though the Indian government has a fairly clear policy, it needs to make the process simpler," says Rebecca Mark, chairman of Enron Development Corp., the Enron subsidiary that has spearheaded the power project. Construction is expected to begin soon.

In the meantime, AT&T and US West are two American-based telecommunications companies waiting for the Indian government to clarify its policies so that they can offer basic phone services. Pharmaceutical manufacturers such as Pfizer Inc. charge that Indian law does not protect their product patents. Indian companies are seemingly free to make a drug—as long as they employ a different chemical process in its production. The absence of significant protection for patents and other kinds of intellectual property is a major barrier to increased American investment in India, reported a recent survey from the U.S.-India Joint Business Council.

The bottom line is that it's going to be some time before India has the same level of attractiveness for foreign investors that, for example, Asia-neighbor Indonesia has today. India is in the early stages of economic reform. How fast and how well the country changes will depend in major measure on the amount of momentum its government can maintain.

Ethics in the Trenches

Robert D. Haas

ROBERT D. HAAS is chairman and CEO of Levi Strauss & Co.

Human-rights violations, child labor— how does a company deal with such problems?

A quick scan of today's headlines shows that ethical dilemmas are everywhere. Prudential-Bache Properties Inc. is sued by its investors, who allege it sold limited partnerships misleadingly; corruption and mismanagement cause the fortunes of Gitano Group Inc. to collapse; and executives of the American subsidiary of Honda Motor Co. Ltd. are charged by federal prosecutors with accepting bribes from dealers in exchange for franchises and hot-selling models.

What's going on? Have our ethical standards deteriorated, or are these headlines just a result of intensive media scrutiny? Can companies afford to be ethical in today's fiercely competitive environment, or are ethics a costly and convenient luxury?

I believe—and our company's experience demonstrates—that a company cannot *sustain* success unless it develops ways to anticipate and address ethical issues as they arise.

Drawing Multinational Lines

At Levi Strauss & Co., we're integrating ethics and other corporate values (such as empowerment and diversity) into every aspect of our business—from our human-resources programs to our vendor relationships. Let me illustrate our approach to linking ethics and business conduct with an area of increasing importance to many multinational corporations—the sourc-

ing of products in the developing world.

Levi Strauss operates in many countries and diverse cultures. We must take special care in selecting our contractors and those countries where our goods are produced in order to ensure that our products are being made in a manner that is consistent with our values and reputation. In early 1992, we developed and adopted a set of global-sourcing guidelines that established standards our contractors must meet to ensure that their practices are compatible with our values. For instance, our guidelines ban the use of child and prison labor. They stipulate certain environmental requirements. Working hours can't exceed 60 hours a week, with at least one day off in seven. Workers must be present voluntarily, have the right of free association, and not be exploited. At a minimum, wages must comply with the law and match prevailing local practice.

We also recognize that there are issues beyond the control of our contractors in some countries, so we developed a list of country-selection criteria. We will not source in countries where conditions, such as the human-rights climate, would run counter to our values and have an adverse effect on our global brand image. Our decision to undertake a phased withdrawal from China, for example, was due largely to human-rights concerns. We remain hopeful that the human-rights climate will improve so we can reverse our decision.

Similarly, we will not source in countries where circumstances expose our traveling employees to unreasonable risk; where the legal environment makes it difficult or jeopardizes our trademarks; and where political or social turmoil threatens our commercial interests. In mid-1992 we suspended sourcing in Peru due to concerns regarding employee safety. Recently, we were able to lift the suspension because conditions in Peru have im-

proved, although we still have not placed any business in that country.

To develop our guidelines, we formed a working group made up of 15 employees from a broad cross-section of the company. The working group spent nine months at the task, during which time its members researched the views of key stakeholder groups— sewing-machine operators, vendors, contractors, plant managers, merchandisers, contract productions staff, shareholders, and others. The working group then used an ethical-decision-making model to guide its deliberations. The model is a process for making decisions by taking into consideration all stakeholders' issues.

Once our guidelines were in place, training sessions were held for 100 in-country managers who would have to enforce them with our 700 contractors worldwide. Training included case studies and exercises in decision-making. The managers then made presentations on the guidelines to our contractors, conducted on-site audits, and worked with them to make those improvements identified as necessary.

Vexing Dilemmas

Drafting these guidelines was difficult. Applying them has forced us to find creative or unconventional solutions to vexing ethical dilemmas.

For example, we discovered that two of our manufacturing contractors in Bangladesh and one in Turkey employed underage workers. This was a clear violation of our guidelines, which prohibit the use of child labor. At the outset, it appeared that we had two options:

● instruct our contractors to fire these children, knowing that many are the sole wage earners for their families and if they lost their jobs, their families would face extreme hardships; or

● continue to employ the underage children, ignoring our company's stance against the use of child labor.

Courtesy Levi Strauss & Co.

Fourteen underage former workers at two Levi Strauss & Co. contractors' manufacturing plants in Bangladesh, including these children, now attend school.

Other companies facing this issue might have simply instructed contractors to fire underage workers on the spot. For Levi Strauss, this was undesirable. But we couldn't ignore our corporate values either. Looking beyond the obvious options, we came up with a different approach that led to positive benefits all around.

The contractors agreed to pay the underage workers their salaries and benefits while they go to school. (They do not work during this time.) Levi Strauss pays for books, tuition, and uniforms. When the children are of working age, they will be offered full-time jobs in the plant, which they are not required to take. Today, 14 children are attending school in Bangladesh, while another six are in school in Turkey.

And how did Levi Strauss benefit? We were able to retain three quality contractors who play an important role in our worldwide sourcing strategy. At the same time, our values and brand image were protected.

At times, adhering to these standards has added costs. To continue working for us, some contractors had to add emergency exits and staircases, improve ventilation or bathroom facili-ties, reduce crowding, and invest in water-treatment systems. The costs of these requirements were passed on to us in the form of higher unit prices. In other cases, we have forgone cheaper sources of production due to unsatisfactory working conditions or concerns about the country of origin.

> **In today's world, an exposé on working conditions on *60 Minutes* can undo years of effort to build brand loyalty.**

Conventional wisdom holds that these added costs place us at a competitive disadvantage. Certainly, they limit our options and squeeze profit margins. But over the years, we have found that decisions that emphasize cost to the exclusion of all other factors do not best serve a company's—or its shareholders'—long-term interests. Our five straight years of record sales and earnings, and a doubling of the size of our business in as many years, support our conclusion.

Moreover, as a company that invests hundreds of millions of advertising dollars each year to create consumer preference for our products, we have a huge stake in protecting that investment. In today's world, an exposé on working conditions on *60 Minutes* can undo years of effort to build brand loyalty. Why squander an investment when, with foresight and commitment, reputational problems can be prevented?

But don't take our word for it. There is a growing body of research evidence from respected groups that shows a positive correlation between good corporate citizenship and financial performance. These studies underscore that companies driven by values and a sense of purpose that extends beyond just making money outperform those that focus only on short-term profits. The former have higher sales, sustain higher profits, and have stocks that outperform the market.

These findings mirror our experience. Our values-driven approach has helped us:

● identify contractors who really want to work for Levi Strauss;

● gain customer and consumer loyalty because they feel good about having us as a business partner or about purchasing our products;

● attract and retain the best employees;

● improve the morale and trust of employees because the company's values more closely mirror their own personal values;

● initiate business in established and emerging markets because government and community leaders have a better sense of what we stand for and what to expect from us; and

● maintain credibility during times of unplanned events or crisis.

The conclusion is clear: There are important commercial benefits to be gained from managing your business in a responsible way that best serves the enterprise's long-term interests. The opposite is equally clear: There are dangers of not doing so.

Cultural Awareness: An Essential Element of Doing Business Abroad

Gary Bonvillian and William A. Nowlin

Gary Bonvillian is an assistant professor of management, and **William A. Nowlin** is a professor of management and associate dean of the College of Business, both at

> *Enough emphasis cannot be placed on the importance of knowing the culture with which you are dealing.*

When traveling to other countries to transact business, Americans usually attempt to make a favorable impression and do their professional best. Unfortunately, behaviors, comments, time orientation, social practices, and etiquette that are considered appropriate professional behavior in corporate America may be perceived as arrogance, insensitivity, overconfidence, or aggressiveness in another culture. This could result in the American business person being perceived as insensitive to other cultures and jeopardize that person's working relationship with international counterparts.

In the domestic market, Americans are comfortable in knowing what to do and how to do it. But to achieve the same objective and success with a minimum of interpersonal and professional errors abroad, advanced preparation is crucial. American corporations have a long way to go in developing executives to function abroad successfully. One retired senior vice president from a major U.S. corporation reports, "We have the technology and we know the business but we are not prepared as a country to deal with cultural differences. . . . I have seen relatively little progress over the past 30 years."

Recent literature cites an acknowledgment by business executives that understanding cultural differences is absolutely essential for doing business abroad. Unfortunately, this same literature reports that surveys of major corporations indicate that relatively few offer this type of preparation for their people. According to one such survey by the consulting firm of Moran, Stahl and Boyer, only 12 percent of the respondents of 51 multinational U.S. corporations indicated that they offered seminars and workshops on cross-cultural differences and doing business abroad (Callahan 1989).

Similarly, the preparation that is being provided appears to be inadequate, resulting in high costs to companies and frustration for employees. According to one source, in a study of expatriates who were forced to return to the United States before completing their assignment, the failure rate (as measured by coming home before the end of tour in-country) ranged from 20 percent to 50 percent, costing the company between $55,000 and $150,000 per person. This translates into approximately $2 billion per year in costs for U.S. corporations (McEnery and DesHarnais 1990).

Training alone will not solve the problem. Many conditions influence the success of doing business abroad; the individual is merely one variable in the equation. It is perhaps the most critical factor, however, for we know that inadequate attention is being given to this important aspect of executive development.

Other factors that influence success abroad include the nature, scope, and location of the project. Of particular note is the location, as studies have shown that although 18 percent of those sent to London will fail, this increases to 36 percent in Tokyo and 68 percent in Saudi Arabia. Such statistics point to a need for companies to carefully consider the unique nature of differing cultures and direct their executive preparation initiatives accordingly.

From *Business Horizons*, November/December 1994, pp. 44-50. © 1994 by the Foundation for the School of Business at Indiana University. Reprinted by permission.

This article examines many cross-cultural differences among 25 or more countries in which there is a practice or behavior dissimilar to that in the United States. They rank among the many complex subjects that must be considered by corporations when designing or contracting training for cultural awareness. Among the cultural elements that will be examined are language and communications, aesthetics, time orientation, social institutions, religion, personal achievement, personal space, social behavior, and intercultural socialization.

Cultures include all types of learning and behavior. They are learned, they vary, and they influence the manner in which people behave.

Communications

Of all the cultural elements that an international traveler must study, the language of the host country is among the most difficult to manage. Although it is beneficial for individuals to know the language, one also needs the competency to recognize idiomatic interpretations, which are quite different from those found in the English dictionary. All cultures have verbal and nonverbal communication systems, and each country's vocabulary reflects its primary value and composition. Words spoken by an American may not have the same meaning when translated into another language.

When visiting a country in which English is not spoken, executives often use an interpreter to translate for them. Yet numerous gestures, facial expressions, and motions send different signals, and an interpreter might not be capable of articulating the full intention of the message. For example, Americans are often direct in their conversations, expecting the truth with no hint of deception. At the same time, Americans also tend to be uncomfortable with silent moments. People in some other countries, though, may prefer not to be direct and may shift their eyes away from the American. To them this is a sign of respect. To the American, however, it may be seen as a gesture suggesting withholding of information. And in some cultures silence is appreciated, giving discussants or negotiators time to think and evaluate the situation.

One of the most damaging demands that can be made of an Asian is "Give me a yes or no answer." Although an American would view this as a mild form of confrontation and would expect to get a "yes" or "no" response, Asians rarely say no. This is because of their reluctance to displease another with a negative answer and also to save them the embarrassment of having to admit an inability. There is no word for "no" in Thailand. Similarly, the French often say "no" when they may actually mean "maybe."

In some countries, if a question is asked, the visitor may be told whatever the native thinks the visitor wants to hear. If you ask for directions in Mexico, Lebanon, or Japan, and the natives don't really know the answer, they may still give you one simply to make you happy. In countries such as Paraguay or Pakistan, if directions are requested, regardless of the distance, the answer is likely to be "not far."

In America, a person who is reluctant to maintain eye contact is called shifty-eyed and arouses suspicion. But in some countries an attempt to maintain eye contact may be perceived as a sign of aggression. Accordingly, in Japan, South Korea, Taiwan, and other Asian countries, maintaining eye contact is not an acceptable behavior. On the other hand, in Saudi Arabia, eye contact and gestures of openness are important and could facilitate communications.

Most people who transact business abroad may not be proficient in the spoken language of the host country. However, nonverbal communications, such as signs, gestures, and body cues, can be learned in a short period. The value of knowing what to do and what to avoid should not be underestimated, so that one will not transmit unintended messages. According to several business executives interviewed, these issues are of much greater importance to closing the deal than actually knowing how to speak the native language.

One executive reported that the English language is used in many regions of the world as the accepted form of business communication. In some countries such as the Philippines, you would be expected to use English or risk being considered of a lower class. Even though they risk isolation from the rest of the world, Filipinos no longer require English as a second language for their young, leaving only the upper class the ability to learn it in private schools or from tutors. Power brokers in most of the developing countries recognize the importance of understanding English. In Singapore, for example, it is not unusual to hear the language spoken in the home just for the purpose of further developing the skills of young people.

In the same respect, such regions as the Middle East may prefer that visiting business people not attempt to use the native language, unless they have a high degree of proficiency. According to one source, it is quite common for Arab businessmen to speak English, because their formal education is likely to have come from Western universities. However, it is also recommended that if a company is intending to do a significant degree of business in the Middle East, its employees should be trained in Arabic. Dialects and accents aside, its written form dominates the region.

Aesthetics

Aesthetics refers to attitudes toward beauty and good taste in the art, music, folklore, and drama of a culture. The aesthetics of a particular culture can be important in the interpretation of symbolic meanings of various artistic expressions.

It is important for companies to evaluate in depth such aesthetic factors as product and package design, color, brand name, and symbols. For instance, some conventional brand names that communicate positive messages in America have a totally different meaning in another country, which may substantially stigmatize corporate image and marketing effectiveness.

When General Motors (GM) introduced its Chevy Nova into the Spanish market, it failed to first investigate whether the product name had an adverse meaning. GM subsequently learned that Nova ("no va") in Spanish means "It won't go." Other American product names, shown in **Figure 1**, impart a negative message when literally translated into another language.

Symbols also are important aesthetic factors that could have an adverse meaning in a different country. For example, the Wise Corporation would have to change or modify its trademark if it decided to test-market potato chips in India. The owl, which is the Wise trademark, is a symbol of bad luck in India even though in America it is associated with intelligence.

This further exemplifies the importance of pre-travel inquiries to avoid making errors that will hamper one's ability to conduct business abroad effectively. They also illustrate the cross-cultural quagmires that can be avoided when a firm leaves little to chance in choosing appropriate and inappropriate behavior or practices.

Time Orientation

Americans are clock watchers. We live by schedules and deadlines and thrive on being prompt for meetings and "efficient" in conducting business. In many parts of the world people arrive late for appointments, and business is preceded by hours of social rapport. In such places, people in a rush are occasionally thought to be arrogant and untrustworthy.

In the United States, a high value is placed on time. If someone waited outside an office for half an hour or so beyond the appointed time, it would be seen as a signal of his or her lack of importance. In the Middle East, a business person may keep a visitor waiting for a long time. But once the host begins the meeting, it may last as long as required to conduct the business at hand. Of course, others with later appointments on the same day also must wait their turn.

Americans are also deadline-oriented. If a deadline is mentioned to an Arab, however, it is like waving a red flag in front of a bull. Forcing the Arab to make a quick decision may very well cost you the deal. What appears to be inefficiency and muddling on the part of Arab businessmen may be a signal of displeasure with the way things are going. Experienced negotiators recommend slowing down and looking for signals that suggest that negotiations are not going well.

Western cultures view time as a resource that is not to be wasted. The efficient use of time is emphasized in such phrases as "Time is money" and "Time is the enemy." In contrast, Eastern cultures view time as unlimited and unending. In America, meetings sometimes begin with phrases such as "Let's get started" and "Let's dispense with the preliminaries." In Japan, casual conversation precedes business matters, because the Japanese are generally more interested than Americans in getting to know the people involved in the transaction.

Furthermore, it is important to the Japanese that consensus be reached and any misunderstandings be cleared up before proceeding on any problems that may surface in negotiations. The Japanese process of consultation (*ring-seido*) could bring to the surface problems not appreciated or known to Americans. This will require further consultations to remove obstacles.

Many cultures value relationships. Europeans and Asians place a high regard on long-term relationships rather than on short-term gains, which runs counter to what most Americans per-

Figure 1
American Brand Names and Slogans with Offensive Foreign Translations

Company	Product	Brand Name or Slogan	Country	Meaning
ENCO	Petroleum	(Former name of Exxon)	Japan	"Stalled car"
American Motors	Automobile	Matador	Spain	"Killer"
Ford	Truck	Fiera	Spain	"Ugly old woman"
Pepsi	Soft drink	"Come alive with Pepsi"	Germany	"Come out of the grave"

(Griggs and Copeland 1985, p. 62)

ceive. Excessive emphasis on speed and time may give the impression that the transaction is more important than the person. This is a fundamental error in professional judgment in many regions of the world.

Social Institutions

Social institutions—business, political, family, or class related—influence the behavior of people. In some countries, for example, the family is the most important social group. So social structures must be examined to understand the culture, because family relationships sometimes influence the work environment and employment practices.

In Latin America and the Arab world, a manager who gives special treatment to a relative is considered to be fulfilling an obligation. From the Latin point of view, it only makes sense to hire someone you can trust. In the United States, however, it is considered favoritism and nepotism. In India there is a fair amount of nepotism. But there too it is consistent with the norms of the culture. By knowing the importance of family relationships in the workplace and in business transactions, embarrassing questions about nepotism can be avoided.

According to the director of sales in the Mideast for a U.S.-based communications company, nepotism is commonplace in this region. He reports that not only are you forced to deal with "large groups of families," but these families often represent the country's aristocracy. Such individuals typically hold high positions in the local government and can rather easily skew a deal in one direction or another. As an outsider, a visiting business executive must learn not only to tolerate but also to appreciate the purpose of these relationships. It is not for us to judge the virtue of these conditions, concludes the sales director, but to adapt and work within the local norms.

Americans should also be cautious of being judgmental or intrusive in the local political structure. Particularly in South America, where each country functions as a distinctive nation-state, it is a mistake to presume that a single political ideology prevails. Rather, these countries have foregone the benefits of functioning as a single market in favor of autonomous units. This results in separate infrastructures of military, customs, currencies, and legal systems.

Religion

Religion is of utmost importance in many countries. In America, substantial effort is made to keep government and church matters separate. Nevertheless, there remains a healthy respect for individual religious differences. In some countries, such as Lebanon and Iran, religion may be the very foundation of the government and a dominant factor in business, political, and educational decisions.

In the United States, employers are required by federal law to "reasonably accommodate" individual religious beliefs that conflict with job demands. There may be quite a number of them, however, because multiple nationalities, ethnic groups, and religions are represented in the diverse U.S. work force. In other countries, there may be fewer religions, but the dominant religion must be respected in professional, supervisory, managerial, and other business behavior. When abroad, any effort to compare religions should be avoided.

When supervising a work group in some countries, an attempt to modify a policy, behavior, or process that is grounded in religion would not only draw the attention of national corporate officials but that of government officials as well. In Saudi Arabia, for example, during the month of Ramadan, Moslems fast from sunrise to sunset. As a consequence, worker production drops. Many Moslems rise earlier in the morning to eat before sunrise and may eat what they perceive to be enough to last until sunset. This affects their strength and stamina during the work day. An effort by management to maintain normal productivity levels will likely be rejected, so managers must learn to be sensitive to this custom as well as to others like it.

Eating pork is forbidden by law in Islam and Judaism. So if hot dogs are an American's favorite lunch, all-beef hot dogs would have to be substituted for pork. The pork restriction exists in Israel as well as in Islamic countries in the Middle East, such as Saudi Arabia, Iraq, and Iran, and Southeast Asia, such as Indonesia and Malaysia.

Islamic religion also frowns upon excessive profit, which is considered a form of exploitation. This is an important consideration in pricing products and services.

The role of women is also different in Islamic countries. They are, among other things, required to dress in such a way that their arms, legs, torso, and faces are concealed. An American female would be expected to honor this dress code while in the host country.

Islamic worshippers pray facing the holy city of Mecca five times each day. Visiting Westerners must be aware of this religious ritual. In Saudi Arabia and Iran, it is not unusual for managers and workers to place carpets on the floor and kneel to pray several times during the day. Although Sunday is a day of rest for most countries in the world, there are several countries in which the rest day is not Sunday. **Figure 2** lists several of these countries.

Personal Achievement

For the most part, Americans strive to achieve, be competitive, land the best job, earn the most money, and be promoted. They consider their position in the organization for which they work

Figure 2
Countries That Have Official Rest Days Other Than Sunday

Thursday	Iran, Egypt, Saudi Arabia
Friday	Afghanistan, Algeria, Bahrain, Egypt, Iraq, Jordan, Kuwait, Libya, Oman, Pakistan, Qatar, Saudi Arabia, Somalia, Syria, Tunisia, United Arab Emirates, Yemen Arab Republic, Yemen Democratic Republic
Saturday	Israel

Brown and Thomas (1981)

as an indication of status. We are an individualistic society and have built a nation based on our tenacity to get things done in as little time as possible and with minimal disruption.

By contrast, Hindu teachings suggest that acquisition and achievement are not to be sought, because they are the major courses of suffering in one's daily life. In Japan, positions are not arranged in a status hierarchy, and promotions are determined based on seniority rather than merit, although there is some evidence of movement from seniority-based rewards. Japanese workers are encouraged to work as teams. Cooperation is an art in Asian countries. It is said in Japan that "the nail that sticks out will be pounded down" (Adler 1986). This illustrates that individual competitiveness is less desirable than teamwork and team spirit.

Even the former Soviet Union encouraged teamwork. If a work group failed to meet production goals, no one was rewarded. But if a group exceeded its quota, everyone would benefit. Although cash rewards are often given to high achievers in America, a Japanese, Chinese, or Yugoslav would be humiliated to receive one.

A great deal has been written in U.S. management literature over the past 10 to 15 years on teamwork and a participatory environment of decision making. The currently popular Total Quality Management movement would suggest that more U.S. companies are adopting this ideology. However, some researchers say that the U.S. cultural orientation on this subject is too embedded for us to adapt the normative working relationships of, say, the Japanese. On this comparison, one individual states, "Harmony has long been important in Japan and is used as a building block to develop consensus in decision-making." In addition, whereas the individual is still the primary unit in American society and the educational system, group welfare prevails in Japan (Fram 1985).

Personal Space

Different cultures have varying rules of personal space and touching. Americans sometimes touch others on the hand or arm or shoulder when talking. In some cultures, such behavior may not be appropriate, especially with the left hand when in the Middle East.

The distance between individuals when talking is another issue that must be known and respected. Although one may not be able to define the exact distance if asked, most individuals have a specific amount of space that they maintain between themselves and others when conversing. Americans are typically made uncomfortable by the close conversation distance of Arabs and Africans. In the same respect, Arabs and Africans may feel rejected by the lengthy personal distance Americans maintain.

Indonesians operate with less empty space than Americans require, and some touching is permissible. However, an Indonesian should not be patted on the head, and a person of the opposite sex should never be touched. It is important to know the rules for personal touching and space of the culture in which a visit is planned. In some cases, personal touching can be viewed as an extreme act; in addition to violating the norms of a culture, it may even be viewed as a criminal offense.

Social Behavior

There are a number of social behaviors and comments that have different meanings in other cultures. For example, Americans generally consider it impolite to mound food on a plate, make noises when eating, and belch. However, some Chinese feel it is polite to take a portion of every food served and consider it evidence of satisfaction to belch.

Other social behaviors, if not known, will

place the American international traveler at a disadvantage. For example, in Saudi Arabia, it is an insult to question a host about the health of his spouse, show the soles of one's shoes, or touch or deliver objects with the left hand.

In Korea, both hands should be used when passing objects to one another, and it would be considered impolite to discuss politics, communism, or Japan. Also in Korea, formal introductions are very important. Although in America it might be acceptable to initiate a visit to a corporate or government office to meet an official, in Korea it is not considered in good taste. In both Japan and Korea, ranks and titles are expected to be used in addressing hosts. In the United States, there is not a clear rule on this behavior, except in select fields such as the armed forces or medicine. In Indonesia, it is considered rude to point at another person with a finger. However, one may point with the thumb or gesture with the chin.

When greeting someone, it is appropriate in most countries, as in the United States, to shake hands. In some countries the greeting includes a handshake and more. In Japan, a handshake may be followed by a bow, going as low and lasting as long as that of the senior person. In Brazil, Korea, Indonesia, China, and Taiwan, a slight bow is also appropriate.

In some countries, the greeting involves more contact. For instance, in Venezuela, close friends greet each other with a full embrace and a hearty pat on the back; in Indonesia, a social kiss is in vogue, and a touching of first the right then the left cheek as one shakes hands. In Malaysia, close friends grasp with both hands; and in South Africa, blacks shake hands, followed by a clench of each other's thumbs, and another handshake.

In most countries, addressing someone as Mr., Mrs., Miss, or Ms. is acceptable, but this is certainly not universal. Monsieur, Madame, and Mademoiselle are preferred in France, Belgium, and Luxembourg, while señor, señora, and señorita are the norm in Spain and Mexico.

It is sometimes the case that conversation occurs as greetings are exchanged. In Sweden, the greeting is "goddag"; in the Netherlands, it is "pleased to meet you"; in the United Kingdom it's "how do you do"; and in Israel it is "shalom." Other greetings vary by country.

In many countries, men do not shake hands with a woman unless she extends her hand first. In India, women, or a man and a woman, greet each other by placing the palms of their hands together and bowing slightly; and in Mexico simply by a slight bow. In some countries, such as India, it is not advisable for men to touch or talk alone with a woman.

Although many of the social behaviors mentioned vary slightly from the American norm, negative judgments should not be made about them. When trying to explain what took so long in closing a deal, home office executives need to understand that drinking tea, socializing, and relationship building are important components in accomplishing corporate international goals.

Intercultural Socialization

In addition to knowing specific courtesies, personal space, language and communication, and social behavioral differences, there are numerous intercultural socialization behaviors that an international business traveler should learn. Knowing a culture means knowing the habits, actions, and reasons behind the behaviors.

Americans often make assumptions about what is culturally proper or incorrect based on their own experiences. For example, in the United States the bathtub and toilet are likely to be in the same room. Americans assume this is the world norm. Some cultures, however, such as that of the Japanese, consider it unhygienic. Other cultures think it unhygienic even to sit on a toilet seat.

It is not always necessary for an international business traveler to understand the "whys" of a culture, but it is important to accept them and to abide by them while on foreign soil. However, if the time is available, becoming thoroughly aware of the culture in which you will be visiting or working will pay excellent dividends.

Pre-Travel Planning and Training

Becoming internationally adept and culturally aware should be a goal of any professional who aspires to do business abroad. This generally means a conscious effort in training and professional development by organizations. The Canadian International Development Agency (CIDA) provides an excellent model. CIDA hosts a five day pre-departure briefing for Canadians that includes travel information, introduction to the geographical area of the host country, and presentations by a host national or a returnee. Cross-cultural communication, information for family members, and information on skills transfer are also included.

There are numerous sources from which to obtain the training necessary for travel abroad. They range from individual consultants and established pre-departure corporations to state and federal offices that center on foreign trade or other foreign relations matters. Universities with international business centers are excellent sources as well.

Many elements of culture that we believe make America such a pleasant place in which to live and work are not the norm in other countries. But when an American travels abroad on behalf of his or her corporation, the more that is known about potential business partners and their culture, the less the risk of engaging in offensive and insulting behavior. This increases the probability of achieving success rather than missing an opportunity simply because of arrogance or ignorance.

References

Nancy J. Adler, *International Dimensions of Organizational Behavior* (Boston: PWS-Kent Publishing Co., 1991).

Harry Brown and Rosemary Thomas, *Brits Abroad* (London: Express Books, 1981).

Madelyn R. Callahan, "Preparing the New Global Manager," *Training and Development Journal*, March 1989, pp. 28-32.

Lennie Copeland, "Making Costs in International Travel," *Personal Administrator*, July 1984, pp. 47-51.

Lennie Copeland and Lewis Griggs, *Going International* (New York: Random House, 1985).

Lennie Copeland and Lewis Griggs, "Getting the Best from Foreign Employees," *Management Review*, June 1986, pp. 19-26.

Eugene Fram, "Consensus on Campus: Lessons for University Decision Making in Japan," *Speaking of Japan*, April 1985, pp. 20-26.

Shari Gaudron, "Surviving Cross-Cultural Shock," *Industry Week*, July 6, 1992, pp. 35-37.

Allen Hixon, "Why Corporations Make Haphazard Overseas Staffing Decisions," *Personnel Administrator*, March 1986, pp. 91-93.

John Ivancevich, James Donnelly, Jr., and James Gibson, *Management* (Boston: Irwin, 1989).

Gavin Kennedy, *Doing Business Abroad* (New York: Simon and Schuster, 1985).

Rose Knotts, "Cross-Cultural Management: Transformations and Adaptations," *Business Horizons*, January-February 1989, pp. 29-33.

Jean McEnery and Gaston DesHarnais, "Culture Shock," *Training and Development Journal*, April 1990, pp. 43-47.

Christopher North, *International Business*, 2d ed. (Englewood Cliffs, NJ: Prentice-Hall, 1985).

Arvind V. Phatak, *International Dimensions of Management* (Boston: Kent Publishing Co., 1983).

Janet Stern Solomon, "Employee Relations Soviet Style," *Personnel Administrator*, October 1985, pp. 79-86.

H.L. Wills, "Selection for Employment in Developing Countries," *Personnel Administrators*, July 1984, pp. 53-58.

Charles F. Valentine, "Blunders Abroad," *Nation's Business*, March 1989, pp. 54-56.

American Involvement in Vietnam, Part II: Prospects for U.S. Business in a New Era

Clifford J. Shultz II, William J. Ardrey IV, and Anthony Pecotich

Clifford J. Shultz II is an assistant professor at the School of Management, Arizona State University, Phoenix, and an associate at the Columbia University Center for International Business Cycle Research. **William J. Ardrey IV** is a vice president of Fiduciary Communication Co., New York. **Anthony Pecotich** is a senior lecturer at the University of Western Australia, Perth. The authors give special thanks to Standard Chartered Bank, Tilleke & Gibbins, the Vietnamese Foreign Ministry in Hanoi, Ho Chi Minh City University, the Ho Chi Minh City College of Marketing, the Hanoi Institute for Research on Market and Price, and the numerous interviewees who graciously consented to give their valuable time.

W ith the stroke of President Clinton's pen last February, the Vietnamese trade embargo ended and U.S. business horizons expanded considerably. Many American firms, having already evaluated the risks and rewards of the Vietnamese market, have moved swiftly to penetrate it; others are only now evaluating the country and are moving more cautiously.

Over the course of the last two decades of the embargo, U.S. corporations were forced to watch and wait as businesses and governments from Australia, Japan, Singapore, Taiwan, Hong Kong, Indonesia, Malaysia, and the former Soviet Union—to name just a few of the major players—invested billions of U.S. dollars in one of the few world economies presently experiencing real GNP growth greater than 5 percent. Now U.S. firms have the unrestricted opportunity to compete in one of the world's most promising markets. But given the present mix of players and current business conditions, what are the prospects for U.S. business in Vietnam?

The purpose of this article is to address that question while providing more general insights into the considerations for market entry in authoritarian East Asian economies. The information we share here is based on data we have collected on site and via secondary sources during the last three years. Our methods included a combination of ethnographic techniques, personal interviews, and analyses of secondary data provided by the United Nations, ASEAN, institutions within the Vietnamese, American, and Australian governments, and various universities in the United States, Vietnam, and Australia.

Vietnam's unique history, its pervasive grip on the American psyche, and its extraordinary—if somewhat perilous—business opportunities make it a compelling study. Thus, this article is an assessment of the investment environment in Vietnam at the start of a new era in U.S. and Vietnamese relations.

> *With the lifting of the trade embargo, Vietnam is poised to grow and prosper. American firms looking to invest had better take note.*

WAITING FOR THE U.S. INVESTMENT FLOOD

T here has long been the perception in Vietnam that once the trade embargo was lifted, money would magically pour into this country of more than 70 million people and wash away the many problems that have inhibited development. Part of this optimism is well justified; the market potential of Vietnam *is* enormous and American firms are understandably eager to penetrate it. But even though the embargo may have deprived many U.S. companies of some potential profits, American trade sanctions and pressure within the international community combined to hurt Vietnam far more.

For years, the United States constricted the total flow of aid and investment into Vietnam, making it difficult for the country to rebuild after decades of war. More specifically, since 1965 the U.S. government has invoked the 1917 Trading with the Enemy Act to prohibit doing business with what was then North Vietnam. After the U.S. withdrawal in 1975, prohibitions against trading or investing in Vietnam continued and were extended to include restrictions on economic and financial assistance from the IMF, the ADB, the World Bank, and other multilateral agencies. This U.S. pressure kept most other countries from supplying needed investment as well. And until Vietnam's withdrawal from Cambodia in 1989, most industrialized nations supported the American-led embargo. Add to these conditions the Vietnamese government's disastrous economic policies and expensive military activities of the 1970s and early 1980s, and one can understand just how close Vietnam came to the brink of economic collapse and social upheaval.

The only real aid flowing into Vietnam in the 1980s—mostly in the form of technical assistance and capital goods, and provided in rubles—came from the Council for Mutual Economic Assistance, controlled by the former USSR. But even that aid fell off in 1991 and, with the disintegration of the USSR, stopped altogether in 1992. Other countries have begun economic assistance in recent years—more than $200 million in 1991 and $600 million in 1992—but aid at this level is not nearly adequate for the task of rebuilding a developing country that has been cut off from capital and technology for decades. Direct foreign investment has flowed at significant levels only since 1991. The Vietnamese hope that the accelerating rate of investment aid from multilateral agencies, and the return of U.S. companies—with cash in hand—will be the catalyst that enables the country to claw its way to the oft-cited objective of "Asian Tiger" status. Indeed, Vietnam has paid a high price for independence, and in many respects the world passed it by. Now, however, with the advent of peace and political stability, most Vietnamese wish to make up for lost time and are urgent to prosper and become part of the world community.

So Vietnam is faced with the formidable task of building an economy that can support a population expected to exceed 81 million by the year 2000. By approving a renewal of IMF lending to Vietnam in July 1993 and lifting the embargo on February 3, 1994, the U.S. government has given heart to businesspeople who have long been optimistic about the prospects for Vietnam's economy. Private American businesses have given an additional vote of confidence to the Vietnamese; IBM, GE, Caterpillar, BankAmerica, Philip Morris, Citibank, IBM, and a host of other

> *"For all Vietnam's progress and promise, the nation continues its three-steps-forward, two-steps-backward transformation called market socialism."*

U.S. companies were setting up offices even before the embargo was lifted, and many more continue to follow.

ECONOMIC TRANSFORMATION

Vietnam would not be such a promising market, of course, had not the Vietnamese government restructured the political and economic foundation of the country. The most fundamental changes occurred in 1986, when the Seventh Party Congress implemented a policy referred to simply as *doi moi*, which loosely translates into "economic renovation" or "change for the new." This policy change included market-determined pricing and a tolerance for free enterprise. Results were striking and immediate as a private sector blossomed and foreign investors flocked to Hanoi and Ho Chi Minh City (HCMC, formerly Saigon). Yet for all Vietnam's progress and promise, the nation continues its three-steps-forward, two-steps-backward transformation called market socialism—a free market economy under the aegis of communist party leadership.

Any discussion about buying, selling, and doing business in Vietnam must bear in mind that Vietnam has been, and will continue to be, an authoritarian, single-party state. Although the economy continues to evolve as the country borrows administrative practices from Singapore, China, and other Asian economic models, support for economic reforms is not universal within the government. The present government continues to be led by the Communist Party of Vietnam (CPV), which intends to stay in power by ensuring that senior positions in government are held by party members.

In a sense, reform was forced upon the communists. Unlike neighboring China, where economic liberalization has enjoyed the unqualified support of both the senior leadership, headed by Deng Xiaoping, and a reformist faction that has kept the new economy marching forward since 1978, reform in Vietnam is supported by ambivalent factions within the CPV. Conservatives know that macroeconomic prosperity is by no means the only outcome of reform policies. These policies have also changed the face of Vietnamese society, and threaten to bring even greater social change, corruption, a widening gap between rich and poor, Western ideas on individual rights, and cries for political freedom that are imported along with investment capital and technology.

Despite the potential threats of "social depravity" and "cultural imperialism," *doi moi* was seen by the CPV as the only answer to Vietnam's desperate economic situation. To stay in power after years of deprivation, the Vietnamese government had to deliver greater prosperity. But the

CPV continues to pepper progressive laws with party rhetoric, so the central leadership in Hanoi remains divided to this day between hard-liners and reformers. Such division could permit the CPV to impede reforms despite the accelerating momentum of the reform movement.

By maintaining many inefficient socialist principles, the central government actually empowers local governments with deciding which line to pursue, conservative or reformist. In the absence of clear guidelines from the central government and the ruling party, local officials will be inclined to exert greater control over the economic development of their regions. American businesses hoping to initiate enterprises may find they will have to receive approval first from Hanoi, then from local governments whose officials will need to be convinced of the benefits of having a new American business in town. All this is despite recent efforts by the Vietnamese government to streamline the approval process for startup operations. In one of the poorest countries in Asia, this opens the system to more corruption and the danger of "foot-dragging" by conservatives in Hanoi at a time when a detailed law on foreign investment, a blueprint for a modern banking system, and rational codified tax policies are long overdue.

Still, the reform movement *is* accelerating, even though the government still holds 75 percent of Vietnam's assets, uses most of the bank credit, and employs a third of the work force, yet only contributes a third of the country's GDP. In the face of extraordinary challenges, the private sector contributes more than 40 percent of industrial output and employs the other two-thirds of the working population. Private sector output is growing exponentially, and statistics on the private sector are indicators of the tenacity, industriousness, and entrepreneurship of the Vietnamese and, more generally, Vietnam's investment potential.

A Foundation for Growth

Vietnamese economic planners are encouraged by the examples of Korea, Indonesia, Thailand, and China. These countries have all turned their economies around in less than two decades. The politically astute Vietnamese leaders can see that citizens of these countries have forgiven many of the sins of their respective governments. Political freedoms may inch along, the gap between rich and poor can widen, corruption can be ignored, the environment can be exploited; in the end, many transgressions will be tolerated as long as the people have a solid belief that greater wealth will be delivered and the quality of life will improve. American firms setting up in Vietnam can gain confidence from the country's economic

performance under *doi moi*, even if government-imposed business policies often seem to be at conflict or, worse, wildly out of sync with Western logic and standard international business practices. And for a transforming economy moving from Marx to market, only serious economic reversals will cause the political instability that authoritarian governments fear—such as the former Soviet Union's inability to deliver basic goods to its citizens, which facilitated the disintegration of the USSR, or the rampant inflation and sociopolitical uncertainties that fueled the Tiananmen demonstrations in China. If Vietnam is progressive but cautious, the government can truly lead the country to an era of rapid growth and rising standards of living for its citizens.

> "By selling rice, oil, and other products, Vietnam has begun to develop links with the more industrially advanced world."

To date, economic reforms have had the most success in the agricultural sector, permitting Vietnam to transform itself from a net importer to a major exporter in less than a decade. In contrast to other transforming economies—such as China, where rural policy is constantly changing, causing farmers to be skeptical of investing heavily for fear of another "great leap forward"—there is a high level of confidence that rural reforms will remain in effect. According to one property developer from Singapore, the Vietnamese people truly believe they will be able to pass their land to the next generation through transferable leases (a significant individual incentive), despite state ownership laws for all land (Ong Beng Kheong 1994).

At the same time, Vietnam has beaten down inflation to about 6 percent, which is superb compared to the 400 percent rate the country experienced in 1988. By selling rice, oil, and other products, Vietnam has begun to develop links with the more industrially advanced world. Its top five export markets in 1992 were Japan, Singapore, Hong Kong, China, and France, and the country recently signed export agreements with the EEC, expanded markets in the Middle East, and resumed trading with other former Soviet bloc nations. Vietnam may now have gained the experience necessary to profit from the opportunity to sell to the United States and gain access to Western technology with fewer restrictions.

At bottom, Vietnam is clearly committed to development. According to Pham Chi Lan (1992), Deputy Secretary General of the Vietnamese Chamber of Commerce and Industry, "Market forces are now the driving force in Vietnam's economic development." And as chairman of the Ho Chi Minh City Foreign Trade and Investment Development Center, which works to promote international trade in HCMC as Vietnam liberalizes its markets, restructures its industries, and becomes active in international trade, Pham Chi Lan stated, "The key will be to bring the right people together and to take full advantage of the opportunities" (1994).

Cautious Optimism

Fundamental statistics seem to support cautious optimism. Vietnamese exports, for example, increased from $2 billion in 1991 to $3 billion in 1993; the imports of consumer goods and other predictor variables of consumer wealth and consumption patterns continue to increase exponentially. Development also continues at a dizzying pace, as 73 projects worth more than $1.5 billion await approval in HCMC alone. Some of these are in property, such as the Saigon Tower joint venture to build commercial office space ($10 million) and a Ba Son shipyard development project ($6.6 million). Moreover, Vietnam supplies 58 percent of its consumer goods domestically, including more than 60 percent of the food, liquor, cigarettes, and even home appliances bought by its citizens, and sells abroad about as much as the nation buys from foreigners, although a troubling trend toward deficit trading is emerging. The most recent statistics from the General Statistical Office (1994) indicated Vietnam's exports for the first half of 1994 totaled $1.6 billion dollars, a 26 percent increase over the same period last year, while imports totaled $1.8 billion dollars, a 30.6 percent increase over that same period.

Particularly noteworthy is a growing concern among Vietnamese about sustainable development. During one of our meetings in January 1994, a senior official in HCMC discussed new forest regulations to prevent exploitation. After learning environmental lessons from their comrades in Eastern Europe and China, and after suffering the effects of defoliants, napalm, and other toxic chemicals used during the war, the Vietnamese seem keenly interested in avoiding any new environmental catastrophes. But here, too, there are conflicts. Many projects and policies, some of which have already begun and some of which are planned, are clearly detrimental to the environment. So we wonder whether "politically correct" conversation is also creeping into Vietnamese policy discussions.

The Vietnamese government also responded positively to a complaint frequently lodged by U.S. companies in Asia—namely, trademark infringement. The Vietnam Union of Cigarette Producers shut down a Marlboro cigarette counterfeiting operation in response to a December 1, 1993, protest by the Philip Morris group. Though this decision was partly a gesture to influence U.S. congressional delegations and other officials to lift the trade embargo, it also suggests that the government is serious about involving U.S. companies in Vietnamese development.

SO, WHERE EXACTLY IS THE OPPORTUNITY?

Vietnam is still a poor country, with an official per capita GDP of about $250 and more than 80 percent of its population living in rural areas, engaged in agriculture. The country has, however, a rural population that continues to benefit from economic reforms, as well as a growing urban population and developing Western-style markets for goods and services.

Partly because of the various wars over the past 50 years, which took a portion of the population off the land, and partly because of the burgeoning economies in the cities, urban areas are growing in wealth and population density. This urban population, which has readily embraced free enterprise, is an emerging force that will help drive much of the economy. Middle classes and even upper classes are forming. These trends suggest that domestic economic successes can now be combined with foreign investment to facilitate more rapid growth. For example, Ho Chi Minh City is expected to grow at about 11 percent and attract more than $1 billion in investment capital. Within a few years, this will be a market with considerable wealth and buying power.

Emerging Consumer Markets

As a traditional Asian culture and an authoritarian socialist political environment, Vietnam is an interesting case study of the diffusion of consumer culture. Some consumers in Vietnam will move slowly toward embracing a purely consumer culture; others are already completely smitten by it. Like many countries with growing economies, the young urbanites are proving to be opinion leaders who prefer imported motorbikes to bicycles, Western-style sneakers to domestic designs, and Western music and popular culture. The pent-up consumer frustration felt by many Vietnamese has been expressed well by Hoang Ngoc Nguyen (1992):

> "Some consumers in Vietnam will move slowly toward embracing a purely consumer culture; others are already completely smitten by it."

After two or three decades of living in a penurious economy and self-imposed austerity, a consumer boom is evident. Japanese scooters, color TV sets, VCRs, refrigerators, and other electronic appliances are common, even in remote areas.

The rate at which this consumer boom is diffusing into Vietnamese society is accelerating and a discernible market segmentation pattern is emerging with the diffusion process. That pattern roughly differentiates consumers along North-South, urban-rural, and old-young lines, though recent observations suggest to us that the North-South differences are dissipating somewhat, at least in terms of consumer needs and wants, whereas others are becoming more apparent. Young consumers, for whom the war with America is a history lesson, have ambitions and consumer desires hardly distinguishable from many youths around the globe.

The university students we recently interviewed were almost unanimous in their career plans: to work for a foreign-owned company or joint venture and enjoy all the material benefits such employment offers. The idea that an entrepreneurial spirit is healthy, not subversive, is slowly becoming accepted by both the government and Vietnamese society. As Vietnam grows in wealth and expands contact with the outside world, demand for American consumer goods ranging from soft drinks to cosmetics is bound to increase.

The desire for Western products and the affinity for Western images indicates that some U.S. firms have product lines perfectly positioned to exploit current Vietnamese market conditions. Not surprisingly, many firms have moved swiftly to leverage such competitive advantages. Pepsi-Cola, for example, began production within hours of the announcement of the ending of the embargo. More than 40 million cases of soft drinks are already sold annually in Vietnam, a figure that is expected to increase fivefold within the next decade; such packaged consumer goods, the easiest Western goods to purchase, are relatively inexpensive.

An increased interest in marketing and consumer behavior has led the government to compile databases to track consumer spending and foreign companies to employ market research firms to measure purchase patterns. The segmentation schema mentioned earlier will segment even further. Consumer behavior will continue to be influenced by returning Viet Kieu (overseas Vietnamese), interaction with tourists and expatriates, and general information diffusion from television and periodicals. If Vietnam's economy manages to grow faster than its population, prospects for a modern consumer market are good.

Export Market

Like many Asian economies, Vietnam's governmental policy and tax code favor foreign businesses that set up to export. Imports of equipment, for example, are free of tariff and tax, and the seafood industry is an excellent illustration of the country's ability to build a healthy, value-added export industry. Petroleum, agricultural products, and minerals are good illustrations as well. Basic low-tech and labor-intensive manufactured goods, such as shoes and textiles, soon will be.

An important benefit of lifting the embargo has been Vietnam's integration into the world economy. Exports for all of 1993 saw Vietnam increasing coffee exports by 25 percent, tea by 30 percent, sea products by 22 percent, and garments by 22 percent. As one of the world's poorest economies, the newly embargo-free Vietnam will be entitled to favorable quotas on its exports to the developed world.

The Multilateral Aid Market

Every businessperson and government official seems quick to point out Vietnam's inadequate infrastructure. Although the Australians are busy upgrading the international telephone system, Vietnam badly needs new roads, power plants, ports, transmission lines, and other investments in infrastructure. More than $2 billion is slated for investment in one project alone to build a major North-South highway. Ten American companies have already registered intentions to bid for two sections of this contract, and American companies that have established some sort of operation in Vietnam clearly have an opportunity to capitalize on the good will fostered by the recent warming of relations between the U.S. and Vietnamese governments. General contracting and heavy equipment companies, for example, are natural suppliers.

Some observers have suggested that many East and Southeast Asian brands have become so firmly entrenched in the market that it will be difficult to acquire significant market share in many industries. Ironically, says Nick J. Freeman (1993), U.S. business now needs Vietnam more than Vietnam needs U.S. business. Despite the absence of Americans from the Vietnamese mar-

> "The idea that an entrepreneurial spirit is healthy, not subversive, is slowly becoming accepted by both the government and Vietnamese society."

ket and the resultant successful efforts by other nations to fill the vacuum created by that absence, American companies still enjoy very good brand image in Vietnam. Coca-Cola, for example, has been smuggled into Vietnam for years and never really left the country. Its advertising slogan in Vietnamese is *Vui Mung Gap Lai Cac Ban*, ("Good to See You Again"), in contrast to the newer Pepsi publicity blitz that declares Pepsi-Cola *Su Lua Chon Cua The He Moi* ("the Choice of a New Generation"). Furthermore, a can of soda, for which a Vietnamese would pay anywhere from 30 cents to a dollar, is equivalent to an American spending about $15 per can—a pretty strong indicator of brand image and customer loyalty.

Nevertheless, American corporations will have difficulty converting existing brand loyalties in the electronics industry, for example, or perhaps even in the personal computer industry. Still, American firms have (at least) two advantages over other players. First, many American products are simply perceived to be superior to many other non-American products. Second, the Vietnamese government is keen to establish mutually beneficial commercial ties—and therefore implicit political ties—that will enable the United States to serve as an important counterbalance to the emerging political clout of historical regional nemeses China and Japan.

This tendency for the communist Vietnamese government to see America as a potential political ally may seem extraordinary (and more than a little ironic) to most Americans. Yet to the Vietnamese, the *realpolitik* of a new era requires good relations with the United States. Twenty years after the fall of Saigon, such vision is both economically and politically expedient. Consequently, some projects have been earmarked specifically for American concerns. For example, Vietnam has long favored U.S. investment in its oil fields; it keeps an eye on China's claims to some choice fields and again welcomes U.S. investment, as much for strategic political reasons as immediate economic value.

Other Opportunities

Finally, the authors have observed a rapid growth of import-export businesses and cash businesses such as hotels, restaurants, and car rentals, many of them managed by Viet Kieu. These companies are reshaping the commercial and physical landscape of urban Vietnam because they often provide services to other investors and deep-pocketed expatriates, and because the return on investment is relatively quick. Generally, however, companies would be well advised to think in terms of long-run returns on investment rather than aiming for the "quick hit."

One of the most striking outcomes of Vietnam's renovation is a feeling of rebirth shared by almost every Vietnamese we have encountered. Indeed, the eagerness of the people to improve their country, their enthusiasm to learn how to accomplish that goal, and the role they expect American business to play in the process are remarkable. With the mutually beneficial support of foreign partners, the nation's prospects are promising, and most Vietnamese consider American businesses to be among the most desirable partners. Many sources say American investment is welcomed for its own sake as well as to balance Chinese and Japanese investments in the region, but investors should also note that most Vietnamese genuinely like Americans as well as American products.

Before the embargo was lifted, a steady flow of businesspeople, U.S. lawmakers, diplomats, and academics visited the major cities and assured themselves that (a) Vietnam was committed to reforms and (b) the benefits to U.S. firms outweighed any ideological differences with the Vietnamese government. Nevertheless, business managers with high expectations may be disappointed if they expect quick returns from their investments. Prudent investors have learned that respect for the following factors is required for any successful operation.

First, Vietnamese workers are dedicated and literate, but their basic accounting and managerial skills are sadly lacking. Even though Vietnamese generally possess a great desire to learn these skills, especially the younger people, U.S. companies can expect to invest heavily in training their employees. This investment in basic human resource development does not include the substantial investments in modern manufacturing facilities and equipment that are necessary for most enterprises.

Second, political forces continue to shape policy and therefore affect business operations; so does individual profiteering. Although the investment climate is very favorable, the Vietnamese governmental authorities, especially at the local levels, have the power to make or break a project. Almost 75 percent of foreign-sponsored projects are joint ventures, which require substantial interaction with local partners, whether provincial governments or individual Vietnamese citizens. Consequently, patience and circumspection will be required in the formative stages of any operation.

To be sure, Vietnam is a resource-rich nation with dynamic and industrious citizens who crave the goods and services consumed by many of their more prosperous Southeast Asian neighbors. At this juncture, however, because of poor infrastructure, the necessary evolution and accompanying confusion of its legal code, and limited managerial acumen, Vietnam still functions much more like a teetering "tiger on a bicycle" (Fforde 1993) rather than a bona fide Asian Tiger. But if U.S. business leaders understand that Vietnam's promise outweighs its peril, there are virtually countless opportunities to sell goods and services to the Vietnamese and set up facilities to produce for the local market and for export. As we embark on a new era, Vietnam is going to grow and prosper. As it does, astute investors stand to prosper as well.

References

Thomas A. Bernstein, "Ideology and Rural Reform: The Paradox of Contingent Stability," in Arthur L. Rosenbaum, ed., *State and Society in China* (San Francisco: Westview Press, 1993).

Laurence J. Brahm, *Foreign Investment and Trade Law in Vietnam* (Hong Kong: Asia 2000, 1993).

Adam Fforde, "Vietnamese Commerce: The 'Tiger on a Bicycle' Syndrome," *Columbia Journal of World Business*, Winter 1993, pp. 48-55.

Nick J. Freeman, "United States' Economic Sanctions Against Vietnam," *Columbia Journal of World Business*, Summer 1993, pp. 12-22.

General Statistical Office, Hanoi, 1993; 1994.

Hoang Ngoc Nguyen, "The Scope and Prospects of Foreign Direct Investment in Vietnam," *Contemporary Southeast Asia*, December 1992, pp. 244-256.

Stanley Karnow, *Vietnam: A History* (New York: Penguin, 1991).

Le Van Minh, Tilleke & Gibbins-HCMC, interview with authors, January 4, 1994, Ho Chi Minh City.

Lee Kuan Yew, "Asia Won't Be a Repeat of Europe's Wartorn Past," interview with Fareed Zakaria, *Singapore Straits Times*, March 12, 1994, p. 34.

Nguyen Xuan Oanh, NXO Associates, interview with authors, January 5, 1994, Ho Chi Minh City.

Ong Beng Kheong, EVP Colliers Jardine HCMC, interview with authors, January 5, 1994, Ho Chi Minh City.

Pham Chi Lan, in the foreword to Laurence J. Brahm, *Foreign Investment and Trade Law in Vietnam* (Hong Kong: Asia 2000, 1992), pp. v-vi.

Pham Chi Lan, Ho Chi Minh City Foreign Trade and Investment Development Center, interview with authors, January 4, 1994, Ho Chi Minh City.

Philip Shenon, "New Vietnam Combat: Coke vs. Pepsi," *New York Times*, February 7, 1994, pp. D1-D2.

Clifford J. Shultz II and Khai Le, "Vietnam's Inconsistencies Between Political Structure and Socio-economic Practice: Implications for the Nation's Future," *Contemporary Southeast Asia*, September 1993, pp. 179-194.

Clifford J. Shultz II and Anthony Pecotich, "Vietnam: New Assessments of Consumption Patterns in a (Re)Emergent Capitalist Society," paper presented at the Association for Consumer Research Conference, Singapore, June 14, 1994.

Clifford J. Shultz II, Anthony Pecotich, and Khai Le, "Marketing and Consumption Activity in the Socialist Republic of Vietnam," in Clifford J. Shultz II, Russell W. Belk, and Güliz Ger, eds.. *Consumption in Marketizing Economies* (Greenwich, CT: JAI Press, 1994), pp. 225-257.

Ton Si Kinh and Pham Vyen Nguyen, *Development Trends of Foreign Direct Investment in Vietnam* (Ho Chi Minh City: Institute for Economic Research, 1993).

Vietnam: A Guide for the Foreign Investor (Washington, DC: Price Waterhouse, May 1993).

Vietnam Investment Evaluation (Ho Chi Minh City: Banque IndoSuez Regional Research, 1993).

Vietnam Investment Review, January 9, 1994, p. 9.

Political Risk Analysis in North American Multinationals: An Empirical Review and Assessment

Frederick Stapenhurst

The author is with the Canadian International Development Agency, Ottawa, Canada.

Political risk analysis (PRA) emerged during the late 1970s as an important component of environmental assessment. This article replicates a 1987 study that examined the approach to PRA in North American corporations, and assesses the changes that have occurred. The principal finding is that while there has been relatively little change within the "continuing practitioners" regarding organizational approach to, and use of, PRA, there are a number of significant differences between these corporations and "late adopters" of PRA.

INTRODUCTION

It is generally recognized that corporations must first assess, and then adapt to their external market and environment if they are to survive and prosper (Stoffels, 1983). In order to do so, corporations must comprehensively scan the business environment for both opportunities and risks (Thomas, 1974; Fahey & King, 1977; Porter, 1980, 1986; Hax and Majluf, 1984).

There was an early emphasis on the assessment of technological and economic factors within the environment but during the 1970s, with such factors as the Iranian Revolution, the social and political upheavals in Latin America, and increased terrorism, political analysis came to the fore and was undertaken by an increasing number of multinational corporations (MNCs) and international banks. The emergence of political risk analysis (PRA) as a "new corporate function" was widely reported (Kobrin et al., 1980; Grosse and Stack, 1984; Stapenhurst, 1990; Preble et al, 1988).

Over the past half decade, the political environment within which corporations operate has become increasingly complex. The integration of the former centrally planned economies of the (former) Soviet Union, Eastern Europe, and China into the world economy and the emergences of a single European market are political developments that have presented oppor-tunities to international corporations. At the same time, the Iraqi invasion of Kuwait, the disintegration of Yugoslavia, and the collapse of various governments in Africa are examples of some of the recent political events that have resulted in heightened political risk.

It could be expected, therefore, that the corporate use of PRA would have become more widespread and more sophisticated and that it would be better integrated into corporate decision making. Despite some largely descriptive reports (Rogers, 1992; Stapenhurst, 1992a), little is known regarding the evolution of the PRA function. The research in this article replicates an earlier study carried out in 1987 (Stapenhurst, 1988, 1990); it seeks to determine how PRA, as a corporate function, has evolved over the past 6 years. In particular, it compares PRA in those corporations that have only recently adopted a formal approach to such assessments with corporations that have been long-time practitioners.

LITERATURE REVIEW

Academic research on PRA has unfolded along three separate lines: studies of individual perceptions of the political environment; conceptual approaches to PRA methodology and processes; and empirical surveys.

Individual Perceptions
First, originating at the microlevel, there were studies of *individual perceptions* of the political environment, which asked the question: "How do individual managers get information about their environment?" Examples include Kobrin et al. (1980), Grosse and Stack (1984), and Low et al. (1989), which built on the earlier research on scanning by Kefalas and Schoderbeck (1973) and Keegan (1974).

Conceptual Approaches
Second, research was conducted on the *methodology and process* involved in environmental scanning and assessment, including PRA. Ansoff (1975) developed a model for detecting

and responding to what he called "weak signals" in the environment and thus managing strategic surprise; systems theory foundations of environmental scanning were articulated by Kahalas (1971) and Neubauer and Solomon (1977) developed a scheme for assessing external strategic pressures. Segev (1977) modeled the process of interaction between strategy making teams and environmental analysis units; Rodriguez and King (1977) wrote on the development of data bases of various kinds of external information required for planning.

Extending this early research on environmental scanning, Kobrin (1981) undertook a major review of the conceptual state of the art of PRA and Brewer (1981, 1983) initially extended the analysis to consider more specifically the links between PRA and capital budgeting decisions and then examined the relationship between political instability, political risk, and the foreign investment decision.

Empirical Surveys

Third, in parallel to this conceptual analysis of the role of scanning and PRA in strategic decision making, several studies examined the *empirical state of the art.* Following reports of a slow adoption of formalized scanning and assessment techniques (Fahey and King, 1977; Stubbart, 1982), Thomas (1980) found that scanning was a permanent, persuasive, and multi-level activity that surveyed social, political, economic, and technological conditions. Similarly, Diffenbach (1983) noted an evolution of corporate environmental analysis from an *appreciation* of the need for such analysis by corporations in the mid to late 1960s, although a focus on *analytical methodology* in the early 1970s to an *application* phase in the late 1970s and early 1980s. Lenz and Engledow (1985) conducted a field study of 10 "leading edge" corporations and determined that the most effective environmental analysis units were those whose activities were integrated into strategic planning processes and who were thus able to influence directly the formulation of strategy.

Surveys have shown that PRA emerged as a *distinct corporate function* in the 1970s (Blask, 1976; Kobrin et al., 1980; Korth, 1981; Burton and Inoue, 1983; Grosse and Stack, 1984; Mascarenhas and Sand, 1985; Hefernan, 1986; Low et al., 1989; Stapenhurst, 1990).

Kennedy's (1984) findings showed that, while prior to 1979 analysts in American corporations spent most of their time on other responsibilities besides PRA, after 1979 more than half of them were employed almost solely for PRA. By contrast, Stapenhurst (1990) showed that most PRA units comprised less than five, and often less than three analysts, all of whom had other responsibilities besides PRA; he also showed that the mean amount of time spent on PRA by North American analysts was 39% (Stapenhurst, 1990).

Regarding the *methodological approach,* in the mid 1970s Blask (1976) found that 5 percent of US banks had NO formal system of country evaluation, and an additional 8 percent had unsophisticated checklists or qualitative systems. Several years later, Burton and Inoue (1983) noted a trend toward greater elaboration by a progression from nonsystematic to systematic,

subjective to objective, and qualitative checklist to other quantitative methods. However, Grosse and Stack (1984) noted a falling back among US MNCs, with 64 percent using a checklist format. More recently, Stapenhurst (1990) indicated a swing back to the use of more sophisticated methodologies, with only 25 percent of corporations using simple checklists, 50 percent using more complex structured/qualitative formats, and nearly 25 percent using scenario development.

Fahey and King (1977) and Stubbart (1982) reported that the most common process for undertaking PRA among American corporations was "irregular" scanning, followed by "regular" scanning. While Fahey and King found that 17 percent of the corporations surveyed undertook "continuous data collection and processing," Stubbart (updating his study 5 years later) found that these "continuous scanners" had slipped back to become "regular scanners." Interestingly, Lenz and Engledow (1985) declared in their study of 10 leading edge corporations, that each firm was using a continuous process of intelligence gathering. Stapenhurst (1990) showed that approximately one-half of corporations used the "non-regular (ad hoc)" approach to PRA, and 30 percent used "regular report periodically updated."

With regard to *integration,* Stapenhurst (1990) confirmed the findings of Kobrin et al. (1980) that PRA tended to serve as an input into decision-makers' subjective impressions on non-economic factors and their likely impact on operations, which in turn serve as a background against which decisions are taken. Indeed, one of the continuing failings of political analysts is the integration of their analyses into corporate decision making; and there appears to be substantial scope to improve the integration of PRA into corporate decision making.

Kobrin et al. (1980) also reported that the PRA assessment responsibilities in American (nonbank) MNCs were most commonly located in the international division, followed by finance/treasury, planning, and legal departments. Kennedy (1984) noted a locational shift, finding that the most usual location was the strategic planning department. In the same year, Grosse and Stack (1984) reported that, for US banks, the PRA was located in the international division (55% of cases) or in economics (36%). Stapenhurst (1990) also noted a locational shift away from finance/treasury and legal to strategic planning and economics.

Kennedy (1994) found that 84 percent of PRA units in (nonbank) US corporations reported directly to a member of the corporation's Board of Directors. Stapenhurst (1990) suggested a trend away from such high level reporting, with most PRA units reporting to a staff or line manager.

Stapenhurst (1990) also found that the principal end uses of PRA was to assist in specific loan/investment decisions and in strategic planning, which confirmed the earlier findings of Kobrin et al. (1980).

Regarding *general corporate characteristics,* Stapenhurst (1990) found that among firms practicing PRA, while a significant minority of corporations were highly international (i.e., with over 80% of total loans/sales to foreign countries), most reported that foreign loans/sales account for less than 40 percent of the total. They were typically active in more than 20 countries and their foreign operations dated from before World War II. With regard to regional breakdown of foreign operations, he noted a heavy concentration in the developed counties of Europe and in Latin America and Australia.

RESEARCH DESIGN AND METHODOLOGY

Using the same corporate data base and survey instrument as reported earlier (Stapenhurst, 1988, 1990), survey research was conducted using a questionnaire mailed to, and subsequent interviews with, corporate political risk analysts, to determine the evolution of PRA over the past 5 years.

The questionnaire was mailed in January 1993 to 40 of the 48 respondents to the Stapenhurst survey (three of the original respondents had not put the name of their company on the completed questionnaire, and thus were not traceable; five other companies had either ceased business or had merged with other corporations). A subsequent mailing to all nonrespondents was undertaken 6 weeks after the initial mailing. Twenty-seven responses were received (67.5% response rate); of these, eight reported that either the PRA function had been discontinued or that international business activities had ceased, and one corporation reported that all information regarding its PRA activities as confidential. There were thus 18 usable responses; for the purpose of this study, these corporations are referred to as the "continuing practitioners." (Occasional reference will be made to the original 1987 population of 48 respondents, which included the continuing practitioners at that time; this group will be referred to as the "original practitioners".)

In addition, the questionnaire was also sent to 17 corporations that had not been part of the earlier survey but were known to have more recently established a formalized PRA system. Ten responses were received (58.8% response rate); these are referred to as the "late adopters."

Comparisons were then made between the initial (1987) responses of the continuing practitioners and their subsequent 1993 responses to determine what change, if any, had occurred in the organizational approach to, and role of, PRA over the past 6-year period. In addition, comparisons were made between the 18 continuing practitioners and the 10 late adopters responding in 1993 to determine if there were any differences within the two groups of companies. Given the broad coverage of corporations, the conclusions drawn are believed to represent a valid overview of the evolution and current practice of PRA in North American corporations.

SURVEY RESULTS

Table 1 indicates that there *were a few significant differences regarding the role of, and approach to, PRA between the continuing practitioners of PRA reporting in 1987 and their reporting today.* The principal differences concern the organizational approach to PRA, and in particular, the relative emphasis on the use of outside consultants, as opposed to in-house analyses, and the extent to which political analysts have additional responsibilities.

By contrast, as Table 2 indicates, there *were a greater number of significant differences regarding the role of, and approach to, PRA in 1993 between the continuing practitioners and the late adopters.* These differences were in the areas of the methodology, the use of outside consultants, relative to in-house analysis and methodological approach; integration of PRA, the extent to which senior management receives PRA reports and the location of the PRA unit; and the percentage of investments made overseas.

Organizational Approach

Regarding organizational approach, the continuing practitioners in 1993 reported *the establishment date of a formalized PRA unit* in the late 1970s or early 1980s (median date: 1977, compared with reported 1978 for the original practitioners). By contrast, most late adopters established their PRA unit in the early to mid 1980s (median date: 1983; see Table 2).

Although not statistically significant (at $\alpha = 0.10$), there was some decline in the *number of analysts* undertaking PRA. The mean number of professionals working in PRA units in the continuing practitioners was 1.4 in 1993, down from 2.2 reported by them in 1987 (and 2.3 reported by all respondents in 1987; see Table 1). Similarly, there was little difference between the continuing practitioners (mean of 1.4 political analysts in 1993) and the late adopters, who reported a mean of 1.7 analysts (Table 2).

Coupled with this downsizing of PRA units was a move toward the greater *use of external consultants.* In 1987, among the continuing practitioners, the mean reported reliance on outside consultants, relative to in-house analyses, was 35 percent (the reported mean for original practitioners was 29%). By 1993, the proportion of political analyses undertaken by external consultants had risen to 47.8 percent for continuing practitioners (see Table 1). However, although for the original practitioners the dispersion around 35 percent was narrow, with only four corporations relying on consultants for 80–100 percent of the analyses, in 1993 there was a concentration of companies at both lower ends, that is using outside consultants for less than 20 percent of the analyses (five corporations), and at the higher end, that is using consultants for at least 80 percent of the analyses (four corporations).

Similarly, as Table 2 shows, there is a clear dichotomy in 1993 between the continuing practitioners and the late adopters: whereas the reported mean reliance on outside consultants for continuing practitioners was 47.8 percent, for late adopters it was only 35 percent. This difference is significant at $\alpha = 0.05$.

According to Rogers (1992), in the late 1980s there was a wholesale downsizing of staff functions, including PRA, in US corporations in response to intense pressure to reduce costs. This led to an increased need for external consultants; at the same time, however, the quality and relevance of external analyses had been brought into question. Ernest Brown, Vice President at Salomon Brothers, states: "We don't consume

Table 1. Difference Between Original and Continuing Practioners

| | Mean/Freq. | | | |
| | 1987 | | 1993 | |
	$(n = 48)^a$	$(n = 18)^b$	$(n = 18)^b$	t-Stat
Organizational approach				
Date established	1978	1977	1977	
No. of analysts	2.3	2.2	1.4	0.46
External consultants	29	35	47.8	− 1.7c
Other responsib, Y/N	47/1	18/0	18/0	
% Time on PRA	40.6	46.9	20.7	2.19d
Methodology				
Checklisting	12	5	6	
Structured reports	25	10	7	
Scenario building	9	5	5	−1.29
Investment modeling	0	0	1	
Other	0	1	2	
Process				
Ad hoc	21	4	7	
Regular studies	15	7	8	− 0.1
Continuous assessments	10	6	4	
Other	1	0	1	
Integration				
Reports received				
Board of Directors	28.8	33.3	29.3	0.54
President/CEO	52.0	52.0	48.8	1.37
Head/strategic planning	57.5	54.5	60.0	0.85
Reporting lines				
Board of directors	0	0	0	
President/CEO	10	4	2	
Other executive officer	13	7	10	0.28
Line manager	4	1	1	
Staff manager	20	6	5	
Location				
Separate unit	3	1	2	
Finance	5	0	1	
Strategic planning	10	4	2	0.85
Economics	13	4	6	
Other	16	9	7	
Purposes^e				
Inv./loan decisions	32	11	10	
Strategic planning	8	11	13	
FX operations	1	5	2	1.47
Day-to-day operations	3	4	2	
Other	2	4	0	
Corp. characteristics				
% Sales/loans overseas	40.6	41.1	47.6	− 0.9
% DFI/total investment	25.0	37.1	42.9	1.3
No. of Countries	16.8	19.6	18.2	0

^{a}Original practitioners.
^{b}Continuing practitioners.
^{c}Significant at α 0.10; tcv (40, 0.10) = 1.684.
^{d}Significant at α 0.05; tcv (40, 0.05) = 2.02.
^{e}Multiple citations.

external stuff much. We find it either too general or so consistently alarmist as to be useless." Another criticism often mentioned regarding external consultants is that they often come from academia, with little corporate experience; as a result, their analyses may be less suited for corporate purposes. According to Paul Sachs, President of Multi-National Strategies, a PRA consulting firm, such academic PRA "Tends to be written by young people ... [who] tend not to have had responsibility for managing money," (*Euromoney,* 1992). Nonetheless, the use of external consultants is often considered useful for those countries where in-house expertise is limited.

With regard to continuing practitioners, the trend has been toward the downsizing of PRA units, a greater use of outside consultants, and somewhat less time spent by each analyst on PRA. This finding is generally consistent with Rogers (1992: 4), who noted that "the global economic threat on U.S. companies found the slashing away at perceived "fat" in the organization. Layers of middle management were pared away, including in-staff functions such as [political risk analysis]." He also noted that, quoting Bill Kelly of Ford Motor Company, "There is a growing need for consultants in specialized, niche areas which are beyond the capabilities of the firm. . . . There will be more contracting out of this type of work" (p. 6). However, it does not explain the trend of the late adopters that have established somewhat larger PRA units, which function with limited reliance on outside consultants. Could it be that these corporations: have viewed "the rise and fall of PRA" in the earlier adopters of PRA; have seen the competitive advantages of undertaking PRA; and have aggressively built up an in-house capability? Or are they simply destined to follow the trend of the earlier practitioners: will we see a retrenching of the PRA function in them as well?

Methodologies Used

Several differences can be seen in Table 2 regarding *methodology used in 1993* by the continuing practitioners and the late adopters. Two-thirds of the continuing practitioners still used unstructured check-listing (six corporations) or the structured qualitative approach (seven corporations) and there was little use of statistical analyses (used by only one corporation), but greater use of scenario building (five corporations) and other, custom-tailored methodologies (two corporations).

Interestingly, none of the late adopters were using the unstructured checklist approach: structured qualitative reports and scenario building were their favored methodologies (used by five and three corporations, respectively). The differences between continuing practitioners and these late adopters is significant at $\alpha = 0.10$.

Regarding the *predominant process* followed in undertaking PRA, there were no significant differences (at $\alpha = 0.10$) between continuing practitioners and the late adopters. Seven continuing practitioners and five late adopters in 1993 used the "nonregular (ad hoc) studies" approach; the second most popular approach was "regular studies, periodically updated" (used by eight continuing practitioners and four late adopters). The "continuous (organized data collection and processing)"

was reportedly used by four continuing practitioners and three late adopters in 1993 (see Table 2).

The late adopters have, on average, adopted relatively more sophisticated methodologies, perhaps drawing on the literature highlighting "best practices" (Kobrin, 1981; Lenz and Engledow, 1985; Mascarenhas and Sand, 1985, among others). By contrast, it seems apparent that the continuing practitioners are generally satisfied with the methodologies and processes they have been following for PRA; there was little change in methodologies used since the mid 1980s. Alternatively, there it could be that a degree of organizational inertia hinders them from adopting new, more sophisticated approaches.

In contrast, there has been relatively little change regarding the predominant process involved in PRA: among continuing practitioners there seems to general satisfaction with the process originally adopted. Among the late adopters there is a wide dispersion of processes adopted, with five corporations opting for the relatively unsophisticated nonregular (ad hoc) studies approach. Perhaps it is misleading to think of a "hierarchy" of approaches, where the nonregular (ad hoc) approach is considered somehow inferior to "regular studies (periodically updated)" that in turn are inferior to the "continuous (data collection and processing)" methodology, as postulated by several authors (Fahey and King, 1977; Stubbart, 1982; Lenz and Engledow, 1985; Preble et al., 1988). Rather, it may be that there is an optimal approach or process for each corporation, which is a function of the needs of that particular organization for PRA. Once this particular approach is in place, there is little incentive to change, unless corporate needs change.

Integration of PRA into Decision Making

With regard to the integration of PRA into decision making, significant differences were noted between the continuing practitioners and late adopters with regard to *the frequency with which senior decision-makers receive PRA reports* as well as with regards to the location of the PRA unit.

In 1987, the continuing practitioners reported that in their corporations, the Board of Directors received PRA reports 33.3 percent of the time (roughly comparable with the 28.8 percent reported by the original practitioners). In 1993, among continuing practitioners the frequency was essentially unchanged, with the Board of Directors receiving the reports 29.4 percent of the time (Table 1). By contrast, among new adopters the frequency was much less, with Directors receiving PRA reports only 11 percent of the time; the difference between continuing practitioners and late adopters is significant at $\alpha = 0.10$ (Table 2).

As Table 1 shows, the frequency with which the Chairman/ President received PRA reports fell slightly from 52.0 percent of the time among original practitioners in 1987 to 48.8 percent of the time for continuing practitioners; Table 2 indicates that it was 52 percent for the late adopters. These differences were not significant at $\alpha = 0.10$.

Similarly, with regard to the frequency with which the Head of Strategic Planning receives the PRA reports, there was again no reported significant difference at $\alpha = 0.10$ (57.5% of the

Table 2. Difference Between Continuing Practioners and New Adopters

	1993 Mean/Freq.		
	Late (n = 10)	Con-tinuing (n = 18)	t-stat
Organizational approach			
Date established	1983	1977	
No. of analysts	1.7	1.4	− 0.59
External consultants	35.0	47.8	2.36[a]
Other responsib., Y/N	8/2	18/0	
% Time on PRA	32.2	20.7	0.6
Methodology[b]			
Checklisting	0	6	
Structured reports	5	7	
Scenario building	3	5	− 1.77[c]
Investment modeling	0	1	
Other	3	2	
Process			
Ad hoc	5	7	
Regular studies	4	8	
Continuous assessment	3	4	0.78
Other	1	1	
Integration			
Reports received			
Board of directors	11.0	29.3	2.03[c]
President/CEO	48.0		− 0.5
Head/strategic planning	2.0	60.0	− 0.3
Reporting lines			
Board of directors	0	0	
President/CEO	3	2	
Other executive officer	3	10	0.71
Line manager	1	1	
Staff manager	3	5	
Location			
Separate unit	3	2	
Finance	2	1	
Strategic planning	2	2	− 3.1[a]
Economics	1	6	
Other	2	7	
Purposes			
Invest./loan decisions	7	10	
Strategic planning	5	13	
FX operations	2	2	− 0.4
Day-to-day operations	4	2	
Other	2	0	
Corp. characteristics			
% Sales/loans overseas	36.7	47.6	1.32
% FDI/total investment	30.0	42.9	1.82[c]
No. of countries	20.0	18.2	− 1.6

[a]Significant at α = 0.05, tcc (28, 0.05) = 2.024.
[b]Multiple citations.
[c]Significant at α = 0.10, tcv (28, 0.10) = 1.701.

time among original practitioners and 54.5% of the time for continuing practitioners in 1987, compared with 60.0 percent of the time for continuing practitioners in 1993 (Table 1), and 52.0 percent of the time for late adopters (Table 2).

There were no significant changes with regard to whom the PRA unit reported. In 1987, none of the continuing practitioners indicated that their PRA unit reported directly to the Board of Directors; in four corporations (21% of reporting corporations) the PRA unit reported directly to the President or Chief Executive Officer. In 1993, among the continuing practitioners, still no PRA units reported to the Board of Directors and in only two (11% of respondents) did the PRA unit report to the President or CEO (Table 1). In contrast, among late adopters the level to which the PRA unit reported was somewhat higher: none to the Board of Directors but in three corporations, or 30 percent, to the President or CEO (Table 2).

As Table 1 indicates, the proportion of units reporting to an Executive Officer other than the President or CEO rose from 38 percent (seven corporations) among the continuing practitioners (and 28% or 13 corporations among original practitioners) in 1987 to 55 percent (10 corporations) of continuing practitioners. Table 2 shows that 30 percent (three corporations) of late adopters reported at this level.

The proportion of units reporting to a staff or line manager declined somewhat from 38 percent of continuing practitioners in 1987 and 50 percent (24 corporations of original practitioners) to 33 percent, or six continuing practitioners in 1993 (Table 1). For late adopters it was 40 percent (four corporations) (Table 2). None of these differences were statistically significant.

Because of the need for better integration of PRA into corporate decision making has been well-documented in the literature (Levinson, 1986; Stapenhurst, 1988, 1990, 1992a, b; Rogers, 1992), this general lack of improvement is surprising. It is possible that PRA is better disseminated within the corporation and is being incorporated into decision making at a lower level of decision making; alternatively, this may again be an example of continuing organizational inertia, in which case the PRA function will continue to be criticized for its "lack of corporate relevance." An example of the former is the practice at Chase Manhattan Bank, where the country-limit setting now takes place in its three annual meetings, in New York, London, and Hong Kong. There is, according to Vice-President Dominique Clavel, " . . . a constant dialogue with the people in the field who clearly have more access to information on local developments but might also run the risk of being less independent." The outcomes of these conferences are subsequently reviewed by the bank's country risk committee (Euromoney, 1992).

Although no significant differences (at α = 0.10) regarding the location of the PRA unit were noted between the continuing practitioners in 1987 and 1993, there was (at α = 0.05) between the continuing practitioners and new adopters (see Tables 1, 2, respectively). In 1987, the most common location for the PRA unit were within economics and strategic planning departments (four corporations in each). By 1993, among continuing practitioners, economics remained the single most common location reported by six corporations, but only two corporations reported the location of the PRA unit within strategic planning (Table 1). Contrastingly among the late adopters, there was a tendency to establish a separate unit (three corporations); two corporations located the function with economics or strategic planning (see Table 2).

With regard to use, an interesting change has occurred: the greater *corporate use of PRA* for single, as opposed to multiple, purposes. Twelve continuing practitioners (66% of respondents) in 1987 stated that PRA was used for multiple purposes within their corporations; this had fallen to nine (50% of continuing practitioners) in 1993. Among the late adopters 60 percent (six corporations) reported multiple uses of PRA. However, these differences are not statistically significant.

PRA was used by continuing practitioners in 1987 primarily as input into specific investment/loan decisions in 1987 (11 citations), followed by strategic planning (26 citations) and day-to-day operations (five citations). By 1993, for continuing practitioners this had changed to 11 citations for specific investment/loan decisions, 13 citations for strategic planning, and two citations for day-to-day operations (Table 1). For late adopters the variation was more even with six citations for strategic planning, five for specific investment/loan decisions, and four for day-to-day operations (Table 2). However, none of these reported differences were statistically significant.

Perhaps the biggest problem facing analysts is ensuring that their analyses are relevant to the corporation. Indeed, they have been criticized for being too absorbed in conceptualization rather than implementation. This is attributable to three factors: an early emphasis on theoretical models, little prior experience by analysts in business issues, and in some cases, spurious results (Rogers, 1991). Currently, at Citibank assessments are used to distinguish between those countries in which the bank will take exposures of up to 1 year, those with 1–5 year exposures, and those where longer term exposures are deemed acceptable. By contrast, Chemical Bank also used its analyses to set country limits by product for each country and even intraday trading limits, in addition to setting more general cross-border financing limits.

Firm Characteristics

Can differences in firm characteristics explain the changes and differences in approach to PRA? There is some, albeit limited, evidence that the degree of globalization affecting a corporation is associated with the extent of adoption of PRA. In 1987, the mean *percentage* of sales or loans made to foreign countries as a proportion of total sales or loans was for the continuing practitioners, 41.1 percent; in 1993 it was 47.6 percent for continuing practitioners and 36.7 percent for late adopters (Tables 1, 2), respectively. Although none of these differences are statistically significant, at $\alpha = 0.10$, the reported differences regarding foreign investment were: the mean proportion of foreign direct investment to total investment had increased, from 37.1 percent for continuing practitioners in 1987 to 42.9 percent in 1993 (Table 1) but was only 30 percent for the late adopters (Table 2).

In 1987, the mean *number of countries* in which original practitioners were active was 19.6; in 1993 the mean number was 18.2 for continuing practitioners and 20 for late adopters.

There was not a great variation for the *regional breakdown of foreign operations* among the original practitioners, continuing practitioners, and new adopters. It was: North America (excluding home country), 16 percent for 1987 respondents, 28 percent for continuing practitioners, and 15 percent for late adopters; Latin America: 16, 4, and 20 percent, respectively; Europe: 27, 28, and 39 percent; Africa: 6, 8, and 3 percent; the ASEAN countries: 12, 7, and 10 percent; Australia/New Zealand/Japan: 13, 8, and 9 percent; other Asia (including the Middle East); 10, 17, and 5 percent, respectively. None of these differences are statistically significant.

In short, with the only exception of the degree to which investment in undertaken overseas, there is little difference in the nature of respondents' overseas operations. In other words, it seems unlikely that differences in firm characteristics can explain the changes and differences in corporate approaches to PRA.

INTERPRETATION

The results of this study only partially confirm earlier research that suggested that corporate PRA has gone through a "shake-out" phase (Levinson, 1986; Rogers, 1992; Stapenhurst, 1992a, b). Although there has been some shedding or scaling back of PRA in certain North American corporations, this has been offset, at least in part, by its adoption in other corporations. Indeed, among those corporations that were practicing PRA in the mid 1980s and are still practicing (the continuing practitioners), the only significant differences are in the areas of organizational approach to PRA, specifically regarding the use of outside consultants (which has increased) and the percentage of time analysts spend solely on PRA (which has declined).

Perhaps more interesting than the reported differences are the similarities. Judging by the relative lack of change in organizational approach to PRA, or the degree of its integration into corporate decision making, it appears that, at least among the continuing practitioners, management is satisfied with the results of PRA.

Also noteworthy are the differences between the continuing practitioners of PRA, which on average adopted a formal approach to PRA in the mid 1970s, and the late adopters, which established the function in the mid 1980s. The late adopters rely to a greater extent than the continuing practitioners on in-house analysis, as opposed to outside consultants; they use more sophisticated methodologies, but are integrating the results of their PRA less well into corporate decision making. What can explain these differences? Whereas it is possible that the late adopters have followed developments in the field, and thus have adopted more sophisticated, and proven, methodologies, why then have they not followed recommendations suggesting that *integration* is critical for PRA? Perhaps definitions and methods for measurement now current in the literature regarding integration need to be revised. Alternatively, perhaps these corporations quite simply have not learned from others' experience and are destined to suffer from the same mistakes. Regarding location, too, the late adopters have tended to shun establishing the PRA unit as part of the strategic planning department, favoring instead a separate independent unit.

It was thought that some of these differences could be explained by differences in corporate characteristics; however, there were few.

CONCLUSIONS

The major finding of this study is the lack of large-scale change regarding the role and importance of PRA in North American corporations over time and the lack of incorporation of "lessons learned" regarding the integration of PRA into corporate decision making.

The tentative conclusions to be drawn are twofold. First, that MNCs still practicing PRA (the continuing practitioners) are generally satisfied with the organizational approach that they have adopted and the degree to which PRA is integrated into decision making. Apart from small, statistically insignificant changes (at $\alpha = 0.10$), the only noticeable differences related to their reliance on outside consultants (which has increased) and the time devoted to in-house analyses (which has declined). The critical question is whether this lack of change represents general satisfaction with the results of PRA, or simply organizational inertia.

The second conclusion is that those corporations that have only more recently adopted PRA (the late adopters) seem to have adopted somewhat different organizational approaches, methodologies, and methods of integration, which are perhaps better suited to their own individual needs for PRA. This may indicate a willingness to adopt lessons learned from other practitioners that have been well-documented in the literature. However, it is surprising that, despite the need for close integration of the results of PRA into corporate decision making (also well-documented in the literature), these companies report a relatively low level of such integration. Perhaps the definitions and methods of measurement of such integration now current in the literature need to be revised. Alternatively, perhaps these corporations quite simply have not learned from the experience of others and are destined to suffer from the same mistakes.

RECOMMENDATIONS FOR FURTHER STUDY

Recommendations for further study are essentially threefold. First, more research is needed into why late adopters of PRA have tended to establish larger in-house capabilities, while continuing practitioners have scaled down on their PRA staff and rely more on outside consultants. What are the relative costs and benefits of each approach? Is the final outcome purely corporation-specific? Or are the late adopters simply destined to follow the trend of the earlier practitioners: will we see a retrenching of the PRA function in them as well?

Second, more research is required into how PRA is incorporated into corporate decision making. There is not discernible trend to better integrate PRA into decision making. Is it *possible* that PRA is better disseminated within the corporation and is being incorporated into decision making at a lower level?

And finally, further examination should be undertaken on the process followed in undertaking PRA. Earlier studies, suggesting a hierarchical approach, with firms moving along a spectrum from irregular, through regular to continuing analyses may be wrong. Perhaps there is an "ideal" process, relevant for each individual corporation, given its particular needs for PRA.

REFERENCES

Ansoff, H. I. (1975) "Managing Strategic Surprise Through Response to Weak Signals." *California Management Review*, 18, 21–35.

Blask, J. K. (1976) *A Survey of Country Evaluation Systems in Use,* Washington: The Export–Import Bank.

Brewer, T. L. (1981) "Political Risk Assessment for Foreign Direct Investment Decisions: Better Methods for Better Results," *Columbia Journal of World Business,* Spring, 5–12.

Brewer, T. L. (1983) "The Instability of Governments and the Instability of Controls on Funds Transferred by Multinational Enterprises: Implications for Political Risk Analysis," *Journal of International Business Studies,* Winter, 147–157.

Burton, F. N. and Inoue, H. (1983) "Country Risk Evaluation Methods: A Survey of Systems in Use," *The Banker,* January, 41–44.

Diffenbach, J. (1983) "Corporate Environmental Analysis in Large U.S. Corporations," *Long Range Planning,* 16, 107–116.

Euromoney, (1992) "How to Rate a State," September, 61–64.

Fahey, L. and King, W. R., "Environmental Scanning for Corporate Planning," *Business Horizons,* 20, 61–71.

Grosse, R. and Stack, J., (1984) "Noneconomic Risk Evaluation in Multinational Banks," *Management International Review,* 24, 41–59.

Hax, A. C. and Majluf, N. S., (1984) *Strategic Management: An Integrative Perspective,* Englewood Cliffs: Prentice Hall.

Hefernan, S. (1986) *Sovereign Risk Analysis,* London: Allen and Unwin.

Kahalas, H. (1971) "Long Range Planning—An Open Systems View," *Long Range Planning,* 10, 78–82.

Keegan, W. (1974) "Multinational Scanning: A Study of Information Sources Utilized by Headquarters Executives," *Administrative Science Quarterly,* September, 411–421.

Kefalas, A. and Schoderbeck, P., (1973) "Scanning the Business Environment—Some Empirical Results," *Decision Sciences,* 4, 63–74.

Kennedy, C. (1984) "The External Environment-Strategic Planning Interface: U.S. Multinational Corporate Practices in the 1980s" *Journal of International Business Studies,* Fall, 99–108.

Kobrin, S. J. (1981) "Political Assessments by International Firms: Models or Methodologies," *Journal of Policy Modelling,* 3, 251–270.

Kobrin, S. J., Basek, J., Blank, S., and Lapalombara, J. (1980) "The Assessment and Evaluation of Non-Economic Environments by American Firms: A Preliminary Report," *Journal of International Business Studies,* 11, 32–47.

Korth, C. M. (1981) "The Seat-of-the-Pants Analyst Needs Professional Help," *Euromoney,* May, 124–127.

Lenz, R. T. and Engledow, J. L. (1985) "Environmental Analysis Units and Strategic Decision-Making: A Field Study of Selected 'Leading Edge' Corporations," *Journal of Business Strategy,* Fall, 61–89.

Levinson, M. (1986) "Where's the Next Revolution?" *Across the Board,* January, 40–46.

Low, P. S., Stening, B. W., and Stening, K. (1989) "The International Political Risk Assessment Activities of Australian Corporations: A Pilot Study," *International Journal of Management,* 6, 341–349.

Mascarenhas, B. and Sand, O. (1985) "Country Risk Assessment Systems in Banks: Patterns and Performance," *Journal of International Business Studies,* Spring 19–35.

Neubauer, F. F. and Solomon, N. (1977) "A Managerial Approach to Environmental Assessment," *Long Range Planning,* 10, 13–20.

Porter, M. E. (1980) *Competitive Strategy.* New York: The Free Press.

Porter, M. E. (1986) *Competition in Global Industries,* Boston: Harvard Business School Press.

Preble, J. F., Rau, P. A., and Reichel, A. (1988) "The Environmental Scanning Practices of Multinational Firms—An Assessment," *International Journal of Management,* 6, 18–28.

Rodriguez, L. J. and King, W. K. (1977) "Competitive Information Systems," *Long Range Planning,* 10, 45–50.

Rogers, J. (1992) "Political Risk Analysis: State of the Art 1989," *Risk Management Review,* Spring, 4–7.

Segev, E. (1977) "How to Use Environmental Analysis in Strategy Making," *Management Review,* 66, 4–13.

Stapenhurst, F. (1988) *Political Risk Analysis in Canadian and U.S. Based Multinational Corporations,* unpublished dissertation, International Graduate School, St. Louis.

Stapenhurst, F. (1990) *Corporate Political Risk Analysis: A Comparison of U.S. and Canadian Approaches,* ASAC Conference, Whistler, British Columbia.

Stapenhurst, F. (1991) "Corporate Political Risk Analysis: A Comparison of U.S. and European Approaches," International Trade and Finance Conference, Marseille, 1507–1518.

Stapenhurst, F. (1992a) "The Rise and Fall of Political Risk Analysis?" *Management Decision,* 30, 54–57.

Stapenhurst, F. (1992b) *Political Risk Analysis Around the North Atlantic,* New York: St. Martin's Press.

Stoffels, J. (1983) "Environmental Scanning for Future Success," *Managerial Planning,* November/December, 4–12.

Stubbart, C. (1992) "Are Environmental Scanning Units Effective?" *Long Range Planning,* 15, 139–145.

Thomas, P. S. (1974) "Environmental Analysis for Corporate Planning," *Business Horizons,* 17, 27–38.

Thomas, P. S. (1980) "Environmental Scanning—The State of the Art," *Long Range Planning,* 13, 20–25.

Group of 7 Defines Policies About Telecommunications

Nathaniel C. Nash

Special to The New York Times

BRUSSELS, Feb. 26—The Governments of the seven largest industrialized countries, seeking to find common ground on the future of the global information network, today backed broad concepts of competition, deregulation, the protection of intellectual property rights and security of data.

The statement came at the end of a three-day meeting of officials of the so-called Group of Seven countries who were trying to prepare a common policy on how to approach the future of telecommunications.

"We made a giant step forward," Commerce Secretary Ronald H. Brown of the United States said at a news conference today, adding that the accord among the group "far exceeded the expectation going into the meeting."

Heading into the conference, some officials believed that France and Canada, worried that the giant American telecommunications and broadcast companies would overwhelm their industries, could set major obstacles to an accord that bases the future of telecommunications on free markets and free competition.

Yet the conference ended in remarkable harmony, as the nations managed to put aside their differences. Even the French, while stressing that governments would need to monitor world information systems, supported a joint statement that effectively embraces a vigorous free-market approach.

"A year ago the question was whether we could reach this kind of agreement," an American official said. "But even they seemed to realize that you have to open these markets. You can't afford to keep them closed."

The conference was sponsored by the European Commission, the executive body of the European Union. Commission officials have strongly supported the opening of telecommunications to competition. Most of its member states, though, including Germany and France, have maintained telecommunications monopolies and do not plan to deregulate telephone and data transmission until 1998. Of all the European Union member countries, only Britain and Sweden are considered to have open markets in telecommunications.

At the conference, the first held by the group to deal with what was called the global information infrastructure, German officials clearly supported open markets. "Private sector competition must be the driving force," Gunther Rexrodt, Germany's Economic Minister, said.

The joint statement, which addressed a number of concerns raised by France and Canada, called for "ensuring universal provision of and access to services," "promoting equality of opportunity to the citizen," "promoting diversity of content, including cultural and linguistic diversity," and "recognizing the necessity of worldwide cooperation with particular attention to less developed countries." The Group of Seven countries comprises the United States, Canada, Japan, Britain, France, Germany and Italy.

Martin Bangemann, the European Community's Commissioner for Industry, said that "we must insure that the information society is not divided up into the have's and have-not's."

Indeed, a tone for the conference was set on Friday night when at the opening dinner, Thabo Mbeki, South Africa's First Deputy President, told conferees, "The reality is that there are more telephone lines in Manhattan, New York, than in the sub-Sahara Africa," adding that half of the world's population had never made a telephone call.

Governments in Europe had earlier expressed fears about deregulation. For example, some were troubled that the privatization of their state-owned telephone monopolies would create significant unemployment in a

Europe that is already saddled with its highest unemployment since World War II, with 17 million people unemployed.

Dismantling those monopolies will probably mean considerable reduction in employment in those sectors, as well as fights with strong telecommunications unions. But conference attendees apparently agreed that the inflow of new investment, and the ensuing economic growth, would more than compensate for the short-term loss of jobs.

And the conference also concluded that open telecommunications markets would not eliminate cultural diversity, but promote it, as it makes access to broadcasting available to small cultural groups.

Some attendees said the meeting helped define a clear set of principles for the speedy opening of markets. Stuart E. Eizenstat, the United States Ambassador to the European Union, said he believed that as a result of the conference, some European countries would deregulate their telecommunications markets before the 1998 deadline set by European Commission regulations.

The conference also proposed 11 pilot projects as the first concrete step in advancing the information superhighway. The projects range from establishing links among libraries, museums and classrooms around the world to sharing information on the environment, natural disasters and disaster management to building compatible links between global information systems.

What GATT Means To Small Business

For many small firms that export, stronger protection for intellectual property will help even more than lower tariffs.

John S. DeMott

GATT is more than an acronym to Barbara Maxwell, marketing executive vice president and part owner of Synergy Software, in Reading, Pa. To her, the new accord under the General Agreement on Tariffs and Trade should help restore order to an international market where U.S. software creators alone lose about $2.5 billion a year when their works are pirated in other countries. "It's really crazy out there," she says.

Implementing legislation for the latest GATT pact, known as the Uruguay Round agreement after the South American country where the trade talks began in 1986, was approved by Congress late last year and signed into law by President Clinton, allowing GATT's provisions to apply to the U.S. beginning Jan. 1.

Although it will take a decade for all of GATT's features to become effective, for Maxwell and many other small-business owners, GATT's most important implication is already apparent. GATT will press its signatory countries, now at 124 but expected to be 144 before the end of the century, into mandating stronger legal protection for patents and other intellectual property.

This will make it possible for U.S. companies to sell abroad with less fear of losing the value of their intellectual and financial capital. Says Andre Schnabl, a partner with the Grant Thornton consulting firm in Atlanta: "GATT makes it easier for smaller manufacturers to protect patents in foreign markets. You'll be far more secure."

The intellectual-property protections included in the GATT agreement commit signatory countries to seven years of protection for trademarks, 20 years for patents, and up to 50 years for copyrights, including those for films, music, and software.

GATT effectively adds global muscle to U.S. efforts under trade legislation of 1974 and 1988 designed to stop pirating of U.S. patented products. These laws allow the U.S. trade representative to put countries on a "watch list" for purposes of restricting U.S. imports from those countries if, among other things, piracy is a problem.

Synergy, an 11-year-old software publisher, suffered because of the lack of intellectual-property protections several years ago. A college professor in Italy at the time purchased and then duplicated one of the company's programs. What had been one copy became 1,200. Says Maxwell: "Everyone on the whole campus was using VersaTerm"—a program allowing easier access to the Internet, the global web of computer networks.

Under Italian law at that time, Synergy had no way to recover any losses from the pirating of the software. "People told me to let it go. I didn't have a choice," says Maxwell. "Until two years ago, there was no law that had the word 'software' in it. The best you could do in an Italian court was try to include software in some very old copyright laws that protected magazines."

But now, under the new trade pact, Italy, as a GATT signatory, is required to provide legal protection for software and is, in fact, upgrading its protections under the agreement. Says Maxwell: "It will be much more reassuring for any smaller software developer to have things like GATT in place."

Businesses large and small almost anywhere in the stream of international commerce will be affected by GATT. It is the weightiest, most comprehensive trade agreement ever negotiated. Totaling 2,000 pages, it touches almost all industries, from agriculture to aviation and pharmaceuticals, allowing products and services to flow much more freely to foreign markets and from foreign markets to the U.S.

GATT reduces import tariffs for a wide range of products from mines, farms, mills, and factories. By early in the next century, GATT should cut prices to consumers on world markets by a total of about $744 billion, and in the U.S. by $122 billion, as tariffs drop an average of 40 percent, say its proponents.

Jim Lozelle, executive vice president of Tower Automotive, in Grand Rapids, Mich., a major supplier of frame and body components to Detroit's auto industry, defines the trade pact's meaning to him in its most elementary terms: "We should be able to buy cheaper [imported] steel."

John Howard, director of international policy and programs for the U.S. Chamber of Commerce, in Washington, D.C., says the new trade pact facilitates the exporting of products by smaller businesses, which generally can't afford to locate in the customer country, as many bigger businesses do. "Anything that levels the export playing field helps small business," he says.

Lower tariffs will benefit small firms even if they don't export. Many will profit indirectly by piggybacking on larger, exporting companies through supplier relationships. Says Michele Fratianni, a professor of business economics at Indiana University: "If you're typically a small company on the fringe of Detroit supplying GM, you'll grow as GM grows."

To settle disputes that arise under the pact, the agreement established the World Trade Organization (WTO), with headquarters in Geneva. The new organization will resolve disputes presented to it.

Details on how U.S. companies will gain access to the WTO are still being worked out. A small firm may decide to sue a patent-infringement violator, for example, but if there is no mechanism for suing in the violating country, the firm can file a complaint with the U.S. trade representative. The USTR would appeal the case on behalf of the small company or its trade association to the WTO. The process won't be easy, but at least there will be a structure for it under GATT. Says Geoffrey Kessler, a small-business consultant in Northridge, Calif.: "You'll need a lawyer, and you'll need money and time." What's most important to small businesses are GATT's Trade Related Aspects of Intellectual Property Rights, or TRIPS, which will be enforced by the WTO. TRIPS establishes minimum levels of protection for patents, trademarks, copyrights, industrial designs, and computer software. When there are violations under TRIPS, the WTO is authorized to act against violators.

The new system, says Kessler, is superior to the old GATT system in which rulings were recommended by panels of representatives from three nations (none involved in the dispute) and accepted or rejected by all GATT members. Countries accused of adverse trade practices effectively had to agree to panel rulings against them for the rulings to be legal.

The WTO's panels, supporters say, will be fairer because representatives of countries involved in certain trade disputes aren't permitted to be members of the panels deciding the disputes. And the WTO is the arbiter; it will resolve disputes. Says Lawrence Chimerine, managing director and chief economist of the Economic Strategy Institute, in Washington: "It should be easier to get complaints addressed and get relief."

Although GATT's requirements for intellectual-property protection and many of its tariff cuts take effect this year, other provisions will take a decade or so to phase in. But the thrust toward freer markets is helpful in and of itself.

Says Kevin Marsh of Marsh & McBirney, a manufacturing firm in Frederick, Md.: "Anytime you make a movement toward more free trade, I know we're going to benefit from it. GATT will only help our sales, period." Marsh and McBirney makes Flo-Totes—devices that measure underwater currents—and it attributes 27 percent of its $10 million in annual sales to exports. Kevin Marsh's father, company owner Larry Marsh, says the firm aims for exports to account for 40 percent of sales by 2000. "We had these plans before GATT," he says. "But it'll be easier with GATT."

The trade agreement, says ESI's Chimerine, should "create the best export environment for small U.S. companies that we've ever had." Larry Liebenow agrees. President and chief executive of Quaker Fabric Corp., in Fall River, Mass., Liebenow says, "We'll have far greater access to foreign markets." Quaker, which makes upholstery for the furniture industry and has sales of $180 million annually, plans to target India, Pakistan, and Brazil, in part because of GATT.

The new trade agreement will not put a stop to intellectual-property piracy immediately, however. China, for example, is not a signatory to GATT, though it wants to be. Its participation has been blocked because the U.S. and other nations believe it may not enforce protections against piracy required under the pact. As China opens up and becomes less directed by a central government, say watchers of that country, Beijing's efforts to control the situation become harder and harder to enforce.

Piracy involving such items as U.S.-made compact disks (CDs) and software is widespread in China. Software companies "cannot expect to export to China now because they know that the first copy they bring in there is probably going to be ripped off, and no one's ever going to buy a legitimate copy," says Steve Metalitz of the International Intellectual Property Alliance, in Washington.

Under pressure from U.S. trade officials, the Chinese government in January put together a 15-page "action plan" to combat theft of intellectual property. Unimpressed, the U.S. in February announced it would impose trade sanctions against some Chinese imports.

The problem with China is of concern not only to America's Microsoft Corp., which is waging a legal battle against theft in China of its popular computer software, but to "a lot of smaller companies wanting to do business in China," says an American official of a Hong Kong trading company.

Some small companies are skeptical about the trade agreement's protections. Vermont Castings of Bethel, Vt., is in good financial shape now, but only after spending $2 million to win a design-patent suit against a company in the Far East that it says stole designs for its famous wood-burning stoves and sold cheap knockoffs in the United States. Says Scott Searle, the firm's marketing director: "It almost bankrupted us."

The same Far Eastern company, Searle says, is again selling another version of a Vermont Castings stove in the United States. "I don't know whether GATT would protect us or not" in the new dispute, says Searle, but he intends to find out.

GATT will hurt some small businesses, particularly those that are labor-intensive. John Connaughton, economics professor at the University of North Carolina at Charlotte, believes lower tariffs under GATT will eliminate the portion of the U.S. clothing industry that depends on low-skilled labor. The industry is already withering under pressure from foreign producers. "Instead of taking 20 years for all those jobs to disappear," he says, "it will take 15 years."

Job losses because of GATT are expected to be minimal, however—about 180,000 U.S. workers, or two-tenths of 1 percent of the U.S. work force, according to Alan Deardorff and Robert Stern, economists at the University of Michigan.

On the other hand, GATT is expected to create 1.4 million jobs in competitive exporting industries by its 10th year, according to the U.S. trade representative. That should benefit many small businesses, which already are exporting more than ever and taking part in world trade expansion of 7 percent a year.

High-Tech Jobs All Over The Map

As training and experience in less developed countries rapidly improve, the West's workers may be left behind

If any megatrend kindles hopes of producing megajobs for skilled Americans, it is the coming of age of the Information Revolution. U.S. companies are already setting industry standards and pioneering virtually all of the key technologies. Plus, America possesses the wealth of creative talents needed to lead the coming wave of newfangled software, multimedia gadgetry, and ingenious programming. There will be jobs enough, it would seem, for anyone with a decent education.

But trek out to the laboratory of Kenneth Chou in a new business park on the outskirts of Beijing, and you begin to wonder. There, 30 artists, software engineers, and computer programmers at Chou's Bilingual Ed-ucational Computing Inc. are busily designing interactive CD-ROM programs, complete with voice and animation, for teaching English. Since 1991, Bilingual has sold 50,000 sets of its First Aid English multimedia lessons, now $55 apiece, to institutes from Japan to Germany.

In fact, practically anywhere you go in Asia these days, local workers can be found doing the same highly skilled tasks you would expect to find in Palo Alto, Boston, or Tokyo. At a Silicon Graphics Inc. joint venture in Bangalore, India, software designers earning $300 a month are developing programs to produce three-dimensional images for diagnosing brain disorders. In a sleek industrial park in Singapore, engineers design future generations of personal digital assistants for Hewlett-Packard Co. In Taiwan, Hong Kong, and South China, research and development teams are at work on multimedia gizmos ranging from digital answering machines to interactive computers for children.

NEW WORLD ORDER. The message is that anybody who still thinks the only competitive edge of developing countries is cheap, unskilled labor has a lot of catching up to do. One of the less-heralded developments in the emergence of a global economy is that there is an increasingly better balance of skills in the world. The worldwide shift to market economies, steady improvements in education, and decades of over-

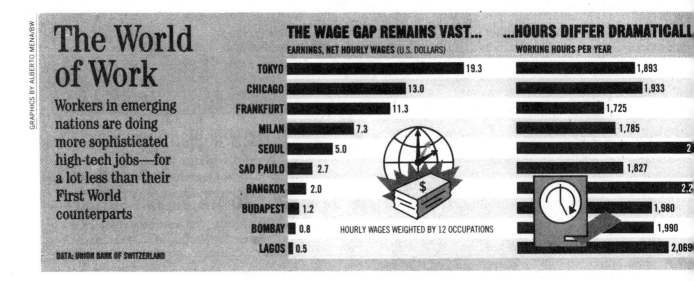

The World of Work

Workers in emerging nations are doing more sophisticated high-tech jobs—for a lot less than their First World counterparts

DATA: UNION BANK OF SWITZERLAND

GRAPHICS BY ALBERTO MENA/BW

THE WAGE GAP REMAINS VAST...
EARNINGS, NET HOURLY WAGES (U.S. DOLLARS)

TOKYO	19.3
CHICAGO	13.0
FRANKFURT	11.3
MILAN	7.3
SEOUL	5.0
SAO PAULO	2.7
BANGKOK	2.0
BUDAPEST	1.2
BOMBAY	0.8
LAGOS	0.5

HOURLY WAGES WEIGHTED BY 12 OCCUPATIONS

...HOURS DIFFER DRAMATICALL
WORKING HOURS PER YEAR

	1,893
	1,933
	1,725
	1,785
	2
	1,827
	2,2
	1,980
	1,990
	2,069

seas training by multinationals are all producing a global workforce in fields ranging from product development to finance and architecture that is capable of performing tasks once reserved for white-collar workers in the West.

What's more, dizzying advances in telecommunications are making these workers more accessible than ever. As a result, just as Westerners learned in the 1970s and 1980s that manufacturing could be moved virtually anywhere, today it is getting easier to shift knowledge-based labor as well.

Conventional notions of comparative advantage are getting blurred in the process. In electronics, cities such as Taipei, Edinburgh, Singapore, and Penang (Malaysia), which are far away from the end-user and technological breakthroughs, already have emerged as global product-development hubs.

Service providers, too, can now spread across the globe. Citibank taps local skills in India, Hong Kong, Australia, and Singapore to manage data and develop products for its global financial services. Houston-based M. W. Kellogg Co., farms out detailed architectural-engineering work for power and chemical plants it builds around the world to a partner in Mexico. And everyone from law firms to U.S. nonprofit groups cuts costs in managing and analyzing documents by hiring "outsourcers" such as International Data Solutions Inc. in Herndon, Va.,

which employs thousands of workers in the Philippines.

What makes Third World brainpower so attractive is price (charts). A good computer circuit-board designer in California, for example, can pull down $60,000 to $100,000 a year. Taiwan is glutted with equally qualified engineers earning around $25,000. In India or China, you can get top-level talent, probably with a PhD, for less than $10,000.

TEDIOUS TASKS. Where the big savings can come is in the "back end" of product development—the painstaking work of turning a conceptual design into blueprints, computer code, or working models and in testing the final product. Take Bilingual's CD-ROMS. With wages ranging from $75 a month for a Chinese keypunch operator to $400 for a good artist, Bilingual can produce a CD-ROM product for anywhere from a quarter to one-tenth of the cost in the U.S. In a business as tough as CD-ROMS, where the few titles that succeed can have a shelf life of less than a year, keeping costs under control is critical.

It doesn't matter that few of the staff speak English. Bilingual writes the scripts, the most creative part, in Taiwan. The rest of the work, from animation to voice-over recording, is done on the mainland. "When you get down to it," says Chou, "about 80% of the labor in producing software is very tedious."

Since marketing and creativity will always be in hot demand, graduates of

Stanford University business school or Massachusetts Institute of Technology probably needn't worry. Trouble is, the back end happens to be where millions of Americans are employed. And they're well-paying jobs: software designers, bookkeepers, mechanical engineers, draftsmen, librarians. Most require a bachelor's degree or at least a few years in a polytechnic institute. Yet in theory, at least, none of these jobs can be regarded as secure from foreign competition. "Just as with the move of manufacturing overseas, you're going to see an increasing flux of technical jobs out of the U.S.," predicts Intel Corp. Chief Operating Officer Craig R. Barrett. "We don't have any protected domains anymore."

NEW VIEW. Policymakers have only begun to ponder what all this means for American, European, and even Japanese white-collar workers. Until recently, it seemed the impact would be minimal. Groups such as the National Science Foundation have been warning that as the Digital Age makes industries technology-intensive, there will be an acute shortage of technicians in the West. Skilled workers displaced by outsourcing would simply move on to higher value-added sectors.

But this view is being challenged. In a jarring keynote speech to the annual convention of the Institute of Electrical & Electronics Engineers (IEEE) in September, Edith Holleman, counsel to the House Science, Space & Technology Committee, warned

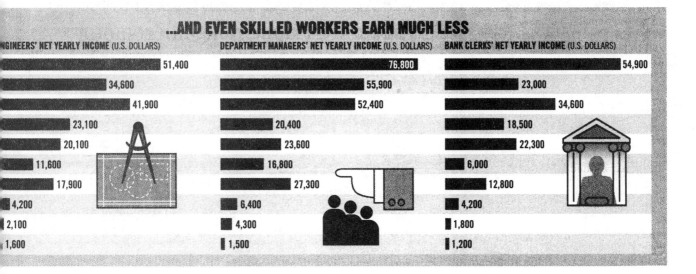

...AND EVEN SKILLED WORKERS EARN MUCH LESS

ENGINEERS' NET YEARLY INCOME (U.S. DOLLARS)	DEPARTMENT MANAGERS' NET YEARLY INCOME (U.S. DOLLARS)	BANK CLERKS' NET YEARLY INCOME (U.S. DOLLARS)
51,400	76,800	54,900
34,600	55,900	23,000
41,900	52,400	34,600
23,100	20,400	18,500
20,100	23,600	22,300
11,600	16,800	6,000
17,900	27,300	12,800
4,200	6,400	4,200
2,100	4,300	1,800
1,600	1,500	1,200

that exciting new high-tech jobs "are not reserved for you in the First World." What's more, she said, high-tech breakthroughs in the U.S. "cannot be counted on to spin off into domestic manufacturing facilities providing employment for many engineers and skilled workers."

Consider what already has happened to the PC motherboard, the circuit card loaded with chips that runs every computer. Five years ago, most motherboards—regarded as the guts of a PC—were produced in-house by U.S. computer makers. Today, some 60% are subcontracted to Taiwanese companies and their army of 150,000 information-technology engineers. And now, the Taiwanese are becoming a major force in customized computer-chip design and local-area networks. Little wonder, it would seem, that unemployment among U.S. electrical engineers hit a record 5.9% this summer, according to the IEEE, and the situation is expected to get worse.

Still, a host of factors suggests that the outflow of skilled work to cheap Third World havens is only a temporary phenomenon. For one, the wage gap is bound to close eventually, as technicians and engineers in the developing world command more. Also, the Information Super-highway is a two-way street, allowing U.S. and European engineers to compete for work in Asia as well as the reverse. Moreover, experts fear that education systems in Thailand, Malaysia, Indonesia, and Mexico, among others, are not producing enough skilled workers for those nations to guarantee advancement up the industrial ladder.

ROBO-TECH What's more, as factories in the Third World turn to state-of-the-art automation to stay competitive with domestic rivals and meet international quality standards, that automation could threaten Third World job growth. Meanwhile, technological leaps in areas such as text and voice recognition and computer-aided design software that reduce the time-consuming code-writing process will wipe out jobs in service industries.

→ *"Today, your location doesn't matter," says a Hong Kong micromotor maker, "it's turnaround time"*

But for now, the ground is shaking under skilled workers as Western companies take advantage of big wage disparities. Anyone who has witnessed the exceptional performances of Chinese, Indian, and Vietnamese emigrés in U.S. schools and labs knows that developing countries are loaded with talent. The rapid growth of Asia's economies means they can now apply their skills at home.

A wild card in the global skills game is telecommunications. Consider Hong Kong's Johnson Electric Holdings Ltd., a $195 million producer of micromotors that power hair dryers, blenders, and auto features such as door locks, windshield wipers, and automatic windows. With factories in South China and an R&D base in a Hong Kong industrial park, Johnson is thousands of miles away from a leading auto maker.

This hasn't stopped the company from virtually cornering the market for the electric gizmos it makes for Detroit's Big Three. "My customer is right here," says Managing Director Patrick Wang Shui Chung, pointing to a videoconferencing unit in the midst of hundreds of engineers. For two hours each morning, design teams "meet" face-to-face with their customers in the U.S. and Europe. Concepts are transmitted from R&D centers in North America and Europe to Hong Kong, where 200 engineers on a network of workstations develop the motors using CAD/CAM software.

Their specifications are programmed directly into Hong Kong production lines. The process is so streamlined that Johnson can take a concept and deliver a prototype to the U.S. in six weeks. To cut that time even further, the company is investing in more advanced telecommunications to link its 9,000-worker operations in China. "Today, your location doesn't matter," says Wang. "It's turnaround time. I want to be the fastest gun in the world."

KNOWHOW. The pioneers in bringing foreign technicians into the global workforce are multinationals such as Motorola, Hewlett-Packard, and Philips Electronics. Originally, they set up plants in Asia chiefly for cheap labor. But many of these assembly shops have gathered so much know-how that they now do critical design- and engineering tasks.

A good example is Motorola Inc. Its paging-device plant in Singapore boasts 75 local engineers and a new $35 million building dubbed the Motorola Innovation Center. There, the Scriptor pager was developed almost entirely by Singaporean industrial designers using Singaporean software.

Hewlett-Packard has gone even further. It encourages each of its manufacturing sites around the world to become the global base of its product. Penang, Malaysia, has become a global center for many components used in HP's microwave products and is taking over responsibility for computer hard-disk drives from Palo Alto. And in Singapore, a plant HP opened in 1970 to assemble keyboards is now the global R&D and production center for its line of portable ink-jet printers. It is also the base for all handheld devices, such as personal digital assistants and calculators.

Intensive training by multinationals is another reason that skills are rising rapidly. A key training locale is the Penang Skills Development Center, a 360-student polytechnic institute funded by 57 foreign companies and the government for local high school and university graduates. Intel donated a $140,000 microprocessor lab. A 20,000-square-foot "team building park" for leadership training and a clean room for vacuum technology came courtesy of Seagate Technology Inc., which has a big hard-disk plant nearby. Motorola Inc. kicked in $320,000 for PC software training and a bachelor-of-science program.

India, China, and Russia are closely watching the successes of Malaysia and Singapore. The potential of all three is staggering given the heavy emphasis their schools place on math and basic science. In these countries, notes Intel's Barrett: "I see a ton of people who are technically well-educated as people in the U.S."

India has the second-largest pool of English-speaking scientific talent in the world, after the U.S. This includes 100,000 software engineers and technicians and hundreds of companies, many locally owned, that supply software to Western customers. The number of engineers could double by the end of the decade. And a monthly salary of $800 for an engineer with five years' experience is enough to place a worker squarely in India's upper-middle class.

Central Europe also is peppered with brilliant scientists rapidly being discovered and unleashed. The most promising spots as production bases by 2020, according to a study of 404 European locations last year by Cologne-based market researcher Empirica, are Bratislava (in Slovakia), Western Bohemia (in the Czech Republic), Györ-Sopron (Hungary), and Poznan (Poland).

Germany's Robert Bosch has been making engine parts in the Czech Republic since last year. "Czech engineers have the technical competence we require," says Heinz G. Grewe, Bosch's head of management systems for gasoline engines. Despite added startup and training costs, industry analysts say auto-parts makers can still save 30% by outsourcing to Central Europe. Farther east, in Russia, most multinationals have been slow to exploit the huge pool of technologists who worked in the former Soviet Union's defense industries. But pioneers such as Sun Microsystems Inc. and ABB Asea Brown Boveri (Holdings) Ltd., which already employ thousands of Russians, are bullish, particularly

Training of Third World Workers Is Improving

PERCENT OF AGE ► GROUP ENROLLED IN EDUCATION (Weighted Average)	SECONDARY (12–17 YEARS)		TERTIARY (20–24 YEARS)	
	1970	1991	1970	1991
LOW- AND MIDDLE-INCOME ECONOMIES	24	45	6	8
HIGH INCOME	31	52	12	17

DATA: WORLD DEVELOPMENT REPORT, 1991, 1994

about the hard-driving younger generation that is eager to get rich.

WELL-STOCKED WATERS. The deepest pool of untapped skills is in China. Dataquest Inc., the research firm, estimates that there are at least 350,000 information-technology engineers in Chinese research institutes, state companies and universities. The average salary: about $105 a month. And with the Chinese government placing electronics, telecommunications, and software industries high on its list of priorities, colleges across the country are preparing to train hundreds of thousands more.

Multinationals are fishing in these well-stocked waters. Northern Telecom Ltd. just opened a lab at the 10,500-student Beijing University of Posts & Telecommunications that will soon employ 250 engineers. NT will work with faculty and students on cellular phones, multimedia-transmission devices, and software. In the northern city of Tianjin, Motorola will have 3,000 workers making semiconductors and telecom equipment by yearend. Meanwhile, AT&T, which is just getting started in China, plans to link up the telecom plants it has scattered across the country.

For now, these facilities will focus on the enormous telecom needs of China. But it's only a matter of time before Chinese engineers start playing key R&D roles in products sold globally. "All of our joint ventures can be technical centers in their businesses," says AT&T China Inc. Human Resources Director Albert Siu. "I've never found people more open to learning. They soak up everything."

Many of the lessons companies are learning in high tech can also be applied to the West's other big job generator: services. There, the potential of offshore skilled labor is just beginning to be tapped. For more than a decade, companies such as American Airlines Inc. and Citicorp have been loading tons of ticket stubs, credit-card receipts, and insurance forms onto planes headed for places such as the Dominican Republic or the Philippines, home of low-paid keypunch operators.

Many experts think high-end services can also be farmed out to overseas workers. Why not let specially trained Filipino accountants do much of the grunt work in preparing tax returns for multinationals? Or how about outsourcing the legal research for expensive product-liability cases? Using CD-ROM libraries, paralegals in India could churn out the mountain of writs and affidavits for such cases at a deep discount. Anupam P. Puri, managing director of McKinsey & Co.'s Bombay office, says such task transfers are long overdue. "Most of our multinational clients are still very behind in seeing how they can redistribute service work around the world," he says.

→ *China has at least 350,000 information-technology engineers in schools, state companies, and institutes. Average salary: $105 a month*

Regulatory hurdles remain, of course. But the technological barriers are falling fast. International Data Solutions, for example, scans case and client files for U.S. law firms and transmits them in digital form via satellite to the Philippines. There, workers organize and index the documents so they can be readily retrieved by a computer network in the U.S. International Data employs two full-timers in Virginia—and up to 3,000 Filipinas. "With the Information Superhighway revolution, this trend is accelerating dramatically," says International Data President Kenneth R. Short. "It really doesn't matter where the work is done as long as quality, price, and service are right."

BROADER VIEW. In the construction industry, Houston's M. R. Kellogg has teamed up with Mexico Bufete Industrial on contracts to build petro-chemical-refining systems worldwide. After developing conceptual drawings on a computer, Kellogg transmits them to Bufete, on which Kellogg owns 21%. The Mexicans turn the drawings into detailed blueprints. The arrangement, says Kellogg Manager Robert Salazar,

"makes us competitive all over the world."

While this flexibility sounds great for corporations, it could be traumatic for professionals who are not well-equipped for a global economy. As gaps between experience levels and wages narrow around the world, skilled workers will compete on a more equal footing. To profit from the emerging trends, workers will require broader training than is now provided by most education systems—in both the East and the West.

Rather than focus on one discipline, for example, professional workers will need to understand the economics and technologies that are revolutionizing their industries. In the banking world, "the pure technologist is already dead,"

says George P. DiNardo, Singapore-based chief technology officer for Citibank's Asian consumer business. "And so is the pure businessperson."

In electronics and telecommunications, engineers discarded by Corporate America are taking advantage of cheaper access to data and video networks by forming their own design houses for Asian manufacturers. In many other fields, professionals may have to similarly redefine their jobs in order to prosper from the globalization of work rather than be at its mercy.

By Pete Engardio in Hong Kong, with Rob Hof in San Francisco, Elisabeth Malkin in Mexico City, Neil Gross in New York, and Karen Lowry Miller in Bonn

Role of Labor, Environmental, and Human Rights Groups in Trade: Is There a New Protectionist Cabal?

Robert F. Housman

Robert F. Housman is a Senior Attorney, Center for International Environmental Law, and Adjunct Professor of Law, The American University's Washington College of Law. He is also Adjunct Professor of Global Affairs in the Washington Program of Syracuse University's Maxwell School of Citizenship and Public Relations.

The dialogue of trade liberalization is dominated by the language of economics. In this language it is tempting, albeit somewhat contorted, to dismiss: environmental harms as mere externalities; efforts to ensure that hard working Americans have a future beyond the employment line as attempts to redistribute wealth; and laws to provide basic labor, environmental, or human rights protections as impingements on the ability of companies to reallocate activities across national borders. Against this semantic backdrop it is easy to label efforts to bring environmental, labor, and human rights concerns into trade policies as neosocial protectionism (Steil, 1994).

Why all this concern about labels and linguistics? The reason why labels and linguistics are so important here is because they tend to focus public and legislative attention on images and prevent further analyses as to the truths or fictions that may underlie these images. Because the debate over trade and other macroeconomic policies are so complex, digestible images govern a debate, that is in turn dominated by name calling.[1] As a whole, these ad hominem attacks defeat the evolution of sound policies. As a result, regardless of one's views on these issues, the flippant use of labels should give grounds for concern.

Thus, the question must be asked: to what extent are these labels accurate? Answering this question requires more than a mere finding that various elements of the environmental, labor, or human rights trade agenda have some element of protectionistic sounding policy; even the most trade oriented industries argue at times for policies that are downright protectionist (Bovard, 1991).[2] The answer requires one to determine whether there is a neosocial protectionist cabal, or in the words of the Economist a "sinister alliance," that seeks to undermine trade liberalization.

This article concludes that generally no such cabal exists. The social trade agenda does not generally require protectionist policy responses. To the extent that protectionism creeps into this agenda, it does so because the core concerns of these social interests are not properly weighed in the formulation of trade policies, requiring these interests to resort to second-best, and at times protectionist responses.

To determine if a protectionist cabal exists it is first necessary to determine what we mean when we say "free trade" and protectionism. In reality free trade is a theory of international economic relations that is, in turn, built largely upon Ricardo's theory of comparative advantage. Comparative advantage theory, as it is now typically discussed, provides that if labor and capital are mobile, and there are no restrictions on international trade, then each nation will focus on producing those goods and services in which they have a comparative advantage over their trading partners (Jackson; Daniel, unpub.)[3] This dynamic increases overall global economic efficiency, and in turn welfare—in theory. Ricardo's comparative advantage theory also focused exclusively on natural, as opposed to man-made, comparative advantages, such as climatic, geographic, and meteorological conditions.

This is all just theory because in reality almost all, if not all, trade is managed in some way (Diamond, 1993). Thus, while it is vogue to be pro free trade, what we really are talking about is not free trade, but liberalized trade, or economic relations that more closely approximate the theory of free trade.

One more caveat on the theory of free trade is that just as with every other political economic theory, while it may function perfectly on paper it does not necessarily function with equal precision in practice. For example, free trade theory

The author wishes to thank John Audley and Lance Compa for their invaluable guidance and review, Brian Chenowith for his research assistance, and Art Farrance for his editorial assistance. Any remaining errors, however, are solely the author's.

depends upon the mobility of labor. However, in the real world there are restrictions on immigration that prevent the unfettered movement of persons across national borders. The result is that when wages, or for that matter the right of free association, are depressed in one country, labor cannot simply pick up and leave until those conditions are corrected and a labor equilibrium is attained. The effect of this dynamic can be seen every day on the United States-Mexico border, where despite the promises of free trade benefits, literally hundreds of Mexican workers still attempt to illegally enter the United States in search of better lives.

As a result of this discrepancy between free trade theory and liberal trade reality, liberalized trade in goods and investment, without liberalized movement of labor, can put downward pressure on labor wages, benefits, working conditions, and rights in nations that exceed the levels of their trading partners. For example, at one US sponsored trade show representatives of Honduras, El Salvador, and Guatemala were recorded by a hidden camera in a minimum wage bidding war, beginning at $0.90 and falling to $0.57 per hour, to lure industry from the United States (Compa). Unfortunately for labor, unlike industry, it could not respond by moving to the United States or some other nation where conditions were more favorable to its interests; it was captive (Collingsworth). Thus, while liberalized trade provides the working man with cheaper bread, if the working man no longer has a job or a decent wage, cheaper yet now unaffordable bread is of little solace.

This bread example also highlights another area where free trade theory falls prey to the viciousness of reality: the "rising tide" theory. This theory provides that because trade creates greater efficiencies it brings about greater overall wealth in all our societies. This aspect of theory may in fact be true. However, the theory goes on to argue that just as a rising tide lifts all boats, free trade driven wealth allows for more environmental protection, higher wages, and better working conditions—in short the trickle down economics answer to social ills now displayed at the international market level. Here the theory simply does not work. As with all trickle down theories, there is nothing to guarantee that any new wealth will, in fact, trickle down. In reality, the gains of trickle down economics usually are captured at the upper echelons of society and are never realized at the lower levels.[4]

Moreover, even if some of this wealth were to trickle down there is no viable way to ensure that it is allocated to first repairing any trade liberalization caused harms. For example, there is no way, shy of a politically unrealistic broad-based consumption tax, to ensure that trade gains will be captured and put to cleaning up the air or water fouled in building the products that were traded. Similarly, while worker A, who is a high technology sector engineer, may be able to obtain a better position here in the United States because of NAFTA, worker B, who is a 60 year old riveter on an assembly line in Detroit, may lose his job and never be able to find a replacement. If the engineer obtains a job that pays her more than the lost salary of the riveter our overall economy shows growth; but our individual economies, and perhaps our unemployment rolls, may not.[5]

Next it is important to define what is meant by the term protectionism. Because there is no precise definition of what

constitutes protectionism,[6] this task is more difficult than one might expect. Defining protectionism is a lot like McCarthy defining communism; protectionism is anything that the prevailing free trade powers say it is. For example, some say it would be protectionist to apply our environmental standards to products made in other countries that fail to meet US production standards (Hall, 1994). Yet many of these same people see no problem in doing precisely the same thing with our standards on antitrust or intellectual property (Committee for Economic Development, 1991). Why the difference? All three areas—environment, antitrust, and intellectual property—regulate the conditions related to the production of a product. None of the three fundamentally alter the product in question. Lamentably, a pilfered Mutant Ninja Turtles doll is still a Mutant Ninja Turtles doll.[7]

To eliminate the circularity of present definitions of protectionism, allow me to use the following imperfect working definition: protectionism, in the trade context, is the use of policies that are intended to benefit domestic or local products or services by eliminating or offsetting the legitimate comparative advantages of foreign producers and service providers, at the expense of the producers or providers of like foreign products or services, solely because the protected products or services are domestic or local in origin (Regan, 1986).

With these definitional clarifications in hand, the position of environmental, labor, and human rights groups in the NAFTA debate provide an appropriate starting point for determining whether these groups are individually inherently protectionist and alliances between these groups are protectionist in nature.

ENVIRONMENTAL CONCERNS IN NAFTA

Before proceeding to generalize about the concerns of environmental groups[8] during the writing of NAFTA, it is important to note that there was no standard environmental position at that time. Each environmental group adopted its own position based upon its own priorities and concerns. Ultimately, some US environmental groups supported the agreement, some groups took no official position on the agreement, and some vehemently opposed it.[9] That said, in general the concerns of these groups were fairly uniform; what differed was their approach to these concerns.

First and foremost, environmental groups were concerned that, absent effective environmental laws and enforcement of these laws in all three NAFTA parties, NAFTA-driven economic growth would endanger human health and environmental security (Audley, 1993; Pastor, 1993). Why the concern? Simple, look at the United States-Mexico border. Until the NAFTA debate, environmental, health, and safety law and law enforcement were virtually nonexistent in the border region. As a result the American Medical Association has described the border region as "a virtual cesspool and a breeding ground for infectious disease." In Brownsville, Texas, which sits directly across the border from the heavily industrialized and overpolluted Mexican city of Matamoros, the rate of anencephaly (babies born with incomplete or nonexistent brains) is over five times the national average. Such an elevated rate defies genetic explanations, and can only be accounted for by some form of environmental exposure (*LA Times,* 1992). To economists these environmental threats are externalities; to the people who live on the border they are realities.

From the beginning of the NAFTA discussion, Mexico had developed a system of environmental law that was largely similar to that of the United States in its stringency. However, to date Mexican environmental law enforcement has not fully developed. Environmentalists therefore placed a great deal of emphasis on the need to develop incentives and checks to ensure that enforcement continued to improve.

In response to this concern environmentalists sought a mechanism in the treaty or in a parallel agreement that would encourage each NAFTA party to fully implement their laws. This need was addressed by the Clinton administration through the development of the environmental supplemental agreement that provides that a party's persistent pattern of the failure to enforce its environmental laws can subject the party to first a fine, and then if the fine is not paid a trade sanction.[10]

Second, environmental groups were concerned that the rules provided for under the NAFTA agreement might be used to undercut high US environmental, health, and safety provisions (Audley, 1993; Pastor, 1993). The reason for this concern can be seen in the rash of trade cases that have been filed or threatened over the course of the past few years to environmental, health, and safety measures (Housman and Orbuch, 1993). While the more radical proponents of free trade would argue that these challenges are merely efforts to do away with nontariff trade barriers, it is important to remember that in the United States each of these nontariff trade barriers is a democratically enacted safeguard against some threat; it is, for example, a law that ensures your food is not tainted with pesticides, or your baby's clothes are flame retardant.

The response of environmentalists here was to seek changes or understanding, as to the standards provisions of the NAFTA (the rules used to judge whether laws are illegitimate trade barriers). During the Bush presidency, in the primary negotiations on the treaty, changes were in fact made to the standards provisions. Environmentalists generally did not believe that these changes went far enough and they sought further assurances from the Clinton administration, Mexico, and Canada. Mexico and Canada, however, refused to either directly or indirectly renegotiate these provisions and so environmental groups that supported the NAFTA had to settle for promises in the implementing legislation's nonbinding Statement of Administrative Action.

Ironically, the US NAFTA implementing legislation validates the fears of environmental groups that NAFTA may diminish our protections. The implementing bill substantially curtails the food safety inspection procedures that are applied to Mexican commodities entering the United States.

Third, environmental groups were concerned that without proper safeguards Mexico might become a "pollution haven" where "dirty" industries would locate to avoid high US environmental regulations. (This argument has been called the "competitiveness argument." [Audley, 1993; Pastor, 1993]) The pollution haven problem was of concern because the United States and Mexico are mutually dependent on fragile shared natural resources that are extremely susceptible to transboundary threats. The pollution haven issue also posed another threat in that if environmental protections were seen as jeopardizing jobs or investments in the United States, then there would be pressures to harmonize our protections downward to the lowest common denominator.

Critics of the pollution haven theory have argued that no such dynamic exists. They argue that the limited empirical data points to the fact that environmental regulatory costs on average are too low to play a role in industrial sitting or investment decisions (Low). These critics, however, miss several key points. Environmental costs are not static; the more aggressively we seek to deal with our problems the more likely they are to increase (Tobey, 1993). Further, dealing with averages means that the costs at the high end (the most dangerous, heavily regulated industries like chemical plants) balance those at the low end (like accounting firms). Lost amid these theoretical calculations is the fact that at the high end environmental costs have already caused US industries to relocate to Mexico. For example, a 1991 GAO study found that almost the entire California furniture finishing industry has relocated to Mexico to avoid the costs of complying with the 1990 Clean Air Act (GAO, 1991).

Last, and most importantly, in political terms the reality of whether environmental costs are substantial enough to play a role in a company's decision making is, to a large degree, irrelevant. What matters here are perceptions. In political fora companies continue to successfully use the "high" costs of environmental protections before Congress, regulator, and the public as a means of lowering their cost and increasing their profits. For example, where were all these economists who now argue that environmental costs make little or no difference during the Quayle Competitiveness Policy Council's assault on US environmental laws? Where are they now during the Congressional debate over the competitiveness aspects of our environmental laws?

To prevent the development of pollution havens, environmentalists sought provisions in the NAFTA investment section that would make the waiver of environmental laws to encourage investments an actionable violation of the treaty's investment chapter. The response of the parties was to include a provision prohibiting such waivers; however, this provision does not make such violations subject to dispute resolution or sanctions. In addition, the environmental supplemental agreement's dispute provisions are also seen as playing a role in preventing the development of pollution havens.

Do these concerns amount to protectionism? None of the environmental concerns enunciated above focused on benefitting American, Mexican, or Canadian products because they were local or domestic in origin. The environmental concerns during the NAFTA were not about benefitting domestic producers; they were about preserving environmental protections and conserving resources.

Further, for the NAFTA environmental concerns to be protectionist in nature one must assume that differences in environmental regulatory regimes, a man-made phenomenon, are a legitimate comparative advantage. In other words, it must be acceptable, as Larry Summers has argued, that certain developing countries are "under-polluted" and that it is more efficient to pollute in these countries because the value of life, as calculated from expected lifetime wages, is lower than in developed nations (Kamen, 1993; Power, 1993). Presumably, the same would hold true for overpopulated countries where there are more people that could be sacrificed to environmental harms? Unless one agrees that there should be no ethical constraints on economic behaviors, and that the value of life is determined solely by economic pricing, there can be no legitimate comparative advantage founded upon a nation's differential assimilative capacity for poison or other environmental demise.

Moreover, in deciding upon the protectionist motives of environmental groups it is important to remember that very few environmental groups willingly came to argue against the treaty. Although the environmental verdict on the NAFTA was ultimately split, the vast majority of even those environmental groups that came out against the treaty had worked feverishly and in good faith with the Clinton administration to develop a NAFTA that they could support. It is ironic that while many try to paint environmentalists as protectionist, there were times during the NAFTA debate, when, in the face of business community indifference, it appeared that the only groups that were actually vocal in their support for the agreement were the pro-NAFTA environmental organizations; an odd stance indeed for protectionists.

LABOR'S CONCERNS IN NAFTA

Although labor groups[11] were more united than environmental groups in their NAFTA positions, there was no uniform labor position on NAFTA. Here again, this analysis relies upon issues of widespread concern throughout the labor groups.

Labor's principle concern with the NAFTA was the prospect of large scale job loss from industrial relocation and investment flight from the United States to Mexico. Taken as a whole, the overall regulatory costs associated with doing business (e.g., environmental, health, safety, equal employment, and anti-discrimination, etc.) clearly favor industrial decisions to invest or site facilities in Mexico over the United States (*Journal of Applied Corporate Finance*). Labor feared that when these costs were coupled with higher US wages the result would be US job losses from NAFTA that could exceed 550,000 (Faux and Lee, 1992, 1993).

Labor's concerns were based on figures that did provide grounds for caution, if not outright concern. In 1988, the average wage for a Mexican *maquiladora* factory worker was $0.98 in low skill jobs, and $1.99 in high skill jobs. The average hourly manufacturing wage for US workers in 1988 was $13.85, with an average hourly wage of $6.20 in sectors comparable to those in the maquiladora plants (CRS, 1991). These figures proved most unsettling because the labor sectors most vulnerable to NAFTA displacement had already seen dramatic employment losses (OTA, 1991). For example, the displacement rate for durable goods manufacturing from 1979 to 1989 was 4.1

percent, 4.8 percent in autos and autos parts, and 4.9 percent in the apparel industry (OTA, 1992).

Proponents of the NAFTA countered that large scale NAFTA-driven employment displacement was unlikely to occur. In fact, government figures as well as those of economists like Gary Hufbauer and Jeffrey Schott, argued that NAFTA's overall impact on US jobs would be minimal,[12] somewhere on the order 130,000–175,000 jobs created (USITC, 1991; Hufbauer and Schott, 1992, 1993).[13] The simple fact is that it is still too soon to tell which predictions will prove accurate over the long run.

Labor, like environmentalists, also feared that various provisions of the agreement could be invoked to undercut a wide range of US labor, environmental, health, and safety laws (Collingsworth). Here labor had reason for their concern. Even before the formal agreement was signed, the Bush administration had agreed in a precursor NAFTA preparatory agreement to eliminate the rights of US states to impose licensing requirements on Mexican truck drivers entering the United States. By eliminating these standards the federal government usurped the traditional powers of the states, diminished the highway protections states can guarantee travelers on their byways, and provided Mexican origin drivers with a competitive advantage over US drivers who continue to be regulated by the several states they drive in (Housman and Orbuch, 1993).

Labor also expressed a corollary concern that the NAFTA would create competitive pressure to lower high US labor, worker health and safety, and environmental standards (Collingsworth). The most troubling aspect of downward harmonization was in the area of wages. Labor feared that industries could use the threat of NAFTA-abetted mobility to force bidding wars between the labor markets of the three parties for jobs (Clinton, 1992). Advertisements like the one run by the Mexican state of Yucatan promoting wages as low as $1 per hour gave credence to these concerns.

Labor's anxieties about downward harmonization were also driven in great measure by the lack of effective labor rights enforcement in Mexico. Although Mexico's laws provide most of the basic labor rights, the Mexican government has failed to enforce these laws (Hollings). Not only has the Mexican government failed to enforce its labor laws, but historically—with much debate over whether to measure history in years, hours, or minutes elapsed—it has engaged in a persistent campaign of repression against the labor movement (Cornelius).

As with the environment, the Clinton administration attempted to address labor's concerns with the agreement by negotiating a supplemental agreement on labor (Clinton). However, because labor's concerns with the NAFTA stemmed directly from one of the core goals of the NAFTA, providing US business with access to cheap labor, and because the Clinton administration had been backed into a no renegotiation corner by the Canadians and the Mexicans, the supplemental agreement could not address the heart of labor's fears. This dynamic secured US labor's opposition to NAFTA. Had NAFTA incorporated effective labor and wage standards into the agreement, labor conceivably might have been able to support the agreement. The parties, however, balked at this approach arguing sovereignty concerns; NAFTA-based standards would interfere with each parties' sovereign right to set their own standards. Such sovereignty protestations notwithstanding, the agreement did make wholesale changes to Mexico's intellectual property protections, judicial system, and investment protections addressed by the agreement's various chapters (Faux and Lee, 1993). One can only speculate why labor rights concerns were subject to sovereignty limitations, although no such limitations hampered areas addressed in the agreement.

Here again let us ask the question, does labor's participation amount to protectionism? Although labor's stance was decidedly anti-NAFTA and elements of labor's anti-NAFTA campaign may have been downright protectionist, it is harder to say that labor was decidedly protectionist here.[14]

Labelling labor's participation in NAFTA is not easy. Labor's opposition to NAFTA centered around the belief that the agreement would lead to a demise of domestic production, and, in turn, harm domestic jobs. Further, throughout the NAFTA process labor did embark on a range of efforts that sought to protect various industries, and jobs in these industries, from NAFTA-based competition. At first glance these types of activities would seem protectionistic. On the other hand, in the area of goods, labor's goal was not to protect domestic products qua products. Rather labor's goal was to protect domestic workers—jobs and labor conditions.

Although this difference may seem semantic, from a future policy formulation standpoint the difference may be more real. Protecting the interests of domestic workers does not *inherently* require protections for domestic products of industries.[15] Thus, one may be able to parcel labor's anti-NAFTA approach off from protectionism. It is possible, albeit admittedly difficult, to conceive of a NAFTA package that would have provided sufficient protection to US jobs and labor conditions, coupled with effective adjustment assistance, to garner labor support. Such a package would not necessarily have been any more protectionist than the protectionist components that are included in the NAFTA. Admittedly, in the services area, because no distinction can be made between protecting a job and protecting the item of value (the service) that is conveyed, such an argument is harder to make.

Moreover, to argue that labor was protectionist in NAFTA one must also determine if there can be a legitimate comparative advantage in lower labor standards or lower wages. Turning first to the standards issue, many of the labor standards that US labor sought to have enforced in the NAFTA arose by way of internationally agreed upon norms, particularly through the International Labour Organization conventions. It would seem to be hypocritical, if not downright abhorrent, for a signatory to the ILO conventions (such as Mexico and Canada), or a nation that has implemented these rights in its laws (such as the United States), to claim a right of comparative advantage in violating these norms. If a country could use such violations to obtain a comparative advantage, would it be protectionist for a nation to refuse to trade with another nation that practices slavery to gain a comparative advantage? Simply put, violations of internationally agreed upon norms or rights should not form the basis of a legitimate comparative advantage. Placed in perspective, labor's participation then does not appear inherently protectionist.

The issue of wages, however, offers a more difficult analytical challenge. Wages are inherently domestic in nature, they are entirely dependent upon the market conditions of each nation, and there are no international norms as to what constitutes a fair minimum wage. Thus, wage differences normally would seem to be a legitimate comparative advantage.[16] To claim wages as a comparative advantage, however, the labor norms discussed above would have to be enforced to ensure that a fair bargaining process set the wage. To the extent that legitimate questions were raised as to the implementation and enforcement of basic labor rights in Mexico, it is difficult to say that low Mexican wages caused a legitimate comparative advantage. For example, it has been reported that Mexican General Electric (GE) workers who merely met with US GE workers about harmonizing the wages of Mexican GE workers up to US levels were dismissed from their jobs (Myerson, 1994). Under these circumstances it is more troubling to argue that wage differentials are a legitimate comparative advantage. Thus, in turn, it becomes more difficult to call labor protectionist in this regard as well.

Even if one dismisses many of labor's efforts in NAFTA as protectionist, the broader pattern of labor participation in trade policymaking argues in favor of not dismissing labor as inherently or necessarily protectionist. Historically, labor has been a strong voice for free trade. Even during NAFTA formulation, the position of labor as a whole was divided on NAFTA: some US unions, ones that saw NAFTA as a job gainer for their particular constituents, and most of Mexican labor supported NAFTA. Labor's post-NAFTA efforts on the Uruguay Round show a similar pattern. Until business and Republicans sought to include antilabor mandates in the fast track provisions of the Uruguay Round implementing bill, labor was noticeably silent on the Round's adoption. Labor entered the fray only after business and Republicans sought to use the Round's implementing bill to foil future trade and labor discussions.

As this analysis reflects, although many of the actions of labor in NAFTA may be dismissed as protectionist, such a dismissal ignores vital nuances that should be taken into account in formulating future trade and labor policies.

DEMOCRACY AND HUMAN RIGHTS CONCERNS

The third leg of social criticism of the NAFTA focused on issues of democracy and human rights. In addition to human rights groups[17] who focused particularly on these issues, these issues also received a great deal of attention from environmental and labor groups. The interest of labor and environmental groups in issues of democracy and human rights stems from the widely held belief that there is a symbiotic relationship between these areas of social concern, namely, that labor and environmental movements play a critical role in advancing democracy and human rights, and the advancement of democracy and human rights, in turn, allows for environmental and labor gains.

These groups together advanced three major concerns with the NAFTA. First, they argued that the NAFTA established undemocratic institutions that would exert major influence over the established national institutions of democratic government.

NAFTA democracy critics pointed to the closed door, un-elected, trade technocratic NAFTA dispute resolution processes, which could be used to challenge, and eventually undermine through economic sanctions, democratically enacted laws passed by the elected legislatures of the NAFTA parties.

Second, democracy critics argued that, from a democracy perspective, Mexico was not yet ready to become so tightly linked a trading partner of Canada and the United States.[18] The record of Mexico on torture and other human rights abuses, government corruption, graft, election fraud, and political repression provided these critics, Northern and Southern alike, with ample grounds for their arguments (Castaneda, 1993; Zinser; Hollings; Santos de la Garza, 1993; Yamin Americas Watch, 1990). For example, in 1992 alone, both the US State Department and the United Nations Committee Against Torture severely criticized the continued use of torture by Mexican government authorities (Hollings). Proponents of the agreement countered that gains in democracy in Mexico would be facilitated by the adoption of the NAFTA, an argument that may bear merit.

Whether or not NAFTA may inspire or inhibit greater democracy in Mexico notwithstanding, do the democracy-based concerns of human rights advocates, labor groups, and environmentalists with the agreement amount to protectionism? It seems difficult to say that they do. These democracy concerns had little to do with protecting any product or service based on the fact that it was domestic in origin.

Moreover, to find that democracy advocates were protectionist one must argue that human rights abuses can form the underpinnings of a legitimate comparative advantage (Zakaria, 1994). As the success of certain Asian nations bears out, a society of citizens too fearful to speak out or to mobilize makes an excellent obedient and docile work force: wages can be dictated by a central authority, strikes can be put down, a questioning press can be silenced. However, underpinning these advantages are violations of universally recognized human rights. Here again, it seems outrageous to say that one can legitimately obtain a comparative advantage by violating basic human rights.

MORAL OF THE STORY

Debunking the myth of an inherently protectionist labor, environment, and human rights cabal in trade policy provides a number of important lessons for how we go about making trade policy. If one believes, as this author does, that these social interests can be brought into the trade policy fold by addressing their concerns, just as trade policy makers attempt to do with individual industries, the key then is not to alienate these interests but to find ways of addressing their concerns while not undercutting the very legitimate goals of trade liberalization.

Ironically, many have argued (Esty) that, at least on the environmental front, NAFTA bears this lesson out. Environmental groups who felt that their concerns had been addressed were some of the more vocal supporters of the agreement. This strategy, however, in the NAFTA context, was never applied to the labor and human rights fronts. The failure to expand this strategy into other areas secured the opposition of these interest groups.

That is not to say that these social groups will, or can, be satisfied by every trade deal. It is to say that it is incorrect to label them protectionist without distinction from inefficient industries that have sought to use trade policies to protect themselves from foreign competition. Perhaps a more accurate label would be dissatisfied, as one might label industries that oppose or criticize a certain trade agreement because it does not address their concerns adequately, such as the motion picture industry's position on the Uruguay Round.

Using the label dissatisfied, as opposed to protectionist, conveys an important message: they can be satisfied. In other words rather than adopting trade policies that are confrontational in nature, it is preferable to attempt to deal with their concerns and make them supporters of our trade policies. The importance of this lesson can be seen in the recent debate over the fast track language proposed for the Uruguay Round.

At the outset of the fast track debate the Clinton administration proposed the most modest, no more than a few cursory sentences, of environmental and labor language for inclusion in the goals of future trade negotiations that would receive fast track consideration (*Inside U.S. Trade,* 1994a; *Inside U.S. Trade,* 1994c). As noted previously business and Republicans fought this language vehemently and the administration in response removed this language from their proposal (Rosenberg). Still unsatisfied, business and Republicans pushed the administration for language that would actively prevent the administration from moving forward on a pro labor and environmental trade policy agenda (*Inside U.S. Trade,* 1994b). Once again, in fear of losing the Uruguay Round, the administration caved to the pressure and included the language in its proposal (*Inside U.S. Trade,* 1994b; *Inside U.S. Trade,* 1994d). This brought about a strong backlash from a number of influential members, such as Senators Moynihan (D-NY, and Chair of the influential Finance Committee), John Kerry (D-MA), Wofford (D-PA), Boxer (D-CA), and Pelosi (D-CA) (*Inside U.S. Trade,* 1994e; *Inside U.S. Trade,* 1994g). The simple fact is that this unfortunate turn of events could have been avoided had a balance been sought on these issues that weighed the concerns of all involved as opposed to the one-sided proposal the administration allowed to be foisted upon itself.

The moral of this story is that to ensure the smooth working of our trade policies it will be increasingly necessary for traditional economic trade policy interests and parties to seek common ground and mutually agreeable policies with labor, environmental, and human rights interests. Only through this approach can we ensure that we can continue to make gains in liberalizing international trade, while at the same time preserving other vital areas of our security and standards of living, such as the air we breathe, the food we eat, the wages that pay our bills and fuel our economy, and the rights that we call inalienable.

NOTES

1. The counterpart attack launched by trade critics at free trade proponents is the "faceless bureaucrat" slight that found its way into several popular press advertisements campaigning against NAFTA and GATT.

2. For example, Lee Iacocca, was one of the main proponents of free trade and NAFTA, however, Chrysler has long sought trade protectionist policies to protect the auto industry.

3. The comparative advantage theory as Ricardo discussed it did not deal with the advantage of one nation over another. Instead it dealt with the advantage of one product over another within the manufacturing scheme of a particular nation (Daniel, unpub.) Over time, however, the theory has taken on the aspects of defining relations between countries.

Because it is directly relevant to the focus of this article, one alternative vision of Ricardo's comparative advantage theory should also be mentioned. Herman Daly has argued that, from a Keynesian perspective, if capital is internationally mobile, investment does not follow comparative advantage, but instead tracks absolute advantage (Daly, 1993; Keynes, 1993). Only if capital is immobile internationally does investment follow comparative advantage. Daly argues that it is this flaw in implementation that causes wholesale social "externalities" to result from the existing free trade paradigm (Daly, 1993).

4. For example, during the boom 1980s, specifically 1984–1988, after adjusting for inflation, the median income in the most affluent fifth of all US households increased by 14 percent. During this same period, however, the median income remained unchanged for the remaining four-fifths of the population (Medoff, 1994: Diamond, 1993).

5. This scenario aptly displays the two major ways in which the NAFTA's positive employment effects will not easily reach those the agreement harms. First, the NAFTA's benefits are being enjoyed by the Southwest (USITC, 1992: Orme, 1993); however, its harms are likely to be diffused over the rest of the nation, with concentrations in certain industries of the East North Central. Pacific, and Mountain census regions (USITC, 1991). Second, while certain industries and job categories, particularly those that support manufacturing in Mexico, may increase, any declines that will be felt will occur in other job categories and industries, particularly in manufacturing line jobs. Increases in the demand for, say, engineers are unlikely to help the situation of the displaced riveter.

6. A range of often times conflicting definitions of protectionism have been offered; however, none of these definitions have received universal acceptance. For example, the *International Relations Dictionary* defines protectionism as "the theory and practice of using governmental regulation to control or limit the volume or types of imports entering a state" (*IRD*, 1982). Moffat instead defines it from a cognitive focus as "the feeling that government should protect domestic sellers from competition with imported goods and services by the use of taxes, quotas, import prohibitions, and other means" (Moffat, 1983). Salvatore defines it with a historical perspective as a "revival of 'mercantilism' whereby nations, particularly the industrial nations, attempt to solve or alleviate their problems of unemployment, lagging growth, and declining industries by imposing restrictions on imports and subsidizing exports" (Salvatore, 1993). Miller, however, looking at the ends, broadly asserts "any policy that increases the price of a bounty's imports or decreases that of its exports is considered protectionism" (Miller, 1989).

7. Increasingly, intellectual property rights (IPR) protections are being recognized as legitimate trade-related factors upon which discrimination can be premised. The author supports this trend. However, from a pure product qua product, or traditional trade analysis, there is no difference in the pilfered product.

8. Unless otherwise provided this article deals only with the positions of US environmental groups.

9. If a protectionist label can be applied to any environmental groups, the case for such a label is arguably strongest as to those environmental and consumer groups that opposed the agreement. Here, however, care should be taken in generalizing. Some groups that opposed the agreement, most notably the Sierra Club, arguably endeavored to bring about an agreement they could support. These groups might be distinguished from other groups that at no point in time sought to endorse any NAFTA.

10. The supplemental agreement provides a dispute resolution mechanism to determine whether such a failure is occurring. The supplemental agreement also provides a reporting mechanism that is triggered by public complaints, which is intended to shine the spotlight of public attention on weak enforcement.

11. Except where otherwise provided this article discusses only US labor groups.

12. Given this small overall impact on the US economy, one can rightly ask why the NAFTA took on such major political significance. If NAFTA would not create major new industrial gains, and hence jobs, for US industries, why were these industries so invested in the agreement's success?

13. These proponents did, however, concede that while NAFTA might be a net job gain, it would cost the United States 150,000 jobs, mostly in manufacturing (Hufbauer and Schott, 1993). Although the net job gain figures for NAFTA were promising, these studies typically did not delve into the plight of workers who might be among those displaced. For

example, although many of these workers might find replacement jobs, one-quarter of all displaced workers laid off between 1979 and 1989 were unemployed for more than 6 months (OTA, 1992). Displaced workers with substantial job experience (older workers) took two to four times longer to find jobs than other workers (OTA, 1992). Displaced workers also face a substantial drop in benefits. For example, one-quarter of displaced workers lost their health insurance (OTA, 1991). The overall economic decline suffered by displaced workers is substantial. Manufacturing workers who were laid off during the 1980s suffered on average a $36,000 loss in income (OTA, 1992).

14. For example, although US labor argued against the agreement, Mexican labor generally cautiously supported the agreement (Diamond, 1993). Thus, under the right conditions labor can be pro free trade.

15. Of course, in the absence of alternative equal job prospects, and without adequate adjustment assistance, labor can be backed into a protectionist posture from which it has no choice but to do everything in its power to protect domestic industries and products from foreign competition.

16. One could, however, conceive of situations where this would not be the case, such as where no free market agreement occurred in setting the wage. For example, if labor is coerced and an illusory wage is paid, can this low wage be claimed as a comparative advantage?

17. Unless otherwise noted this article discusses only the concerns of US human rights groups.

18. Some critics went further, arguing that the changes NAFTA would bring to Mexican society might create barriers to the necessary political evolution of the country. Ironically, the barriers to democracy that critics of the agreement feared served as core concerns of the predemocratization Zapatista uprising that coincided with the NAFTA's implementation. In this unwitting way the NAFTA may have proven critical to advancing democracy in Mexico.

REFERENCES

Americas Watch (1990) "Human Rights in Mexico: A Policy of Impunity," June.

Audley, John (1993) "Why Environmentalists Are Angry About the North American Free Trade Agreement," in Durwood Zaelke, et al. (Eds.), *Trade and the Environment: Law Economics and Policy*, Washington, D.C.: Island Press, 191.

Bovard, James (1991) *The Fair Trade Fraud*, New York: St. Martin's Press.

Castaneda, Jorge G. (1993) "Can NAFTA Change Mexico?", *Foreign Affairs*, 66, 72.

Clinton, Bill (1992) "Expanding Trade and Creating American Jobs," remarks at North Carolina State University, October 4.

Collingsworth, Terry, Goold, William, and Harvey, Pharis (1994). "Time for a Global New Deal," *Foreign Affairs*, 8, 73.

Committee for Economic Development (1991), *Breaking New Ground in U.S. Trade Policy*, Boulder, CO: Westview.

Compa, Lance (1993) "International Labor Rights and the Sovereignty Question: NAFTA, Guatemala, Two Case Studies," *American University Journal of International Law and Policy*, 117, 8.

Congressional Research Service (CRS) (1991) "North American Free Trade Agreement: Issues for Congress," March 25.

Cornelius, Wayne (1994) "Mexico's Delayed Democratization," *Foreign Policy*, 53, 95.

Daniel, Royal, III "Comparative Advantage," unpublished manuscript. Continental Bank NAFTA Executive Roundtable (1993) *Journal of Applied Corporate Finance*, 64.

Daly, Herman (1993) "Problems with Free Trade: Neoclassical and Steady-State Perspectives," in Durwood Zaelke, et al. (Eds.), *Trade and the Environment: Law Economics and Policy*, Washington, D.C.: Island Press, 147.

Diamond, Stephen (1993) "U.S. Labor and North American Economic Integration: Toward a Constructive Critique," in Ricardo Grinspun and Maxwell Cameron (Eds.), *The Political Economy of North American Free Trade*, New York: St. Martins.

Economist (1993) "GATT Comes Right," Dec. 18, 1993, 13.

Ely-Yamin, Alicia (1993) "Six Months after the U.N. Verdict: An Update on Impunity in the Mexican Federal Judicial Policy," *World Policy Institute Report*.

Esty, Daniel (1993) "Integrating Trade and the Environment: First Steps in the North American Free Trade Agreement, in Durwood Zaelke, et al. (Eds.), Trade and the Environment: Law, Economics, and Policy, Washington, DC: Island Press, 45.

Faux, Jeff and Lee, Thea (1992) "The Effect of George Bush's NAFTA on American Workers: Ladder Up or Ladder Down?", Economic Policy Institute, July.

Faux, Jeff and Lee, Thea (1993) "Implications of NAFTA for the United States: Investment, Jobs, and Productivity," in Ricardo Grinspun and Maxwell Cameron, *The Political Economy of North American Free Trade*.

General Accounting Office (GAO) (1991) "U.S.-Mexico Trade: Some U.S. Wood Furniture Firms Relocated from Los Angeles to Mexico," report to the Chairman, Committee on Energy and Commerce, House of Representatives, GAO/NSIAD 91-191, April.

Greider, William (1992) "Bushism Found: A Second-Term Agenda Hidden in Trade Agreements," *Harpers*, September, 44.

Hall, Khristine, (1994) "Trade and the Environment: The Business Point of View," in *Proceedings of the 88th Annual Meeting*, American Society of Internal Law, 495, 88.

Hollings, Ernest (1993-1994) "Reform Mexico First," *Foreign Policy*, 91, 93.

Housman, Robert and Orbuch, Paul (1993) "Integrating Labor and Environmental Concerns into the North American Free Trade Agreement: A Look Back and a Look Ahead," *American University Journal of International Law and Policy*, 719.

Hufbauer, Gary and Schott, Jeffrey (1992) "North American Free Trade: Issues and Recommendations," Institute for International Economics.

Hufbauer, Gary and Schott, Jeffrey (1993) "Prescription for Growth," *Foreign Policy*, 104, 93.

Inside U.S. Trade (1994a) "Congressional Fight Brewing Over Fast-Track Proposal in GATT," June 21, S1, S24.

Inside U.S. Trade (1994b) "Administration Offers New Fast-Track Concessions to Business, GOP," August 12, S1–S8.

Inside U.S. Trade (1994c) "Democrats, Environmental Groups Propose Fast Track Alternative," August 19, 3–4.

Inside U.S. Trade (1994d) "Danforth Threatens to oppose Administration Fast Track Proposal," August 19, 3–4.

Inside U.S. Trade (1994e) "Moynihan, Packwood Urge Clean GATT Bill, Better Funding Options," September 2, 1, 16.

Inside U.S. Trade (1994f) "Pro-Labor Environment Democrats seek to Exclude Fast Track," September 2, 5–6.

Inside U.S. Trade (1994g) "Officials Acknowledge Fast Track May Be Dropped from GATT Bill," September 9, 1, 16.

Jackson, John (1994), *The World Trading System: Law and Policy of International Economic Relations*, Cambridge, MA: The MIT Press.

Kamen, Al (1993), "On the Front Line," *The National Journal*, June 19, p. 1556.

Keynes, John Maynard (1993) "National Self-Sufficiency," in Donald Moggeridge (Ed.), *The Collected Writings of John Maynard Keynes*, Vol. 21, New York: Macmillan and Cambridge University Press.

Levinson, Jerome (1993) "Unrequited Toil: Denial of Labor Rights in Mexico and Implications for the NAFTA," *World Policy Institute Report*.

Los Angeles Times (1992) "Hunt Goes on For Cause of Brain Defects in Babies Born on Border: Anencephaly: Theories Include Chemicals Emitted by Factories, Solvents in Gulf of Mexico, or Fathers Exposed to Chemicals at Work," July 26, A1.

Low, Patrick, (1992) "Do Dirty Industries Migrate?," in World Bank, *World Bank Discussion Papers: International Trade and the Environment*, Washington, DC: 89.

Medoff, James (1994) "The Demand for Labor 1990-1993," *Center for National Policy Paper*.

Miller, Helen V. (1989) *Resisting Protectionism: Global Industries and the Politics of International Trade* (Princeton, NJ: Princeton University Press).

Moffat, Donald W. (1983) *Economic Dictionary*, 2nd ed., New York: Elsevier.

Myerson, Allen R. (1994) "Big Labor's Strategic Raid in Mexico," *New York Times*, September 12, D1.

Office of Technology Assessment (OTA) (1992) "U.S.-Mexico Trade: Pulling Together on Apart."

Orme, William J. (1993) *Continental Shift: Free Trade and the New North America*, Washington Post.

Pastor, Robert (1994), "NAFTA's Green Opportunity," in Ambler Moss (Ed.), *Assessments of the NAFTA*, New Brunswick, NJ: Transaction Publishers.

Plano, Jack and Olton, Roy, *The International Relations Dictionary* (1964) 3rd ed. Santa Barbara, ABC-Clio, 143.

Power, Thomas and Rauber, Paul (1993) "The Price of Everything: Free-Market Environmentalism," *Sierra*, Nov. 86.

Regan, Donald (1986) "The Supreme Court and State Protectionism: Making Sense of the Dormant Commerce Clause," *Michigan Law Review*, 1091, 84.

Ricardo, David (1977) *On the Principles of Political Economy and Taxation*, Toronto: Toronto University Press.

Rosenberg, Robin (1994) "Trade and the Environment: Economic Development versus Sustainable Development," *Journal of Interamerican Studies*, 129, 36.

Salvatore, Dominick (1993) *Protectionism and World Welfare*, New York: Cambridge University Press.

Santos de la Garza, Luis (1993) "Ineffective Suffrage: The Denial of Political Rights in Mexico," *World Policy Institute Report*.

Steil, Ben (1994), "Social Correctness Is the New Protectionism," *Foreign Affairs*, 8, 73.

Tobey, James (1993) "The Impact of Domestic Environmental Policies on International Trade," in *OECD, Environmental Policies and Industrial Competitiveness*.

United States International Trade Commission (USITC) (1991) "The Likely Impact on the United States of a Free Trade Agreement with Mexico," Report to the Committee on Ways and Means of the United States House of Representatives and the Committee on Finance of the United States Senate on Investigation No. 332-297 Under Section 332 of the Tariff Act of 1930.

United States International Trade Commission (USITC) (1992) "Economy-wide Modeling of the Economic Implications of FTA with Mexico," Addendum to the Report on Investigation No. 332-317 under Section 332 of the Tariff Act of 1930.

Zakaria, Fareed (1994) "Culture is Destiny: A Conversation with Lee Kuan Yew," *Foreign Affairs*, 109 73.

Zaelke, Durwood, et al., (Eds.) (1993) *Trade and the Environment: Law Economics and Policy*, Washington, D.C.: Island Press.

Zinser, Adolfo (1993) "Authoritarianism and North American Free Trade: The Debate in Mexico," in Ricardo Grinspun and Maxwell Cameron, (Eds.), The Political Economy of North American Free Trade, New York: St. Martin's Press, 205.

The Harmonization of Standards in the European Union and the Impact on U.S. Business

Tom Reilly

Tom Reilly is a consultant in the New York office of Ernst & Young's Performance Improvement practice.

> *Despite problems, American businesses have a chance to help themselves by participating in the European standard-setting process.*

The goal of the European Union is to strengthen Europe's economy by creating an internal free market among the community's 15 member nations with common external trade barriers to the rest of the world. This internal market is based on the removal of barriers to allow for the free movement of products, labor, and capital. The 15 nations include: Belgium, France, Italy, Luxembourg, Netherlands, and Germany (as established by the 1957 Treaties of Rome); Denmark, Ireland, and the United Kingdom (added in 1973); Greece (1981); Spain and Portugal (1986); and Austria, Finland, and Sweden (1995).

The success of the single European market depends on three major developments: the elimination of internal customs barriers and immigration restrictions; the reduction of fiscal barriers and the possible creation of a single European currency; and the harmonization of product standards among the 15 member nations. And although all of these developments are sure to have a profound impact on European firms, the creation of pan-European product standards is likely to have the most far-reaching effects on U.S. companies. To predict the consequences of European standardization on American firms, an understanding of the EU's standard-setting process is needed.

EUROPEAN STANDARDIZATION

Although the term *standard* is used in various ways throughout the European Union (EU), a broad definition refers to a commonly accepted set of principles, practices, or requirements that goods or services must meet to be marketed within a particular jurisdiction. Standards may be voluntary or mandatory, and may be set by a governmental or private standard-setting body. They may define necessary product features or mandatory elements of a production process.

There are several motivating factors behind the harmonization of standards within the European Union. First, uniform standards are designed to promote minimum health and safety requirements for workers and consumers across the community. Nations have traditionally set minimum qualifications on a wide variety of products and work-related situations, ranging from motor vehicle passenger protection to meat production procedures. Health and safety standards often translate into technical specifications, such as requiring a lawn mower to have specific guards (safety standard) and maximum noise level (health standard). Manufacturers may be forced to make major design changes to conform with a particular health or safety standard imposed in a nation or trading area. Recent EU product liability laws have intensified the need for manufacturers to meet health and safety standards.

Harmonized standards are also a means of eliminating trade barriers disguised as national standards. Because standards dictate the requirements a product must meet to be marketed in a

From *Business Horizons*, March/April 1995, pp. 28-34. © 1995 by the Foundation for the School of Business at Indiana University. Reprinted by permission.

particular area, they are often viewed as Non-Tariff Barriers (NTBs) to trade. Problems may arise when governments set standards in such a way that a national industry is protected from competition. Some examples of standards as NTBs include the French standard that all tractors must be equipped with automobile-style headlights, whether they travel on roads or not; this favors French manufacturers who traditionally designed equipment in this way. The Belgium standard stating that margarine must be packed in cubes favors local producers. International agreements such as the General Agreement on Tariffs and Trade (GATT), to which the U.S. and EU are signatories, have also striven to eliminate unnecessary national standards. GATT, which operates by granting Most Favored Nation (MFN) status to members, bars the use of unnecessary national standards when the standard results in a restraint of trade. GATT also outlines many situations in which standards are necessary, such as in cases involving health and safety.

As part of the completion of the internal market, the EU has done much to prevent its member states from banning imports on the basis of nonconformance to local regulations. The EU, however, has made a major exception and left member states with control of local regulations in health and safety standards. This gap creates problems for companies in industries such as pharmaceuticals, engineering, foodstuffs, and precision medical equipment, and adds cost to industries such as motor vehicles.

Uniform standards facilitate cooperation among firms by promoting compatibility of product specifications. They serve to ensure that a part built in one plant will be compatible with parts in another plant, and that the product will be able to be used in various parts of the world. Standardization simplifies the coordination of firms, which can avoid costly mistakes by specifying that all products must be *produced to EU standards."* German companies, for example, have traditionally noted "Specification According to DIN" (*Deutshes Institut fur Normung,* or German Institute for Standardization) with no additional explanation necessary. This simplifies transactions, ensures that parts from different suppliers will be compatible, and helps avoid costly misunderstandings. The compatibility of parts allows for economies of scale. In the past, lack of cooperation has resulted in varying operating environments in areas as fundamental as electrical equipment, weights and measures, and automotive regulations. Currently, for example, the electrical systems in Europe have widely varying voltages, quality, and plugs and fixtures. And though most European countries converted weights and measures to a decimal system in the second half of the twentieth century, many still

use more than one measurement system, such as in measuring temperature. Creation of a single set of European standards will allow producers to take advantage of economies of scale in production and distribute a single product on a European-wide basis.

Although the importance of uniform product standards is generally acknowledged throughout the European Union, nations remain divided over such basics as sizes of clothing, electrical plugs, and units of measurement. Fundamental differences in culture and custom are still widespread in Europe. And there are nine different languages in common use in the EU's product packaging and labeling.

History of European Standardization

Traditionally, many European countries had centralized national standard systems and standard-setting organizations. In Germany, the DIN has existed for more than 70 years and has created more than 20,000 standards. Similar standard-setting bodies, such as the British Standards Institute (BSI) and the *Association Française de Normalisation* (AFNOR), have been in place throughout Europe and have developed national guidelines ranging from testing nuclear reactors to the standard height of automotive headlights. European national standards systems normally dictate regulations and minimum requirements in the form of mandatory codes. Although individual nations have had centralized national standards, companies wishing to sell products across Europe historically have had to meet as many as 19 sets of varying standards.

The diversity of European standards seems relatively mild compared to the standard-setting system in the United States, which is highly decentralized with more than 400 organizations producing standards. The U.S. relies on voluntary standards developed and enforced by private organizations rather than a uniform national policy. Most U.S. standards are coordinated through the American National Standards Institute (ANSI), which is a private, industry-supported organization. ANSI has become actively involved in the European standard-setting process, and has recently opened an office in Brussels.

Attempts at the harmonization of European standards can be traced to the April 1951 signing of the Treaty of Paris and the inception of the European Coal and Steel Community. After the signing of the 1957 Treaties of Rome, the current standard-setting institutions of the EU were established. The European Commission, in its 1985 White Paper, condemned varying national standards as creating additional costs, hampering cooperation between nations, and hindering the common European market. A European Court

Figure 1
Areas in Which European-wide Essential Requirements Have Been Set

- Building products
- Gas appliances
- Lifting and loading equipment
- Machine safety
- Medical devices
- Mobile machines
- Earth movers
- Personal protection equipment
- Rollover protection equipment
- Simple pressure vessels
- Light industrial trucks
- Telecommunications equipment
- Toys

ruling known as the "Casis de Dijon" did much to establish the idea that EU members should not ban certain imports on the basis of a product's nonconformance to local regulations. Again, this ruling provided latitude in the case of local health and safety standards.

Originally, the task of harmonization was to be conducted by a central standard-setting body that would draft detailed descriptions of minimum requirements to be accepted throughout Europe. It was estimated that the EU would have to harmonize standards in more than 10,000 product categories simply to meet the 1992 deadline set by the Single European Act. The size and scope of European standardization proved easier said than done, however, and some negotiations promised to take years to settle. To speed the process, the EU implemented a *new approach* that focused on 1,500 of the most vital product categories that had to be completed for 1992.

The "New Approach"

The EU's new approach put into place a system of mutual recognition of member states' standards in some areas while setting new European-wide minimum standards in a number of other areas. Theoretically, a producer that is allowed to sell products in one country cannot be prevented from selling the same product in another member country; a product will only have to meet one European standard, not a dozen different ones. Instead of preparing individual directives aimed at removing trade-related problems (as

in the old approach), the EU will prepare broad technical directives to cover such areas as health, safety, and environmental protection. Specific directives will be made only in areas where serious conflict exists between member nations. If a serious conflict exists and a specific Europe-wide standard cannot be agreed upon, the standard-setting bodies will prepare a *harmonization document,* which specifies essential requirements that must be met and outlines customized local versions for each member.

The caveat to this new approach is that every EU member is obliged to acknowledge that products meeting the guidelines of this system are suitable for sale and use in the local market. Overall, conforming to a local standard, whether or not a specific EU directive applies, should ensure acceptance throughout the EU. A single set of European-wide essential requirements has already been agreed upon in some areas (see **Figure 1**), while proposals to cover other areas are in the works.

Administration of Standards

The task of harmonizing standards for the EU falls upon the European Commission, which works closely with international standard-setting bodies. The implementation of new EU standards is conducted by a common European decision-making body, which is consulted by various government and non-government standardization committees. Within the standard-setting bodies there is fierce debate among committees trying to influence the final version of the standard.

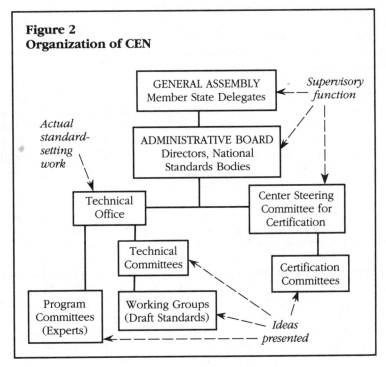

Figure 2
Organization of CEN

GENERAL ASSEMBLY
Member State Delegates

Supervisory function

Actual standard-setting work

ADMINISTRATIVE BOARD
Directors, National Standards Bodies

Technical Office

Center Steering Committee for Certification

Technical Committees

Certification Committees

Program Committees (Experts)

Working Groups (Draft Standards)

Ideas presented

Several committees have been charged with the development of standards in specific areas. The organization that handles product standards in general is the CEN (*Comité Européen de Normalisation,* or European Committee for Standardization), which is made up of subcommittees from various parts of the EU. The CEN is organized into three major segments: a *supervisory* segment, a *technical standardization* segment, and a *certification* segment. An outline of its structure is presented in **Figure 2**.

The supervisory work of the CEN is conducted by its general assembly, which is made up of delegates from each EU member nation, and the administrative board, comprising the directors of participating national standards organizations. All proposed standards and requirements must be approved first by the administrative board and finally by the general assembly. The technical office, relying on consultation from program committees or technical committees, does the actual standard-setting work. Program committees are made up of experts who supply necessary advice for specific standardization issues. Technical committees are made up of working groups that propose drafts of standards. It is important for outsiders to monitor the work going on in the technical committees, since this is where various countries and industries present concerns and lobby to have their version of a standard adopted for all of Europe. By the time the proposed standards leave the technical office for submission to the administrative board, almost all of the major issues have been resolved.

The standard-setting process, as illustrated in **Figure 3**, is conducted by the CEN and experts from interested countries. Before a standard can be formally accepted, it must pass the CEN general assembly's voting process. Each of the member nations receives a number of votes proportionate to its relative size in the European market. The criteria for passing the voting process are that a majority must accept the proposed standard, there must not be more than 22 "No" votes, and there must be no more than three countries voting "No." The process typically involves eight months or more of intense negotiation.

The desired result of the process is a European-wide standard that is the same in all member countries. When members decide that a single European standard will be impractical, unnecessary, or too difficult to agree upon, a harmonization document is created.

Mutual Recognition and Testing

The *Global Approach to Certification and Testing* was initiated in 1989 to promote confidence in product safety, manufacturers, testing laboratories, and certification bodies. This approach is

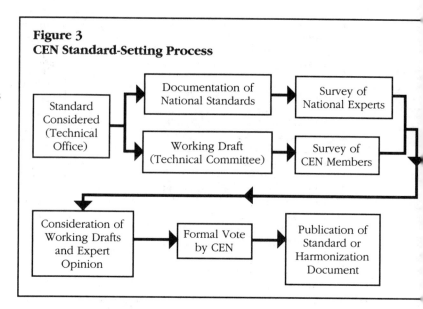

Figure 3
CEN Standard-Setting Process

designed to measure a product's conformity to an EU directive and attach a recognizable certification mark on satisfactory products. The mark for products on which a European standard has been agreed upon is the "CE" mark shown in **Figure 4**. Each member must allow all certified products to be marketed as complying to local standards, regardless of the product's origin. An example of the conditions a product must meet to earn a "CE" mark is shown in **Figure 5**.

Producers in non-EU nations must follow the same certification procedures and have products pass the same requirements as producers within the EU. In accordance with the principles covering technical barriers to trade set forth in GATT, non-EU products have the same rights to certification systems and to bear the "CE" mark as native EU products.

Quality

Product quality is probably the broadest aspect covered by European standardization. This is because of its wide application in business and its importance in the area of product liability. In 1985, the EU issued a *Product Liability Directive* stating that a producer will be liable, regardless of fault or negligence, if a person is harmed or an object damaged by a faulty product. Because EU law places the burden of proof on the producer (in other words, guilty until proven innocent), a firm will have to prove that its products are free from defects and deficiencies to avoid liability. When defending a product liability claim, a producer must demonstrate that a certified quality assurance program was in use during production.

Figure 4
European Union Certification Symbol

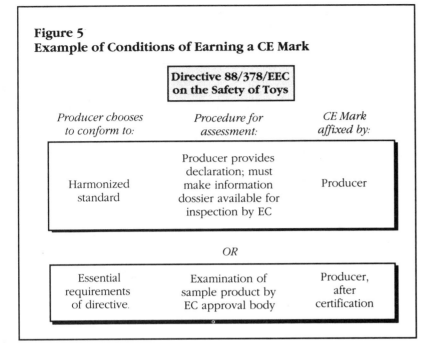

Figure 5
Example of Conditions of Earning a CE Mark

	Directive 88/378/EEC on the Safety of Toys	
Producer chooses to conform to:	Procedure for assessment:	CE Mark affixed by:
Harmonized standard	Producer provides declaration; must make information dossier available for inspection by EC	Producer
	OR	
Essential requirements of directive.	Examination of sample product by EC approval body	Producer, after certification

Current EU quality standards are guided by the International Standards Organization (ISO). They are based on the ISO 9000 series standards, and are appropriately named EN9000. (In the U.S. they are known as the Q90 series.) Many European firms require suppliers and subcontractors to meet European-quality standards or have quality systems audited through third-party certification. Contracts may be written or bids awarded on the grounds that design, development, installation, and servicing meet ISO criteria.

Current trends suggest an increasing role of quality standards in Europe. Some proposed regulations may require producers and importers to permanently monitor the safety of a product throughout its useful life. European firms already require that quality standards be met in about 50 percent of its contracts.

EFFECTS OF EUROPEAN STANDARDIZATION ON AMERICAN FIRMS

The unification of European standards presents both enormous opportunities and threats to U.S. producers. American companies may soon be able to market a single product to 368 million EU consumers, or they may be shut out by protectionist European policies. The stakes are high for companies planning on entering this market as well as for those with an established European presence.

U.S. Role in International Standardization

Many American firms had little problem operating in Europe's old regulatory environment. After all,

the American standardization system had nearly as many regional variations. At home, U.S. firms were used to meeting varying, often conflicting standards, set by organizations as diverse as the American National Standards Institute (ANSI), the Department of Defense, the Food and Drug Administration, or the Environmental Protection Agency. As mentioned earlier, the U.S. system of standardization is based on a combination of mandatory government regulation and voluntary standards put in place by various public and private standard-setting bodies.

American firms now need to become involved in international standard harmonization, both as a tool to combat regional protectionism and to promote possible economies of scale and scope. The United States has actively worked to further the acceptance of worldwide product standards by entering bilateral agreements and participating in institutions such as the ISO. American firms can also maintain a role in international standard-setting through the representation of ANSI, which is heavily involved in the ISO and has even had a delegate serve as its president.

U.S. participation in the EU's standardization process is limited, since outside nations do not have formal representation in standard-setting proceedings (with the exception of the remaining European Free Trade Association, or EFTA, nations that participate in the standardization process). American influence can be asserted, informally, through the European subsidiaries of U.S. companies and in the form of passive participation and commentary during EU talks. Often, European standards unintentionally favor European products, since the process is heavily influenced by European designs and preferences.

U.S.-EU Agreements

In 1989, the U.S. and the EU entered into an agreement to make it easier for U.S. companies to receive advance notice of planned standards and make comments to EU regulatory bodies. This agreement actually gave U.S. companies the right to sit in on EU standardization negotiations and is often cited as an illustration of the EU's genuine concern for the removal of technical barriers to trade.

Efforts have also been made to adopt international standards that transcend both the United States and Europe. In 1991, the two governmental bodies agreed to remove conflicting U.S. and EU standards when consensus international standards were developed. Cooperation between the United States and the EU is conducted by ANSI, the American Society for Testing and Materials, the European Committee for Norms, the European Telecommunications Standards Institute, and the ISO. Currently, unplanned technical barriers still exist between the two trading regions in such basic areas as voltages for electrical items and sizes of industrial fasteners, such as nuts and bolts.

Potential Threats to U.S. Companies in Europe

One of the biggest fears among American producers is that the protectionist politics of the EU will result in standards that are created in favor of European products. These fears are compounded by events such as a recent EU ban on U.S. pork and beef, which was condemned because of "substandard" slaughterhouse practices. Whether or not the meat ban was appropriate, at least one U.S. official took offense and stated, "We would not welcome any additional restraints on U.S. exports to Europe."

Some EU members have been accused of stalling standardization talks in an effort to retain the last bits of control over foreign imports. Italy, France, and Spain have been consistently disagreeable when talks focus on automotive safety standards that would allow cars to be sold freely throughout Europe. Blatant attempts to use standards to block competition help enforce the stereotype of "Fortress Europe," in which American products are not welcome.

Many European standards, notably in health and safety, are criticized for being overambitious with no foreseeable benefits. Some products have had to undergo expensive design changes that do not improve—and may even hinder—product performance. The price of making major changes that have not been demanded by customers may be so high that producers will be discouraged from the European market.

Potential Opportunities and Benefits

Even with the problems, though, U.S. firms face tremendous gains from the harmonization of European standards. The sheer size of the unified European market holds great promise for producers who seek economies of scale or broad marketing reach. The potential of meeting a single standard for 368 million Europeans provides incentive for products that previously did not find the fragmented Europe attractive.

European standardization has also helped pave the way for what may some day be truly worldwide product standards. Global standards are becoming a reality in many areas, allowing U.S. firms to conduct business freely with companies throughout the world. At the very least, the harmonization of standards among regional trading blocks has called attention to the benefits of early cooperation among nations.

Another potential benefit for the United States may arise from the need to implement strict quality control practices for products marketed in Europe. American companies that have not properly implemented comprehensive quality systems will now be forced to do so to compete in Europe. Higher quality is sure to benefit U.S. consumers and producers, who will be able to reap the rewards of better products.

Considering the size and scope of the standards to be harmonized, it is safe to assume that a completely harmonized set of European standards is still far in the future. The process is painstakingly slow because of the wide variety of factors that must be considered. The size of the European market—368 million people with a combined GDP of almost $6 trillion—will surely mean that standards set there will affect global product and process norms.

Unfortunately, it is quite difficult for outside interests to exert as much influence as EU members during the harmonization process. European standard-setting bodies are naturally influenced by European process designs and products. American firms, on the other hand, must work through representatives of European subsidies and standard-setting bodies.

In the short run, EU standards could hurt the ability of some U.S. firms to compete in Europe. Standards are apt to mean expensive product design changes and the loss of varying degrees of competitiveness to native European firms. Non-European companies may also run into difficulty and expense when trying to meet certification criteria for health, safety, and quality standards. During the early stages of harmonization, many firms may continue to experience unplanned complications in their European operations.

Over the longer term, however, the harmonization of standards could be a boon to U.S. companies by reducing the multiplicity of standards in Europe. American firms and consumers may also benefit from the focus on product quality. Ultimately, after the costs of meeting standards are paid, the cost of operating in Europe could be drastically reduced.

Since the EU has granted the U.S. the right to receive advance notice of standardization and to comment on proposed standards, U.S. concerns have a unique chance of influencing the standards that will affect all of Europe. The benefits to be reaped by those who get involved early and stay on top of the work being done are substantial. Influence may be gained by focusing on the work of standard-setting committees through passive participation or local subsidiaries. Companies that monitor the progress of harmonization can gain valuable insight that will allow them to take active steps in areas that will affect their operations.

U.S. firms should also make an effort to influence the setting of worldwide standards through ANSI representation to global standard-setting bodies. This is especially important since the U.S. and the EU have agreed to allow international standards to supersede conflicting local standards.

Overall, the United States should become aggressively involved in European and inter-regional standardization. This will allow American companies to learn of anticipated changes and possibly help shape future standards.

References

"EC Calls U.S. Meat Unsanitary," *Wall Street Journal,* October 26, 1990, p. A12.

INDUSTRIAL SEA CHANGE

How Changes in Keiretsu Are Opening the Japanese Market

Kiyoshi Mori

Kiyoshi Mori, a guest scholar in the Brookings Economic Studies program last year, is an official of the Japanese Ministry of International Trade and Industry. The views expressed here are his own, not those of his agency.

KEIRETSU. Americans have spilled much ink trying to come to grips with the cooperative business structure that links Japanese companies into industrial groups and that, Americans widely believe, keeps U.S. companies out of the Japanese market. Many strategies have been proposed to combat keiretsu—from using Japanese antitrust enforcement to break up monopolistic transactions among members of industrial groups to forcing Japan's government to loosen restrictions against U.S.-style mergers and acquisitions with which to oppose them. So far, however, none of these strategies has been very successful. The penetration of foreign manufacturers in the Japanese market remains low.

It is time to try a different approach. Over the past decade the keiretsu relationship has been undergoing changes, and those changes offer an expanded opportunity to gain entry into the Japanese markets.

The Changing Keiretsu Relationship

The heart of the keiretsu relationship has been the affinity of Japan's business culture, both corporate managers and employees, for long-term cooperative relationships. Traditionally Japanese managers have opted for long-term contracts with a limited number of partners. Employees have favored a system of lifetime employment. And the two sets of preferences have reinforced each other.

Throughout the post–World War II era, the managers of Japan's largest companies have kept their companies slim, preferring to contract large amounts of labor-intensive work out to smaller firms rather than to absorb new contracts through mergers and acquisitions, as many U.S. managers have done. One reason large Japanese companies began contracting work out was the substantial wage difference between large and small companies: in 1960 salaries in small firms were only about 60 percent of those in large firms. Another was the need to finance every new employee position for the jobholder's lifetime. Managers who know they are expected to keep employees on the payroll until retirement are particularly cautious about hiring more workers.

Other characteristics of the keiretsu relationship, from cross-shareholding among partner companies and their banks to the kanban system of just-in-time delivery, with the manufacturer depending on its supplier to furnish inventory as needed, also knit keiretsu member companies together in long-term cooperative relationships.

Lately, however, the rationale of the keiretsu system has begun to weaken. First, dealings between contractors and subcontractors have been strained by purchase practices that subcontractors find objectionable. Some subcontractors, for example, especially in the service and retail industries, must do their work on extremely short notice and at quite low fee rates. In addition, with the Japanese economy in recession and industry no longer expanding, subcontracting companies have been unable to depend on the traditional single long-term relationship. In 1986, when a sudden appreciation of the yen slowed the Japanese economy, even Toyota advised its subcontractors to build up business with other contractors.

The perspective of employees is also changing. Well-educated workers, especially women, are beginning to have second thoughts about the lifetime employment system, viewing it less as a source of social status and more as an impediment to their self-development as professionals who might want a variety of business experience.

Shrinking wage differences between large and small companies (salaries in small firms are now nearly 80 percent of those in large firms) have erased much of the cost advantages of keiretsu relationships for managers of larger firms.

Even the just-in-time delivery system has recently come under fire. Although the frequent deliveries of parts are useful for manufacturers, they worsen traffic congestion and impose onerous work schedules on the suppliers.

These changes in the value of the keiretsu relationship offer American companies a way to break into the Japanese market. Americans may, for example, be able to negotiate subcontracts with suppliers of high-quality goods or services who are seeking multiple long-term relationships with companies outside the old keiretsus. They will be able to hire workers who already have substantial work experience in Japan and want to change their careers. Mobil Sekiyu, the second largest foreign petroleum company in Japan, is already trying to attract talented workers by offering high-quality employee training, promoting women aggressively, and improving working conditions.

U.S. companies can use these strategies to establish a substantial base in the Japanese economy and then penetrate the institutional barriers of the Japanese industrial system through offering cooperation in newly emerging technologies and product development—areas in which even the older large companies that dominated the keiretsu system are less effective.

Changes in Financing

Even more important to U.S. business are major changes in the system of financing used within the keiretsu structure. Just after World War II, Japanese business, having no significant capital to invest, had no choice but to borrow money. Financial markets were immature, and the government encouraged banks to be the primary intermediaries between savers and investors and to set interest rates low to enable businesses to borrow money.

Beginning in the early 1970s, Japanese managers began to derive more of their funds directly from the bond and equity market. Yamaha, a large musical instrument, motorcycle, and sports equipment company, issued new stock at the market price for the first time in Japan in 1969. Over time the debt-equity ratio of domestic companies gradually fell, from an average of more than 70 percent in the 1950s to under 50 percent in the 1980s. Their dependency on the banks has declined even further.

Still, bank loans continued to play an important role in financing, with three factors leading companies to continue to borrow. First, interest rates remained low. Second, government restrictions in the financial sector slowed the development of the bond, commercial paper, and asset-backed securi-

ties markets. Finally, newly accumulated equity was often used as collateral for new loans. When a keiretsu member asked the group's main bank to purchase its newly issued stock, the bank almost invariably asked it to borrow money in return, using some of its increased capital as collateral. But despite the continued reliance on borrowing, in fact the primary role of banks has changed—from one in which they lend money to their group companies to one in which they hold newly issued stock.

Cross-Shareholding: A Core of Keiretsu?

At the close of World War II cross-shareholding among related businesses offered a way to absorb liquidated stocks (resulting from the breakup of major Japanese prewar holding companies) that the market could not otherwise have handled. It also helped protect Japanese companies from takeovers by foreign investors or companies. It can still serve that purpose—and did in 1984, when members of the Mitsubishi Group protected the Mitsubishi Oil Company from being acquired by Texaco.

As a result of cross-shareholding, banks hold more than 40 percent of all stock listed on all Japanese stock exchanges, other companies 30 percent, and individuals only a little more than 20 percent.

But cross-shareholding, too, has begun to change. In particular there is less cross-shareholding within keiretsu groups. Keiretsu member companies have begun seeking transactions with companies outside the group. In 1989 Nikkei Newspaper reported that five Japanese companies, all unconnected, made cross-shareholding arrangements for reasons of business strategy and access to new technologies, not historical ties. As Kenicki Imai, of Stanford University, has noted, "technological and engineering perspectives," rather than keiretsu relationships, are increasingly determining interfirm linkages. Finally, cross-shareholding purely for the purpose of providing finance rather than corporate control has increased since the 1980s.

Why Is It Easy to Issue New Stock in Japan?

In the United States, stockholders traditionally oppose plans to issue new stocks to a third party because stock prices generally fall as a result. By contrast, Japanese companies can, and often do, choose to issue new stock—and the price of their stock often *increases* after the new shares are made available. The explanation for the sharply different experience in Japan is twofold: the price-earnings ratio of Japanese companies is quite high, and dividends are extremely low. When stock prices are high, a company can raise a considerable amount of money by issuing a small amount of new stock. Yet a low dividend pay-out implies only a negligible increase in future cash payments. Thus the cost of issuing new stock is often lower than interest rates for loans. These conditions, however, seldom happen in the United States, where high dividend rates and relatively low price-earnings ratios make the cost of is-

Banks hold more than 40 percent of all stock listed on all Japanese stock exchanges, other companies 30 percent, and individuals only a little more than 20 percent.

suing new stocks the same as, or higher than, interest rates for loans.

Why do Japanese stockholders accept such low dividends? The answer used to be that Japanese companies preferred participating in the keiretsu cross-shareholding system over receiving and paying a higher dividend. But increasingly the answer is that domestic companies that create new cross-shareholding networks can mutually increase the potential value of their assets by issuing new stock and then borrow money cheaply by using these stock assets as collateral for new loans. The Japanese accounting system, which for tax purposes does not require companies to change their balance sheets in accordance with the increase in the "hidden value of assets" (the difference between book value and actual market value), also undergirds the system.

The Japanese business system, especially its financial component, will not be able to remain isolated from U.S. or European systems permanently.

Recession and the Financing System

During 1987–90, the period of Japan's "bubble economy," most of the major Japanese companies engaged in aggressive equity financing and built strong cross-shareholding relationships with main banks.

These business strategies, however, were abandoned abruptly in 1990, in the aftermath of several huge downturns in the Japanese stock market. The consequences for both Japanese banks and corporations in the early 1990s were severe. Large banks and insurance companies suffered as the hidden asset values on which they had relied heavily for expanding their businesses fell sharply. Most major companies' operational profits fell dramatically during the severe economic recession that began in 1991. And since 1992 companies have been obsessed with redeeming convertible bonds that they had issued during the bubble economy and that have not been converted to stocks.

All this is further straining the keiretsu system. No longer able to rely on the old certainty that stock prices would be going up, Japanese companies and banks are far less willing than before to hold stock in keiretsu-member companies. The volatile state of the Japanese stock market has driven off most substantial purchasers. Even if some companies wanted to issue new stocks, there is no one to buy them.

This situation, painful as it is for Japanese companies, offers U.S. business an important opening into the Japanese market. Although some economists believe that the Japanese cross-shareholding financial system collapsed completely with the end of the bubble economy, the conditions in Japan's stock market that encouraged equity financing and cross-shareholding have not changed substantially: equity prices remain relatively high, and dividends, extremely low. Most notably, because stock prices have not dropped as dramatically as average company profits, the average price-earnings ratio has increased nearly to 80 (compared with about 25 in the United States).

How Can U.S. Companies Invest in Japan?

Despite its unique nature over the postwar period, the Japanese business system, especially its financial component, will not be able to remain isolated from U.S. or European systems permanently. Japan's traditional financial system is under pressure on many different sides.

For example, although the continuous asset price increase (gradual at first, and then dramatic during the bubble economy) nurtured by the postwar financing system has contributed to the rapid progress of Japan's economy, it has also kept Japan's people from being able to buy property—a state of affairs that Japanese appear less and less willing to tolerate.

And given the current strains on the keiretsu system, Japanese banks and stock companies will surely begin developing international risk management methods independent from the other keiretsu members.

In addition, recent amendments to Japanese commercial law have made it easier for stockholders to sue their company, a change that may encourage company managers to increase dividends in accordance with their profits.

Finally, capital standards set by the Bank for International Settlement (BIS), which are supposed to be strengthened further in the near future, may prevent Japanese banks from holding large amounts of equities in their asset portfolio.

But the adjustment of the Japanese financial system to the international financing systems will be gradual, and in the interval elements of the old keiretsu-style financing structures will continue to operate, particularly as long as the two key stock market conditions (high price-earnings ratio and low dividends) remain.

The gradual weakening of both the keiretsu relationship and the cross-shareholding systems offers U.S. companies opportunities to use equity financing of the sort that boosted industrial growth in Japan. They can even establish temporary cross-shareholding relationships with Japanese companies for the purpose of arranging efficient financing. A Japanese company issuing new stock in the domestic market and a U.S. company issuing convertible bonds in the Euro-market could enter a cross-shareholding arrangement to increase their respective potential assets. They could also use these assets as collateral for new loans, as the big Japanese companies did before the bubble economy. U.S. companies can pursue these strategies because, not having previously acquired substantial stocks and property in the Japanese market, they, unlike many Japanese keiretsu companies, have not been hit by the decrease in the value of these hidden assets.

I do not mean to suggest that U.S. companies should always follow Japanese business methods when they operate in Japan. They can protest

Japanese business structures they think unfair. But at the same time, they should take advantage of the current business opportunities, particularly those related to financing.

Now is a turning point for the Japanese economy. Since World War II the keiretsu-style cross-shareholding system and the hidden assets of property and stocks have been the chief risk absorbers in corporate and financial management. But from now on, Japan must rely more on strict risk-management financing and operating systems, which can no longer be guaranteed by the keiretsu membership ties. Success in this reform will help create Japan's future prosperity—a prosperity it will enjoy under a more mobile system of labor management, a more deregulated financial market, and a simpler distribution system. Farsighted U.S. companies will invest in the Japanese market now—a move the highly appreciated yen has made harder, but not impossible.

How Management Deals with Environmental Forces

Managers of international organizations are faced with the problem of having to deal with a changing and varied global environment. To be successful, managers cannot just sit back and wait for things to happen. They need to be proactive in their approach to the opportunities and problems associated with doing business on an international basis.

One of the major tools that managers have to help their organizations become successful on the global stage is marketing, and in particular, marketing analysis. Managers need to realize that while all markets have certain similarities, they are all different in their own way. The various levels of marketing are also different in their own way, while at the same time having certain similarities (see Kim Howard's report, "Global Retailing 2000"). Yet certain practices are different and will probably remain so for the foreseeable future.

In the case of industrial sales, trade shows play a much larger role in Europe than they do in the United States. Trade shows require proper preparation, and some help in preparing for trade shows is presented in "Planning for International Trade Show Participation: A Practitioner's Perspective."

An easy way for a firm to get into international trade is through import/export channels. Quite often, when a small firm first starts to engage in international trade, it is not a deliberate action on the part of the company. The company might place an advertisement in one of the industrial magazines, or will have a booth at a trade show, or will have an article about them in the news, and one day they get an order from someone outside of their domestic market. It may be for a very small order that in so many words says, "Send us one of these, we would like to look at it!" This is frequently followed by a much larger order, and the small domestic firm suddenly finds itself doing business abroad. This can happen on either side of the equation; as an importer or an exporter. As time passes, the foreign business often grows at a faster rate than the domestic business, especially if it involves one of the more rapidly developing economies, and all of a sudden, a significant amount of business is being done overseas. The essays "Forming International Sales Pacts" and "Export Channel Design: The Use of Foreign Distributors and Agents" address the challenges firms face when performing international business.

An especially difficult area for firms has been the recent developments in Eastern Europe and the former Soviet Union. Certainly there is great opportunity in these markets, but there is also great risk. Many people in these societies simply do not know how to operate in a developing capitalist system. Commercial laws have not been developed, and an understanding of the fundamental aspects of capitalism has not been achieved by much of the population, including important government officials, as well as quasi-capitalists, such as factory managers. As the article "Yes, You *Can* Win in Eastern Europe" implies, it is possible to succeed in Eastern Europe trade, but it is not easy. International managers must be prepared for setbacks and disappointments before they will be able to experience success.

Of particular concern in international trade has always been the monetary issue. Currency trading and fluctuations have caused managers sleepless nights and terrible days. Some of the currencies from the developing world, in particular, are difficult to deal with. As Ben Edwards discusses in "Negotiating the Honeyed Knife-Edge," the rewards can be very high, but, unfortunately, so are the risks. Managers who engage in world trade need to develop a set of risk-management goals. In "A Framework for Risk Management," the authors advise how managers should deal with the financial aspects of their global business if they are going to be successful.

An additional factor that needs to be considered is that of production. A world economy means not only worldwide customers but worldwide production. To be competitive, organizations must be able to produce worldwide and to coordinate those activities to the greatest advantage of the organizations. This is demonstrated in Peter Buxbaum's report, "Timberland's New Spin on Global Logistics." With the introduction of the North American Free Trade Agreement (NAFTA), firms in North America are not just American, Canadian, or Mexican firms, but they are North American firms with an entire continent as their backyard. These organizations are in the process of seeking integration, and, as the essay "North American Business Integration" reports, many of them are well on their way to achieving that goal.

Organizations that are going to produce, distribute, and sell overseas must realize that they cannot do this without workers, the people who perform the necessary tasks for the organization's success. Generally speaking, labor relations are very different outside North America. The relationship between labor and management in Germany, for example, frequently involves a highly cooperative arrangement between union and management. On the other hand, in some lesser developed countries, child labor is often common and a living wage, let alone

benefits, is as rare as a union organizer. This does not mean that organizations from developed countries should emulate all these practices, but they should select those aspects that are the best (see the articles "Lesson from HR Overseas" and "A Global Glance at Work and Family").

International managers must learn to combine all of these parts of the new global business environment. They must plan strategically to include marketing, production, finance, and labor to be successful, and they must learn to control this highly diverse and sometimes contentious brew by using the most modern management technologies available. Controlling a business on an international scale is certainly not easy, and, as the essay "Transnational Management Systems: An Emerging Tool for Global Strategic Management" advises, management information systems will be needed in the future so that managers will be successful.

In conclusion, there are many challenges facing managers in the international environment. But, fortunately, managers do have some of the tools they will need to deal with these challenges. The task will not be easy, and new problems and opportunities are certain to arise in the future. Managers will have to develop all of the tools necessary to deal with these challenges, so that they will be successful in the developing international business environment.

Looking Ahead: Challenge Questions

What are some of the things that marketers can do to market more effectively on the international level?

Doing business in the former Soviet Union and Eastern Europe blocs is difficult, but it is possible. What are some of the things that can be done when doing business in this particular part of the world?

The challenge for managers in the future will be in a new and changing international environment. How can managers strategically plan for success in the future?

The New *Sexenio*

Fraught with opportunity and peril, Mexico continues to entice foreign investors.

Joan Rothman

Joan Rothman is Vice President of Market Planning and Development for Dun & Bradstreet Information Services, Murray Hill, N.J. She is responsible for several strategic initiatives with particular focus on database services and new market development. In addition, Joan served on the executive committee of the Electronic Services Division of the Information Industry Association and is currently a member of the IIA's Global Development Council. She received her MBA in 1984 from Baruch College.

Mexican President Ernesto Zedillo began his six-year term in December at the Latin American crossroads of free markets and free elections. Zedillo's task was to maneuver safely through the intersection, complete the economic liberalization program of outgoing President Carlos Salinas de Gortari, and democratize the nation's electoral system.

Unexpectedly, however, the new administration veered sideways. Deep fissures emerged in Zedillo's ruling Revolutionary Institutional Party, conflict resumed in rebel strongholds in the southern state of Chiapas, and the peso's value plunged by one-third, falling prey to an economic formula irreverently dubbed the "Tequila hangover."

All of this appeared to undermine, if not repudiate, the Salinas *sexenio*—the Mexican term for six-year political epochs—and imperil Zedillo's own.

But, even as fair-weather free traders took flight, Mexico's economic foundation remained sound and new opportunities emerged. Mexico spends 70¢ of every import dollar on U.S. goods, and, in the first year of the North American Free Trade Agreement (NAFTA), two-way commerce between the United States and Mexico expanded to more than $100 billion.

As the United States pledged essentially unlimited assistance to help Zedillo prop up the peso, Japanese and Korean investors poured tens of millions of dollars into new Mexican manufacturing ventures.

Global investors, moreover, began assessing a new wave of Mexican privatization programs that will include railroads, telecommunications, airports, and seaports. Zedillo himself, in a speech at the height of the peso debacle, said, "In the same way as the crisis situation that we face demands sacrifices of us, we should also identify and take advantage of the opportunities it affords."

Partners of Choice

Invariably, the first year of a new *sexenio* is marked by the crossed swords of victors and vanquished, optimism and uncertainty, progress and pain. Ultimately, it inspires reconciliation and consolidation.

Even now, olive branches are being extended to the first coalition presidential cabinet since the 1910 revolution. Broad new social and financial initiatives are being devised to convert Mexico's recent economic largess to the benefit of all Mexicans. A new infrastructure—roads, bridges, rail trestles—is being constructed to quicken the pace of North American integration.

And a new *infostructure* is being laid as well—beginning with capital investment in the nation's intellectual resources and extending to technology transfers, joint ventures, and the arrival of cross-border financial services including banking, brokerages, insurance, and credit. Eighteen foreign banking institutions are coming to Mexico. Among them are Citicorp, Chemical Banking Corp., Chase Manhattan Corp., and American Express Bank.

Executive Briefing

Newly installed Mexican president Ernesto Zedillo's six-year term got off to an inauspicious start as the peso plunged in December, throwing the economy into turmoil. But many U.S. corporations are keeping the faith and increasing their investment in Mexico. Free-trade treaties, backing from the Clinton Administration, and Zedillo's vow to maintain fiscal discipline combine to bolster confidence in Mexico's ability to wrench itself out of the Third World by the early part of the next century.

American business has heeded Mexico's call for expanding cooperation and assistance. In the first year of NAFTA, U.S. exports to Mexico rose more than 21%, averaging $1 billion a week and generating more than 100,000 jobs, according to the U.S. Commerce Department. During the same time, Mexican exports to the United States increased about 23%.

Moreover, at a time when Latin America generally, and Mexico specifically, emerged as a touchstone for global investment, the United States remained by far the region's partner of choice. In the second half of the Salinas *sexenio*, when his reforms started taking effect, foreign investment in Mexico rose from $30.3 billion to $42.4 billion by the end of 1993. U.S. investment, 74.2% of the total, grew during that same time period from $19.1 billion to $26.3 billion. Trailing far behind the United States were the United Kingdom (which represents 6.4% of the total foreign investment in Mexico), Germany (5.7%), Switzerland (4.6%), Japan (4.3%), and Korea (4%).

The leading individual U.S. investors were the Big Three automakers—General Motors, Ford, and Chrysler—followed by IBM, Celanese, Kimberly Clark, American Express, Anderson-Clayton, Xerox, Dupont, Hewlett Packard, and Vitronatic. Retail trade represents 39.4% of the Mexican marketplace, followed by wholesale trade (19.8%), services (11.4%), manufacturing (9%), and construction (8.9%). Other sectors are far smaller.

Enduring Model

Though it is impossible to gauge perfectly what the next six years will bring, the Zedillo *sexenio* inherits and embraces a broad, enduring framework for the future. Mexico's participation in NAFTA and GATT (the General Agreement on Tariffs and Trade), and its election last year to the Organization for Economic Co-operation and Development—the international policy-making body of the world's 25 largest market-economies—all follow from Salinas's neoliberal model. In a nation where the politics of personality traditionally rule, these cross-border pledges will outlive the men who made them.

NAFTA itself establishes a schedule for the prompt abolishment of tariffs between the United States, Canada, and Mexico. It promotes nondiscriminatory treatment for cross-border ventures, eliminates the need for government approval of most foreign investments, clears the way for profits and royalties to be remitted and capital repatriated, protects against uncompensated expropriations, and establishes a system of arbitration to enforce investor rights.

Failures Haunt

The Salinas *sexenio* also was characterized by failures. The Chiapas Indian uprising, which

EXHIBIT 1

Macroeconomic Mexico

	1988	1990	1992	1994E	1995E
Population (million)	82.8	86.2	89.5	93.0	94.7
GDP (billion)	171.8	244.0	323.4	387.7	410.1
GDP Real Growth (%)	1.2	4.4	2.6	3.2	4.7
Per Capita Growth ($)	-0.8	2.4	0.7	1.3	2.7
Inflation	51.7	29.9	11.9	6.5	5.0
U.S. Inflation	.4	6.2	3.0	3.0	3.0

Source: Smith Barney Shearson

erupted a year ago after decades of neglect, lingers yet. Fears of high-level assassinations, fueled by the death of a leading presidential candidate, persist. Prominent kidnappings and political disarray can be expected to continue in the aftermath of last August's presidential elections until Zedillo establishes his personal authority and until his commitment to extending Salinas's reforms are understood as unequivocal.

It's important to understand that the Mexican peso crisis, though perhaps mismanaged by Zedillo, was an accumulated problem inherited from past presidential administrations. Salinas's economic reforms left Mexico's industrialists needing vast sums of foreign capital to modernize. At the same time, an emergent middle class suddenly was introduced to an appealing array of imported consumer goods. A large current-account deficit—the difference between exports and imports—resulted, totaling $77 billion in the last four years.

The deficit was financed by government sales of short-term debt and foreign investment capital. But when enough investors concluded that the deficit was too great, they pulled out of Mexico, draining the Central Bank of foreign exchange and forcing Zedillo to allow the peso to trade freely against the U.S. dollar for the first time in Mexico's modern history.

Zedillo, an economist, explained, "One clear opportunity lies in freeing our economy of the burden implied by an overvalued exchange rate. The burden was preventing us from translating the structural changes we undertook with so much hard work into more dynamic economic growth."

Defining Realms

The success of Zedillo's efforts over the next six years will be measured in three broad realms: improving Mexico's social and economic demographics, extracting maximum benefit from NAFTA, and laying a blueprint—through legal and political means—for developing Mexico's economy into the 21st century.

Social and Economic Demographics

Three times the size of Texas, Mexico is the third largest country in Latin America, after Brazil and Argentina, and 13th largest in the world.

Mexico's per capita gross domestic product, the best measure of a nation's productivity, and ultimately its wealth, doubled during the Salinas *sexenio* from $2,074 to an estimated $4,169. Unemployment declined by nearly half, from 15.4% to 8%. And inflation, the parasite that robs any economy of its strength and promise, fell from 160% in Salinas's first year to about 6.4% at the *sexenio*'s close (see Exhibit 1).

If the Zedillo government is able to stabilize the peso exchange rate at about 4.5 to $1, it will be able to contain domestic inflation at about 19% this year and quickly begin pushing it back down again.

Mexico is a young, educated, fast-growing nation—Latin America's MTV generation. About 57% of its 86 million population is under age 30; nearly one-third is between ages 16 and 30. This means another 12 million workers will join Mexico's 26 million member labor force over the next decade.

It is widely known that 25 Mexican families control 54.2% of the nation's wealth, with half of Mexico's assets held by six conglomerates: Grupo Carso, Visa, Vitro, Telmex, Alfa, and Grupo Mexico. Under Salinas's watch, that wealth concentration increased. According to Mexico's National Statistics Institute, the elite upper-tier absorbed an additional .6% of the nation's resources during the Salinas *sexenio*, whereas the poorest 20% lost .11% and now accounts for just 4.28% of the total economy. Except for Brazil, that is the greatest skew between haves and have-nots in Latin America.

All told, 37 million Mexicans live in poverty. The Mexican Social Security Institute, the nation's largest public health care provider, covers only 38% of the working population, and just 7.7 telephone lines serve every 100 inhabitants, compared to about 20 per 100 in most developed countries and 50 per 100 in the United States.

Malnutrition, the surest sign of poverty, touches 66% of all Mexicans. "The most important cause of malnutrition is lack of purchasing power," notes Hector Bourges, M.D., of the Mexican government's National Nutrition Institute.

Remedying these inequities can be viewed as an obligation or an opportunity; the solution can be perceived as either a cost or a potential return. Increasingly, it appears that the task of modern nation-building in Mexico is being seen as an unmitigated opportunity not only by domestic power brokers and international investors, but by all elements of society, including opposition political factions.

To lay the foundation for Mexico's next generation—and its dramatically restructured economy—about 1,000 technical schools countrywide are educating skilled, motivated workers with vastly growing purchasing power. Moreover, even though only 3% of the population has a college degree, the literacy rate is about 88%. That means Mexican labor is prepared to adapt to the increasing technological and productivity demands of the global economy. And it demonstrates that Mexico itself is fast becoming a lucrative market in which to sell.

Case in point: Union Pacific Railroad, which links the industrial Midwest to Mexico City through a north-south rail line that crosses the border at Laredo, Texas, saw its loads increase 17.4% in the first 10 months of 1994; Union Pacific spent $4 million in 1994 to add six new tracks to its intermodeal transfer yard in Laredo; and it petitioned the Mexican government to build a $62.7 million border bridge beginning sometime in 1995—all to support increased cross-border trade between the two nations.

Doubters insist that U.S. investment in Mexico drains American jobs and destroys northern industry through low-cost export platforms that ultimately will serve American, rather than Mexican, customers. Every major U.S. government indicator points to the contrary, notably the U.S. merchandise trade surplus with Mexico, which, through the third quarter, was running at a record annual rate of $2.8 billion.

Even excepting government data, consider the example of Wal-Mart stores, which in December 1993 opened a 208,000 square foot superstore in the northern Mexico city of Monterrey: First-day turnout was so great that security personnel blocked the entrances and allowed new customers in only as others exited. A few months later, Kmart Corp. opened a store just outside of Mexico City. Since then, a daily average of 40,000 customers have been swarming its aisles.

The U.S. Commerce Department has identified the following trades as enjoying the best export prospects in Mexico: automotive parts and service equipment, chemical production machinery, plastics materials and resins, industrial chemicals, machine tools and metalworking equipment, laboratory and scientific equipment, computers and peripherals, telecommunications equipment, oil and gas field machinery, and franchising and services. In fact, almost any reputable product with an American moniker has better-than-average prospects in Mexico.

Here are a few prominent examples of NAFTA-inspired investments:

• Bell Atlantic Corp. announced plans to pay $1.04 billion for 42% of Grupo Iusacell, Mexico's second-largest cellular telephone company. In October 1993, Bell Atlantic paid a first-installment of $520 million for 23% of Iusacell's shares. Mexico is deregulating telephone service and aggressively seeking to increase the number of standard and cellular telephone lines nationwide.

• General Electric Co. subsidiary NBC formed a joint venture with Television Azteca under which it received the option to buy up to 20% of Azteca's stock for $328 million. The venture partners also agreed to develop programming, advertising sales, and technology for U.S. and Mexican markets.

• Anheuser-Busch Cos. acquired 10% of Mexican brewing giant Grupo Modelo S.A. de C.V. for $207.3 million, with an option to double the investment within two years. Busch, the world's biggest brewer, thus buys into the second most popular U.S. beer import, Corona Extra, and lays the groundwork for establishing distribution in Mexico, the world's eighth-largest beer market.

• Major automakers Chrysler, Ford, General Motors, Honda, Nissan, and BMW earmarked $2.4 billion in investment for Mexico last year.

That reflects industry predictions that Mexico will produce more than 2 million vehicles annually by the year 2000, up from 1.2 million now, and that its auto parts trade will double the existing $6.5 billion annual sales in the next six years. (Ford expected its sale of U.S. and Canadian-built cars to Mexico to rise to 25,000 cars in 1994, from 1,500 a year earlier, claiming that figure would double in 1995 and again in 1996. Meanwhile, General Motors planned to export 10,000 cars to Mexico last year compared to just 1,700 in 1993, and Chrysler said it would export to Mexico 2,500 Dodge Intrepids from its Newark, Del., plant.)

Doing Business in Mexico

Each morning, two-dozen buses convey 540 first-shift employees to Ford Motor Co.'s Chihuahua, Mexico, engine plant. Roughly 1,500 miles to the north, hundreds of cars fill an employee parking lot outside an older Ford engine plant in Lima, Ohio. "Separated by an international border, language, and an average age difference of 30 years, the two groups of workers are nevertheless part of the same corporate web. They produce for the same market with largely the same technology, answer to the same executives, and generate dividends for the same shareholders," social economist Tom Barry observes in his 1994 primer, *The Great Divide: The Challenge of U.S.-Mexico Relations in the 1990s.*

Ford's intricate interconnects demonstrate the remarkable degree to which North and South already are integrated. "International trade no longer conforms to the textbook model of an exchange of British cloth for Portuguese wine," according to the New York-based Committee for Economic Development (CED), which consists of top executives from most U.S. blue-chip corporations.

"An American automobile may be designed in Japan, assembled in Canada or Mexico, and consist of parts manufactured in Taiwan, Brazil, or just about anywhere," the CED's recent paper, "U.S. Trade Policy Beyond the Uruguay Round," notes. "Globalization, therefore, means increased trade in parts, components, and semi-finished goods. It also implies an increase in intra-firm trade... .

"In short, the traditional horizontal pattern of trade in final products is being overtaken by a form of vertical trade in which countries specialize in different parts or stages of the production chain for individual products."

Consequently, today's corporation must view itself from a global perspective even if it doesn't function as such. "Cross-cultural, cross-functional, and multilingual knowledge and fluency," assert Institute of the Future researchers Mary O'Hara-Devereaux and Robert Johansen, "will be among the most highly valued assets in the emerging managerial landscape—whether one works in a global, regional, or national organization."

But important differences between the United States and Mexico also persist. As Mexico City

Cardinal Ernest Carhop Ahumada was helping a nun out of his car one day last May, thieves rode up on a motorcycle and stole the vehicle at gunpoint. They also made off with keys to the shrine of the Virgin of Guadalupe. If the papal representative in heavily Catholic Mexico is not sacred, then nothing is.

The laments are many in Mexico, including but not limited to official corruption, cartel-like competition, high-level kidnappings, and assassinations that reach even the upper strata of Mexican society. Mexican leaders are in a quandary, as evidenced by the ruling party's muted response to the Chiapas rebellion.

Heavy-handed repression, the one-time answer, fosters resentment and potential for even greater violence. Unanswered assaults on civil society, however, threaten to undermine Mexico's economic gains and sully its international reputation. Salinas's view, dented but not discredited, was that economic development would create expanded opportunities for all Mexicans over time and, thereby, lessen the nation's social disequilibrium.

More encouraging to outsiders is the increasing sophistication of Mexico's legal system. U.S. Ambassador to Mexico James R. Jones, the former head of the American Stock Exchange, credited Zedillo in a recent speech for "expanding political reform, further increasing cooperation in fighting narcotrafficking, and undertaking a complete reform of the judicial system." For instance, the Law to Promote Mexican Investment and Regulate Foreign Investment, overhauled in 1989, provided foreigners with entry to two-thirds of Mexico's economy. Under pressure from global technologists, Mexico also enacted strong intellectual property safeguards.

And in June 1993, the national legislature passed the Federal Economic Competition Act, a cartel- and monopoly-busting law that is the rough equivalent to three landmark pieces of U.S. legislation: the 1890 Sherman Antitrust Act, 1914 Clayton Act, and 1914 Federal Trade Commission Act. The new law prohibits price fixing, production and distribution restraints, bid-rigging, and shared market arrangements. It authorizes exclusive distributorships, however, and exempts both the Federal Electricity Commission and semi-private Telefonos de Mexico utilities.

At the same time, certain Mexican customs will continue to depart from the U.S. norm for generations to come. Mexico is a hierarchical society dominated by paternalistic institutions: family, church, employer, and government. The United States, as revealed by the cars parked outside the Ohio Ford plant, remains an individualistic culture. American investors and marketers in Mexico must distinguish those differences.

Several alternatives exist for conducting business in Mexico, including product licensing, direct investment for export to the United States (exemplified by the in-bond plants), direct investment for sale in Mexico and Latin America, and joint venturing, whether to capitalize on Mexican markets or Mexican labor savings (see Exhibit 2 on page 47). At an individual level, opportunities exist for direct and door-to-door marketing.

RJR Nabisco provides an example of the go-it-alone approach in Mexico. After a 20-year partnership with Monterrey-based Gamesa, RJR's Nabisco S.A. de C.V. subsidiary bought out Gamesa in 1992 and spent $125 million to increase its 10% share of the Mexican cookie and cracker market. Sears Roebuck de Mexico, which owns 46 department stores in Mexico, plans to invest $300 million through 1999 to add 30 outlets. RJR and Sears are confident of their prowess in Mexico. Others, less so, seek partners.

Joint ventures, once strictly controlled by the Mexican government, are highly flexible instruments in the NAFTA era in which up to 100% ownership can be vested in the foreign partner. U.S. investors often view joint ventures as the surest way to land securely in a new market. Mexicans, in turn, see the partnerships as a means to secure the capital, technology, product and management strategy needed to succeed in the post-NAFTA environment. "It does not mean losing our sovereignty but rather making the best use of our resources," observes Jorge Diaz Saran, former director general of state-owned energy monopoly Petroleos Mexicanos.

Promise and Peril

Long before NAFTA, Mexico created a duty-free trade zone along its northern flank known as the Zona Libre, or free zone, which played a fundamental role in the development of small towns along both sides of the border in the late part of the last century. It succeeded so well, in fact, drawing commerce away from central Mexico and traditional U.S. channels, that by 1905 it was taxed and regulated into extinction (see "Back to the Future" on facing page).

With NAFTA, GATT, and the beginning of the new *sexenio*, a vastly improved framework exists for trading and investment in Mexico whose nation-building efforts are unfinished but advancing. Due in large part to its expanding economic partnership with the United States, Mexico is destined to become a developed nation by the early 21th century. It follows that opportunities for doing business in Mexico are proliferating, in part because the nation's young, mobilized work force is creating a dynamic new social and economic infrastructure.

As U.S. Ambassador Jones observed in a recent speech: "The road to the First World, to a free-market economy, and to full democracy is not a smooth one. The events of 1994 brought that point home very clearly. An uprising in Chiapas, the murders of prominent politicians, and the sudden devaluation of the peso all shocked Mexico and the international community.

Back to the Future

During the 35-year rule of Gen. Porfirio Diaz from 1876–1910, Mexico relied on foreign capitalists to develop the nation's infrastructure and economy. Railroads, mines, oil wells, banks, ports, and large-scale agricultural projects—financed largely from abroad, mostly with U.S. dollars—remade the landscape.

"Order and progress," was Diaz's dictum. Ultimately, however, Mexico's popular classes grew sufficiently frustrated by the enrichment and corruption of the nation's elite to lead an assault on the *Porfiriato*—as Diaz's reign was known—and force the septuagenarian ruler into exile.

The civil war that followed, a protracted struggle that incorporated agrarian, class, economic, and religious conflicts, culminated in a new constitution in 1917. Article 27 of the new constitution gave the state authority to limit foreign investment in the Mexican economy. It also granted government ownership of all lands and waters, and the right to expropriate private property.

Mexico thereafter joined the rest of Latin America in what is known as the import-substitution model of development. Its design: Develop a strong national industrial base by encouraging domestic production of imported goods.

"Mexico was one of the most vigorous and successful exponents of [import-substitution]. Starting in the 1920s and accelerating after World War II, Mexico raised tariffs and imposed other barriers to imports, assigning the highest duties to those goods that economic planners felt would be easiest to produce domestically, such as apparel, footwear, and bottled beverages," write Tom Barry, Harry Browne, and Beth Sims in *The Great Divide: The Challenge of U.S.-Mexico Relations in the 1990s.* These are the very conditions that the tariff-abolishing NAFTA compact would reverse.

Over time, Mexico's economy became increasingly self-reliant and isolated. Foreign capital fell from 66% of total investment at the end of the *Porfiriato* to about 10% in the 1950s, 5% in the 1960s, and less than 3% in the 1970s.

Oil remained the elixir, however, with petroleum exports an important lubricator of the nation's increasingly inefficient economic engine. Even after Mexico otherwise disengaged from the global power train, oil offered collateral for tens of billions of dollars of foreign borrowings, and a hard currency-equivalent for state financing of giant domestic hydroelectric projects, jungle roads, and beach resorts.

Only after oil prices plummeted in 1982 did the chronic deficiencies in Mexico's development model become inescapable. Government-directed debt payments sapped the nation's economy, forcing the leadership to abandon its ambitious infrastructure projects and contributing to massive job dislocations, particularly in such neglected, undeveloped regions as Chiapas. President Jose Lopez Portillo subsequently nationalized the nation's banks and devalued the peso by more than 90%. Real wages dropped by as much as half.

Portillo's successor, Miguel de la Madrid, began the necessary policy reversals by scrapping Mexico's import-substitution model, and, in 1986, making Mexico a signator to GATT. (In fact, de la Madrid reduced tariffs more rapidly than GATT required.)

In 1989, the successor Carlos Salinas de Gortari administration signed a debt-reduction agreement—named for U.S. Treasury Secretary Nicholas Brady—that reversed Mexico's net external transfers abroad, generating net capital inflows equal to 5% of gross domestic product. And the creditors agreement enabled Mexico to sell bonds on international markets and attract significant new investment to Mexico's stock exchange, the Bolsa de Valores.

Salinas went on to privatize more than 1,000 state enterprises, raising better than $23.7 billion. According to the World Bank, 10 of the world's 20 largest privatizations since 1988 were undertaken in Latin America, 5 in Mexico. Seeking to consolidate Mexican reforms and accelerate its gains, Salinas proposed a free-trade compact with the United States in June 1992 that served as the basis for NAFTA.

Prior to NAFTA, the average tariff on goods entering the United States from Mexico was 3%–4%, and about 10% for goods leaving the United States to enter Mexico. NAFTA reduces most such duties to zero within 15 years.

—*Joan Rothman*

"And yet," he says, "by looking beyond the headlines, we can put these events into better perspective and get a better picture of where Mexico stands today."

NAFTA-inspired trade will slow in the near-term, and foreign investors will take some losses as a result of the peso's temporary collapse. But foreign capital already is pouring back into Mexico. Carlos Fernandez Ruiz, Baja, Calif.'s secretary of economic development says that Korean and

EXHIBIT 2

Mexican labor costs

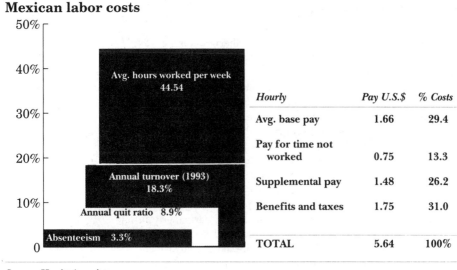

Hourly	Pay U.S.$	% Costs
Avg. base pay	1.66	29.4
Pay for time not worked	0.75	13.3
Supplemental pay	1.48	26.2
Benefits and taxes	1.75	31.0
TOTAL	5.64	100%

Source: Hewitt Associates

Japanese industrialists made "concrete plans to invest $40 million" in new border-area factories within days of the crisis.

Wages, too, will pick up quickly. "Even though we pay...people in pesos, we analyze [costs] in terms of dollars," says Dave Sanderson, president of SKB Corp., a musical-instrument case manufacturer with a factory in Mexicali. "Certainly, we have room to pay them what we were paying them before."

In addition, American businesspeople selling in Mexico are adjusting their terms. Steve Eggers, CFO of San Diego-based Imex Corp., which sells a powdered milk substitute, says, "We're looking to cut our margins significantly just to help our distributors get through this."

And Wal-Mart International President Bob Martin attests that "The Mexican economy offers a growing market and an avid group of potential new customers."

Clearly, Salinas directed tectonic shifts in Mex-

ico's social, political, and economic borders, restoring Mexico to the community of world nations and elevating it to a status it never before had enjoyed. And Zedillo appears determined to maintain the fiscal discipline of the former administration.

No doubt perils remain, but with risk comes reward. Today's framework, in fact, is not very different from what John Gunther observes in his 1941 work, *Inside Latin America*. "I asked four eminent Mexicans of different professions what the country needed most," Gunther related. "One was a musician. He answered, 'education and public health.' One, a soldier, said, 'steadfastness and organization.' The third was a high-ranking jurist. He answered, 'More sense of responsibility in public men.' The fourth was an ex-president of the republic. He said, 'capital, technicians, education, and hard work.'"

All remain true in 1995 at the outset of the new *sexenio*.

Additional Reading

Banco de Mexico (1994), "The Mexican Economy 1994." Mexico City: Banco de Mexico.

Barry, Tom, Harry Browne, and Beth Sims (1994), *The Great Divide: The Challenge of U.S.-Mexico Relations in the 1990s*, New York: Grove Press.

Bell, Samuel E. and James M. Smallwood (1982), *The Zona Libre: 1858-1905, A Problem in American Diplomacy*, Monograph No. 69, Southwestern Studies. El Paso, TX: University of Texas.

Committee for Economic Development (1994), *U.S. Trade Policy Beyond the Uruguay Round*. New York: CED.

El Financiero International, Weekly Edition, Feb. 22, 1993-June 6, 1994.

Gunther, John (1941), *Inside Latin America*, New York: Harper.

KPMG Peat Marwick NAFTA News Bureau (1994), May 9 and May 23.

Kandell, Jonahan (1988), *La Capital: The Biography of Mexico City*, New York: Random House.

La Jornada (1994), May 29.

Newman, Gray and Anna Szterenfeld (1993), *Business International's Guide to Doing Business in Mexico*. New York: McGraw-Hill Inc.

OECD Letter (1994), Vol. 3/5 (June).

O'Hara-Devereaux, Mary and Robert Johansen (1994), *GlobalWork: Bridging Distance, Culture &*

Time. San Francisco: Jossey-Bass Publishers.

U.S. Department of Commerce (1994), "NAFTA: The First Nine Months." Washington, DC: Government Printing Office.

Winsor, Anita (1994), *The Complete Guide to Doing Business in Mexico*. New York: American Management Association.

RESEARCH NOTES AND COMMUNICATIONS

A NOTE ON INTERNATIONAL MARKET LEADERS AND NETWORKS OF STRATEGIC TECHNOLOGY PARTNERING

JOHN HAGEDOORN
Maastricht Economic Research Institute on Innovation and Technology (MERIT), University of Limburg, Maastricht, The Netherlands

Interfirm partnering has become a familiar aspect of corporate behavior as it is found in a large number of industries with many companies participating in strategic alliances. This paper focuses on questions that are related to market structural issues of this phenomenon in an international context. It raises the question whether alliances establish stable networks of firms, and whether market leading firms dominate the world of strategic partnering. Our contribution stresses the need for a further understanding of cooperative behavior in terms of the increase of corporate flexibility and the extension of core competences of companies.

INTRODUCTION AND THEORETICAL BACKGROUND

The growth in strategic partnering and interfirm R&D cooperation, the possible implications of these phenomena for (international) competition and the strategic consequences for participating companies are widely reported in the popular business press as well as in the more academic publications. In this research note we will explore two aspects of strategic interfirm partnering:

— the extent to which strategic technology alliances establish stable networks of cooperating firms; and
— whether market share leading firms also

Key words: Strategic partnerships, networks, market structures

participate disproportionately in strategic technology partnerships.

So far different bodies of research have studied strategic partnering from the point of welfare gains, competitive rivalry, firm size, and interfirm networks. Tirole (1988), d'Aspremont and Jacquemin (1988), and Katz (1986) discuss the possible economic effects of cooperative R&D and joint ventures in terms of welfare gains or losses and R&D spillovers to participating companies. In Chesnais (1988), Harrigan (1985), Kogut (1988), Link and Bauer (1989), and Mytelka and Delapierre (1987) the role of joint ventures or strategic partnering is discussed in the context of corporate strategic behavior and competitive rivalry through which (international) market power of participating companies is enhanced. In a related line of study, regarding the size of companies engaged in partnerships, Berg, Duncan and Friedman (1982), Ghemawat,

Porter, and Rawlinson (1986) and Hagedoorn and Schakenraad (1994) found that larger companies are more engaged in building strategic alliances than their smaller competitors. Mytelka (1991) and Casson (1987) submit that strategic partnering should be seen in the light of oligopolistic rivalry through which international market leaders set up networks of strategic partnering in which they act as nodal companies. This oligopolistic interpretation of strategic partnering is qualified by Hagedoorn and Schakenraad (1992) suggesting that networks of strategic alliances are moderately flexible 'modes of governance' in between markets and hierarchies (Williamson, 1985; Hakansson, 1989) with repositioning, exit and entry of companies (Thorelli, 1986).

Some themes that emerge across these research bodies suggest that:

— collaboration in early parts of the value chain may result in collusion that limits entry;
— market leaders could further increase their market power in a repetitive game of cooperation and increasing industrial concentration;
— the combination of industrial concentration, firm size and cooperative efforts by market leaders could create more or less stable networks of cooperation.

However, the empirical base of many of these studies fails to measure market structure adequately in the sense that international oligopolistic market structures or the degree of industrial concentration are somewhat loosely defined in terms of the role played by large, diversified multinational companies. This is probably partly due to a major problem for empirical research regarding industrial concentration and market structures in an international context. For instance, finding appropriate statistical indicators of international industrial concentration is practically impossible as the size of worldwide markets is in most instances unknown. Returning to national concentration indices is not feasible as strategic partnering is to a large extent an international game. Combining firm size and market structural aspects we propose to introduce the concept of market structural hierarchy that indicates a (rank) order of major companies in relevant international sectors of industry. This enables us to find reliable data on the international distribution of a sufficiently large group of companies through which we can explore the following research questions:

— The first issue is whether in recent years strategic technology partnering coincides with a growth of stable networks of companies. Hence, if the density of networks of strategic partnering has increased, do these networks also represent configurations in which a limited and similar group of companies is found for a substantial period of time that could characterize a static oligopolistic structure?
— Is the international market structural hierarchy of companies reflected in a parallel hierarchy of interfirm strategic technology partnering, which would indicate that world market leading firms also dominate interfirm collaboration?

DATA AND OPERATIONAL CONSTRUCTS

For the analysis of strategic partnering we use data from the MERIT-CATI data bank which contains information on thousands of cooperative interfirm agreements (see the Appendix). Our data do not refer to strategic partnering at large but are in particular related to technology cooperation. Therefore, the present paper addresses only those interfirm agreements for which a combined innovative activity is aimed at the long-term improved product-market positioning of at least one of the participating companies. The period covered is the 1980s; if relevant we will compare the first half of the 1980s with the second half to detect changes over time.

To achieve an across-the-board understanding of market structural aspects of strategic technology partnering we have chosen seven industrial sectors which are quite diverse in terms of their technological opportunities and broader industrial setting (see Table 1). The present state of theory, however, does not suggest a clear set of hypotheses on sectoral differences and network attributes, for differences in industrial concentration for which we, as mentioned above, unfortunately lack appropriate statistical information. Apart from the argument of a grouping of alliances over industries with different sectoral features, these particular sectors were chosen because of the availability of reliable indicators of hierarchies of substantial numbers of internationally leading companies.

To analyze the structure of networks in each sector we will have to apply some operational constructs for network density and the stability of networks. To uncover some aspects of structural

Table 1. Some characteristics of the industrial sectors studied

Sector	Technological opportunities[a]	Industrial setting
Computers	High tech	IT
Microelectronics	High tech	IT
Telecommunications	High tech	IT
Automotive	Medium	Engineering
Aviation/defense	High tech	Engineering
Chemicals	Medium	Process
Food and beverages	Low tech	Process

[a]See OECD (1990).

centrality of a network a density index is computed. This density index is defined as the ratio of the actual number of links between companies (k) to the possible number of links $\frac{1}{2}n(n-1)$, where n denotes the number of points in the network. For practical reasons we will restrict this measure of network density for each sector to the 45 most cooperating companies. For network stability we take the rank correlation of the top 45 cooperating firms at two different periods of time to see whether the hierarchy of firms with respect to their participation in strategic technology alliances has changed. Furthermore, we have to determine the share of a group of the most cooperating companies, for which we have taken 10 companies with the largest number of strategic technology alliances in each sector and set the number of their alliances against all alliances in their sector.[1] We will discern these groups of companies as 'nodal' companies, i.e., companies that have the largest numbers of interfirm linkages which position them in the core of sectoral networks.

For the analysis of the possible reflection of market structural hierarchies in strategic technology partnering a simple rank correlation between world leading companies in terms of their international market shares and strategic technology alliances is computed. As the actual market shares are unknown for many of these sectors, the rankings of company turnover in these seven sectors are taken as 'proxies' for market shares. Apart from the fact that we think that the 'quality' of international market structure indicators does not justify more sophisticated statistical methods, the use of fairly coarse

---

[1] More precisely we counted the share of the 10 most collaborating companies in the total number of interfirm linkages for each sector. As alliances can have more than two inter-firm linkages, depending on the number of partners, this gives a more precise indication of the participation rate of the most collaborating companies.

statistical measures suggests that if there is any dependency between both variables it will show up in a Spearman rank correlation. For each of the seven industries we compare the rank order of the leading technology partnering firms during the second half of the 1980s with a worldwide hierarchy of firms according to their turnover in 1 year from the same period. For most of the industries we have taken rank orders of the top 20 firms, unless a lack of information or a trivial lower end of the market hierarchy forced us to choose somewhat smaller sets of companies.

EMPIRICAL FINDINGS

Information on some structural aspects of strategic technology partnering is presented in Table 2. From this table one learns that these outcomes present a somewhat diverse picture. The share of the 10 most cooperating companies in strategic technology partnering has decreased in some sectors and increased in others. If there was an increase this was rather small compared to some of the larger decreases for the most cooperating firms in other sectors. These results suggest that by and large leading cooperating firms have not improved their nodal position during the 1980s. Consequently, a much larger group of companies are responsible for the increase of technology partnering in sectors such as computers, telecommunications, automotive, and food and beverages.

On the other hand the network densities of larger groups of the 45 most cooperating firms have increased during the 1980s, although large differences between sectors were found. In chemicals, telecommunications, aviation/defense, and microelectronics the network density increased to 0.200 or more, which means that during the second half of the 1980s over 20 percent of all theoretically possible links between the 45 most cooperating firms are also empirically observed. So, for these sectors one can find rather dense networks of a relatively large group of companies. For computers and the automotive industry networks are characterized by a somewhat modest density, whereas the density of strategic technology partnering in the food and beverages industry remains low.

The next step in our analysis is to examine the stability in the group of most cooperating firms. In case strategic technology partnering would be part of a static oligopolistic structure the group of most cooperating companies would resemble a relatively closed system with little or no entry and a more or less stable rank order if

Table 2. A comparison of some network aspects for different sectors, 1980–1984 and 1985–1989

	Share of the 10 most cooperating companies		Network density for top 45 firms		Rank correlation between top 45 firms in 1980–84/1985–89			
	1980–84	1985–89	1980–84	1985–89	No. of stayers	(% of 45)	r	N
Computers	42%	32%	0.082	0.093	25	56%	0.11 n.s.	65
Microelectronics	34%	37%	0.183	0.269	29	64%	0.41*	61
Telecommunications	30%	29%	0.093	0.227	28	62%	0.27(*)	62
Automotive	38%	33%	0.072	0.094	33	73%	0.61**	57
Aviation/Defense	34%	36%	0.187	0.233	36	80%	0.46**	54
Chemicals	21%	25%	0.121	0.200	33	73%	0.57**	57
Food and beverages	28%	23%	0.027	0.030	29	64%	0.54**	61

(*)Marginally significant (0.10 level). 1-tailed.
*Significant at 0.05 level, 1-tailed.
**Significant at 0.01 level, 1-tailed.

one would compare these cooperating companies at different time intervals. Based on our conceptualization of networks of strategic technology alliances as moderately flexible modes of governance, we can expect interfirm networks that are partly open to new entrants but still with some moderate domination by a large group of companies that build the core of these networks, otherwise the increase of network density would be difficult to explain. In other words, we anticipate a relatively stable and large group of intensively cooperating companies which, however, does not exclude entry or changes in the rank order.

This is supported by the findings of rank correlations and the percentage of firms that remain among the leading cooperating firms, which are also presented in Table 2. If we look at the presence of companies amongst the group of leading cooperating companies during both periods of the 1980s we find that, with the exception of the computer industry, between 60 and 80 percent of the top cooperating firms remained in this group of companies. The Spearman rank correlations, comparing the rank orders of cooperating firms during the first and the second half of the 1980s, are significant for all sectors, again with the exception of the computer industry. Given these rank correlations and the percentage of 'stayers' we can conclude that for most of the industries that are analyzed the hierarchies of partnering firms are relatively stable. Some firms indeed do leave and others enter the group of most collaborating companies, but the rankings of the remaining companies did not change significantly.

In addition to the hierarchy within groups of cooperating firms we still have to analyze strategic technology partnering in terms of a possible

domination by international market leaders. In Table 3 one can find the lists of companies having most strategic links during the second half of the 1980s and the listings of companies according to international market shares. Spearman rank correlations can indicate to what extent the existing hierarchies in terms of strategic technology partnering are associated with rank orders in terms of market shares. The results we found do not suggest a strong relation. For most sectors we did not find a significant correlation or we found a negative correlation. Only for computers and the automotive industry did we find a positive and (marginally) significant association between the rank order of firms for their market shares and their position in strategic technology partnering. Sectoral differences according to general technological and industrial characteristics, as presented in Table 1, do not explain the variation in rank correlations.

However, we can also learn from the above that many of the international market leaders are well represented in the strategic technology partnering arena. For these leading firms strategic alliances might play an important role in their corporate strategy, but this does not imply that their links with other companies are also concentrated in their core businesses or activities that are of most crucial interest to these companies. Unfortunately, it is extremely difficult to determine the core businesses for larger groups of companies, e.g., all companies in Table 3. Furthermore, such an exercise is also highly questionable because many of these companies are rather diversified, which makes it difficult to delineate core businesses uniformly. Also many of the less diversified companies listed above will define their core business quite narrowly, which makes it troublesome to place these companies

Table 3. Rank correlations between leading companies in market shares and strategic technology alliances during the second half of the 1980s (number of alliances)

Computers		Microelectronics	
Market share (1988)	Strategic alliances (1985–89)	Market share (1989)	Strategic alliances (1985–89)
1 IBM	1 Olivetti (22)	1 NEC (Sumitomo Group)	1 Intel (59)
2 Digital Equipment	2 Control Data (20)	2 Toshiba	2 Thomson (59)
3 Fujitsu (DKB Group)	3 Sun Microsystems (16)	3 Hitachi	3 Motorola (57)
4 Unisys	4 Unisys (16)	4 Motorola	4 Adv. Micro Devices (55)
5 NEC (Sumitomo Group)	5 Fujitsu (DKB Group) (12)	5 Fujitsu (DKB Group)	5 Siemens (54)
6 Hitachi	6 NEC (Sumitomo Group) (11)	6 Texas Instruments	6 National Semicond. (48)
7 Hewlett-Packard	7 Hitachi (10)	7 Mitsubishi	7 Hewlett-Packard (39)
8 Siemens	8 Siemens (10)	8 Intel	8 Texas Instruments (39)
9 NCR	9 Bull (9)	9 Matsushita	9 Philips (37)
10 Bull	10 Hewlett-Packard (9)	10 Philips	10 General Electric (35)
11 Olivetti	11 IBM (9)	11 National Semicond.	11 Digital Equipment (33)
12 Apple	12 Digital Equipment (8)	12 Sanyo	12 Harris (31)
13 Toshiba	13 Sequent (8)	13 Thomson	13 IBM (31)
14 Control Data	14 Toshiba (8)	14 Samsung	14 Toshiba (29)
15 Wang	15 Intel (7)	15 Sharp	15 Control Data (28)
16 Nixdorf	16 STC/ICL (7)	16 Siemens	16 AT&T (27)
17 Matsushita	17 Apple (6)	17 Oki (Fuyo Group)	17 Honeywell (27)
18 STC/ICL	18 Honeywell (6)	18 Adv. Micro Devices	18 Fujitsu (DKB Group) (25)
19 Philips	19 Matsushita (6)	19 Sony	19 NEC (Sumitomo Group) (23)
20 Compaq	20 AT&T (5)	20 AT&T	20 Unisys (19)

Source: Arthur D. Little	Source: MERIT/CATI	Source: Dataquest	Source: MERIT/CATI
Spearman rank correlation: 0.45*		Spearman rank correlation: −0.06 n.s.	

Notes: missing values are given lowest rank.

1-tailed significance: **0.01 level

*0.05 level

(*)0.10 level (marginally significant)

n.s. not significant

These lists are usually not provided by 'official' statistical services and they are published at irregular intervals, which explains the different years for which these data are given in this table.

Telecommunications	
Market share (1989)	Strategic alliances (1985–89)
1 AT&T	1 Siemens (57)
2 Alcatel (CGE)	2 NEC (Sumitomo Group) (56)
3 Siemens	3 AT&T (52)
4 Northern Telecom	4 Fujitsu (DKB Group) (48)
5 NEC (Sumitomo Group)	5 British Telecom (41)
6 Motorola	6 IBM (33)
7 Ericsson	7 Alcatel (CGE) (31)
8 IBM	8 STET (IRI) (31)
9 Fujitsu (DKB Group)	9 Mitsui Group (31)
10 GPT (GEC)	10 Mitsubishi Group (30)
11 Bosch	11 Philips (30)
12 Philips	12 Oki (Fuyo Group) (28)
13 Matsushita	13 Ericsson (26)
14 STET (IRI)	14 NTT (26)
15 GTE	15 CTNE (25)

Source: CEC	Source: MERIT/CATI
Spearman rank correlation: 0.24 n.s.	

(continued)

Table 3.   Continued

Automotive		Aviation/defense	
Market share (1985)	Strategic alliances (1985–89)	Market share (1987)	Strategic alliances (1985–89)
1 General Motors	1 General Motors (29)	1 Boeing	1 Daimler (95)
2 Ford	2 Mitsubishi Group (27)	2 McDonnell Douglas	2 British Aerospace (52)
3 Toyota	3 Fiat (25)	3 General Electric	3 Aérospatiale (48)
4 Nissan	4 Nissan (25)	4 Lockheed	4 IRI (45)
5 Volkswagen	5 Isuzu (24)	5 United Technologies	5 Thomson (38)
6 Renault	6 Toyota (22)	6 British Aerospace	6 Fiat (32)
7 PSA	7 Mazda (21)	7 General Motors	7 General Motors (31)
8 Fiat	8 Ford (18)	8 Northrop	8 Mitsubishi Group (30)
9 Chrysler	9 Renault (16)	9 General Dynamics	9 GEC (28)
10 Honda	10 Chrysler (15)	10 Raytheon	10 Siemens (26)
11 Mazda	11 PSA (15)	11 Rockwell	11 SNECMA (26)
12 Mitsubishi Group	12 Volvo (15)	12 Allied-Signal	12 United Technologies (26)
13 Daimler	13 Daimler (10)	13 Aérospatiale	13 DKB Group (23)
14 British Leyland	14 Honda (10)	14 Martin Marietta	14 Fokker (22)
		15 Textron	15 General Electric (22)
		16 Daimler	16 Rolls-Royce (21)
		17 Rolls-Royce	17 Boeing (20)
		18 Dassault	18 INI (20)
		19 Grumman	19 Ferranti (18)
		20 Mitsubishi Group	20 McDonnell Douglas (18)

Source: L'Argus   Source: METIT/CATI   Source: DG III/EC   Source: MERIT/CATI
Spearman rank correlation: 0.31[*]   Spearman rank correlation: −0.29[*]

Chemicals		Food and Beverages	
Market share (1988)	Strategic alliances (1985–89)	Market share (1985)	Strategic alliances (1985–89)
1 Du Pont	1 Mitsubishi Group (57)	1 Unilever	1 Ajinomoto (6)
2 BASF	2 Shell (43)	2 Nestlé	2 Allied-Lyons (4)
3 Bayer	3 Mitsui Group (40)	3 BAT Industries	3 Guinness (4)
4 Hoechst	4 Enimont (38)	4 Philip Morris	4 BSN (3)
5 ICI	5 Sumitomo Group (38)	5 Beatrice	5 DKB Group (3)
6 Dow Chemical	6 DKB Group (37)	6 RJR Nabisco	6 Goodman Fielder Wattie (3)
7 Ciba-Geigy	7 Hoechst (36)	7 General Foods	7 Meiji Seika (3)
8 Rhône-Poulenc	8 Du Pont (35)	8 Sara Lee	8 Mitsubishi Group (3)
9 Enimont	9 Solvay (34)	9 Pepsico	9 Philip Morris (3)
10 Norsk Hydro	10 Dow Chemical (28)	10 Dart & Kraft	10 Staley Continental (3)
11 Akzo	11 Fuyo Group (27)	11 Coca Cola	11 Suntory (3)
12 Union Carbide	12 ICI (26)	12 American Brand	12 Tate & Lyle (3)
13 Monsanto	13 ELF-Aquitaine (23)	13 Grand Metropolitan	13 H.J. Heinz (2)
14 Asahi (Mitsubishi)	14 Akzo (22)		
15 Sumitomo Group	15 Allied-Signal (22)		
16 Solvay	16 BASF (20)		
17 W.R. Grace	17 DSM (18)		
18 DSM	18 Exxon (18)		
19 Elf-Aquitaine	19 SABIC (18)		
20 American Cyanamid	20 Sayer (17)		

Source: Anizon   Source: MERIT/CATI   Source: UNCTC   Source: MERIT/CATI
Spearman rank correlation: −0.21 n.s.   Spearman rank correlation: −0.78[**]

under identical denominators. Nevertheless, some illustration of the restricted role of core businesses in alliance building can be found in Table 4. From this table we learn that for nearly all market leaders, in the industries that we discuss, their links with other companies in their core business are only a relatively small share of their total strategic technology linkages (the food and beverages industry was not included because of small numbers). In the three subfields of information technology that we analyzed, market leaders such as IBM, NEC and ATT have only

Table 4. The relative importance of core business alliances in the total of companies' strategic technology links, percentage of total, 1985–89

Sector	Company	Share of core business
Computers	IBM	5.8%
Microelectrics	NEC (Sumitomo)	9.3%
Telecom.	ATT	16.8%
Aviation/defense	Boeing	50.0%
Automotive	General Motors	28.7%
Chemicals	Du Pont	35.4%

a small minority of their strategic technology links in their core businesses. Although the shares of noncore business strategic links of market leaders in the other fields, such as General Motors, Du Pont and Boeing, are substantially smaller, they still take at least half of the total number of strategic technology linkages of these companies. These figures have to be interpreted with some care as they also illustrate some of the problems with the description of core businesses mentioned above. The 'specialization ratio' in terms of core business partnerships is obviously affected by the degree of diversification of these companies, the sectoral homogeneity, and above all the 'wider' or 'narrower' definition of sectors. If, for instance, the definition of the computer industry is somewhat narrow a market leader will easily appear more diversified in its strategic alliances than in the case of a broadly defined sector such as the chemicals industry. Nevertheless, Table 4 provides a good illustration of the point that market leaders might not take a leading position in strategic technology partnering in their core business but still be quite active in forming alliances in their other business interests.

DISCUSSION AND CONCLUSION

The exploratory character of this research note demands a brief discussion of its main findings on general patterns as well as some further directions for future research.

One of the main findings is that it appears beyond doubt that large international companies play a leading role in strategic technology collaboration at large. Following Thorelli (1986) this partnering behavior has to be seen in the context of competitive (re-)positioning games. At first this seems to coincide regularly with oligopolistic rivalry between a small number of companies. However, if one takes a closer look at the issue matters become somewhat more complicated. The increase of strategic technology partnering in the past decade has indeed led to tighter webs of partnering for many international industries, but this increase of network densities has in the first place affected a relatively large group of companies and less so a smaller group and exclusive inner circle of nodal companies. In other words, there is little evidence that strategic partnering itself causes or is affected by a tight and static oligopolistic structure. For a further understanding of corporate partnering strategies and their effect on competitive positioning it seems more interesting for future research to pay detailed attention to the game of strategic partnering behavior itself. In particular a more in-depth analysis of the role of alliance-initiating companies, the steps taken by their main competitors and the counter-moves made by other companies are expected to improve our understanding, not only of the structure of networks, but also of the reciprocal effects of partnering strategies on participating companies and the relevant changes in industry structures at large.

In general flexibility and gradual changes within the moderately stable structures of networks of strategic technology cooperation seem to describe the pattern we found. Strategic technology alliances create relatively steady networks of cooperating companies, but these networks are unlike closed circuits. Over time the population of companies that play a leading role in these networks is transformed through exit and entry but a core structure of heavily partnering companies remains intact. In that sense networks of strategic technology partnering can be described as moderately flexible and dynamic structures as the hierarchy of leading partnering firms and the pattern of networks are still subject to change. It comes as somewhat of a surprise that these features do not seem to be fundamentally distinct for the variety of industries studied in the above.

Research on the general characteristics of these interfirm networks could also profit from a more detailed analysis of the barriers to entry. In addition to the topic of the strategic game of incumbents, the evidence found on the entry of players warrants further research into entry behavior of companies through alliances. Without implying that such a line of investigation would change the current general research agenda in strategic management, it does affect the scope of main issues on the agenda reaching from the resource base of companies to corporate diversification and the boundaries of firms.

Returning to the flexible character of networks

of strategic partnering we found that this aspect is also reflected in relation to the relevant market structural counterparts. A possible interpretation of hierarchies of strategic technology partnering as a reproduction of existing international market hierarchies has to be rejected as too mechanistic and simplistic. Market hierarchies, in terms of a rank order of market shares for leading companies, are not mirrored in a corresponding participation in strategic technology partnering. However, there is also little evidence of strategic partnering being dominated by 'second-tier competitors and companies trying to catch up' as suggested by Porter (1990: 67). Although this does not necessarily mean that the 'truth is somewhere in the middle,' it appears worthwhile to search for a more subtle explanation that could improve our theoretical understanding of these phenomena. In such an understanding strategic technology partnering is to a large extent dominated by large, multinational and often diversified companies. These companies apply their alliances with a wide variety of partners to improve their technological and strategic capabilities. However, only part of the alliances are found in their core businesses; a large share of their joint efforts is related to other activities that are relevant to their diversified present and future corporate interests. In other words, the existing hierarchies in strategic technology partnering do not merely reproduce existing market structures, but they are so much more a reflection of the flexibility found in the wider setting of complex interfirm networks and strategic behavior of companies.

Although by no means an easy task for further empirical research, Prahalad and Hamel's (1990) contribution to the debate on core competencies of companies seems worthwhile to consider in the context of strategic partnering as well. If core competencies build the competitive strength of companies and this strength goes beyond the demonstrated capabilities for an existing portfolio of products and businesses, the analysis of alliances for core businesses and other corporate interests has to be expanded. For a further understanding of the rationale behind the partnering behavior of companies a clear delineation of core competencies can reveal the pros and cons of concrete interfirm linkages. From that perspective interfirm complementarity has to be redefined in terms of core competencies that are not necessarily related to existing product–market combinations. New combinations of core competencies of potential partners can open new perspectives going beyond traditional business unit perspectives for interfirm partnering. In that

sense future analysis of strategic partnering behavior in the light of building core competencies and learning through interfirm partnering takes us back to an earlier suggestion for further research stressing the need for a more detailed understanding of the effect of alliances on strategic positioning behavior within complex environments.

The implications of the future research suggestions made in the above are that both qualitative and quantitative research methods will be necessary to increase our understanding of strategic technology partnering. Following Parkhe's (1993) suggestions for research on joint ventures, the need for more in-depth understanding of corporate partnering behavior implies that this will depend on both multiple-case studies and research on large data sets. In particular the analysis of strategic and behavioral aspects of technology partnering and the internal organizational consequences of cooperative strategies require an in-depth understanding through case-study approaches that can supplement and enrich more standard multivariate analysis.

ACKNOWLEDGEMENTS

The author would like to thank Francois Chesnais, Lynn Mytelka, Jos Schakenraad, Bart Verspagen and two anonymous reviewers for their detailed comments that considerably improved this paper. Any remaining errors and omissions are mine.

REFERENCES

Berg, S.V., J. Duncan and P. Friedman (1982). *Joint Venture Strategies and Corporate Innovation*. Oelgeschlager, Cambridge, MA.

Casson, M. (1987). *The Firm and the Market*. Blackwell, Oxford.

Chesnais, F. (1988). 'Multinational enterprises and the international diffusion of technology'. In G. Dosi, C. Freeman, R. Nelson, G. Silverberg and L. Soete (eds), *Technical Change and Economic Theory*. Pinter, London, pp. 496–528.

d'Aspremont, C. and A. Jacquemin (1988). 'Cooperative and noncooperative R&D in duopoly with spillovers', *American Economic Review*, **78**, pp. 1133–1137.

Ghemawat, P., M.E. Porter and R. A. Rawlinson (1986). 'Patterns of international coalition activity'. In M. E. Porter (ed.), *Competition in Global Industries*. Harvard Business School Press, Boston, MA, pp. 345–365.

Hagedoorn, J. and J. Schakenraad (1992). 'Leading companies and networks of strategic alliances in information technologies', *Research Policy*, **21**, pp. 163–190.

Hagedoorn, J. and J. Schakenraad (1994). 'The effect of strategic technology alliances on company performance', *Strategic Management Journal*, **15**(4), pp. 291–309.

Hakansson, H. (1989). *Corporate Technological Behaviour*. Routledge, London.

Harrigan, K. R. (1985). *Strategies for Joint Ventures*. Lexington Books, Lexington, MA.

Katz, M. L. (1986). 'An analysis of cooperative research and development', *Rand Journal of Economics*, **17**, pp. 527–544.

Kohut, B. (1988). 'Joint ventures: Theoretical and empirical perspectives', *Strategic Management Journal*, **9**(4), pp. 319–332.

Link, A. N. and L. L. Bauer (1989). *Cooperative Research in U.S. Manufacturing: Assessing Policy Initiatives and Corporate Strategies*. Lexington Books, Lexington, MA.

Mytelka, L. K. (ed.) (1991). *Strategic Partnerships and the World Economy*. Pinter, London.

Mytelka, L. and M. Delapierre (1987). 'The alliance strategies of European firms in the information technology industry and the role of Esprit', *Journal of Common Market Studies*, **26**, pp. 231–253.

OECD (June–July, 1990), *OECD Observer*.

Parkhe, A. (1993). '"Messy" research, methodological predispositions, and theory development in international joint ventures', *Academy of Management Review*, **18**, pp. 227–268.

Porter, M. (1990). *The Competitive Advantage of Nations*. Free Press, New York.

Prahalad, C. K. and G. Hamel (1990). 'The core competence of the corporation', *Harvard Business Review*, **68**(3), pp. 79–91.

Thorelli, H. B. (1986). 'Networks: Between markets and hierarchies', *Strategic Management Journal*, **7**(1), pp. 37–51.

Tirole, J. (1988). *The Theory of Industrial Organization*. MIT Press, Cambridge, MA.

Williamson, O. E. (1985). *The Economic Institutions of Capitalism*. Free Press, New York.

APPENDIX: THE COOPERATIVE AGREEMENTS AND TECHNOLOGY INDICATORS (CATI) INFORMATION SYSTEM

The CATI data bank is a relational data base which contains information on nearly 10,000 cooperative agreements involving some 3,500 different parent companies. Systematic collection of interfirm alliances started in 1988. If available, many sources from earlier years were consulted, enabling us to take a retrospective view. In order to collect interfirm alliances we consulted various sources, of which the most important are specialized journals which report on business events.

This method of information gathering which we might call 'literature-based alliance counting' has its drawbacks and limitations:

— In general we have only come to know those arrangements that are made public by the companies themselves.

— Newspaper and journal reports are likely to be incomplete, especially when they go back in history and/or regard firms from countries outside the scope of the journal.

— A low profile of small firms without well-established names is likely to have their collaborative links excluded.

Despite such shortcomings, which are largely unsolvable even in a situation of extensive and large-scale data collection, we think we have been able to produce a clear picture of the joint efforts of many companies.

The data bank contains information on each agreement and some information on participating companies. The first entity is the interfirm cooperative agreement. We define cooperative agreements as common interests between independent (industrial) partners which are not connected through (majority) ownership. In the CATI data base only those interfirm agreements are being collected that contain some arrangements for transferring technology or joint research. We also collect information on joint ventures in which new technology is received from at least one of the partners, or joint ventures having some R&D program. Mere production or marketing joint ventures are excluded.

We regard as a relevant input of information for each alliance: the number of companies involved; names of companies (or important subsidiaries); year of establishment, duration and year of dissolution; field(s) of technology; modes of cooperation. Depending on the form of cooperation we collect information on equity sharing; the direction of capital or technology flows; the degree of participation in case of minority holdings; some information about motives underlying the alliance; the character of cooperation, such as basic research, applied research, or product development possibly associated with production and/or marketing arrangements.

The second major entity is the individual subsidiary or parent company involved in one (registered) alliance at least. We ascertain its nationality and we determine the main branch in which it is operating and classify its number of employees. In addition to this time-series for employment, turnover, net income, R&D expenditures and numbers of assigned U.S. patents have been stored.

Global Retailing 2000

Kim Howard

Kim Howard is the associate editor of Business Credit.

"International business"..."regional economic trading bloc"..."global retailing" are all buzzwords of the '90s. Wait a minute, what is global retailing?

Retailing traditionally has been "local" because it required knowledge of the needs and habits of specific groups of consumers. However, with more trade barriers dropping, retailing has been added to the list of businesses that must sell globally to stay competitive. More businesses are tapping into other country's markets and learning how to succeed overseas. A continuing slow economy in the U.S. has forced many companies to look elsewhere for profits.

Management Horizons, a retail consulting division of Price Waterhouse, has produced a report entitled "Global Retailing 2000" which profiles global retailing trends. The economic forecasting team at Management Horizons noticed a trend about the U.S. retail environment: it is difficult to operate in and is growing slowly.

"We began to notice that a number of the more successful retailers were looking overseas for opportunities and we thought, 'Maybe there's a trend here,'" said Ira Kalish, Ph.D., one of the three authors of "Global Retailing 2000."

Dr. Kalish is an expert in forecasting and analyzing the consumer sector of the U.S. economy, as well as the effects of financial and economic trends on the retail industry. He contributes to several Management Horizons economic publications such as the *Retail Economist*, the *Five Year Forecast*, and the *Retail Previews*. After receiving his doctorate in economics from the John Hopkins University, he was an economist with the Eastman Kodak Company consulting on trends in consumer spending, business capital spending, and financial markets.

The Global Retailing 2000 report contends that markets will be divided into three regional blocs: The Americas, Europe, and the Far East, with little integration between the three. All are economically diverse, so business professionals must have prior knowledge about each in order to succeed.

"Globalization is the way to go for retailers who want to keep growing," said Dr. Kalish.

Follow the Yellow Brick Road to Consumer-Oriented Countries

The '80s was the decade of excess: the Trump Towers, huge government spending, and "Dynasty" lifestyles. The '90s started out "lean and mean" and some economists predict they will stay that way: rightsizing, total quality management, and reengineering are "Roseanne" realities.

According to the report, as a result of rising taxes, a declining dollar, and tighter controls of lending institutions, the retail industry in the United States faced a period of long-term slow growth. Baby Boomers who are now approaching middle-age and slowing their spending habits are another reason for suppressed consumer spending. The trade balance also influences consumer spending.

Countries other than the consumer-oriented U.S. are experiencing rapid economic growth causing a dramatic increase in their living standards, thus encouraging them to become consumer-oriented societies. Retail is moving toward specialization of stores as occurred in the U.S. during the 1980s with such stores as Home Depot, The Limited, and Toys "R" Us. In the other economic blocs, the shift toward specialty stores means electronic superstores are replacing manufacturing stores and national chains are replacing independents. Foot Locker is one speciality retailer that has gone global and been successful in North America, Europe, Asia, and Latin America. Small businesses will find it hard to keep up with the retail giants.

"Small businesses have difficulty achieving the efficiencies that come from scale and technology that larger retailers have. We have already seen the disappearance of large numbers of mom-and-pop stores in this country. As American firms go global and firms elsewhere do the same, retailing becomes more consolidated and in other countries, small businesses will disappear as well," Dr. Kalish said.

Retail Holds Its Own

Retail cannot be ignored: In 1991, the top 100 retailers in the world represented over $1 trillion in sales. Today, the average top-100 company generates sales of approximately $10 billion, profits of nearly $240 million, and operates over 1,900 outlets. Supermarkets, diversified companies, and department stores account for nearly three-fourths of total sales of the top 100 companies.

As of 1991, the European marketplace led the retail race holding 51.9 percent of sales. The Americas are no longer in the number one spot: Their share is under 36 percent. Although the Pacific Rim experienced the highest sales growth between 1987 and 1991, retailers in the Far East only account for 12.3 percent of the top 100 global retailers sales.

Some growth trends seen in Management Horizon's "Top 100 Global Retailers":

• Over 55 percent of the top 100 have expanded retail operations outside their base country.

• When measured by the number of countries in which they operate, European retailers are the most active outside their own country (due to their own small market size and geographical proximity of most European countries).

• U.S. retailers remain highly focused on operations within the states.

• Of the five lines of trade significantly represented in the top 100 (supermarkets, diversified companies, department stores, discount stores, and hypermarkets), hypermarkets are clearly leaders in the global arena. (Hypermarkets are very large department stores that include a supermarket).

• Certain lines of trade seem to be particularly disastrous to global operations; for example, the department store confirms the traditional view of the department store as a very localized concept.

• U.S. supermarkets operate predominately within the country. Supermarkets in Europe and the Far East tend to operate on a much more global level. For example, several European supermarket giants have grown globally through investments in U.S.-based retailers: Delhaize "Le Lion" (Food Lion), Tengelmann (A&P), J. Sainsbury (Shaw's Supermarkets), and Ahold (Giant Food, BI-LO, First National Supermarkets, and Tops Markets).

• Retailers of the Americas lag behind the other trade blocs in terms of their globalization effort. However, of the top 10 companies, five are based in the U.S.

Predictions of Diversity Among Regional Blocs

General conclusions about the next decade of retailing are as diverse as the areas profiled. The report finds:

In the Far East, rapid expansion will occur. It will be relatively easy to prosper with growth in living standards and the emergence of consumer orientation in society and government policy.

In ever-changing Europe, expansion and consolidation will keep management alert. With rapid economic growth, political and economic intergration, changing patterns of shopping leading to increased use of specialty stores, and increasing sophistication of technology, expansion and consolidation will occur.

The Americas are a melting pot. In the U.S., where the economy will grow more slowly, consumer spending will decline as a share of the economic activity, policy will be anti-consumer, and shopping will become a less important aspect of social life; retailing will be in retrenchment. Consequently, growth for individual retailers will come not from a growing market, but from capturing market share. It will be a zero sum game, with some winners and many losers. The result will be massive consolidation and that is already underway.

For Latin America, an expansion, similar to that of the Far East, will take place. Canada will continue to undergo a restructuring of the retail industry.

Strategies for Success

"Micro-marketing" strategy is the buzzword for retailers who want profits to outweigh the losses on the P&L statement. Retailers must "manage at the lowest possible level of aggregation" and be "right for every customer in their target market every time, differentiating each store and each line of goods to capitalize on different tastes and customs," the report states. This type of management requires good technology for processing information and a decentralized system of control.

"Many retailers use electronic data interchange (EDI), transmitting data electronically directly to the manufacturers and then the stock is automatically replenished. You essentially cut out middle-level management and speed up the process by getting the goods to the store quickly," Dr. Kalish said.

For innovators, technology will go far beyond merely speedy transactions and managing inventory. It will enable greater micro-marketing, greater cost control, and greater labor productivity. For those playing catch up, there will be a great leap toward joining the innovative retailers. This will be partly because they will have to compete directly with American retailers: Levels of technology depend on how developed and consolidated the local industry is.

"American companies are certainly the pioneers in retail technology and have an advantage over foreign retailers. Computerized point-of-sale machines record what merchan-

> " . . . technology can also be used to better understand what customers like and what sells well in each store, thereby differentiating stores by merchandise assortment and making the store more efficient by serving customer needs."

dise is being sold when, allowing stricter inventory control and speedier shipments of new inventory from the manufacturer. It also reduces the amount of inventory in the distribution pipeline at any given time. This technology can also be used to better understand what customers like and what sells well in each store, thereby differentiating stores by merchandise assortment and making the store more efficient by serving customer needs," he said.

Those retailers who keep the consumer in mind when dealing with suppliers have a strategic advantage. This relationship can provide greater value, selection, or convenience to the customer. Wal-Mart, for example, forged a relationship with Proctor and Gamble to reduce distribution costs.

In the year 2000, successful retailers will be those that operate on a massive scale, enabling not only strong relationships with suppliers, but the huge investment in technology needed to achieve effective micro-marketing.

A Helping Hand Increases Profits

"Investing in a consultant or a local partner can help make the transition into international business much smoother. It's important to understand the local laws, regulations, business procedures, and culture. A local partner is a common method of globalization. The partner has an equity investment and understands the market, helps get real estate, and walks retailers through rules and regulations," Kalish said.

Customer service will be extremely important. Bad service means low profits. Adding to that pressure, retailers must present a unique image in order to keep up customer awareness and focus on loyal shoppers by knowing target markets and rewarding best customers.

Triumphant managers will have a flexible management style and be able to shift gears quickly. The retail race cannot be won standing on the sidelines. Management must continuously reevaluate strategies to see if they are in line with the business environment.

The report concludes, "American retailers will push the global retailing industry in the direction of high-volume, low-cost operations with an emphasis either on specialization by commodity or by price point. The emergence of a more fully integrated world economy can only facilitate this movement."

Note: resource material taken from "Global Retailing 2000," produced by Management Horizons, a division of Price Waterhouse.

Planning for International Trade Show Participation: A Practitioner's Perspective

Henry W. Vanderleest, *Ph.D., Department of Marketing, Ball State University*
*Dr. Vanderleest teaches international marketing
and is also a general partner of the international
marketing consulting firm of Kuieck, Vanderleest, and Associates in Muncie, Indiana.*

Introduction

Exhibiting at international trade shows can be
an extremely effective way to promote export
products, particularly for small, new-to-exporting manufacturing firms. Data supplied by a
leading trade organization show that in 1991
nearly 2,000 trade shows took place in over 75
countries, with the number of trade shows
doubling in the last ten years.[1] The reason for
this growth is simple. As more U.S. firms
(many of them small) look to global markets,
they soon realize that international trade shows
are generally cheaper and more efficient than
most other ways of making quality sales
contacts.

Other trade association data show that in 1991
the average cost for a salesperson working for a
U.S. industrial goods firm to travel to western
Europe to meet with prospective customers was
about $850 per call. This compares with under
$350 for each quality lead resulting from a
firm's participation in a European trade show.
Additional data show that 54% of all qualified
leads developed by surveyed U.S. exporters
selling industrial products at such trade shows in
1991 were closed with a fax, letter, or phone
call. This compared with the 4.8 in-person visits
that were needed to complete the sale.[2] New-to-
exporting firms, particularly those with limited
promotion budgets, that are aware of these
numbers are quick to recognize that it is "smart"
business to exhibit at overseas trade shows.
From a cost and efficiency standpoint, most
exporters cannot afford not to participate in
these shows.

Almost every industry has a foreign trade
show in which a small exporter can participate.
However, shows can be an expensive waste of
time if a firm does not properly prepare for
them. With an increasing number of small U.S.
firms wanting to sell abroad, it is important that
they know how to properly plan for and participate in international trade shows.

Unfortunately, the author's experience in
nearly three decades of successfully developing
and implementing export programs for manufacturing firms is that most do not follow a well-
organized, systematic approach to trade show
participation. The purpose of this article is to
assist top management in small manufacturing
firms to organize and prepare successfully for
international trade show participation. Although
much of what is discussed can apply to U.S.
exporters in general, this article is specifically
directed at small, new-to-exporting firms that are
often overwhelmed at the thought of participating in an international show.

Although there are numerous references in the
international business literature to trade show
participation by U.S. exporters, most just discuss
in general terms the importance of attending
(Norton, 1989; Humbert, 1987). Others investigate only one or two specific issues facing firms
who participate (e.g., Browning and Adams,
1988; Kern and Crow, 1987). There appear to be
no published articles that approach successful
international trade show participation in a step-
by-step, systematic fashion, from pre-show
preparation through post-show follow-up. What
follows is a work plan that can be used to

prepare for international shows. Although the work plan covers the basics of pre-show preparation, participation, and follow-up, it is not all inclusive. Rather, it is an idealized game plan, and some time frames and specific points may not be appropriate for all companies and trade shows.

It is generally true that international trade shows are not at all what U.S. companies have come to expect from most domestic shows, where booths are often manned simply to maintain a presence or image. At international shows, U.S. exhibitors must be prepared to meet with show visitors who usually have a single purpose: to do business. After a firm determines that its product is suited for export and has decided how trade shows will fit in its overall exporting plans, it is ready to begin following the work plan.

One Year Before the Show

1. Determine why you want to participate in an international trade show. Typical reasons include one or more of the following:
   a. To research the demand for your product in foreign markets.
   b. To assess the competition.
   c. To establish a presence in the market and meet others in your industry.
   d. To introduce your product to the foreign market with the hope of writing orders at the show.
   e. To find suitable distributors or manufacturers' agents who will handle your product in international markets. Most small, new-to-export manufacturing firms lack established distribution channels, so shows represent a good opportunity to get this important aspect of an export program organized. In most instances, locating overseas distributors and agents should be one of the primary tasks of those attending international trade shows, particularly the first time.
2. Decide on what fair(s) you wish to attend during the next fiscal year. This is an important decision, since foreign trade participation represents a significant investment of your time and money. Appropriate overseas show leads can be obtained from your trade association and the U.S. Department of Commerce. Fiscal year planning for shows is recommended because it coincides with budgeting. A survey by the National Trade Show Exhibitors Association revealed 34 criteria used by exporters in selecting which trade shows to attend. The 15 criteria shown in Table 1 were rated in rank order as the most important.

TABLE 1 Table Show Critieria	
Criteria	Rank
Audience Quality	
Proportion of decision makers among visitors	1
Proportion of visitors in your target market	2
Show limited to specific types of exhibitors	8
Number or percent of new contracts last year	9
Screening of visitors	15
Audience Quantity	
Number of visiting exhibit	3
Extent of promotion by show organizers	5
The show's audience size in past years	6
Display Location	
Booth position/location on floor	4
Ability to specify/negotiate size, location, etc.	7
Aisle traffic density	13
Logistic Aspects	
Easy registration or pre-registration	10
Security	11
Easily available move-in/out assistance	12
Move-in/out facilities	14
Source: National Trade Show Exhibitors Association	

3. Once the decision to exhibit is made, assign one person in your firm overall responsibility for coordinating everything associated with the show.
4. Ask the show manager for information on the nature of the audience attracted. Each show has its own kind of audience, so do not assume just from the name of the show that it delivers the audience you want to reach. If at all possible, visit a show before signing up. Seeing what is going on will give you a feel for the nature of the show. Talking with exhibitors and getting answers to questions about such things as benefits, costs, problems, and procedures can be useful.
5. Obtain from show organizers a preliminary program providing such information as the show's days and hours, space rental fees, availability of translators, map of booth locations, set-up requirements, show program and fees, and special equipment availability. Be aware that overseas video systems may not be able to play U.S. produced tapes. It is also important to recognize that exhibit hall rental fees for such things as video equipment are generally steep. It may be better to bring your own with an adapter.
6. Develop a tentative budget that includes such things as cost of booth space, travel, promo-

tional materials, and freight costs for shipping display materials. You will generally find that expenses will double or triple over a comparable domestic show, particularly in Europe. Information in Table 2 shows the eight major components of an international trade show budget, including average compo-

TABLE 2	
Major Components of an International Trade Show Budget	
Components	Percent of Total Budget
Display Construction	17
Transportation Costs	14
Space Rental	11
Specialty Advertising	11
Set-up & Tear-down	10
Personnel	9
Miscellaneous	7
Display Maintenance	6
Source: National Trade Show Exhibitors Association	

nent percentages as determined in 1991 by a leading industry trade organization.

7. Start collecting names of international distributors and agents. If one of your objectives of attending the show is to line up distribution, it is not too early to begin collecting names and addresses of potential channel partners. An often overlooked way to collect names is to ask noncompeting firms in your industry for recommendations. Another way is to look for distributors and agents who may be members of your U.S.-based trade association. State trade offices located overseas may also help in providing names of appropriate distributors and agents. You can also use services of the U.S. Department of Commerce such as the Agent/Distributor Service and the *Commercial News*. You may also find names in various indices such as that published by the Manufacturers Agents' National Association based in Laguna Beach, California. Commercial officers at U.S. embassies in foreign countries may also be able to provide you with appropriate names. For a modest fee, they can also arrange for candidates to meet with you at the show.

Nine Months Before the Show

1. Apply for booth space. If cost is a problem, consider co-oping for booth space with a noncompeting exhibitor. The earlier you apply the more likely you will be awarded the space you desire. Although location is important, it is often outweighed by what you show in your space, how you promote your participation, and how your staff handles visitors to your booth. Make sure that all arrangements relating to space dimensions, exhibit layout, private conference areas, and set-up costs are spelled out clearly in writing, preferably in English. Clarifying this information in advance will guard against unpleasant surprises when you arrive.

2. Begin building display materials if long lead time is required. A professionally designed booth will impress buyers and is an essential part of trade show success. Remember that your trade show booth is an extension of your sales room. Pick the right design. To create maximum impact, you may want to hire a professional display designer.

3. Contact potential new distributors and agents by personal letter. Include a questionnaire for them to complete and return which will provide information to help you decide if a proper match exists. Also send personal invitations to potential buyers encouraging them to visit your booth.

Six Months Before the Show

1. Determine exactly which products you will display at the show. Remember to check, and update if needed, your patent, trademark, and copyright protection. Others may see your products at the show and register them, which may require you to buy back your own intellectual property right before the product can be sold in a particular foreign country. Also check with a foreign freight forwarder about shipping your booth materials and display products to the show city. You need to decide whether to leave sample products after the show ends. Consider giving away or selling locally to reduce customs and return freight charges.

2. Place an ad in the show guide to inform all interested parties, particularly potential new distributors and agents, that you will be participating. Include the booth number if it is available at press time. If possible, ensure that your product is listed precisely by category, sub-category, and description.

3. Select appropriate potential distributors and agents from returned questionnaire informa-

tion. Write a personal letter to each asking them to meet you at the show to further discuss distribution or representation of your product in foreign markets.

4. Make travel arrangements, including plane reservations. Economy coach fares booked well in advance can save a lot of money. Early booking of hotel space is also recommended, since nearby business classrooms sell out early, particularly in major exhibition cities in Europe. This is also the time to decide if a separate hospitality room is required. In Germany, separate closing rooms are common in which exhibitors make deals right on the spot.

5. Arrange to have sales literature translated if necessary. Multi-lingual and metrics system translation may be required if the show is truly international. To save costs, it is recommended that material to be distributed from your booth be condensed to attractive, informative, single page handouts. Providing elaborate sales materials to literature collectors is expensive. You can provide serious prospects additional information at a later date.

6. Decide who from your firm will attend the show. Each should have at least one specific role to perform such as staffing the booth, meeting with prospects at another location, and checking the competition. There are to be no sightseers. You want your booth staffed by people who are knowledgeable about your products, prices, and policies and can talk easily about them without hesitation. People who visit trade shows usually have very specific needs and they are looking for answers to immediate questions. Give authority to one person attending the show to make final decisions on behalf of your firm. If the show is considered major and prestigious, it is recommended that top management also attend to lend the dignity of their office.

7. Check to be certain that all U.S.-based personnel attending the show have valid passports and any necessary visas.

Four Months Before the Show

1. Complete shipping arrangements to include proper timing, clear labeling of crates, and special handling instructions. Make sure your exhibits comply with local import regulations and that any needed foreign customs and other licenses have been applied for. Do not forget insurance coverage for equipment. Develop a shipping schedule to ensure that exhibits arrive in good time. In some instances, there may be congestion at ports or airports at the time of exhibition. You may want to use a local exhibit management company in conjunction with your freight forwarder to coordinate exhibit set-up after arrival.

2. Make final staff arrangements. Ensure that price lists are accurate and complete and that policies stipulating delivery schedules, credit, payment and discount terms, warranties, parts, and service have been established. Be prepared to convert CIF prices to foreign currencies if necessary. Advance preparation in these areas is critical if you are to be responsive to sales inquiries and possibly write orders at the show.

Two Months Before the Show

1. Reconfirm personal travel and hotel reservations as well as arrangements for exhibit shipment.

2. Send a list of booth personnel to the show director to assure that entry passes and proper identification are in order upon arrival.

3. Be certain that all staff attending the show have travelers checks or cash for personal expenses (no need to convert to foreign currency before leaving U.S.). It is wise to take a large number of $1 U.S. bills for taxis, tips, and baggage handling upon arrival prior to exchanging currency.

4. Check to see that sales literature and gift giveaways are finished and ready to be packed. Plan to carry a small stock of giveaways and sales literature in your personal luggage in case freight shipments are delayed or lost.

5. Prepare a tool kit for emergency repairs of display units and equipment. Items such as a pocket knife, duct tape, screwdriver, and extension cords with adapters could come in handy.

6. Determine from show organizers what union rules apply regarding display set-up, maintenance, and repair and how payment is to be made for these services. Knowing this in advance will guard against excessive overcharges and "extra" fees for these services after arrival.

Ten Days Before the Show

1. Confirm with the freight forwarder that your shipment is safely at the show and assure that set-up begins as soon as allowed.

2. Make a list of important phone numbers to leave at home, e.g., show manager, booth

number, hotel number, local American consulate or embassy.

3. Plan your personal wardrobe, arrange to take personal medication (pack in carry-on luggage), and take extra passport photos. Take more business cards than you may think are necessary.

Arrival at the Show

1. Check to see if exhibits are properly set up, testing moving parts if necessary. This should be done a minimum of 24 hours before the show begins.
2. Scout your competition as soon as you can—if possible, while the show is being set up. You don't want any surprises. More than a few firms have had their carefully laid plans destroyed by not knowing what their competitors were doing.
3. Locate the nearest fax machines, secretarial services, and medical facilities.
4. To save time in case of emergency, telephone or fax home so your company and family know the exact name of hotel, room number, and telephone number.
5. If the hotel is not adjacent to the exhibition hall, make a trial run noting route and travel time.
6. Conduct a final check of booth and equipment.
7. Meet with field staff to review final work schedules, sales policies, and literature available.

Working the Show

1. Continue surveying competitors and try to obtain prices, sales literature, and names of potential customers, distributors, and agents if needed.
2. Make sure your booth is properly staffed without overcrowding. Allow for adequate meal breaks and business calls away from the exhibition hall if required.
3. Make visitors to your booth feel that they are welcome and not intruding. Be sure there is always someone available who can answer technical questions and demonstrate your products.
4. If you expect to write orders at the show, make sure that someone has authority to negotiate price, credit, and delivery terms. This may require hiring appropriate interpreters.
5. Even though managing a trade show exhibit is hard work and you will be exhausted after most days, your booth staff should never sit down while on duty unless talking to visitors

who prefer to sit. During slow periods, they can introduce themselves to visitors in the aisle or check the competition.

6. Develop a system to remind you to record what you need to remember about visitors to your booth, including the quality of the leads. It is recommended that you staple each prospect's business card on a clean sheet of paper and make notes on that paper.
7. You want to avoid passing out too much literature at the show. Literature is expensive. Instead, it is recommended that you take names and addresses and mail the desired literature back to the visitors' offices.
8. Evaluate better booth sites for future trade shows.

After the Show

1. Arrange for one person to remain 24 hours after the show closes to oversee the clearing of exhibits. Assure that your exhibit is repacked and stored or shipped home. Alternatives are to sell samples locally or give them to your local distributor or agent.
2. Review all bills and charges, seeking adjustments on the spot if warranted. Be sure that the person who stays behind has an adequate amount of local currency to settle local accounts.
3. Remain a few extra days to follow-up on local contracts and, if time permits, visit the local market to note competitive products and prices.
4. Analyze your company's performance and consider what, if anything, can be done to improve it. If anything went wrong, decide how to avoid the same mistake next time. Consider recommendations for making the next exhibition more efficient and less costly. The market potential needs to justify the cost in time and money of attending.

After Returning Home

1. Compile a complete list of names and addresses of distributors, agents, prospects, and other contacts.
2. Write or fax personal thank you letters to the appropriate people.
3. After reviewing questionnaires, appoint new distributors and agents or send a follow-up letter requesting the return of your questionnaire.
4. Follow-up on requests for more information that you could not provide at the show. Quick responses impress potential customers.

Conclusion

Many pitfalls await the exporter who is not properly prepared to participate in an international trade show. Although such participation represents a major investment in terms of time, effort, and money, with proper planning and commitment, it can be one of the best investments in exporting that your firm can make. Remember that a trade show is only a part of your firm's total export promotion effort and is no substitute for a well-designed, professionally managed, long-term exporting program.

Endnotes

1. Information provided by the National Trade Show Exhibitors Association.
2. Information provided by the Trade Show Bureau.

REFERENCES

Bello, D. C. and H. C. Barkdale. "Exporting at Industrial Trade Shows," *Industrial Marketing Management*, Spring 1986, 197–206.

Bertrand, K. "Talking Turkey on Trade Shows," *Business Marketing*, March 1987, 94–103.

Bonoma, T. V. "Getting More Out of Your Trade Shows," *Harvard Business Review*, 61 January–February 1983, 75–83.

Browning, J. M. and R. J. Adams. "Trade Shows: An Effective Promotional Tool for the Small Industrial Business," *Journal of Small Business Management*, October 1988, 31–36.

Firks, R. "Pick Up Your Profits With Trade Shows," *Agency Sales Magazine*, June 1990, 28–33.

Friedman, S. F. "Planning and Knowledge Are Keys to Success at European Trade Shows," *Marketing News*, July 9, 1990, 10.

Humbert, R. P. "Trade Fairs Are an Excellent Way to Take Advantage of Growing Opportunities in Western Europe," *Business America*, December 21, 1987, 3–5.

Kerin, R. and W. L. Crow. "Assessing Trade Show Functions and Performance: An Exploratory Study," *Journal of Marketing*, 51, March 1987, 87–94.

Lelyweld, M. S. "European Trade Shows Are All Business," *Chicago Tribune*, November 17, 1989, 21.

Motwani, J., G. Rice and E. Mahmoud. "Promoting Exports Through International Trade Shows: A Dual Perspective," *Review of Business*, Spring 1992, 38–42.

Norton, J. H. "How To Make Foreign Trade Shows Pay Off," *World Trade*, Winter 1989, 92.

Smith, H. "Special Training for Trade Shows," *Sales and Marketing Management*, February 3, 1986, 67–87.

"Taking Advantage of Trade Fairs for Maximum Sales Impact," *Business International*, October 12, 1987, 321–22.

Weiss, J. "Trade Fairs Draw U.S. Firms to the E.C.," *Europe*, June 1988, 21–23.

Forming International Sales Pacts

U.N. Convention rules govern import/export activities in a growing number of countries.

Gila E. Gellman

Gila E. Gellman is an attorney in the Litigation Department of the New York-based law firm, Milbank, Tweed, Hadley & McCloy.

When American businesses sell goods to other companies within the United States, the rights and obligations of both buyers and sellers generally are set forth in the Uniform Commercial Code (UCC). The UCC is a relatively uniform law, adopted by states across the country to govern the sale of goods (as well as other commercial transactions), that is well-known to senior marketing and sales executives.

In a growing number of cases, however, U.S. exports to and imports from foreign companies are not governed by the UCC but by the United Nations Convention on Contracts for the International Sale of Goods. This is significant because the rules of the U.N. Convention differ from those of the UCC in many ways.

As the economies of the United States and large sections of the world begin to emerge from recession, international trade is poised to expand. It is therefore especially important for companies involved in international sales agreements to understand the Convention's provisions and the ways in which they diverge from those of the UCC.

This awareness can better guide business negotiations and, invariably, limit potential disputes and international litigation arising from conflicting expectations and the collapse of agreements.

Scope of the Convention

The U.N. Convention applies to contracts for the sale of goods between parties whose principal places of business are in at least two signatory countries to the Convention. Thus, without a choice of law provision to the contrary, a sales agreement between a U.S. business and a company located in any other signatory country will be governed by the Convention. (The Convention generally does not cover sales to consumers or transactions where labor or other services dominate the contract.)

> *The UCC is a relatively uniform law, adopted by states across the country to govern the sale of goods.*

As of this writing, more than three dozen countries have signed or ratified the Convention. They are: Argentina, Australia, Austria, Belarus, Bosnia, Bulgaria, Canada, Chile, China, Czech Republic, Denmark, Ecuador, Egypt, Estonia, Finland, France, Germany, Ghana, Guinea, Hungary, Iraq, Italy, Lesotho, Mexico, Netherlands, Norway, Poland, Rumania, Russian Federation, Singapore, Slovakia, Slovenia, Spain, Sweden, Switzerland, Syrian Arab Republic, Uganda, Ukraine, United States, Venezuela, Yugoslavia, and Zambia.

It is important to emphasize that the Convention (like the UCC, in certain cases) permits parties to agree expressly that its terms will not govern their contracts. That is, parties can "opt out" of the Convention and negotiate their own terms instead. This can be particularly important for large, individualized transactions or when businesses believe that UCC provisions will better serve their interests.

Irrevocable Offers. The rules of the Convention and the UCC diverge beginning with contract formation—the making of an offer and the acceptance of that offer. As an example, the Convention states that an offer, including an oral one, is automatically irrevocable if it indicates a fixed time for acceptance or if it is reasonable for the person receiving the offer to rely on the offer as being irrevocable. An irrevocable offer may not be revoked before the offer expires on its own terms at the acceptance date.

In contrast, under the UCC, an offer is irrevocable only if it so states in writing and is signed by the party making the offer. Whereas the Convention does not impose a time limitation, the UCC limits irrevocable offers to three months.

In the United States, businesses frequently make offers to purchase or sell goods that contain a date beyond which an offer may not be accepted. This date restriction sets an outside time limit on the offer that is generally subject to revocation by the party making the offer prior to this date. In contrast, under the terms of the Convention, including a date restriction in an offer keeps it open until that date. This can be perilous for the party making the offer, who might find profits thus disappear in a fluctuating market.

Mirror Image. Often, when a buyer agrees to purchase goods from a seller, the seller will send the buyer a document confirming the sale. This confirmatory document usually has a number of preprinted terms designed to protect the seller's interests. Similarly, the buyer then may send a document confirming its intention to purchase the seller's goods. This document likewise may contain various preprinted terms the buyer believes protect its interests.

Prior to the adoption of the UCC, U.S. courts employed a "mirror image" rule that provided that the terms of an acceptance must be the same as—or mirror—the terms of an offer. In the event the terms of the offer and acceptance differed, courts attempted to find, and define, a contract based on the terms set forth by the party who "fired the last shot." Thus, the party who sent the last form was deemed the new party making the offer and the contract was accepted—and formed—by performance from the other side, either by delivery of goods or payment for goods received.

The UCC resolves the confusion created by this situation, known as the "Battle of the Forms," by allowing a contract to be formed even though an acceptance includes terms not found in the offer. Thus, a definite and timely expression of acceptance or a written confirmation sent within a reasonable time operates as an

> *Whereas the Convention does not impose a time limitation, the UCC limits irrevocable offers to three months.*

acceptance even though it states terms additional to or different from those previously offered or agreed upon.

Under the UCC, these additional terms are to be construed as proposals for additions to the contract. Between two businesses, these terms become part of the contract unless (1) the offer expressly limits acceptance to the terms of the offer; (2) the terms materially alter the contract; or (3) notification of objection to them already has been given or will be given within a reasonable time after notice is received.

Under the Convention, however, contract formation requires that an acceptance match the offer (except for minor differences). In the event the acceptance—made by statement or other conduct—is not symmetrical with the offer, it is deemed a rejection and a counteroffer, which then can be accepted, forming a new contract. The Convention provides that an acceptance containing additional or different terms relating to the price, payment, quality, and quantity of the goods, place and time of delivery, extent of one party's liability to the other, or the settlement of disputes—such as a clause that requires arbitration—is a counteroffer.

Thus, contract formation is more diffi-

> *Under the Convention, a contract for the sale of goods of any value is enforceable even if it is not in writing.*

cult under the U.N. Convention—whose rules are similar to the pre-UCC mirror image rules—than under the UCC.

Open Terms. Although contract negotiations do not always resolve all important issues, the parties nonetheless may believe that they have reached an

enforceable agreement. In many instances, the UCC addresses this scenario. For example, the UCC provides that a contract may be enforceable absent a contract price, with the price to be determined later based on, among other things, the market price of the goods.

The Convention, in contrast, is unclear on the enforceability of open-price contracts. Although one provision clearly requires the party making the offer to set a price, another dictates that in an otherwise validly concluded contract, when price is left open, the price for the goods under the contract is the price "generally charged at the time of the conclusion of the contract." It remains to be seen how courts will interpret this apparent inconsistency.

Necessity of a Writing. Another important contract formation issue is whether an agreement needs to be in writing to be enforceable. Under the UCC Statute of Frauds, a contract for the sale of goods with a value of $500 or more must be in writing. This rule is aimed, at least in part, to limit litigation spurred by the fallible memories of parties to negotiations.

By contrast, under the Convention, a contract for the sale of goods of any value is enforceable even if it is not in writing. Moreover, unlike the UCC, the Convention allows for both oral and written contracts to be amended orally. (The Convention does provide, however, that once a contract is in writing, a provision may be included requiring that any amendment to the contract also be in writing.)

Breach of Contract

Both the UCC and the Convention contain provisions dealing with the rights of a seller and a buyer in the event of a breach of contract by the other.

Suppose an American company reaches an agreement with a buyer to sell the buyer certain goods. To try to ensure payment, the seller might insist that the buyer obtain a letter of credit from a bank, allowing the seller to rely on the creditworthiness of the bank rather than the buyer. Under the UCC, if the buyer fails to provide the letter of credit, the seller may be able to claim the buyer has breached the contract, thus terminating it.

Under the Convention, however, it is more difficult to invalidate a contract because termination will only be granted if there is a "fundamental breach." Although the Convention does not delineate what constitutes a fundamental breach, a buyer's failure to provide a letter of credit to the seller may not meet this standard. Parties to a contract governed by the Convention would be well-advised to clarify the events that will be deemed "fundamental."

Contract Disputes. The Convention takes a different view than the UCC as to the admissibility of evidence in the event a contract dispute results in litigation. In interpreting a contract, the Convention provides that courts may consider both the parties' intentions and "all relevant circumstances of the case, including the negotiations."

By contrast, under the UCC, extrinsic evidence, known as "parol evidence"—including the parties' intentions, prior agreements, and contemporaneous oral statements contradicting the terms of the contract—is not admissible in court. The UCC does permit contractual terms to be explained by course of dealing, trade usage, or course of performance and by evidence of consistent additional terms, unless the court finds the written contract to have been intended also "as a complete and exclusive statement of the terms of the agreement."

Damages for Breach. On a number of key issues, the Convention deals with the issue of damages for breach of contract differently from the UCC. For example:

- Under the Convention, a seller or buyer may be able to recover damages suffered as a result of a breach of contract if it can show that the other party to the contract knew or ought to have known that those damages were "a possible consequence" of the breach.

  The "possible consequence" standard allows for a larger damages recovery than under the UCC, which permits a party to recover damages for a loss only if it can prove that the breaching party had reason to know that damages were a "substantial probability." Thus, depending on whether an American business is more or less likely to face a breach and resulting injuries, it may want to try to limit the availability of damages.

- Under the Convention, a buyer that receives nonconforming goods may reduce the price payable to the seller—even after having paid the

> *Under the Convention, a buyer that receives nonconforming goods may reduce the price payable to the seller—even after having paid the seller—by the difference between the value conforming goods would have had at the time of delivery and the value of the nonconforming goods.*

seller—by the difference between the value conforming goods would have had at the time of delivery and the value of the nonconforming goods. The UCC only permits reduction of the purchase price for amounts still due; in other words, a party may no longer claim a reduction in price once payment has been made.

The right granted under the Convention could be particularly important in a fluctuating marketplace. Even when the Convention applies, American sellers may want to try to limit the effects of this provision by setting forth in the contract, as the Convention permits, the specific damages to which the buyer is entitled in the event of nonconforming goods.

- The Convention imposes a strict obligation on the buyer to examine the goods it receives within as short a period as is practicable under the circumstances. The buyer must give notice to the seller of the lack of conformity within a reasonable time after the buyer discovers or should have discovered it, and no

later than two years from the date of delivery. A buyer that fails to fulfill this obligation loses the opportunity to recover damages for nonconforming goods.

The two-year time period can cause problems for a seller, however; for example, by the time the buyer notifies the seller of nonconformity of the goods, any claim that the seller may have against a carrier for damage to the goods during shipping may be barred by the relevant statute of limitations. The UCC permits buyers and sellers to reduce the statute of limitations for breach of contract suits to one year, thus compelling a buyer to give notice to a seller of any lack of conformity during the time within which the seller could bring an action against the carrier.

Evolving Rules

It should be noted that while idealistically motivated, adoption of the Convention has not resulted in a perfect system. In the same way states in this country have adopted varying interpretations of the UCC—and even on occasion have interpreted the same provisions of the UCC differently—so too have the countries ratifying the Convention adopted somewhat different versions. The Convention on its face permits this, allowing countries to release themselves from certain provisions, which adds another layer of complexity to the analysis of the rules and standards.

Moreover, the Convention is not comprehensive. For example, it does not address letters of credit or security interests—both important in sales transactions and covered in the UCC—nor does it deal with personal injury claims stemming from defective goods.

However, the Convention does provide a uniformity of law that did not exist before its enactment; as a result, American and foreign parties no longer need to debate "choice of law" provisions in their contracts.

As business executives become more familiar with the U.N. Convention, and as courts begin to examine and interpret this multinational agreement, its framework should help bring a degree of certainty and stability to importers and exporters.

Export Channel Design: The Use of Foreign Distributors and Agents

Daniel C. Bello
Ritu Lohtia

Georgia State University

Daniel C. Bello is an associate professor of marketing at Georgia State University. He received his Ph.D. from Michigan State University. His research interests include distribution strategy and international marketing. He has published in the *Journal of Marketing, European Journal of Marketing, Journal of International Business Studies, Journal of Business Research, Industrial Marketing Management,* and *Journal of Advertising.* He serves on the editorial review boards of various professional journals including the *Journal of Marketing* and the *Journal of Business Research.*

Ritu Lohtia is an assistant professor of marketing at Georgia State University. She received her Ph.D. from the University of Maryland. Her research interests include buyer-seller relationships and business-to-business marketing. She has published in the *Journal of Business Research, Industrial Marketing Management, Journal of Global Marketing,* and in the proceedings of various professional conferences.

Because many manufacturers are unable to integrate vertically into global distribution, the nonintegrated market entry modes of foreign distributor and agent are frequently used. Unfortunately, little is known about choosing efficiently between distributor and agent because research has only partially examined the importance of transaction and production costs in determining institutional arrangements. To specify efficient channel design, this article develops and tests hypotheses linking the characteristics of export exchange to the cost-minimizing mode of export channel governance. Based on a sample of 269 manufacturers, results suggest that market diversity, type of transaction-specific asset, and production cost economies all affect the choice between foreign-based agents and distributors. The article concludes with the implications of these results for export management and future export research.

In contrast to integrated corporate channels (foreign sales office or subsidiary), nonintegrated channels (independent agents or distributors) provide a relatively easy form of foreign-market entry (Root 1994). Experts note that the majority of world trade is handled through independent middlemen and that these export intermediaries possess strong local-market knowledge, crucial contacts with foreign buyers, and the ability to provide sophisticated marketing services (Clasen 1991). Despite the importance of middlemen, most theoretical studies using transaction cost analysis (TCA) merely address the question of whether a firm will adopt an integrated or nonintegrated international channel (Anderson and Coughlan 1987). The research shows that firms subject to strong transaction cost pressures choose vertical integration, but the decision of which nonintegrated mode to use is typically not addressed. This leaves unanswered the important question of how best to choose between the nonintegrated modes (agent or distributor).

In this article, the choice between foreign distributor or agent is framed as a question of efficient governance for the direct export channel. Distributor and agent are viewed as alternative institutional arrangements or governance modes for conducting the marketing-distribution functions that are necessary for export exchange (Root 1994). In determining the most cost-effective mode, international writers traditionally rely on the analysis of production costs (the costs of producing the export functions) (Clasen 1991; Cateora 1994). The major economic criterion is a mode's ability to exploit economies of scale and perform export tasks such as foreign-market promotion, pricing, delivery, and after-sale service at the lowest possible cost (Terpstra 1984). Williamson (1979, 1985) criticized sole reliance on the production cost criterion and suggested that the key efficiency criterion in channel design is the minimization of transaction costs (the costs of running or managing the channel). According to TCA, the object is to match governance structures to the attributes of transactions in a discriminating (i.e., transaction cost economizing) way (Williamson 1981). Although he acknowledges the need to minimize the sum of transaction and production costs, his thesis retains the primacy of transaction costs. However, TCA theorists recognize that the situational context in question will affect the relative importance that the attributes of an exchange play "in crafting an appropriate governance structure" (Noordewier, John, and Nevin 1990, p. 82).

For the export context, researchers generally have not addressed the way export exchange influences the choice between the basic types of international middlemen. In a key exception, Klein, Frazier, and Roth (1990) examined agent and distributor modes in conjunction with integrated forms of foreign-market entry. In this pioneering study, production and transaction cost indicators were found to discriminate significantly between integrated and nonintegrated modes, consistent with prior findings. Unfortunately, however, the study failed to find any transaction cost indicators that discriminate significantly between the nonintegrated choice of distributor or agent. Several study limitations may account for their results: the export setting was mostly North American (63% of their Canadian manufacturers exported to the United States), joint ventures and commissioned agents were comingled into a single-agency category, and very few cost indicators were examined.

Thus there remains a compelling need to understand how transaction and production costs affect the efficient design of the nonintegrated export channel. Theorists note that "performance will be enhanced when there is congruence (or a match) between the governance structure employed and the underlying dimensions of exchange" (Noordewier, John, and Nevin 1990, p. 82). Yet the specific way in which attributes of export exchange are efficiently matched to the nonintegrated governance choice (distributor or agent) has not been empirically specified. We examine the linkage or match between exchange attributes and governance mode by looking at the impact that multiple cost indicators have on middleman choice in a global setting. The study will specify the efficient use of international middlemen by analyzing the impact of (1) the transaction costs associated with writing, monitoring, and enforcing foreign distribution contracts; and (2) the production costs incurred while performing export functions.

TCA theory suggests that firms will use full-function distributors in the absence of significant market frictions and scale economies (Williamson 1985). These manufacturers spin off functions such as stocking foreign inventories, granting buyer credit, processing orders, and foreign delivery to a title-taking distributor who is compensated by a profit margin (Shipley, Cook, and Barnett 1989). In terms of channel governance, the distributor mode represents market governance because the export transaction is controlled through market contracting of export functions with an independent foreign firm. In this way, "the distributor assumes a fuller range of functions, but is more difficult to control than the agent" (Root 1987, p. 62). Agents, who do not take title, represent a quasi-integrated mode because the manufacturer self-performs most of the export functions and typically only spins off selling-related functions to an agent who earns a sales commission (Jackson and d'Amico 1989). The foreign selling and buyer contact functions performed by agents are the most difficult for firms to integrate because these functions require unique familiarity with local-market conditions and acceptance by local buyers (Anderson 1985; Clasen 1991). Thus firms subject to moderate transaction and production cost pressures may only quasi-integrate, finding it efficient to spin off the difficult-to-perform foreign selling function to a foreign agent. In this sense, the agent mode is an intermediate governance form because it has characteristics of market (contracting out the selling function) and hierarchy (self-performing other export functions).

We first review transaction cost forces and develop hypotheses about their effects on the choice between the nonintegrated export modes. Next, production cost forces are introduced and hypotheses are developed. Finally, a methodology to test the hypotheses through a multivariate model is introduced, and implications for export theory and practice are drawn.

TRANSACTION COST INDICATORS

TCA predicts that a manufacturer, having committed specific assets to a trading relationship in an uncertain environment, will experience efficiency gains from lowered transaction costs if it vertically integrates. For export transactions involving high levels of asset specificity and uncertainty, it is expected that export activities can be performed most efficiently within the firm by employees in a foreign subsidiary (hierarchical governance) rather than outside the firm by distributors or agents. However, the TCA prescription to integrate into global distribution "is simply irrelevant" for firms that "cannot consider vertical integration as a feasible alternative" (Heide and John 1988, p. 21). Complete integration by setting up a foreign sales subsidiary may be unappealing to a firm for a number of operational and strategic reasons (Root 1994). Although it may lack the desire or ability to integrate completely, a firm that is subject to moderate transaction cost pressures may be motivated to quasi-integrate to the extent feasible. When a firm's export transaction is characterized by asset specificity and uncertainty, it is likely to use the quasi-integrated agent mode.

Specific Assets

Asset specificity refers to a manufacturer's investments that are dedicated to a trading relationship and cannot be redeployed to alternative middlemen or other uses. Manufacturers make such investments when they tailor order, payment, and logistical procedures to suit a middleman's requirements; provide specialized technical and sales training; and commit managerial and physical resources (Rosson and Ford 1982). Because these assets are dedicated to a particular trading partner their value to the manufacturer would be lost if the middleman was terminated. This potential loss of value diminishes the firm's ability to replace a nonperforming middleman because the firm will be reluctant to terminate the middleman, even if the intermediary "is abusing his/her agreement with the firm" (Anderson and Coughlan 1987, p. 72). Lacking a credible termination threat, the manufacturer is exposed to the unchecked opportunistic behavior of its foreign trading partner.

Empirical research in an international context provides partial support for a relationship between the transaction specificity of assets and quasi-integration in foreign markets (Anderson and Coughlan 1987; Gatignon and Anderson 1988). Unfortunately, the research has not fully explored the effect of asset specificity because studies tend to examine only one type of specific investment at a time. For example, Anderson and Coughlan (1987) analyzed dedicated human investments in training; Gatignon and Anderson (1988) examined a product specificity indicator reflecting the proprietary content of technological products; and Klein, Frazier, and Roth (1990) employed a single indicator that combines human and physical investments. Because these studies treat each asset type in isolation, the various specific investments have not been simultaneously examined and little is known about their relative impact on export channel design. To understand the salience of different specific investments, the following discussion examines the contribution of each asset toward the quasi-integrated mode of agent use.

Specific Product Assets

In terms of product specificity, sophisticated export products are posited to trade through agents rather than distributors because "transaction costs . . . are high for technologically complex products" (Johanson and Vahlne 1990, p. 17). The proprietary content of sophisticated products increases monitoring and control costs, making distributor use inefficient and encouraging manufacturers to self-perform most export functions (Anderson and Gatignon 1986). Employees are less costly to manage because safeguarding technology and negotiating over complex, proprietary items with an outside contractor are much more difficult and costly compared to doing so with an employee (Williamson 1985). Consequently, firms with such product-based specific assets tend to self-perform most functions and only spin off the difficult-to-duplicate selling and buyer contact functions to an agent.

Specific Human Assets

Human specificity refers to the specialized knowledge and skills required to perform the export functions used in marketing a firm's brand abroad (John and Weitz 1988). Idiosyncrasies associated with a brand's export procedures and processes require the manufacturer to train its middlemen in many troublesome export functions (Root 1994). Likewise, customer idiosyncrasies may lead to investments in training necessitated by the learning requirements of the foreign selling situation (Anderson and Coughlan 1987). To sell effectively to complex foreign buyers, manufacturers must provide foreign salespeople with specialized knowledge about the buying motives associated with its market offering. Because the time and effort spent training a foreign partner in export tasks are not redeployable, firms economize on transaction costs by self-performing as many tasks as feasible (Anderson 1985). Thus such firms are likely to integrate most tasks and spin off only the difficult customer contact functions to an agent.

Specific Physical Assets

In terms of physical assets, a manufacturer may tailor investments to the particular marketing requirements of its foreign partner. A partner's unique circumstances and existing infrastructure may lead the manufacturer to invest in specialized warehouses, demonstration facilities, repair and service centers, and other capital items needed to support the foreign marketing of its brand (Ward 1984). However, firms committing physical and capital investments risk being held "hostage" because these nonredeployable assets make it difficult to dismiss an opportunistic trading partner (Williamson 1985). Consequently, firms are motivated to bring such transactions under their control by self-performing most functions.

To summarize, the above reasoning suggests that the quasi-integrated mode of exporting (agent use) is an appropriate match to export exchanges involving specific assets. In analyzing this governance match, the relative contribution of each type of specific asset to agent use is of interest. Although theory does not address the relative potency or salience of the different asset types, the sensitivity of governance choice to these requisite investments is a crucial practical issue for export managers. Hypothesis 1 tests the extent to which each type of specific asset is associated with the prescribed channel configuration of agent use.

H1: Agent use is matched or associated with export transactions characterized by specific investments, as indicated by

H1a: highly specific product assets for agent users.

H1b: highly specific human assets for agent users.

H1c: highly specific physical assets for agent users.

Environmental Uncertainty

Environmental uncertainty is defined as unanticipated changes in circumstances surrounding an exchange (Williamson 1985). Uncertainty raises problems in export exchanges that motivate firms to seek governance structures that minimize transaction costs. When it is difficult to predict future contingencies that might confront an exchange relationship, the uncertainty becomes another aspect of market failure. The inability to predict contingencies undermines the firm's ability to write efficient contingent contracts with its foreign middleman. This creates a "hold up" potential for an opportunistic partner when a contractually unaccounted contingency arises. In fact, "one of the principal drawbacks of dealing with independent intermediaries is the difficulty of renegotiating agreements in light of changed circumstances" (John and Weitz 1988, p. 341). TCA suggests that, given specific assets, environmental uncertainty motivates a more integrated mode of governance to lessen the need to monitor, to enforce, and to rewrite contracts.

Because asset specificity is typically nonzero in export settings, highly volatile international markets make it extremely difficult for manufacturers to write formal, comprehensive agreements with foreign distributors (Clasen 1991, Root 1994). Further, Klein, Frazier, and Roth (1990) noted that foreign markets are sufficiently more volatile than are domestic markets that uncertainty "should influence transaction costs independently of the level of asset specificity" (p. 199). More important, these authors also stress the importance of examining the impact of two dimensions of uncertainty on the degree of channel integration—volatility and diversity. Volatility is formally defined, in line with the definition used by Leblebici and Salancik (1981), as "the extent to which the environment changes rapidly and allows a firm to be caught by surprise" (p. 200). Such variability can arise from unexpected changes in customer behaviors and from fluctuations in competitive activities. In a volatile foreign market, it is difficult to write a contingent claims contract; therefore, when unforeseen contingencies arise, an opportunistic partner can interpret the contract to its advantage. Unpredictable customer and competitor actions increase the bargaining and monitoring costs associated with a distribution contract and "motivate suppliers to appropriate control over their downstream channel partners" (Dwyer and Welsh 1985, p. 401). Thus high transaction costs in volatile environments make full-function independent distributor use inefficient, prompting a firm to quasi-integrate through agent usage. This reasoning suggests the following:

H2: Agent use is matched with export transactions characterized by high environmental volatility.

In contrast, diversity is the "extent to which there are multiple sources of uncertainty in the environment" (Klein, Frazier, and Roth 1990, p. 200). Diverse foreign markets are characterized by many competitors and large numbers of intermediate customers or final users with dissimilar buying habits (Seifert and Ford 1989). Diversity affects channel design by making it difficult for the firm (1) to collect and process information relevant to each customer and competitor and (2) to formulate strategic programs and responses appropriate to each (Dwyer and Welsh 1985). Thus a firm operating in a diverse international market needs to develop multiple strategies to effectively address the different customer and competitor demands. However, developing multiple strategies is problematic for firms because complex and unstructured market information is difficult to assimilate and process. Consequently, coordination and communication problems between a firm and its limited-function agent frustrate the adaptation of marketing-distribution functions. However, full-function distributors can adapt quickly because they are embedded in their local markets and can adjust all tasks in response to complex market conditions (Moore 1992).

Thus a firm exporting to a highly diverse foreign environment may be motivated to use a nonintegrated distributor channel because of its superior adaptation characteristics. In a supporting empirical study, Gatignon and Anderson (1988) found that in uncertain risky countries, firms use less integrated modes so as to permit greater flexibility to react to environmental diversity. Therefore, the following is hypothesized:

H3: Distributor use is matched with export transactions characterized by high environmental diversity.

PRODUCTION COST INDICATORS

Production costs are the costs of producing export marketing-distribution functions in the foreign market such as selling, granting credit, warehousing, and providing after-sale service (Cateora 1994; Williamson 1985). The conventional explanation for why manufacturers use foreign middlemen rather than self-perform these export functions is basically a production cost argument (Terpstra 1984). Manufacturers find it uneconomical to perform these activities because foreign sales volume is too low, and the firm's capital and labor resources cannot be efficiently used in the foreign market. Because production cost economies can be derived from various facets of foreign operations, several factors uniquely contribute to the scale effects that lower production costs. On the basis of the extant literature, the magnitude of scale-sensitive export activities are reflected by three indicators: two indicators of export volume (absolute sales volume and rate of sales growth) and one indicator of organizational capacity for exporting (export intensity).

Export Volume

Production costs have only been partially examined because prior export research has tended to focus mainly on the impact of a firm's current foreign sales volume (Terpstra 1984). This traditional approach is based on the notion that at a high sales volume a firm can exploit the production cost advantage enjoyed by middlemen. Williamson (1985) also observed that the high-volume firm "is simply better able to realize economies of scale as its own requirements become larger in relation to the size of the market" (p. 94). Thus firms with a high foreign volume can economically self-perform most export functions and are likely to spin off only the difficult-to-perform selling function to an agent. Unfortunately, supporting empirical studies (John and Weitz 1988; Klein, Frazier, and Roth 1990) consider current volume in isolation from other scale-sensitive factors, thus ignoring other facets of foreign operations that also lower production costs.

A second, but often not considered, volume-related factor is market sales growth. Sales growth is defined as the rate of change in foreign market sales and indicates future levels of foreign sales volume. Because a firm's choice of governance mode for an export market is a relatively long-term decision that may be difficult to change, the governance decision is likely to be influenced by anticipated future channel volume (Root 1994). In contrast to the absolute amount of current sales, the rate of sales growth indicates anticipated levels of production cost economies (Terpstra 1984). Higher growth rates tend to be matched with agent use, in anticipation of future production efficiencies. Consequently:

H4: Agent use is matched with export transactions characterized by a high export volume, as indicated by

H4a: high current foreign sales for agent users.

H4b: high rates of sales growth in the foreign market for agent users.

Organizational Capacity

Another often ignored aspect of foreign operations is a firm's capacity to export, which refers to the ability to exploit scale economies in the use of managerial and labor resources (Welch and Luostarinen 1988). A basic indicator of a manufacturer's capacity to conduct export activities is its export intensity, defined as the percentage of a firm's total sales attributable to exporting. This key capacity indicator reflects management's commitment and involvement with international markets (Cavusgil 1984). When exports are a small fraction of total sales, the firm's managerial resources tend to be devoted to the domestic market to the neglect of foreign efforts. However, for the high-intensity firm, the greater managerial time and effort devoted to foreign decision making greatly enhances the organizational capacity to engage in foreign marketing. Further, the increased capacity economizes on production costs because managerial resources are used more efficiently for export purposes as the frequency and continuity in foreign decision making increases. Anderson (1985) noted that production costs are reduced because of economies of scale in developing and using management skills, allowing the manufacturer to economize on decision making for export marketing functions. Enhanced managerial productivity reflects the scale of managerial involvement in foreign-market decisions that encourages firms to self-perform many functions and export through the quasi-integrated agent mode.

H5: Agent use is matched with export transactions characterized by manufacturers who possess a high export intensity.

METHOD

Subjects and Pretest

A national sample of manufacturers who export through middlemen was drawn from the *Journal of Commerce United States Importer & Exporter Directory* (1991). To best adapt questionnaire items, a series of 20 in-depth field interviews were conducted with export managers drawn from the directory. Following the fieldwork, a pretest of 100 firms was conducted to estimate the percentage of firms using middlemen, to examine the psychometric properties of the questionnaire items, and to fine-tune the

telephone prenotification procedure. Of the 100 firms, 63 use middlemen in one or more markets, whereas the remaining 37 either no longer export or export without middlemen. A single-wave mail survey was used for the 63 middlemen users, yielding a response rate of 57 percent. Analysis of pretest results and a telephone debriefing with respondents suggest that the key informant for this study should be the manager within the manufacturing organization (hereafter referred to as the export manager) who has primary responsibility for the firm's relationship with the export middleman. Rosson (1987) found that this key manager is typically the major contact for the export middleman and consequently is the most informed respondent. Similarly, Williamson (1985) noted that this type of boundary-spanning manager is most responsible for adapting the organizational interface.

Data Collection

For the formal study, a systematic random selection method (every 30th name) was used to draw a sample of 600 firms from the directory. For each of the 600 firms, a telephone prenotification methodology was used to identify the key export manager. The procedure entails contacting a senior executive listed in the directory who then identifies a manager most likely to have middleman responsibilities. The manager is then contacted by phone and his or her responsibilities are verified or a new candidate name is solicited. The procedure identified 398 firms that export through middlemen, with the remaining firms either no longer exporting or doing so without middlemen. The export managers of the 398 firms were mailed a questionnaire with a cover letter instructing them to respond in terms of a single, focal export middleman and foreign market. Three weeks later a follow-up phone call was made to nonrespondents and a second questionnaire was sent. These procedures yielded 94 refusals, 35 questionnaires with substantial missing values or unusable responses, and 269 usable questionnaires for a response rate of 68 percent. Table 1 shows characteristics of the responding firms. A comparison of early and late respondents yielded no significant differences in individual or organizational characteristics relevant to the study, suggesting that nonresponse is not a problem (Armstrong and Overton 1977). Of the 269 responding firms, 162 (60%) export through foreign distributors, whereas 107 (40%) export through foreign agents.

Measurement

The three asset specificity indicators are measured by averaged summative scales composed of items derived from prior research. Table 2 assesses the measurement quality and psychometric properties of the specificity indicators. The confirmatory factor analysis (CFA) evaluates the unidimensionality of the scales and the coefficient alphas assess their reliability. For product specificity, five semantic differential items adapted from Anderson (1985) that describe the technical complexity of the exported product are used. This operationalization is appropriate because the proprietary content of sophisticated products is associated with product-based asset specificity (Gatignon and Anderson 1988). For human specificity, three items adapted from Anderson and Coughlan (1987) are used. The items tap the training necessitated by the learning requirements of the foreign selling situation. The three physical specificity items are adopted from Heide and John (1990) and assess the manufacturer's investment in equipment and other capital items needed to support the foreign trading partner.

As Table 2 shows, the measurement model is judged to provide an acceptable fit because the chi-square goodness of fit is not statistically significant ($\chi^2_{(41)} = 51.75, p > .121$). Additional favorable diagnostics include a goodness-of-fit index (GFI) of .97 and a root mean square residual (RMSR) of .037. The scales are adequately reliable and are typical of those reported in the business literature (Churchill and Peter 1984). Convergent validity is evidenced because items load significantly on their posited indicators, and discriminant validity is indicated because the confidence interval (± two standard errors) around the correlation estimate between any two indicators never includes 1.0 (Anderson and Gerbing 1988, p. 416). Discriminant validity is also indicated by the low to moderate correlations between the scales (Table 3). The highest correlation is between the product and human scales ($r = .36$), meaning that these scales share only a modest amount of variance ($r^2 = .13$).

Table 4 displays the two uncertainty indicators (diversity and volatility) adapted from Klein, Frazier, and Roth (1990). The three diversity items assess the extent to which the foreign market is composed of multiple customer and competitor entities. The four volatility items assess the extent to which the market changes rapidly because of unexpected changes in customer and competitor behaviors. As Table 4 shows, the measurement model is judged to provide an acceptable fit because the chi-square goodness of fit is not statistically significant ($\chi^2_{(13)} = 11.63, p > .559$) and has a GFI of .98 and a RMSR of .031. The data also suggest that the scales are adequately reliable and show evidence of convergent and discriminant validity (Anderson and Gerbing 1988). Production cost indicators are numerical values supplied by respondents, following Cavusgil (1984). Export sales are annual dollar sales through the focal middleman to the focal market, and sales growth is the percentage increase in sales during the past year. Export intensity is the percentage of the firm's total sales that are due to exports.

Hypothesis Testing

Before testing the five hypotheses, which posit specific differences between distributor and agent users, multivariate analysis of variance (MANOVA) is used to test for an overall relation between the cost factors and export modes (Green 1978). The MANOVA uses the eight cost indicators shown in Table 5 as dependent variables and export mode

TABLE 1
Characteristics of Surveyed Export Manufacturers

Characteristic	Number of Firms	Percentage of Firms
Total annual sales (domestic and foreign)		
Under $5 million	66	25
$5 million to $15 million	64	24
$15 million to $30 million	66	25
More than $30 million	71	26
Not reported	2	—
Total	269	100
Foreign export markets		
Canada	23	8
Mexico	18	7
South America	24	9
England	29	11
Germany	18	7
Austria	11	4
France	8	3
Other Europe	25	9
Middle East	19	7
Japan	31	11
Korea	24	9
Other Asia	18	7
Pacific Rim	15	6
Africa	6	2
Total	269	100
Types of products exported		
Electronics, instrumentation	34	13
Engines, power equipment	27	10
Pumps, valves, hydraulics	24	9
Chemicals, adhesives, plastics	22	8
Nonelectrical components, parts	20	7
Small machinery, tools	18	7
Automotive, transportation items	16	6
Aviation, avionics	14	5
Large machinery, equipment	13	5
Household appliances, items	11	4
Agriculture, food processing	10	4
Metal working items	8	3
Miscellaneous others	52	19
Total	269	100

(distributor or agent) as the independent two-level factor. Bartlett's test of sphericity (Bartlett's = 139.49 with 28 df, $p < .001$) indicates that MANOVA is appropriate for examining the overall relation between costs and modes (Cooley and Lohnes 1971). In terms of the individual cost relationships posited in H1 to H5, each is tested directly by an F ratio from a univariate analysis of variance (ANOVA) (Stevens 1972). Further, multiple discriminant analysis (MDA) is typically used in conjunction with MANOVA to help determine the intensity of each variable's impact on overall group differences (Green 1978; Dant, Lumpkin, and Bush 1990). MDA is the appropriate statistical technique for identifying the impact of metrically scaled variables (i.e., the eight cost indicators) on respondent membership in a priori defined groups (distributor or agent user). Of particular interest are discrimi-

TABLE 2
Asset Specificity Measurement Summary:
Confirmatory Factor Analysis and Scale Reliability

Item	Item Description Summary	Standardized Loading (λ_{ij})		Coefficient α
Product[a]				
P1	Unsophisticated - sophisticated	.85	—[b]	.77
P2	Nontechnical - technical	.79	(13.7)	
P3	Simple - complex	.76	(13.2)	
P4	Low engineering content - high	.58	(9.6)	
P5	Commodity - customized	.31	(4.9)	
Human[c]				
H1	It takes a long time to learn about the product	.69	—	.65
H2	It is difficult to learn customer's needs	.61	(6.8)	
H3	It takes a lot of time to understand customer	.58	(6.7)	
Physical[c]				
Ph1	Resources are committed to physical assets	.88	—	.82
Ph2	Special investment in equipment is needed	.80	(12.8)	
Ph3	Capital expenditures are required	.70	(11.7)	

NOTE: Fit statistics for confirmatory factor analysis: $\chi^2_{(41)} = 51.75$, $p = .121$, goodness-of-fit index = .97, root mean square residual = .037.
a. Respondents were asked to describe the product sold through their middleman to the focal foreign country by using a 7-point semantic differential.
b. Dashes are fixed parameters; t values are in parentheses.
c. For the human-asset items, respondents were instructed to respond to statements describing the foreign selling situation. For the physical-asset items, they responded to statements describing the manufacturer's investments made to support the foreign middleman. Response scale for the items was a 7-point Likert-type scale on which items ranged from 1 (*strongly disagree*) to 7 (*strongly agree*).

TABLE 3
Correlation Coefficients Among Study Variables

Variable	Product	Human	Physical	Volatility	Diversity	Sales	Growth
Product	—						
Human	.36**	—					
Physical	.16*	.18**	—				
Volatility	−.06	−.01	.22**	—			
Diversity	−.24**	−.08	−.02	.07	—		
Sales	.13*	.16*	.25**	.01	.03	—	
Growth	.04	.03	−.03	−.09	.00	.01	—
Intensity	.25**	.11	.16*	.03	−.05	.24**	−.01

*$p \leq .05$; **$p \leq .01$.

TABLE 4
Environmental Uncertainty Measurement Summary:
Confirmatory Factor Analysis and Scale Reliability

Item	Item Description Summary	Standardized Loading (λ_{ij})		Coefficient α
Diversity[a]				
D1	Few customers for product (reversed)	.75	—[b]	.63
D2	Many final users for product	.72	(4.9)	
D3	Many competitors in this market	.38	(4.7)	
Volatility[a]				
V1	Resellers act in unexpected ways	.82	—	.77
V2	Surprised by reseller's behaviors	.79	(11.8)	
V3	Surprised by competitor's actions	.69	(10.8)	
V4	Customer reaction often surprising	.48	(7.5)	

NOTE: Fit statistics for confirmatory factor analysis: $\chi^2_{(13)} = 11.63$, $p = .559$, goodness-of-fit index = .98, root mean square residual = .031.
a. Respondents were asked to evaluate statements about the business environment in their focal foreign country. Using a Likert-type response scale, respondents evaluated statements about the numbers of environmental elements and the dynamism of those elements. The items on the 7-point response scale ranged from 1 (*strongly disagree*) to 7 (*strongly agree*).
b. Dashes are fixed parameters; t values are in parentheses.

TABLE 5
Summary of Results: Multivariate Analysis
of Variance and Multiple Discriminant Analysis

Cost Indicator	Discriminant Loadings	Means for Middleman Users		F Ratio	p Value
		Distributors	Agents		
Product	.426	4.71	5.17	3.10	.002
Human	.265	4.77	5.05	1.93	.054
Physical	.303	3.01	2.60	2.21	.028
Volatility	.178	3.23	3.04	1.30	.200
Diversity	.578	4.70	3.95	4.21	.001
Foreign market sales[a]	.325	1.59	3.29	2.37	.018
Market sales growth[b]	.458	9.10	21.94	3.34	.001
Export intensity[c]	.396	17.58	23.37	2.89	.004
Multivariate summary					
Wilks's lambda	.834				
Multivariate significance level	.001				
Percentage correctly classified (hit ratio)					
Analysis sample	69.31%				
Holdout sample	67.16%				
Proportional chance criterion	52.09%				

a. Foreign market sales is dollar sales (in millions) through middleman.
b. Market sales growth is percentage increase in middleman's dollar sales in past year.
c. Export intensity is percentage of firm's total sales that are due to exports.

nant loadings—the correlations between the cost indicators and the discriminant function—that aid in establishing each indicator's contribution to the separation of the groups (Hair et al. 1992).

RESULTS

As shown in Table 5, the MANOVA results (Wilks's lambda = .834, $p < .001$) indicate that overall differences exist between the distributor and agent users across the set of cost indicators. The univariate F ratios indicate that most indicators differ between groups, but volatility ($p < .200$) does not differ and human specificity ($p < .054$) only marginally differs across the groups. The MDA results show that most of the indicators from the transaction and production cost categories discriminate between type of middleman user. In addition, the percentage correctly classified in the analysis sample (69% hit ratio for 202 cases) and the relative stability of the classification across a holdout sample (67% hit ratio for 67 cases) supports the discriminant function's ability to differentiate between distributor and agent users. Moreover, both the analysis sample's hit ratio and the holdout sample's exceed the proportional-chance criterion (52%) by the requisite improvement of 125 percent in classification, supporting the predictive validity of the discriminant function (Hair et al. 1992).

In terms of specific hypothesis tests, H1a and H1b are accepted but H1c, although significant, is not in the direction hypothesized. Whereas agent users make higher product ($p < .002$) and human ($p < .054$) investments, distributor users make higher physical-asset ($p < .028$) investments. Apparently, when export transactions are

characterized by higher levels of equipment and other capital expenditures, distributors rather than agents tend to be used. It appears that TCA motives to protect specific physical investments are offset by the unique skills and marketing-distribution infrastructure offered by foreign distributors. Firms may choose distributors despite investment risks because, as Ward (1984) noted, agents often lack the ability and willingness to accommodate the manufacturer's physical investments in installation, repair, and service facilities. However, these conclusions should be tempered by the fact that the mean for physical assets is low for both groups, indicating that only a few specialized physical assets are required for these exports.

For environmental uncertainty, H3 is accepted because diversity is higher for distributor users, but H2 is rejected because volatility does not differ by middleman type. One reason why volatility does not discriminate between middlemen may be due to the low levels of volatility experienced by the respondents (3.23, 3.04 in Table 5). The studied channels simply are not volatile because both middlemen groups score well below 4.0, the midpoint of the 7-point volatility scale. In contrast, respondents perceived relatively high levels of diversity. The diversity measure for distributors (4.70) is above the scale midpoint, whereas the measure for agents (3.95) is below the midpoint, which is consistent with H3.

Both of the production cost hypotheses (H4, H5) are accepted at the $p < .05$ level. Agent users have much stronger export sales ($3.29 million, 22% growth) than do distributor users ($1.59 million, 9% growth), which is consistent with H4. Similarly, agent users have a greater organizational capacity to export (exports are 23% of sales) than do distributor users (exports are 18% of sales).

With higher sales and greater capacity to export, agent users are much better able to exploit the economies of scale inherent in foreign marketing than are the slower growing distributor users.

DISCUSSION

Implications for Practice

The research suggests that both the transaction costs associated with enforcing contracts as well as the production costs involved in performing export functions influence the choice of entry mode.

Transaction Cost Implications

The data show that the asset specificity related to a firm's export transaction is a key discriminator between distributor and agent use. Because the product-based asset loading (.426) is the highest discriminant loading of the three assets shown in Table 5, the governance process seems to be particularly sensitive to the exchange and safeguarding requirements of sophisticated products. By using agents, firms are able to export technically complex products by self-performing most of the export functions, and they use foreign middlemen only to find customers. By having the manufacturer's own employees perform most export tasks, transaction costs are minimized because safeguarding technology and negotiating over proprietary items is less costly with an internal employee than with an outside distributor.

Similarly, agents are indicated when human specificity is high because it reflects complex buying motives on the part of foreign customers. Agent users are better able to safeguard their training investments compared to distributor users, who are unable to ensure that their specific human investments are implemented properly. Because distributors have a wholesaler's wide product assortment, they tend not to coordinate a particular manufacturer's training with the other elements of a brand's export marketing mix (Shipley, Cook, and Barnett 1989). In terms of physical-asset specificity, the results suggest that motives to safeguard an investment are somewhat offset by a trading partner's ability to employ an investment properly. Unlike foreign distributors, agents tend to lack the extensive physical facilities necessary to accommodate a firm's specific investments in materials handling equipment, repair and service centers, and other specialized capital items (Ward 1984).

The results for environmental uncertainty suggest that low to moderate volatility in a foreign market does not influence the choice between distributor and agent. Both export modes appear capable of adapting to modest variability in customer and competitor behaviors. Because the data did not include highly volatile environments, it remains possible that great variability can raise bargaining and monitoring costs to a point that contracting with a full-function distributor is inefficient. However, the data suggest that highly diverse environments favor the use of distributors: diversity's discriminant loading (.578) is the highest among all the cost indicators in Table 5. Large numbers of customers and competitors place a premium on a distributor's ability to process complex, local market information and to formulate multiple strategies that comprehensively adapt all marketing-mix elements (Jackson and d'Amico 1989). An implication of the adaptation advantage is the need for firms to provide distributors with the marketing support they require to react quickly to diverse market conditions. Diversity increases a distributor's reliance on the product and promotional services a firm provides to increase its distributor's marketing performance (Cavusgil and Zou 1994).

Production Cost Implications

The findings suggest that agents are most appropriate for high-export-intensity firms that export to foreign markets with a high rate of sales growth. Compared to slower growing distributor users, agent users have faster growing export operations (22% versus 9% per year) that represent a larger percentage (23% versus 18%) of their total sales volume. Such sales growth and export intensity create cost-effective conditions that permit the firm to gain control over its export activities by self-performing most of the marketing-distribution functions. The discriminant loadings for sales growth (.458) and intensity (.396) are the highest among the three production cost indicators, suggesting that these indicators are the most critical to mode choice. Sales volume may be less influential because it represents a firm's current ability to realize production cost economies rather than the firm's future economizing ability that is reflected by the more important sales growth rate indicator. This suggests that firms should take a long-term focus and consider indicators of future economizing ability before choosing the channel intermediary.

Similarly, firms should recognize the important role that export-oriented managerial personnel play in their channel design decisions. The indicator of organizational capacity to export—export intensity—discriminates between entry mode, suggesting the pivotal role of personnel commitments. As Welch and Luostarinen (1988) emphasized, "International personnel development remains as a prime indication of the internal extent to which a company has effectively become internationalized" (p. 42). The organizational-capacity indicator suggests that, compared to distributor users, agent users have a much greater internal ability to perform export tasks efficiently. This occurs for high-export-intensity firms because their executives devote substantial time and effort to foreign matters, enabling them to exploit scale economies in developing and using international managerial skills.

The survey data also reveal that the number of full-time employees devoted to exporting differs for the middleman user groups: agent users average 68 export employees compared to only 6 for distributor users. The survey also found that the average duration of the channel relationship is 9 years for agent users compared to 13 years for distributor users. Perhaps, because the employees of companies using agents perform most export functions, experience and knowledge enable these exporters to replace an incumbent middleman or even to set up a foreign subsidiary easier than can distributor users. Thus agent use not only entails a greater commitment of personnel to exporting but also achieves a greater flexibility in export distribution because of the knowledge and experience of employees.

Implications for Research

To extend these findings, future research should examine the governance impact of other categories of specific assets identified by Williamson (1985) such as site, brand capital, and temporal. Also, given the complexity of global distribution, finer distinctions among market-entry choices (piggyback arrangements, import jobbers, trading companies, etc.) should be examined from both a transaction and production cost perspective.

Because the specific uncertainty measures in this research are somewhat narrow, future research should use more sophisticated measures of diversity and volatility that better assess the full domains of these key constructs. With broader measures, future research should validate and extend this study's uncertainty findings. In particular, it is important to examine whether higher levels of volatility would affect the choice of foreign middlemen. Relatedly, research should also examine the impact on entry mode of other types of environmental uncertainty such as technological change, political risk, and internal uncertainty. For example, internal uncertainty exists when a firm cannot accurately assess its trading partner's performance by available output measures (Williamson 1985). Anderson and Gatignon (1986) suggested that uncertainty internal to the international transaction makes higher control entry modes more desirable regardless of the level of asset specificity involved.

Whereas previous research uses sales volume as the sole proxy for production costs (Klein, Frazier, and Roth 1990), this research employs additional indicators to examine the impact of production costs on channel choice. Because all three of the indicators aid in determining middleman type, a more integrated export channel is indicated when any of these production cost advantages can be realized. However, the discriminant loadings (see Table 5) suggest that some aspects of production costs are more influential in discriminating between distributor and agent users. Future research should examine the relative importance of these and other production cost proxies in identifying users of different types of agents (import brokers, sales representatives, etc.) and distributors (import jobbers, trading companies, etc.). When combined with transaction cost indicators, multiple indicators of production costs should allow future researchers to better identify the factors that determine market-entry modes.

Further, future research should examine the impact on channel mode of factors other than transaction and production costs such as a firm's risk tolerance, a competitor's

strategy, and government regulations. It may well be that a highly risk-averse management would choose to shift all foreign marketing activities to a full-function distributor in spite of cost pressures favoring agent use. However, prominent among all the noncost factors that might merit examination is the impact of a firm's own strategic considerations on channel design. For example, speed of development refers to the need for rapid market action because of a timely opportunity. A firm that needs to enter a foreign market rapidly to exploit an opportunity might very well use a full-function distributor rather than delay entry until its internal resources are capable of supporting a foreign agent.

To conclude, this study uses multiple indicators of transaction and production costs to investigate the efficiency-based aspects of export channel design. The findings show that market diversity, nature of specific assets, and production cost economies have an impact on a firm's choice of a foreign-based distributor or agent. Clearly, a better understanding of the factors affecting the selection of foreign trading partners is necessary for more effective market-entry strategies.

ACKNOWLEDGMENTS

The authors would like to thank Li Zhang and Harash Sachdev for their help in collecting the data for this study. Thanks are also extended to three anonymous reviewers for their detailed and constructive comments on previous versions of this article.

REFERENCES

Anderson, Erin. 1985. "The Salesperson as Outside Agent or Employee: A Transaction Cost Analysis." *Marketing Science* 4 (3): 234-254.

Anderson, Erin and Anne T. Coughlan. 1987. "International Market Entry and Expansion via Independent or Integrated Channels of Distribution." *Journal of Marketing* 51 (January): 71-82.

Anderson, Erin and Hubert Gatignon. 1986. "Modes of Foreign Entry: A Transaction Cost Analysis and Propositions." *Journal of International Business Studies* 17 (3): 1-26.

Anderson, James C. and David W. Gerbing. 1988. "Structural Equation Modeling in Practice: A Review and Recommended Two-Step Approach." *Psychological Bulletin* 103 (3): 411-423.

Armstrong, J. Scott and Terry S. Overton. 1977. "Estimating Nonresponse Bias in Mail Surveys." *Journal of Marketing Research* 14 (August): 396-402.

Cateora, Philip R. 1994. *International Marketing*. Homewood, IL: Irwin.

Cavusgil, S. Tamer. 1984. "Differences Among Exporting Firms Based on Their Degree of Internationalization." *Journal of Business Research* 12 (June): 195-208.

Cavusgil, S. Tamer and Shaoming Zou. 1994. "Marketing Strategy-Performance Relationship: An Investigation of the Empirical Link in Export Market Ventures." *Journal of Marketing* 58 (January): 1-21.

Churchill, Gilbert A. and J. Paul Peter. 1984. "Research Design Effects on the Reliability of Rating Scales: A Meta-Analysis." *Journal of Marketing Research* 21 (November): 360-375.

Clasen, Thomas F. 1991. "An Exporter's Guide to Selecting Foreign Sales Agents and Distributors." *Journal of European Business* 3 (November): 28-32.

Cooley, William W. and Paul R. Lohnes. 1971. *Multivariate Data Analysis*. New York: Wiley.

Dant, Rajiv P., James R. Lumpkin, and Robert P. Bush. 1990. "Private Physicians or Walk-in Clinics: Do the Patients Differ?" *Journal of Health Care Marketing* 10 (June): 25-35.

Dwyer, Robert F. and M. Ann Welsh. 1985. "Environmental Relationships of the Internal Political Economy of Marketing Channels." *Journal of Marketing Research* 22 (November): 397-414.

Gatignon, Hubert and Erin Anderson. 1988. "The Multinational Corporation's Degree of Control over Foreign Subsidiaries: An Empirical Test of a Transaction Cost Explanation." *Journal of Law, Economics, and Organization* 4 (2): 305-336.

Green, Paul E. 1978. *Analyzing Multivariate Data*. Hinsdale, IL: Dryden.

Hair, Joseph F., Rolph E. Anderson, Ronald L. Tatham, and William C. Black. 1992. *Multivariate Data Analysis*. New York: Macmillan.

Heide, Jan B. and George John. 1988. "The Role of Dependence Balancing in Safeguarding Transaction-Specific Assets in Conventional Channels." *Journal of Marketing* 52 (January): 20-35.

Heide, Jan B. and George John. 1990. "Alliances in Industrial Purchasing: The Determinants of Joint Action in Buyer-Supplier Relationships." *Journal of Marketing Research* 27 (February): 24-36.

Jackson, Donald M. and Michael F. d'Amico. 1989. "Products and Markets Served by Distributors and Agents." *Industrial Marketing Management* 18 (1): 27-33.

Johanson, Jan and Jan-Erik Vahlne. 1990. "The Mechanism of Internationalisation." *International Marketing Review* 7 (4): 11-24.

John, George and Baron A. Weitz. 1988. "Forward Integration into Distribution: An Empirical Test of Transaction Cost Analysis." *Journal of Law, Economics, and Organization* 4 (2): 337-355.

Journal of Commerce United States Importer & Exporter Directory. 1991. New York: Journal of Commerce.

Klein, Saul, Gary L. Frazier, and Victor J. Roth. 1990. "A Transaction Cost Analysis Model of Channel Integration in International Markets." *Journal of Marketing Research* 27 (May): 196-208.

Leblebici, Huseyin and Gerald Salancik. 1981. "Effects of Environmental Uncertainty on Information and Decision Processes." *Administrative Science Quarterly* 26 (December): 578-596.

Moore, Richard A. 1992. "A Profile of UK Manufacturers and West German Agents and Distributors." *European Journal of Marketing* 26 (1): 41-51.

Noordewier, Thomas G., George John, and John R. Nevin. 1990. "Performance Outcomes of Purchasing Arrangements in Industrial Buyer-Vendor Relationships." *Journal of Marketing* 54 (October): 80-93.

Root, Franklin R. 1987. *Entry Strategies for International Markets*. First Edition. Lexington, MA: Lexington Books.

———. 1994. *Entry Strategies for International Markets*. Second Edition. Lexington, MA: Lexington Books.

Rosson, Philip J. 1987. "The Overseas Distributor Method." In *Market Entry and Expansion Modes*. Eds. Philip J. Rosson and Stan D. Reid. New York: Praeger, 296-315.

Rosson, Philip J. and I. David Ford. 1982. "Manufacturer-Overseas Distributor Relations and Export Performance." *Journal of International Business Studies* 13 (2): 57-72.

Seifert, Bruce and John Ford. 1989. "Export Distribution Channels." *Columbia Journal of World Business* 24 (Summer): 15-21.

Shipley, David, David Cook, and Eileen Barnett. 1989. "Recruitment, Motivation, Training and Evaluation of Overseas Distributors." *European Journal of Marketing* 23 (2): 79-93.

Stevens, John. 1972. "Four Methods of Analyzing Variations in the K-Group MANOVA Problem." *Multivariate Behavioral Research* 7 (1): 442-454.

Terpstra, Vern. 1984. "The Role of Economies of Scale in International Marketing." In *Marketing Aspects of International Business*. Eds. Gerald M. Hampton and Aart P. van Gent. The Hague, the Netherlands: Kluwer-Nijhoff, 59-72.

Ward, James J. 1984. "Your Export Middleman: Making a Wise Selection." *International Trade Forum* 20 (April): 14-34.

Welch, Lawrence S. and Reijo Luostarinen. 1988. "Internationalization: Evolution of a Concept." *Journal of General Management* 14 (Winter): 34-55.

Williamson, Oliver E. 1979. "Transaction Cost Economics: The Governance of Contractual Relations." *Journal of Law and Economics* 22 (October): 3-61.

———. 1981. "The Economics of Organization: The Transaction Cost Approach." *American Journal of Sociology* 87 (3): 548-577.

———. 1985. *The Economic Institutions of Capitalism: Firms, Markets, Relational Contracting*. New York: Free Press.

Moving Mountains to Market: Reflections on Restructuring the Russian Economy

Terry Clark

Terry Clark is an assistant professor of marketing at the Emory Business School, Emory University, Atlanta, Georgia.

> *". . . whoever shall say to this mountain, be removed and be cast into the sea, and shall not doubt in his heart—shall have whatever he says."*
> *(Mark 11:23)*

> For Russia, it is not the economy, stupid.

I t is no great shame to misinterpret events, but it is usually costly. Most analysts examining the problems of the former Communist nations of Eastern Europe see an economic problem: how to transform a centrally planned economy into a free market economy. For solutions, economic theories and models provide a starting point. Most give lead billing to some combination of price liberalization, privatization, and establishment of financial institutions. The hot debate rages more around how quickly the transition should be made than on whether the problem being addressed is the right one.

The problem being addressed is *not* the right one. Someone who begins hiccuping after gulping down poison will never be made well by a medicine to cure hiccups. Attempts at transforming the former Soviet Union by economic prescription alone aim at hiccups. Bamboozled by the lack of markets and free prices, analysts have failed to take full measure of the more pressing human realities in some of these nations.

The Marxist experiment was not a scholarly excursion to be amended by a footnote. It was written in blood, at incalculable cost in human suffering. To categorize the problem as merely economic is to dismiss habit, memory, and human nature as irrelevant facts in people's lives. As we ponder solutions to Eastern Europe's woes, we would do well to remember Keynes's comment: "[On] the surface Communism enormously overestimates the significance of the economic problem. The economic problem is not too difficult to solve—the real problem, lying behind, is quite different."

Whether done gradually or all at once, introducing free market variables into the East European equation will never alone produce a Singapore or a California. East Europeans have been critically conditioned by hard experience. They have learned to think and act in certain ways. Reward structures have shaped their hopes and fears along particular lines, and the challenges facing them have as much to do with hearts and minds as anything.

Clearly, there are economic dimensions, and economic tools should be part and parcel of any solution. But the economic dimensions are symptoms, not the disease. The frustration is that much of the analysis is giving economic prescription far too prominent a place. It should be subordinate.

Economic models are easily adjusted to account for the time needed to move from one set of parameters to another. Real people often cannot adjust so readily. They may not in parts of Eastern Europe for two very fundamental reasons:

1. Ordinary people often cannot comprehend what their rulers are trying to do.

2. The system under which they were nurtured did not prepare them very well in the self-reliance needed to survive the transition to a free economy.

Markets, free prices, and private ownership are not well understood by ordinary people. They barely understand the basic economic vocabulary; the grammar and syntax may be beyond them. But stable free markets presuppose a certain quality of hope and trust in people so they will venture and risk. Finding these in some parts of Eastern Europe is no easy task. Creating them will require more skill in psychology and statecraft than economics. Free markets do not exist in a vacuum, and they cannot be willed into existence. Where their moral basis is absent, free prices, private ownership, and markets will result in a neo-feudalistic anarchy. The fit will survive and enslave (again) the not-so-fit. So the great task to be accomplished is to restore balanced human existence.

THE WORST CASE: RUSSIA

Of all the nations unleashed from the grip of Marxism in recent years, none has such a formidable array of problems facing it as Russia. It is the worst case of a bad lot. On almost every point, considering the factors weighing in for and against successful restructuring, Russia comes in last. For Hungary, Poland, even Albania, the prospects are brighter.

The transition will be easier for nations that had communism imposed on them from the outside. For them, the system—the ideology—the results—were always seen as an alien force that overpowered and crushed their sense of national destiny. For these nations, the problem now is one of organizing the chaotic stampede away from Marxism/Leninism toward something more healthy. On this count, Hungary, the Czech Republic, and Poland have a lot going for them. Russia, the fountain of communist expansion in Europe, does not. Strike one.

Furthermore, nations with a living memory of life before communism will fare much better. These have a human link to former times. No matter what life was like then, most believe or remember that it was better than communism. Wherever the past remains alive in the minds of the men and women who lived before communist rule, it will be easier to rebuild. The simple stories of life before, told by parents and grandparents, multiplied by millions, are a powerful energizing force in the life of these nations.

Transactions ventured, land owned and worked, houses bought and sold—in all these stories, children are shown what things are possible by those who did them. For Russia, with its revolution now more than 70 years in the past, the revitalizing power of living memory is all but spent. Strike two.

Moreover, nations whose store of human capital, entrepreneurial and otherwise, was least damaged by the Marxist experiment will have the easier job of restructuring their economies. Specialized practical knowledge is a wonderfully delicate thing that each generation of practitioners inherits from its predecessors, amends a bit, and bequeaths to its successors. No generation starts from scratch. We all get most of our practical knowledge from those who preceded us.

Take, for example, the farmer. His specialized know-how is built on a network of inscrutable learned behaviors: sifting casual chat among colleagues to determine market conditions and what to plant; assessing weather patterns and soil conditions to determine planting times; examining ripening plants to determine optimal harvest times. All expert knowledge systems are made up of myriad important details, which are as much breathed in as learned.

To one degree or another, the Marxists damaged the national stores of human capital they inherited when they took over. In doing so, they broke the chain that passes along practical knowledge hand to hand, from one generation to another. In some cases the damage was relatively mild. In other cases, human capital was literally destroyed as new powers began ideological purges. The damage was both personal and national. The individual lives destroyed are irreplaceable. The collective practical knowledge of the classes of occupations these individual deaths represent, though not irreplaceable, is an incalculable loss.

The most brutal class and occupation purges under communism occurred before World War II, before most of the recently liberated nations had become communist. The damage to human capital in these nations has been correspondingly small. Russia has sustained the most devastating blows to its stock of human capital, for its leaders have hacked most persistently, systematically, and suicidally at the national vitals since the revolution in 1917. Strike three Russia.

The Ordeal of Change

Eric Hofer said, "We can never be really prepared for that which is wholly new." Russians are experiencing great change. And change of such magnitude is frightening and painful. As dismal as the Soviet regime was, it at least delivered three of the great necessities of life for most people: food, shelter, and security. The Soviets could deliver these because they had a system ordinary people could understand and trust. It provided jobs, direction, and cradle-to-grave security for everyone who behaved. The Gorbachev revolution began to change this. In doing so, it opened a Pandora's box of insecurity for the ordinary Russian.

This vortex of change is a powder keg that will certainly explode if exposed to the right (or should we say, to the wrong) spark. Thirty years ago, Eric Hofer reflected on the problems the centrally planned economies would face if they tried to reverse their revolutions. His words dampen optimism: "It needs a rare constellation of circumstances if the transition from a communal to an individual existence is to run its course without being diverted or reversed by catastrophic complications."

It is far from clear that Russia currently possesses this rare constellation, or that it is being assembled by the responsible parties. On the contrary, her constellations seem to be star-crossed, and her fate catastrophic. As Keynes put it, there "is no massive resistance to a new direction [in the Soviet Union]. The risk is of a contrary kind—lest society plunge about in its perplexity and dissatisfaction into something worse." The question "Can Russia be changed into a Western-style democratic economy?" should first be prefixed with the more pessimistic "Can she be prevented from falling into the abyss?"

Ambitious and ruthless players wait for opportunities. Should they obtain them, they will deliver the basic securities ordinary Russians crave, but at great cost. The danger of leaping the chasm between central planning and free markets in a single bound is that one may fall into the chasm. It would be better to build a bridge, and move a little more slowly. Something is better than nothing, though it is not everything we want.

ROMER'S RULE AND THE RUSSIAN PROBLEM

Paleontologists formerly explained the transition from fish to land dwellers this way: Fish grew legs so they could crawl out of the sea to live on land. A.S. Romer saw it differently. He argued that as seas receded, fish became stuck in shallow pools. *So they grew legs to get back into the sea!* As it turned out, Romer explains, the legs proved very useful for the life nature was preparing for the fish—on land.

Romer's explanation has an interesting application in the management of social and economic change. It suggests that during times of change, people will adopt behaviors that promise to help them recapture the stability they are losing. Thus Romer's Rule: People will gladly change to stay the same!

Russians are suffering from change. Naturally many yearn for their lost stability. The reformers, far from producing the personal security expected, are accelerating change and undermining

what solid ground remains. Privatization, free prices, and markets make theoretical sense, but in the minds of ordinary Russians they spell pain. The goal (one supposes) is for Russia to move from a command to a market economy. The fear is that chaos may erupt in the meantime. There is the real possibility that citizens, reeling from the changes to be absorbed, will take to the streets to find themselves an autocrat, right or left, who will speak iron order into existence through the barrel of a gun—as is the tradition in Russia.

The application of Romer's Rule to the Russian case provides the right sort of framework for workable solutions and the proper context for economic prescription. How can the Russian people be coaxed into growing legs that, while promising to help them back to the sea of stability they crave, really prepare them for survival in the world they fear? Solutions to this query may help divert disaster. Thinking along the lines of Romer's Rule, what sorts of policy initiatives will promise to reduce current pain while preparing the way for the rigors of the market? Desperate diseases require desperate cures.

Restoration of the Czarate

One policy strategy applying Romer's Rule would be to restore a Romanov to a ceremonial position as Czar of Russia. Such a move is not without precedent, though it has not always been effectively implemented. For example, the restoration of Charles II to the English throne after the death of Cromwell was a brilliant idea ruined by poor material. More recently, the stabilizing effects in times of national crisis of the Emperor of Japan after World War II, of Prince Sihanouk in Cambodia, and King Bhumibol in Thailand are as paradoxical as they are revealing. The strategic value of royalty as a positive democratizing force is also seen in the role of King Juan Carlos of Spain after the death of Franco.

A similar move in Russia, if handled well, would offer national inspiration and stability during the testy, tumultuous years that surely lie ahead. Paradoxically, a czar could be a crucial element in Russia's uncertain progress toward democracy and a liberal economy. The trick would be to find the right person for the job.

Given the right pick, many factors will work for success. The mystical, almost religious, attachment of Russians to their motherland has historically gone hand in hand with the popular conception of the czarate. A czar would give coherence and rationality to the struggle to piece together a healthy sense of nationhood. At present, right-wing extremists are poised to capitalize on these neglected elements of state-craft should the opportunity arise. The forces of moderation and stability should preempt them. Boris Yeltsin (or his democratically elected successor) should hold the power, while the czarate, modeled after (for example) the British monarchy, would create an emotional center of gravity for the Russian people.

Hand in hand with this, judiciously drawing from Russia's prerevolutionary traditions—removing the capital from Moscow back to St. Petersburg, resurrecting some of Russia's genuine pre-1917 history and heroes (the Decembrists, for example), and placing an emphasis on ceremony and symbol in public life—would probably do as much for the health and vibrancy of the nation as a truckload of Harvard economists could achieve.

Put Political Reforms on Hold

Another application of Romer's Rule to the Russian situation would be for Yeltsin (or his successors) to put democratic reform on the shelf for the time being and concentrate instead on reforming the economy and its institutions at a more manageable rate. This could be achieved by imposing real performance standards on managers. The process would be slow, and certain freedoms and efficiencies would be sacrificed. The hard reality is that this might be the best hope of actually producing a viable system. Nations as diverse as China, Singapore, and Chile have achieved substantial structural and economic reforms in the absence (we might almost say, in defiance) of democracy. Purists will desire all or nothing. More practically minded people will prefer something over nothing.

Reimposing some level of central control with a view to commanding orderly reform would create stability, reduce unemployment, and relieve many shortages and anxieties. Observers in the West should resist the temptation of judging such a move in terms of more enlightened democratic standards. Russia's reformers should not be scored on the basis of a hypothetical standard but in terms of the real catastrophes that have been averted in the real world.

Infrastructure

If the West had been asked by some cosmic hitman in the early 1980s how much it would be willing to pay to be rid of the Soviet threat, few would have grudged a generous national appropriation to get what then seemed impossible. Its ideological energy spent, the Soviet empire has fallen into its composite parts. Astonishingly, we have obtained that impossibility without cost. Having gained freely what we would have paid dearly for, wisdom demands we follow up with the capital investment to secure it.

A percentage of the peace dividend, earmarked for specific projects in Russia, is a small price to pay for the astonishing opportunity we have been given, and a real steal as the cost of securing it. A WPA-type scheme for Russia funded by the West would provide jobs and therefore stability in the short run, while building the type of infrastructure needed for the develop-

ment and long-run viability of the Russian economy. Housing, roads, river works, environmental cleanups, and telecommunications systems should be tackled this way. Creating a competent infrastructure would grease the tracks and inject balanced dynamism into the nascent private sector. However, if the West is to pay for such a project, professional Western multinational project teams should manage it if possible.

Capital funds would have to come from a consortium of industrialized nations. The cost will be large, but the benefits proportionate. Such a scheme has the double benefit of absorbing current anxieties while helping develop a system capable of supporting a more healthy economy.

Many parts of the Soviet puzzle are still capable of being reassembled into new and frightening combinations. Should that happen, what would we be willing to pay to recapture what is now within our grasp?

MOVING MOUNTAINS TO MARKET: THE ROLE OF WESTERN BUSINESSES

Those who reduce the plight of Russia to an economic problem are disastrously off base. Vigorous free markets exist where human psychological conditions permit—conditions that do not currently exist in Russia. Though markets can be easily destroyed, it is far from clear that they can be created at will. They are complex, fragile, and rare. Given the record and capacity of humankind for acting contrary to its own interest, the marvel is not that Russia does not immediately fall in line with the free market democracies, but that the free market democracies do not fall out. Our failings at home ought to temper our zeal in instructing others overseas. Those who have succeeded in transforming a centrally planned system into a free economy may feel confident in lecturing our Russian friends. The rest of us should be more cautious. A child once asked Walt Whitman what grass was. He replied: "How could I answer the child? I do not know what grass is anymore than he."

We could learn a lot from this refreshingly honest answer as we approach the question so relevant to the Russian problem: "What are markets?" We neither conceived nor created the economic system we enjoy. Like explorers discovering subterranean stalagmites, we behold and wonder. Free market economies are great inexplicable miracles. The sample of successful specimens is small, and our explanations of them are the crude finger paintings of children.

Russians should have a free economy because markets are the best tool imperfect humanity has found to meet its needs and improve its lot. If ordinary Russians are able to improve themselves, their nation may avoid the abyss and the world will be spared the consequences.

However, transitions are dangerous. For Russians, the very real danger is that either they will be tempted to seek again the security of totalitarianism, or else they will fall into an abyss of chaos and violence in attempting to cross the chasm between central planning and markets. Neither of these alternatives is good for Russia or the world.

The Alchemy of Enterprise: How Western Businesses Can Help

The greatest perversity of the Soviet system was that it turned human nature against itself. The urge to venture, create, and risk, and to reap profit, was stifled. Wherever private property becomes public property, the strong force "to take care of mine" is replaced by the infinitely weaker force "to take care of everyone else's." The spirit of enterprise needs the crude fuel of self-interest. It cannot live on weaker stuff. Self-interest is the negentropic force driving all healthy economies. The centrally planned economies have been starved on the entropic vapor of communism's ideal—"from each according to his ability, to each according to his needs." Enterprise dies in this soil. Such has been the lot of the Russian people for more than 70 years.

Productive risk taking has been missing from Russian life for a long time. It cannot be taught. It can only be learned in the context of a dry mouth and a palpitating heart as one steps out onto a limb and assumes risks. Seminars by the most seasoned Western business leaders and consultants, or the most astute business school professors, can do little here. They only confuse matters. The boy selling newspapers on a street corner is more eloquent on this matter than bond theorems and the term structure of interest rates. The boy is flesh and blood risking something for a profit. What that "something" is, is less important than the fact of risk—personal risk.

Like lion tamers and fire eaters, entrepreneurs best explain their craft by acting. They are most compelling when in action. The reason is that the dynamism of risk and the possibility of gain and loss are best displayed—and therefore understood—in the messy laboratory of the real world. The alchemy of enterprise can sweat worlds into existence for a profit, but it has to be seen to be believed!

Therefore, the greatest service Western business leaders can offer in the grand endeavor of saving Russia is to be themselves. They should cast commercial altruism to the wind, put self-interest on center stage, and venture and risk in the hope of big gains in Russia. Our Russian friends will learn much by watching. By billboarding self-interested commercial dreaming—by investing, daring and creating—our business people can help ordinary Russians to begin to see and understand how the alchemy of enterprise might turn the Russian desert into a garden.

Arguably, Muscovites have learned more by watching the Moscow McDonald's come into existence, observing it in action, and shouldering the disciplines and joys of work in an honest-to-goodness Western style operation than a roomful of expensive consultants could have taught them in a lifetime. Every Western business engaged in self-interested enterprise in Russia provides a seminar for any Russian who cares to observe.

Western governments can help by putting together packages of incentives to encourage entrepreneurs to dive into the Russian challenge. Clearly the risks are enormous—too big for many reasonable entrepreneurs to bear. Yet Western governments have a clear interest in Russia's making it across the chasm. The proper interest of business is self-interest. They damage the alchemy of enterprise when they focus on anything else. Western governments can help by developing policies that harmonize the legitimate self-interest of enterprise with the legitimate foreign policy self-interest of state. To be most helpful, our businesses must enter Russian markets as tigers, not pussycats.

The investment in reasonable risk reduction for these businesses will pay off in profits for them, real learning opportunities for Russians, and greater stability for the world. Three guidelines should steer policy formation in these areas:

- Programs should aim at risk reduction, not risk elimination.
- They should channel the sophisticated self-interest of Western entrepreneurs into Russia, not mold it to other policy ends.
- They should be structured to encourage long-term commitment to the Russian market.

The U.S. has already made great strides in this direction with the Freedom Support Act and with programs run by the Eximbank and the Trade Development Program. However, more efforts by more nations embracing more aspects of the problem are needed to help move these mountains to market.

References

Eric Hofer, *The Ordeal of Change* (New York: Harper and Row, 1963).

John Maynard Keynes, "Shaw on Wells on Stalin," *The New Statesman and Nation*, Nov. 10, 1934.

A.S. Romer, *Man and the Vertebrates* (London: Penguin Books, 1960).

YES, YOU CAN WIN IN EASTERN EUROPE

It's not just a market for Western goods, says Percy Barnevik, CEO of Swiss-based ABB, but also a place to make high-quality products at low cost.

Paul Hofheinz

WESTERN INVESTORS have poured some $15 billion into Eastern Europe in the five years since the Berlin Wall came down, but not everyone is happy. General Electric had to put an additional $400 million into its Hungarian light bulb maker, Tungsram, before it saw a dime of profit. Dow pulled out of a $200 million deal in the Czech Republic after accusing the Czechs of grossly overstating assets. Negotiators from Germany's industrial giant Siemens have little to show for their marathon 28-month negotiating session with the heavy-engineering arm of Skoda, the Czech industrial group.

One Western company stands out, both for the breadth of its commitment and for its proven ability to run businesses in Eastern Europe. When Swedish robotics maker ASEA merged with Switzerland's stodgy Brown Boveri power engineering group in 1988, few could have dreamed of the immense opportunities that would shortly appear in the East. When the Iron Curtain parted a year later, CEO Percy Barnevik saw a one-time chance to expand his $28-billion-a-year conglomerate.

Now, ABB Asea Brown Boveri is the most important investor in the former Warsaw Pact countries. ABB has even opened sales offices in such backwaters as Albania and Bulgaria. Through shrewdly managed acquisitions, it controls 58 companies with 20,000 employees in 16 Eastern countries and is on the prowl for more. Siemens has an equal number of joint ventures, but it operates in four fewer countries. United Technologies' Otis Elevator division is another major investor. It has 14,000 employ-

REPORTER ASSOCIATE *Thomas J. Martin*

ees in Russia and is hoping to refurbish, or replace, the country's creaky elevators.

Most of ABB's companies—from turbine makers in Poland to a full-scale power plant assembler in Russia—have already been integrated into the parent company's global production network. The resulting economies of scale have helped ABB cut prices on some major products by as much as 50%. And the company is well positioned in a part of the world where most of what it makes—heavy, infrastructure-based power engineering components and devices—will be in great demand for years.

ABB can use the boost. Despite aggressive cost cutting, its performance has disappointed many analysts in recent years. Sales slumped to $28.3 billion last year from a record $29.6 billion the year before. Profits have fallen too—to a disappointing $68 million, largely because of a $569 million one-time charge in connection with the closing of 15 factories in Europe and the U.S. Nor has the company attained the 10% operating margins and 25% return on assets that Barnevik set as a goal in 1990.

Still, Barnevik says he is confident that ABB's long-range strategy is on the right track. Since ABB is so dependent on infrastructure projects, recession in Europe and Japan has hurt the company more than others. Also, he argues that ABB has been investing heavily in the past few years in order to be competitive when the global economy improves. Barnevik's dramatic push into Eastern Europe is a logical extension of his well-known take-no-prisoners approach to restoring competitiveness to Europe's bloated, high-wage industry. Says Dariusz Karwacki, 31, general director of ABB Dolmel in Poland: "The other companies have focused mostly on the market

opportunities here. Only Barnevik has been production potential here too."

In this, Barnevik may be unique. Europe's deep competitive crisis has cut sharply into the willingness of its companies to invest in the East. Some have made small investments or moved the manufacture of some simple components east, but most companies have been wary. Given the region's astonishing competitive edge—wages in Eastern Europe are, on average, about 6% of Germany's—their investment has been small and tentative. Partly, European companies have been reluctant to trigger the massive layoffs that would result if they moved a lot of production to neighboring low-wage countries. All told, Barnevik has cut 47,000 jobs in the U.S. and Europe—roughly twice as many as he has created in the East. But he claims that by failing to invest in Eastern Europe, the West is harming itself more than it is helping to protect jobs. Says he: "If we become more competitive in Europe by using the opportunities that the East offers us, we can be stronger in Asia."

Barnevik likes to say that his biggest investment in Eastern Europe has been less the cash paid up front for these companies than the amount of management time he and his top aides have put into revamping the state-owned enterprises he took over. He has a point. Though he won't reveal figures, estimates put ABB's total investment at around $300 million—peanuts considering all the assets it acquired.

Barnevik follows a simple turnaround formula. First, he rarely buys whole companies, preferring potentially profitable divisions among the detritus of the huge, usually bankrupt, socialist enterprises. Once the jewels are identified, ABB negotiators begin devising a business plan while still talking terms. Then they look for local managers. Often this means bypassing older command bureaucrats in favor of younger people, whom ABB finds more adaptable—and hungrier. ABB has already trained more than 5,800 Eastern Europeans.

ABB refuses to accept a minority position. Once in control, it divides the company into profit centers, installs a Western accounting system, starts English lessons for middle managers so they can communicate with headquarters in Zurich (English is ABB's official language), and puts in new testing devices to help raise quality to Western levels. Says Barnevik: "My experience is that within two years you can restore a typical Eastern European company to profitability. It is not a ten-year proposition. It is a two-year proposition. But you have to believe in the people."

Tactics like these have helped ABB avoid the pitfalls of others. Says Barnevik: "You have to move fast but be very selective. And don't overpromise on investment." Adds Eberhard von Koerber, the feisty head of ABB's recently reorganized European division, which unites the growing eastern empire with the original Brown Boveri and ASEA holdings: "These markets will develop because they have to develop. Companies like us have to be there."

ABB'S BIGGEST investment is in Poland, where it controls four of the country's five makers of power-generating equipment. After four years, ABB's Polish operations now generate nearly $220 million of revenues and make a small profit on sales within Poland, as well as on exports. ABB is selling Polish-made gas turbines and low-pressure turbine rotors in the U.S. Equally important, ABB is able to produce high-voltage switching gear, turbine blades, rotors, and other products for use in the power plant equipment it assembles in

Germany and Switzerland—at about half the cost of Western European factories.

Right behind Poland in importance to ABB is the Czech Republic, where the company has aggressively expanded in recent months. Already, Brno (pop. 385,000), the capital of the Czech state of Moravia, has become something of an ABB company town. Three joint ventures producing turbines and medium-voltage switching gear have 5,700 employees among them. Across town, more than 200 engineers are busy at ABB Lummus Chemoproject, a joint venture in which Czech designers draw specifications for components of petrochemical plants. ABB officials say that the engineers' work is excellent and that similar advanced engineering would cost roughly three times as much to do in the West.

Now that ABB has a major presence in Poland and the Czech Republic, it has begun moving even farther east. In the past 12 months it has added four joint ventures to its eight existing companies in Russia, and it continues to expand despite recent political turmoil. "We can't wait for the region to stabilize," says Barnevik. "We want to create a home market there now."

Barnevik insists that the outlook for Russia is rosy—in the long term. He has authorized country manager Maxwell Asgari, 56, an Armenian-born American who once ran Combustion Engineering's Russian ventures, to assemble a chain of production facilities capable of putting together complete power plants. Among Asgari's recent additions are Nevskii Zavod, a 1,200-employee full-scale power plant maker in St. Petersburg, where final assembly will be done, and an engineering-based joint venture with Saturn, a government military design bureau that produced high-performance jet engines for the Sukhoi-27, a fighter plane. With these acquisitions—and perhaps more like it—Barnevik vows that Russia will be one of ABB's four or five largest home markets within ten years.

INCREASED REVENUES from acquisitions have helped ABB double its R&D since 1988, to $2.2 billion. The payoff: Last year nearly half of the company's $29.4 billion in orders came from products introduced since 1990. The East has done its share of new-product development. ABB is producing more efficient large gas turbines now because of gas- and liquid-dynamics technology developed with Uniturbo, a Russian joint venture.

There are already remarkable displays of loyalty among ABB's employees in the East. Ewa Nowak, 33, an ABB-trained controller at Dolmel—the Polish generator maker that ABB saved from bankruptcy four years ago—says that she has turned down lucrative offers from other Western firms operating in Poland because she appreciates ABB's long-term commitment.

By contrast, ABB's Westerners have been less shy about cashing in their chips. ABB executives, it seems, have become headhunters' delights, much as General Electric alums are in the U.S. One of the architects of ABB's Eastern policy, Swiss-born Barbara Kux, 40, is now heading Nestlé's push into Eastern Europe. Gerhard Schulmeyer, who headed U.S. operations, will become CEO of Siemens-Nixdorf, the struggling German computer company.

Now that the world economy is turning up, Barnevik wants to switch from cutting costs and people to growth. Last fall he summoned 400 top managers to Norway for a conference. "The period of restructuring is over," he announced. "This year, the message is simple: Go for growth." The Eastern European investments are meant to play a major part in that push.

For a moment, set aside your image of Percy the hatchet man. Like it or not, he is building a company—not just paring one down. The only difference is that the new company will have a geographic center about 1,000 kilometers east of the current corporate headquarters in Zurich. And it will be far more competitive as a result.

A FRAMEWORK FOR RISK MANAGEMENT

Kenneth A. Froot, David S. Scharfstein and Jeremy C. Stein

Kenneth A. Froot *is a professor at the Harvard Business School in Boston, Massachusetts.*

David S. Scharfstein and Jeremy C. Stein *are, respectively, the Dai Ichi Kangyo Bank Professor and the J. C. Penney Professor at the Massachusetts Institute of Technology's Sloan School of Management in Cambridge, Massachusetts.*

n recent years, managers have become increasingly aware of how their organizations can be buffeted by risks beyond their control. In many cases, fluctuations in economic and financial variables such as exchange rates, interest rates, and commodity prices have had destabilizing effects on corporate strategies and performance. Consider the following examples:

In the first half of 1986, world oil prices plummeted by 50%; overall, energy prices fell by 24%. While this was a boon to the economy as a whole, it was disastrous for oil producers as well as for companies like Dresser Industries, which supplies machinery and equipment to energy producers. As domestic oil production collapsed, so did demand for Dresser's equipment. The company's operating profits dropped from $292 million in 1985 to $149 million in 1986; its stock price fell from $24 to $14; and its capital spending decreased from $122 million to $71 million.

During the first half of the 1980s, the U.S. dollar appreciated by 50% in real terms, only to fall back to its starting point by 1988. The stronger dollar forced many U.S. exporters to cut prices drastically to remain competitive in global markets, reducing short-term profits and long-term competitiveness. Caterpillar, the world's largest manufacturer of earth-moving equipment, saw its real-dollar sales decline by 45% between 1981 and 1985 before increasing by 35% as the dollar weakened. Meanwhile, the company's capital expenditures fell from $713 million to $229 million before jumping to $793 million in 1988. But by that time, Caterpillar had lost ground to foreign competitors such as Japan's Komatsu.

In principle, both Dresser and Caterpillar could have insulated themselves from energy-price and exchange-rate risks by using the derivatives markets. Today more and more companies are doing just that. The General Accounting Office reports that between 1989 and 1992 the use of derivatives—among them forwards, futures, and swaps—grew by 145%. Much of that growth came from corporations: one recent study shows a more than fourfold increase between 1987 and 1991 in their use of some types of derivatives.[1]

In large part, the growth of derivatives is due to innovations by financial theorists who, during the 1970s, developed new methods—such as the Black-Scholes option-pricing formula—to value these complex instruments. Such improvements in the technology of financial engineering have helped spawn a new arsenal of risk-management weapons.

Unfortunately, the insights of the financial engineers do not give managers any guidance on how to deploy the new weapons most effectively. Although many companies are heavily involved in risk management, it's safe to say that there is no single, well-accepted set of principles that underlies their hedging programs. Financial managers will give different answers to even the most basic questions: What is the goal of risk management? Should Dresser and Caterpillar have used derivatives to insulate their stock prices from shocks to energy prices and exchange rates? Or should they have focused instead on stabilizing their near-term operating income, reported earnings, and return on equity, or on removing some of the volatility from their capital spending?

Without a clear set of risk-management goals, using derivatives can be dangerous. That has been made abundantly clear by the numerous cases of derivatives trades that have backfired in the last couple of years. Procter & Gamble's losses in customized interest-rate derivatives and Metallgesellschaft's losses in oil futures are two of the most prominent examples. The important point is not that these companies lost money in derivatives, because even the best risk-management programs will incur losses on some trades. What's important is that both companies lost substantial sums of money—in the case of Metallgesellschaft, more than $1 *billion*—because they took positions in derivatives that did not fit well with their corporate strategies.

Our goal in this article is to present a framework to guide top-level managers in developing a coherent risk-management strategy—in particular, to make sensible use of the risk-management fire-power available to them through financial derivatives.[2] Contrary to what senior managers may assume, a company's risk-management strategy cannot be delegated to the corporate treasurer—let alone to a hotshot financial engineer. Ultimately, a company's risk-management strategy needs to be integrated with its overall corporate strategy.

Our risk-management paradigm rests on three basic premises:

■ The key to creating corporate value is making good investments.

■ The key to making good investments is generating enough cash internally to fund those investments; when companies don't generate enough cash, they tend to cut investment more drastically than their competitors do.

■ Cash flow—so crucial to the investment process—can often be disrupted by movements in external factors such as exchange rates, commodity prices, and interest rates, potentially compromising a company's ability to invest.

A risk-management program, therefore, should have a single overarching goal: to ensure that a company has the cash available to make value-enhancing investments.

By recognizing and accepting this goal, managers will be better equipped to address the most basic questions of risk management: Which risks should be hedged and which should be left unhedged? What kinds of instruments and trading strategies are appropriate? How should a company's risk-management strategy be affected by its competitors' strategies?

From Pharaoh to Modern Finance

Risk management is not a modern invention. The Old Testament tells the story of the Egyptian Pharaoh who dreamed that seven healthy cattle were devoured by seven sickly cattle and that seven healthy ears of corn were devoured by seven sickly ears of corn. Puzzled by the dream, Pharaoh called on Joseph to interpret it. According to Joseph, the dream foretold seven years of plenty followed by seven years of famine. To hedge against that risk, Pharaoh bought and stored large quantities of corn. Egypt prospered during the famine, Joseph became the second most powerful man in Egypt, the Hebrews followed him there, and the rest is history.

In the Middle Ages, hedging was made easier by the creation of futures markets. Rather than buying and storing crops, consumers could ensure the availability and price of a crop by buying it for delivery at a predetermined price and date. And farmers could hedge the risk that the price of their crops would fall by selling them for later delivery at a pre-determined price.

It is easy to see why Pharaoh, the consumer, and the farmer would want to hedge. The farmer's income, for example, is tied closely to the price he can get for his crop. So any risk-averse farmer would want to insure his income against fluctuations in crop prices just as many working people protect their incomes with disability insurance. It's not surprising, then, that the first futures markets were developed to enable farmers to insure themselves more easily.

More recently, large publicly held companies have emerged as the principal users of risk-management instruments. Indeed, most new financial products are designed to enable corporations to hedge more effectively. But, unlike the farmer, the consumer, and Pharaoh, it is not so clear why *a large public corporation* would want to hedge. After all, such corporations are generally owned by many small investors, each of whom bears only a small part of the risk. In fact, Adolph A. Berle, Jr., and Gardiner C. Means argue in their classic book, *The Modern Corporation and Private Property*, that the modern corporate form of organization was developed precisely to enable entrepreneurs to disperse risk among many small investors. If that is true, it's hard to see why corporations themselves also need to reduce risk—investors can manage risk on their own.

Until the 1970s, finance specialists accepted this logic. The standard view was that if an investor does not want to be exposed to, say, the oil-price risk inherent in owning Dresser Industries, he can hedge for himself. For example, he can offset any loss on his Dresser Industries stock that might come from a decline in oil prices by also holding the stocks of companies that generally benefit from oil-price declines, such as petrochemical firms. There is thus no reason for the corporation to hedge on behalf of the investor. Or, put somewhat differently, hedging transactions at the corporate level sometimes lose money and sometimes make money, but on average they break even: companies can't systematically make money by hedging. Unlike individual risk management, corporate risk management doesn't hurt, but it also doesn't help.

Corporate finance specialists will recognize this logic as a variant of the Modigliani and Miller theorem, which was developed in the 1950s and became the foundation of "modern finance." The key insight of Franco Modigliani and Merton Miller, each of whom won a Nobel Prize for his work in this area, is that value is created on the left-hand side of the balance sheet when companies make good *investments*—in, say, plant and equipment, R&D, or market share—that ultimately increase operating cash flows. How companies finance those investments on the right-hand side of the balance sheet—whether through debt, equity, or retained earnings—is largely irrelevant. These decisions about financial policy can affect only how the value created by a company's real investments is divided among its investors. But in an efficient and well-functioning capital market, they cannot affect the overall value of those investments.

If one accepts the view of Modigliani and Miller, it follows almost as a corollary that risk-management strategies are also of no consequence. They are purely financial transactions that don't affect the value of a company's operating assets. Indeed, once the transaction costs associated with hedging instruments are factored in, a hard-line Modigliani-Miller disciple would argue against doing any risk management at all.

Over the past two decades, however, a different view of financial policy has emerged that allows a more integral role for risk management. This "postmodern" paradigm accepts as gospel the key insight of Modigliani and Miller—that value is created only when companies make good investments that ultimately increase their operating cash flow. But it goes further by treating financial policy as critical in *enabling* companies to make valuable investments. And it recognizes that companies face real trade-offs in how they finance their investments.[3] For example, suppose a company wants to add a new plant that would expand its production capacity. If the company has enough retained earnings to pay for the cost of the plant, it will use those funds to build it. But if the company doesn't have the cash, it will need to raise capital from one of two sources: the debt market (perhaps through a bank loan or a bond issue) or the equity market.

It is unlikely that the company would decide to issue equity. Indeed, on average, less than 2% of all corporate financing comes from the external equity market.[4] Why the aversion to equity? The problem is that it's difficult for stock market investors to know the real value of a company's assets. They may get

it right on average, but sometimes they price the stock too high and sometimes they price it too low. Naturally, companies will be reluctant to raise funds by selling stock when they think their equity is undervalued. And if they do issue equity, it will send a strong signal to the stock market that they think their shares are overvalued. In fact when companies issue equity, the stock price tends to fall by about 3%.[5] The result: most companies perceive equity to be a costly source of financing and tend to avoid it.

The information problems that limit the appeal of equity are of much less concern when it comes to debt: most debt issues—particularly those of investment-grade companies—are easy to value even without precise knowledge of the company's assets. As a result, companies are usually less worried about paying too high an interest rate on their borrowings than about getting too low a price for their equity. It's therefore not surprising that the bulk of all external funding is from the debt market.

However, debt financing is not without cost: taking on too much debt limits a company's ability to raise funds later. No one wants to lend to a company with a large debt burden, because the company may use some of the new funds not to invest in productive assets but to pay off the old debt. In the extreme, high debt levels can trigger distress, defaults, and even bankruptcy. So while companies often borrow to finance their investments, there are limits to how much they can or will borrow.

The bottom line is that financial markets do not work as smoothly as Modigliani and Miller envisioned. The costs we have outlined make external financing of any form—be it debt or equity—more expensive than internally generated funds. Given those costs, companies prefer to fund investments with retained earnings if they can. In fact, there is a financial pecking order in which companies rely first on retained earnings, then on debt, and, as a last resort, on outside equity.

What is even more striking is that companies see external financing as so costly that they actually cut investment spending when they don't have the internally generated cash flow to finance all their investment projects. Indeed, one study found that companies reduced their capital expenditures by roughly 35 cents for each $1 reduction in flow.[6] These financial frictions thus determine not only how companies finance their investments but also whether they make investments in the first place. Internally generated cash is therefore a competitive weapon that effectively reduces a company's cost of capital and facilitates investment.

This is the most critical implication of the postmodern paradigm, and it forms the theoretical foundation of the view stated earlier—that the role of risk management is to ensure that companies have the cash available to make value-enhancing investments. Although the practical implications of this idea may seem vague, we will demonstrate how it can help to develop a coherent risk-management strategy.

Why Hedge?

Let's start with the case of a hypothetical multinational pharmaceutical company, Omega Drug. Omega's headquarters, productions facilities, and research labs are in the United States, but roughly half of its sales come from abroad, mainly Japan and Germany. Omega has several products that are still protected by patents, and it does not expect to introduce any new products this year. Omega's main uncertainty is the revenue it will receive from foreign sales. The company can forecast its foreign sales volume very accurately, but the dollar value of those sales is hard to pin down because of the uncertainty inherent in exchange rates. If exchange rates remain stable, Omega expects the dollar value of its cash flow from foreign and domestic operations to be $200 million. If, however, the dollar appreciates substantially relative to the Japanese yen and the German mark, the Omega's cash flow will fall to $100 million, since the weaker yen and mark mean that foreign cash flows are worth less in dollars. Conversely, a significant dollar depreciation would increase Omega's cash flow to $300 million. Each of these scenarios is equally likely.

Like most multinational corporations, Omega frequently receives calls from investment bankers trying to persuade the company to hedge its foreign-exchange risk. The bankers typically present an impressive set of calculations showing how Omega can reduce the risk in its earnings, cash flow, stock price, and return on equity simply by trading on foreign-exchange markets. So far, Omega has resisted those overtures and has chosen not to engage in any substantial foreign-exchange hedging. "After all," Omega's top-level officers have argued, "we're a pharmaceutical company, not a bank."

Omega has one thing going for it: a healthy skepticism of bankers trying to sell their financial services. But the bankers also have something going for them: the skill to insulate companies from financial risk. What neither the company nor the bankers have is a well-articulated view of the role of risk management.

The starting point for our analysis is understanding the link between Omega's cash flows and its strategic investments, principally its R&D program. R&D is the key to success in the pharmaceutical business, and its importance has grown dramatically during the last two decades. Twenty years ago, Omega was spending 8% of sales on R&D; now it is spending 12% of sales on R&D.

Last year, Omega's R&D budget was $180 million. In the coming year, the company would like to spend $200 million. Omega arrived at this figure by first forecasting the increase in patentable products that would result from a particular level of R&D. As a second step, managers valued the increased cash flows through a discounted-cash-flow analysis. Such an approach could generate only rough estimates of the value of R&D because of the uncertainty inherent in the R&D process, but it was the best Omega could do. Specifically, the company's calculations indicated that an R&D budget of $200 million would generate a net present value of $90 million, compared with $60 million of R&D budgets of $100 million and $300 million. (See Table 1, "Payoffs from Omega Drug's R&D Investment.")

The company took comfort in the knowledge that the $200 million budget was, on a relative basis, roughly in line with the budgets of its principal competitors.

Given its comparatively high leverage and limited collateral, Omega is not in a position to borrow any funds to finance its R&D program. It is also reluctant to issue equity. That leaves internally generated cash as the only funding source that Omega's managers are prepared to tap for the R&D program. Therefore, fluctuations in the dollar's ex-

TABLE 1 PAYOFFS FROM OMEGA DRUG'S R&D INVESTMENT (IN MILLIONS OF DOLLARS)	R&D Level	Discounted Cash Flows	Net Present Value
	100	160	60
	200	290	90
	300	360	60

TABLE 2 THE EFFECT OF HEDGING ON OMEGA DRUG'S R&D INVESTMENT AND VALUE (IN MILLIONS OF DOLLARS)	The Dollar	Internal Funds	R&D without Hedging	Hedge Proceeds	Additional R&D from Hedging	Value from Hedging
	Appreciation	100	100	+100	100	+130
	Stable	200	200	0	0	0
	Depreciation	300	200	-100	0	-100

change rate can be critical. If the dollar appreciates, Omega will have a cash flow of only $100 million to allocate to its R&D program—well below the desired $200 million budget. A stable dollar will generate enough cash flow for the program, while a depreciating dollar will generate an excess of $100 million. (See Table 2, "The Effect of Hedging on Omega Drug's R&D Investment and Value.")

Will Omega be better off if it hedges? Suppose Omega tells its bankers to trade on its behalf so that the company's cash flows are completely insulated from foreign-exchange risk. If the dollar appreciates, the trades will generate a $100 million gain; if the dollar depreciates, they'll post a $100 million loss. The trades will generate no gain or loss if the dollar remains at its current level. Effectively, the hedging program locks in net cash flows of $200 million for Omega—the cash flows that the company would receive at prevailing exchange rates. Whatever the exchange rate turns out to be, Omega will have $200 million available for R&D—just the right amount.

If Omega doesn't hedge, it will be able to invest only $100 million in R&D if the dollar appreciates. By hedging, Omega is able to add $100 million of R&D in this scenario, increasing discounted future cash flows by $130 million (from $160 million to $290 million). On the other hand, if the dollar depreciates, Omega will lose $100 million on its foreign-exchange transactions. However, the $130 million gain clearly outweighs the $100 million loss. Overall, Omega is better off if it hedges.

Although this example is highly stylized, it illustrates a basic principle. In general, the supply of internally generated funds does not equal the investment demand for funds. Sometimes there is an excess supply; sometimes there is a shortage. Because external financing is costly, this imbalance shifts investment away from the optimal level. Risk management can reduce this imbalance and the resulting investment distortion. It enables companies to better align their demand for funds with their internal supply of funds. That is, risk management lets companies transfer funds from situations in which they have an excess supply to situations in which they have a shortage. In essence, it allows companies to borrow from themselves.

Here's another way to look at what happens. As the dollar depreciates, the internal supply of funds—Omega's cash flow—increases. The demand for funds—the desired level of investment—is fixed and independent of the exchange rate. When the company doesn't hedge, demand and supply are equal only if the dollar remains stable. If the dollar depreciates, however, supply exceeds demand; if it appreciates, supply falls short of demand. By hedging, the company reduces supply when there is

excess supply and increases supply when there is a shortage. This aligns the internal supply of funds with the demand for funds. Of course, the average supply of funds doesn't change with hedging, because hedging is a zero-net-present-value investment: it does not create value by itself. But it ensures that the company has the funds precisely when it needs them. Because value is ultimately created by making sure the company undertakes the right investments, risk management adds real value. (See Figure 1, "Omega Drug: Hedging with Fixed R&D Investment.")

When to Hedge—or Not

The basic principle outlined above is just a first step. The real challenge of risk management is to apply it to developing strategies that deal with the variety of risks faced by different companies.

What we have argued so far is that companies should use risk management to align their internal supply of funds with their demand for funds. In the case of Omega Drug, that means hedging all the exchange-rate risk. Since we have assumed that the demand for funds—the desired amount of investment—isn't affected by exchange rates, Omega should stabilize its supply by insulating its cash flows from any changes in exchange rates. This assumption may be reasonable in the case of Omega because it is unlikely that the value of investing in R&D in pharmaceuticals would depend very much on exchange rates. But there are many instances in which exchange rates, commodity prices, or interest rates do affect the value of a company's investment opportunities. Understanding the connection between a company's investment opportunities and those key economic variables is critical to developing a coherent risk-management strategy.

Take the case of an oil company. The main risk it faces is changes in the price of oil. When oil prices fall, cash flows decline because existing oil properties produce less revenue. Therefore, the company's supply of internal funds is exposed to oil-price risk in much the same way that a multinational drug company's cash flows are exposed to foreign-exchange risk.

However, while the value of pharmaceutical R&D investment is unaffected by exchange rates, the value of investing in the oil business falls when oil prices drop. When prices are low, it's less attractive to explore for and develop new oil reserves. So when the supply of funds is low, so is the demand for funds. On the flip side, when oil prices rise, cash flows rise and the value of investing rises. Supply and demand are both high. For an oil company, much more than for a pharmaceutical company, the supply of funds tends to match the demand for funds even if the company does not actively manage risk. As a

FIGURE 1
OMEGA DRUG: HEDGING
WITH FIXED R&D
INVESTMENT

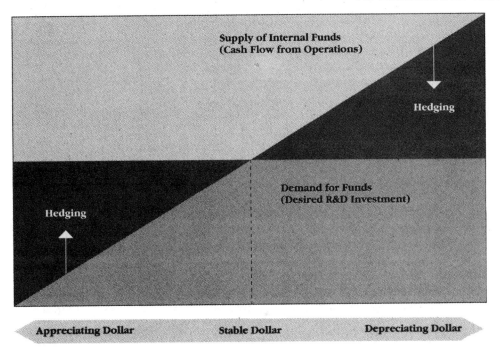

result, there is less reason for an oil company to hedge than there is for a multinational pharmaceutical company.

To illustrate the difference more clearly, let's change some of the numbers in our Omega Drug example and rename the company Omega Oil. Let's suppose there are three possible oil prices—low, medium, and high—which generate cash $100 million, $200 million, and $300 million, respectively. The higher the oil price, the more revenue Omega Oil generates on its existing reserves.

So far, the example is exactly the same as before. Where it differs is on the investment side. The optimal amount of investment in the low-oil-price regime is $150 million; in the medium-oil-price regime, it's $200 million; and in the high-oil-price regime, it's $250 million. Thus, higher oil prices make exploring for and developing oil reserves more attractive. In this example, the supply of funds is not too far off from the demand for funds even if Omega Oil doesn't hedge. Omega Oil sometimes has an excess demand of $50 million and sometimes an

FIGURE 2
OMEGA OIL: HEDGING
WITH OIL-PRICE-SENSITIVE
INVESTMENT

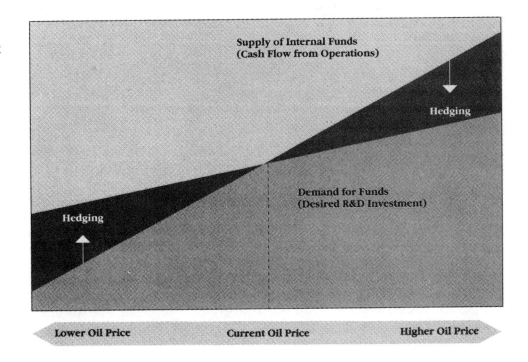

excess supply of $50 million; with Omega Drug, the excess demand and excess supply were $100 million. Omega Oil, therefore, doesn't need to hedge its oil-price risk as much as Omega Drug needed to hedge its foreign-exchange risk. Roughly speaking, the optimal hedge for Omega Oil is only half that for Omega Drug.

Here the demand for funds increases with the price of oil. (See Figure 2, "Omega Oil: Hedging with Oil-Price-Sensitive Investment.") The difference between supply and demand is smaller in the example of the oil company than it is when the investment level is fixed, as it was with Omega Drug. To align supply with demand, Omega Oil doesn't need to hedge as much as Omega Drug did. Essentially, Omega Oil already has something of a built-in hedge.

An important point emerges from this example: A proper risk-management strategy ensures that companies have the cash when they need it for investment, but it does not seek to insulate them completely from risks of all kinds.

If Omega follows our recommended strategy and hedges oil-price risk only partially, then its stock price, earnings, return on equity, and any number of other performance measures will fluctuate with the price of oil. When oil prices are low, Omega is worth less: the company's existing properties are less valuable, and it will invest less. It's simply less profitable to be in the oil business, and this will be reflected in Omega's performance measures. But there's nothing a risk-management program can do to improve the underlying bad economics of low oil prices. The goal of risk management is not to insure investors and corporate managers against oil-price risk per se. It is to ensure that companies have the cash they need to create value by making good investments.

In fact, attempting to insulate investors completely from oil-price risk could actually *destroy* value. For example, if Omega Oil were to hedge fully, it would actually have an excess supply of funds when oil prices fall: its cash flow would be stabilized at $200 million, and its investment need would be only $150 million. But when oil prices are high, just the opposite would be true: the company would lose so much money on its hedging position that it would have a shortage of funds for investment. Its net cash flows would still be only $200 million, but its investment needs would rise to $250 million. In this case, hedging fully would prevent the company from making value-enhancing investments.

This approach helps managers address two key issues. First, it helps them identify what is worth hedging and what isn't. Worrying about stock-price volatility in and of itself isn't worthwhile; such volatility can be better managed by individual investors through their portfolio strategies. By contrast, exces-

sive *investment* volatility can threaten a company's ability to meet its strategic objectives and, as a result, is worth controlling through risk management.

Second, this approach helps managers figure out how much hedging is necessary. If changes in exchange rates, commodity prices, and interest rates lead to large imbalances in the supply and demand for funds, then the company should hedge aggressively; if not, the company has a natural hedge, and it does not need to hedge as much.

Managers who adopt our approach should ask themselves two questions: How sensitive are cash flows to risk variables such as exchange rates, commodity prices, and interest rates? And how sensitive are investment opportunities to those risk variables? The answers will help managers understand whether the supply of funds and the demand for funds are naturally aligned or whether they can be better aligned through risk management.

Guidelines for Managers

What follow are some guidelines for how managers can think about risk-management issues. Although these are by no means the only issues to consider, our suggestions should provide managers with useful direction.

Companies in the same industry should not necessarily adopt the same hedging strategy. To understand why, take the case of oil. Even though all oil companies are exposed to oil-price risk, some may be exposed more than others in both their cash flows and their investment opportunities. Let's compare Omega Oil with Epsilon Oil. Omega has existing reserves in Saudi Arabia that are a relatively cheap source of oil, whereas Epsilon gets its oil from the North Sea, which is a relatively expensive source. If the price of oil falls dramatically, Epsilon may be forced to shut down those reserves altogether, wiping out an important source of its cash flow. Omega would continue to operate its reserves because the cost of taking the oil out of the ground is still less than the oil price. Therefore, Epsilon's cash flows are more sensitive to the price of oil. Hedging is more valuable for Epsilon than it is for Omega because Epsilon's supply of funds is less in sync with its demand for funds.

Similar logic applies when the two oil companies differ in their investment opportunities. Suppose instead that Omega and Epsilon both have essentially the same cash-flow streams from their existing oil properties, but Epsilon is trying to develop new reserves in the North Sea, and Omega in Saudi Arabia. When the price of oil drops, it may no longer be worthwhile to try to develop reserves in the North Sea, since it is an expensive source of oil, but it may be worthwhile to do so in Saudi Arabia.

Thus, the drop in the oil price affects both companies' cash flows equally, but Epsilon's investment opportunities fall more than Omega's do. Because Epsilon's demand for funds is more in line with its supply of funds, Epsilon has less incentive to hedge than Omega does.

Again, a simple message emerges: To develop a coherent risk-management strategy, companies must carefully articulate the nature of both their cash flows and their investment opportunities. Once they have done this, their efforts to align the supply of funds with the demand for funds will generate the right strategies for managing risk.

Companies may benefit from risk management even if they have no major investments in plant and equipment. We define investment very broadly to include not just conventional investments such as capital expenditures but also investments in intangible assets such as a well-trained workforce, brand-name recognition, and market share.

In fact, companies that make these sorts of investments may need to be even more active in managing risk. After all, a capital-intensive company can use its newly purchased plant and equipment as collateral to secure a loan. "Softer" investments are harder to collateralize. It may not be so easy for a company to raise capital from a bank to fund, say, short-term losses that result from a policy of pricing low to build market share. For companies that make such investments, internally generated funds are especially important. As a result, there may be an even greater need to align the supply of funds with the demand for funds through risk management.

Even companies with conservative capital structure—no debt, lots of cash—can benefit from hedging. At first glance, it might appear that a company with a very conservative capital structure should be less interested in risk management. After all, such a company could adjust rather easily to a large drop in cash flow by borrowing at relatively low cost. It wouldn't need to curtail investment, and corporate value would not suffer much. The basic objective of risk management—aligning the supply of internal funds with the demand for investment funding—has less urgency in this type of situation because managers can easily adjust to a supply shortfall by borrowing. To be sure, hedging wouldn't hurt, but it might not help much either.

But managers in this position should ask themselves why they have chosen such a conservative capital structure. If the answer is, The world is a risky place, and you never know what can happen to exchange rates or interest rates, they have more thinking to do. What they have done is use low leverage instead of, say, the derivatives markets to

protect against the risk in those economic variables. An alternative strategy would be to take on more debt and then hedge those risks directly in the derivatives markets. In fact, there's something to be said for the second approach: it's no more risky in terms of the ability to make good investments than the low-debt/no-hedging strategy; but, in many countries, the added debt made possible by hedging allows a company to take advantage of the tax deductibility of interest payments.

Multinational companies must recognize that foreign-exchange risk affects not only cash flows but also investment opportunities. A number of complex issues arise with multinationals, but many of them can be illustrated with two examples. In each example, a company is planning to build a plant in Germany to manufacture cameras. In Example 1 it will sell the cameras in Germany, while in Example 2 it will sell them in the United States. In both cases, most of the company's cash flows come from its other businesses in the United States. How aggressively should it hedge the dollar/mark exchange rate?

Example 1. If the dollar depreciates relative to the mark, it will become more expensive (in dollar terms) to build the plant in Germany. But this does not mean that the company will want to build a smaller plant—or scrap the plant altogether—because the marks it receives from selling cameras in Germany will also be worth more in dollars. In other words, because the plant's costs and revenues are *both* mark-denominated, as long as the plant is economically attractive today, it will still be attractive if the dollar/mark rate changes. Therefore, just as Omega Drug wants to maintain its R&D despite the dollar's appreciation, this company would want to maintain its investment in Germany despite the dollar's depreciation. This calls for fairly aggressive hedging against a depreciation in the dollar to ensure that the company has enough marks to build the plant.

Example 2. The answer here is a bit more complex. Since the company is now manufacturing cameras for export back to the United States, a depreciation in the dollar makes it less attractive to manufacture in Germany. Dollar-denominated labor costs are simply higher when the mark is more valuable. Thus, any depreciation in the dollar raises the dollar cost of building the plant. But it also reduces the dollar income the company would receive from the plant. As a result, the company might want to scale back its investment or scrap the plant when the dollar depreciates. The value of investing falls, so there's less reason to hedge than in Example 1. This case is analogous to that of Omega Oil in that risk that hurts cash flows—namely, a depreciation of the dollar relative to the mark—also diminishes the appeal of investing. As a result, there is less reason to hedge the risk.

Of course, this assumes that the company hasn't yet committed to building the plant. If it has, then it would make sense to hedge the short-term risk of a dollar depreciation to ensure that the funds are available to continue the project. But if it hasn't committed, it is less important to hedge the longer-term risks.

Companies should pay close attention to the hedging strategies of their competitors. It is tempting for managers to think that if the competition doesn't hedge, then their company doesn't need to, either. However, there are some situations in which a company may have even greater reason to hedge if its competitors *don't*. Let's continue with the example of the camera company that is considering building capacity to manufacture and sell cameras in Germany. Suppose now that its competitors—other camera companies with revenues mostly in dollars—are also considering building capacity in Germany.

If its competitors choose not to hedge, they won't be in a strong position to add capacity if the dollar depreciates: they will find themselves short of marks. But that is precisely the situation in which the company *wants* to build its plant—when its competitors' weakness reduces the likelihood of industry overcapacity; this makes its investment in Germany more attractive. Therefore, the company should hedge to make sure it has enough cash for this investment.

This is just another example of how clearly articulating the nature of investment opportunities can inform a company's risk-management strategy; in this case, the investment opportunities depend on the overall structure of the industry and on the financial strength of its competitors. Thus, the same elements that go into formulating a competitive strategy should also be used to formulate a risk-management strategy.

The choice of specific derivatives cannot simply be delegated to the financial specialists in the company. It's true that many of the more technical aspects of derivatives trading are best left to the technical finance staff. But senior managers need to understand how the choices of financial instruments link up with the broader issues of risk-management strategy that we have been exploring.

There are two key features of derivatives that a company must keep in mind when evaluating which ones to use. The first is the cash-flow implications of the instruments. For example, futures contracts

are traded on an exchange and require a company to mark to market on a daily basis—that is, to put up money to compensate for any short-term losses. These expenditures can cut into the cash a company needs to finance current investments. In contrast, over-the-counter forward contracts—which are customized transactions arranged with derivatives dealer—do not have this drawback because they do not have to be settled until the contract matures. However, this advantage will probably come at some cost: when a dealer writes the company a forward, he will charge a premium for the risk that he bears by not extracting any payments until the contract matures.

The second feature of derivatives that should be kept in mind is the "linearity" or "nonlinearity" of the contracts. Futures and forwards are essentially linear contracts: for every dollar the company gains when the underlying variable moves in one direction by 10%, it loses a dollar when the underlying variable moves in the other direction by 10%. By contrast, options are nonlinear in that they allow the company to put a floor on its losses without having to give up the potential for gains. If there is a minimum amount of investment a company needs to maintain, options can allow it to lock in the necessary cash. At the same time, they provide the flexibility to increase investment in good times.

Again, the decision of which contract to use should be driven by the objective of aligning the demand for funds with the supply of internal funds. A skillful financial engineer may be good at pricing intricate financial contracts, but this alone does not indicate which types of contracts fit best with a company's risk-management strategy.

An important corollary to this point is that it probably makes good sense to stay away from the most exotic, customized hedging instruments unless there is a very clear investment-side justification for their use. Dealers make more profit selling cutting-edge instruments, for which competition is less intense. And each additional dollar of profit going to the dealer is a dollar less of value available to shareholders. So unless a company can explain why an exotic instrument protects its investment opportunities better than a plain-vanilla one, it's better to go with plain vanilla.

Where do managers go from here? The first step—which may be the hardest—is to realize that they cannot ignore risk management. Some managers may be tempted to do so in order to avoid high-profile blunders like those of Procter & Gamble and Metallgesellschaft. But, as the Dresser Industries and Caterpillar examples show, this head-in-the-sand approach has costs as well. Nor can risk management simply be handed off to the financial staff. That approach can lead to poor coordination with overall corporate strategy and a patchwork of derivatives trades that may, when taken together, reduce overall corporate value. Instead, it's critical for a company to devise a risk-management strategy that is based on good investments and is aligned with its broader corporate objectives.

NOTES

1. The study, reported in *Derivates: Practices and Principles*, was conducted by the Group of Thirty, an independent study group in Washingon, D.C., made up of economists, bankers, and policymakers.

2. A more technical article on this subject, "Risk Management: Coordinating Corporate Investment and Financing Policies," was published by the authors in the *Journal of Finance*, vol. 48, 1993, pp. 16-29.

3. This view has been advanced in an influential series of papers by Stewart C. Myers of MIT's Sloan School of Management: "The Determinants of Corporate Borrowing," *Journal of Financial Economics*, vol. 4, 1977, p. 148; "Corporate Financing and Investment Decisions When Firms Have Information That Investors Do Not Have," coauthored with Nicholas Majluf, *Journal of Financial Economics*, vol. 13, 1984, p. 187; and "The Capital Structure Puzzle," *Journal of Finance*, vol. 39, 1984, p. 575.

4. See, for example, Jeffrey MacKie-Mason, "Do Firms Care Who Provides Their Financing?" in *Asymmetric Information, Corporate Finance, and Investment*, ed. R. Glenn Hubbard (Chicago: University of Chicago Press, 1990), p. 63.

5. Paul Asquith and David Mullins, "Equity Issues and Offering Dilution," *Journal of Financial Economics*, vol. 15, 1986, p. 61.

6. See, for example, Steven Fazzari, R. Glenn Hubbard, and Bruce Petersen, "Financing Constraints and Corporate Investment," *Brookings Papers on Economic Activity*, no. 1, 1988, p. 141.

Negotiating the honeyed knife-edge

Collapsing prices in Russia, ill-judged intervention in Malaysia, volatilities touching 200% in the Turkish lira and political turmoil in Mexico – on top of all the other horror stories of 1994, the exotic currency markets should leave traders weak at the knees. Instead, some are sitting on substantial profits. So what's the secret? Ben Edwards finds out

It's not easy to make an honest buck these days. Bond traders still nurse wounds inflicted in February. Equity strategists are coming to terms with overvalued markets. The mortgage-backed rocket scientists would do well to look again at their prepayment models. Derivative traders are in the dock. With the Christmas bonus season looming, it is difficult to know where to turn to meet the downpayments on the Ferrari.

Salvation is at hand, says Charles Valentin, fixed income director at the Paris-based emerging market fund manager FP Consult. Why not try your hand at the Zambian kwacha market? The bad news, says Valentin, is that the market is not altogether liquid. Bid-offer spreads on the kwacha can be hefty, often capturing 1% of the total trade. As for the good news, once you have your kwachas you can invest them in Zambian 28-day treasury bills, and the government will pay you an interest rate of 60% for your good faith.

But best of all, the kwacha is appreciating: "The Zambian economy is highly geared to rising commodity prices. More dollars from export production mean support for the currency." Also, argues Valentin, because of the high domestic interest rates, local subsidiaries of multinational companies are now funding themselves cross-border. In turn, these hard currency flows are propping up the kwacha, which has climbed 6% against the dollar since April.

Valentin's eccentric tastes have served him well. While colleagues who manage FP Consult's emerging market equity and bond portfolios are struggling to get into double figures, Valentin's local currency and money market investments are about to post an enviable annual performance of 35%. He has made 70% returns in Brazil, 30% in the Polish zloty market and 8% in Thai baht. Despite the

recent collapse in the rouble, he is now itching to get into Russia.

Valentin is not alone. As the world's capital markets collapse, exotic currency traders are recording some unusual results. Ezra Zask, a former currency manager with Manufacturers Hanover Trust and Mellon Bank, runs an exotic currency trading boutique out of Norfolk, Connecticut. His 16-strong team of traders, researchers and support staff manage about $180 million around the clock for clients ranging from middle eastern central banks to New York brokers.

Last year, they were rewarded with returns of over 18%. This year, says Zask, his performance is likely to be more modest. To date, he has made a return of 5.4%. He counts himself lucky. "Both the dollar/mark and the dollar/yen have been horrendous for traders this year. There have been no trends in the markets," he says. So, for traders who have been operating on last year's technical models, says Zask, "just when the model tells them to change their positions, the market swings the other way. The only people who have made any money are the ones active in the markets we operate in."

So what's the key to a successful trading strategy? Banks operating in the exotic markets are predictably coy about their proprietary trading activities. Currency speculation is often frowned upon by central banks, and the markets can be tightly regulated. "I know of one bank which did a lousy five [million] dollar interest rate cap in Singapore," says one source. "The Singapore Monetary Authority insisted that they unwind the trade. They even called the counterparty and told them the news."

Central banks slap wrists

Even when banks are trading offshore this grip

is rarely relaxed. The biggest players in the exotic markets, such as Citibank, HSBC, Bank of America and Chase Manhattan, all have a well-developed international network of branches. A failure to toe the line in London could result in punitive action in Kuala Lumpur. "In some markets we operate in, every day we will get a call from the central bank, establishing exactly who's been buying and selling," says one London-based trader. "Now if you have a branch operating under a central bank retail licence, the incentive is to cooperate."

But although individual trades can be highly complex, the rationale underpinning high-yield currency investments is disarmingly simple. It helps to have a nose for capital

Zambian kwacha vs $ and T-bill yields

Source: Bloomberg, Barclays Bank (Zambia)

Kwacha/$ T-bills %

flows. Valentin is invested in the Lebanese treasury bill market. High inflation has led to high interest rates, and one-year T-bills yield about 19%. At the same time, the Lebanese pound is appreciating against the dollar at a steady annualized 2%. "Flight capital is returning to the Lebanon to invest in the reconstruction of Beirut," argues Valentin.

These flows were bolstered last month, says Valentin, when Merrill Lynch launched a $400 million, three-year Eurobond for Lebanon. The deal met with strong demand from retail and institutional accounts in Europe and the Gulf states, together with investors from the Lebanese diaspora. The Lebanese central bank estimates the potential pool of Lebanese flight capital at $40 billion.

Zask treats currencies as a separate asset class. He works on the principle that, just like any other emerging market asset, there is a premium built into exotic currency money market interest rates, and hence forward exchange rates, to attract offshore capital and prevent domestic capital flight.

For reserve currencies like the Deutschmark or the yen, argues Zask, interest parity law relates forward exchange rates to spot exchange and short-term interest rates to eliminate arbitrage gains. Investors expect that, over time, the yield pick-up implied in the

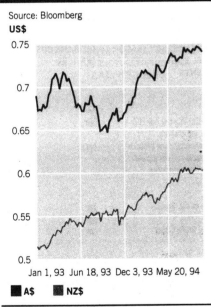

A$ and NZ$ versus US$

Source: Bloomberg

US$

0.75
0.7
0.65
0.6
0.55
0.5

Jan 1, 93   Jun 18, 93   Dec 3, 93   May 20, 94

■ A$ ■ NZ$

forward quote should offset money market interest rate differentials between the two currencies. Buying yen forward with dollars, for example, ought only to produce the domestic risk-free rate of return, in this case US treasury bill yields.

In the exotic markets, this relationship breaks down, says Zask. Implied in the forward rate is a premium which investors should expect to receive for the additional risks they are running. In other words, all else being equal the currency should not devalue as quickly as the forward rate implies. The trick

is to calculate this risk premium and measure it against the interest rate differential.

If the resulting spread looks attractive, then Zask invests. "Where there are significantly high interest rate differentials, this is an indication that we want to invest, with the caveat that there will be enough of a spread to cover our risk," he says. At the moment, for example, there is a 6% interest rate differential between the Thai baht and the yen. "We've invested in Thai, and hedged in yen," says Zask. He trades this both ways. If he judges that the forward quote has not fully priced in the risk premium spread between two currencies, then he will go long in the lower-risk currency and short the higher.

This strategy can be supplemented with more complex plays. Where currency pairs show strong historical correlation, there are further arbitrage opportunities. "We look out for closely matched pairs," says Zask. "Take Australia and New Zealand, or Singapore and Malaysia, or even Spain and Portugal. Here you have high correlations, and low risk. So when currencies start trading out of line, we arbitrage the correlation between the two."

Aiming for onshore exposure

Also, because of counterparty, custody and legal risks in the onshore markets, there is often a yield pick-up over quoted offshore rates. Valentin aims for onshore exposure wherever he can get it. "Some people are more comfortable working offshore, say going through Hong Kong if you're investing in Thailand. We are more aggressive. We are willing to take the additional risk, working under local laws and with local counterparties, for the additional return," he says.

This spread can also be arbitraged. "Because of the poor arbitrage relationships in some of these currencies, there are some very interesting trading opportunities," says Ron Liesching, research director and partner at the London-based risk management specialists Pareto Partners. "Theoretically, [domestic] forward rates should correspond to the difference between two currencies' Euro-rates. But because of the lack of capital flows and tight central bank regulation, you get a discrepancy between the two." One way to take advantage of this, says Liesching, could be to create a synthetic onshore deposit through the swaps markets, and arbitrage the additional yield through the offshore forward markets.

In the most liquid exotic currency markets, these trades can be rare. In Asia, for example, such arbitrage opportunities have rapidly evaporated as the currencies have become more actively traded. "Because of the number of players in the market, there is very little difference now between offshore and onshore rates," argues Chris Tinker, chief economist at Standard Chartered's treasury operations in London.

Fundamentally undervalued

James Leslie, a fund manager with Guinness

Flight in Hong Kong, confirms this. "We don't do this sort of arbitrage," he says. "You're trading too hard for a small margin." Instead, Leslie, who manages a $43 million Asian currency and bond fund launched at the height of the bull market last December, is after longer-term currency appreciation. He argues that outside Japan, Asian currencies are

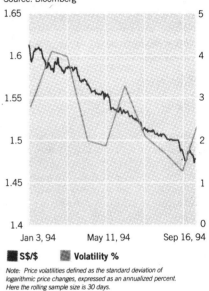

Singapore dollar vs US$ and volatilities

Source: Bloomberg

1.65   5
1.6   4
1.55   3
1.5   2
1.45   1
1.4   0

Jan 3, 94   May 11, 94   Sep 16, 94

■ S$/$ ■ Volatility %

Note: Price volatilities defined as the standard deviation of logarithmic price changes, expressed as an annualized percent. Here the rolling sample size is 30 days.

fundamentally undervalued. "What the US administration has signally failed to realize is that the enemy is not just Japan. It is the whole of Asia. We believe that these countries will eventually have to pay for their economic success through their exchange rates," he says.

The conviction has served him well. His strategy since the outset has been to hedge dollar-denominated investments, such as Eurobond issues from Asian borrowers, into Singapore dollars and Malaysian ringgits through the forward markets. Any local-currency investments in Hong Kong, where the local dollar is pegged tightly to its US counterpart, are treated similarly. As a consequence, although his bond investments have performed poorly as the markets have sold off, most of the losses have been offset by gains made on his exotic currency exposures. His fund is up about 1% since its launch.

But Asian currencies pose other problems. Volatilities are often very low. "These markets don't move very far," says Leslie. "It's all happening very slowly. You might call them exotics, but I'd actually describe them as rather dull currencies."

One way to get around this is to use leverage. Take the Thai baht, says Valentin. "The baht has been one of the most stable currencies for the last 10 years. You would imagine that most people are comfortable taking leverage. So you use a structured note instead of the currency and money markets." Typically, says

Valentin, such leverage might multiply exchange rate exposure by between three and five times. Sometimes, he says, he may also ask for a layer of protection in the form of an embedded put option.

Of course, this also leverages your potential losses. "Asia is a real dilemma," says Zask. "Most of the currencies are very stable. You have the world's capital flows in your favour. But they are also developing countries. Thailand, for example, is susceptible to coups." As a result, Zask tries to strike a balance. "In the case of a French franc/Belgian franc cross, for example, we are comfortable leveraging at about seven or eight to one. In Asia, we leverage as little as three or four to one."

Risks remain

Elsewhere, Zask keeps his risks within strict limits. He trades about 20 currencies, and will not consider anything that is not fully convertible, for example the Taiwan dollar or the Indian rupee. Liquidity is therefore held at a premium. He also trades with a limited number of counterparties. "We trade through 10 banks. We use only American, European and Japanese banks, and everything we do is through interbank forward contracts."

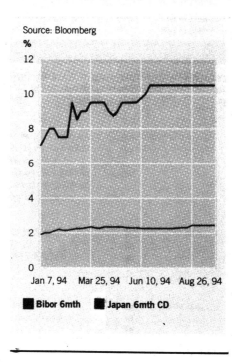

Source: Bloomberg

Thai and Japanese six-month rates

Bibor 6mth   Japan 6mth CD

But turmoil in the ringgit market earlier this year has proved a timely, if ironic, reminder of the risks exotic currency traders are exposed to. Towards the end of 1993, Bank Negara, the Malaysia central bank, bought large quantities of dollars to revalue its reserves and reduce paper losses caused by its own speculation in the foreign exchange markets. Last year, forex losses were officially put at M$5.7 billion ($3.3 billion). In 1992, the bank lost M$9 billion.

The result was a sharp drop in the exchange rate. Trading at around M$2.55 to the dollar for most of last year, by late February the ringgit had plunged to M$2.80. But even before the crisis, the ringgit looked undervalued, perhaps by as much as 40% according to some estimates. As the ringgit fell, speculators poured into local-currency deposits and the money markets. Bank Negara then acted ruthlessly, imposing negative interest rates on foreign-held ringgit accounts and banning foreign investment in short-dated paper.

Market liquidity quickly disappeared, and traders began to suffer losses. "There's a Tibetan saying for this sort of behaviour," says Liesching. "Beware of honey offered on a sharp knife."

TIMBERLAND'S NEW SPIN ON GLOBAL LOGISTICS

The rapidly growing footwear and apparel maker revamps its supply chain to handle burgeoning sales and geographic diversity.

Peter Buxbaum

Senior Editor

In 1979, an Italian distributor walked into The Timberland Company and expressed interest in shoe #100-81, a hand-sewn moccasin with a lug sole. He just had the feeling it would sell in Italy. He bought a supply and they sold like hotcakes.

That was Timberland's first international sale. From there, things almost spun out of control.

Fifteen years later, 50% of Timberland's $419 million in annual sales comes from outside the United States. The Hampton, N.H.-based company manufactures its own footwear in three countries and sources footwear and apparel from dozens of countries in Asia, Europe and the Americas. At the same time, it distributes its products to customers in 50 countries worldwide.

How does a truly global company get its goods from factories all over the world to customers all over the world?

In the case of Timberland, the answer is, "Differently than we did it before."

"Right now, we have an extremely complex supply chain," says Joe Barrell, Timberland's director of distribution. "But we're now a year and a half into a process of re-engineering the supply chain to make it more flexible and integrated. We're trying to reduce cycle-time and optimize costs."

Considering the rapid changes that are taking place at Timberland, it's no wonder Barrell and his team are trying to bring Timberland's logistics into a more manageable orbit.

Company sales have more than tripled in the last five years, and have increased by 44% in the last year alone. Timberland is relying more on sourcing than ever. Footwear manufacturing, as a percentage of units of goods sold, has decreased by one-third in the last three years. Sourcing has increased concomitantly.

"That's not the direction we want to go in," says Barrell. "We'd rather have all of our footwear made on a proprietary basis. But with the rapid growth we've experienced, we have no choice."

What are some of the logistics changes taking place at Timberland?

"When you're in a rapid-growth phase," explains Barrell, "you have an increased need for warehousing space. And when you're expanding globally, you generally have to lease a large number of smaller warehouses. With rapid expansion, warehousing becomes a variable cost rather than a fixed asset. The point has come at Timberland where it no longer makes sense to keep on doing that."

The reason: with footwear shipments averaging less than 23 pairs of mixed SKUs, Timberland makes an enormous number of shipments. This translates into a huge information burden that is impossible to handle with the company's current distribution network.

"The product moves only as fast as the information flows," says Barrell. "We needed a new system."

The plan Timberland came up with was to streamline its logistics information pipeline, first, and then streamline the cargo pipeline accordingly.

The information challenge was to come up with a system that would enable Timberland to track product from the factory to its final destination. The problem was that the links in the supply chain were not talking to one another and therefore not sharing information.

"At every link in the chain, you can make a decision about the cargo that would make it flow better," explains Barrell, "but only if you have the information about the product at its current location and the ability to communicate with that location in real time to direct the product."

For example, when product leaves the factory, you can instantaneously direct the freight forwarder to send it by air instead of by ocean carrier, or vice versa. You can direct cargo arriving in Los Angeles from Asia to a distribution center or directly to a customer, depending on the need of the moment. But you can do that only if you bring together all the information links in the supply chain.

To develop the information system Timberland wants, it chose partners to help it: the Timberland information people are working hand-in-glove with ACS and the Rockport Group.

ACS, a San Francisco-based freight forwarder and part of American President Companies, has overall responsibility for developing the system by identifying its needs and requirements. Rockport is a software house based in Rockport, Mass.—no relation to the shoe company—and it is developing the database programs supporting the international tracking system. The people at Timberland's headquarters are repositioning information and setting boilerplates for use in the system.

"What we have now are shipments going separately from Korea, Hong Kong, Malaysia, and other Asian coun-

From *Distribution*, May 1994, pp. 32-34, 36. © 1994 by Chilton Company, part of Capital Cities/ABC, Inc., New York, NY. Reprinted by permission.

BEHIND THE EIGHT BALL

Even high-tech companies can have problems reaching the logistical leading edge.

In the case of Digital Equipment Corp., a three year attempt to re-engineer its transportation and distribution operations has been compounded by $3 billion in losses in three years, repeated reorganizations and a shift to low margin, volume driven products.

The Maynard, Mass.-based computer maker is only in the early stages of cutting excessive costs out of its inbound supply chain. They are still heavily dependent on the systems and technologies of their carriers and service providers.

"We don't have a single system in place yet for tracking inbound supply," says Paul McGovern, Digital's Asia-Pacific distribution manager. "On the inbound side, we're reliant on our transportation providers. We track product through our carriers' and forwarders' systems."

It's not that digital has done nothing to improve its logistics in recent years. They've reduced the number of carriers and consolidated some of their distribution facilities. They contracted for a third-party distribution facility in California. That way product does not have to be routed from Asia to the West Coast to the East Coast and then back to West Coast customers, as before.

However, it appears Digital is lagging behind other shippers who have made more significant strides toward driving their own supply chain.

Now in the process of developing an Asia-Pacific Logistics Strategy, Digital's McGovern says, "We believe that business requirements will be different in the future."

In the case of low margin PCs and off-the-shelf products such as cables and printers, McGovern says, "There's no customer loyalty for those products, so there is very little room for error. Delivery has to be quick, predictable and cheap while creating an intelligent balance between service and cost."

It's a different ballgame when it comes to more complex orders, such as large built-to-order CPUs. Lead time is longer, the products are not inventoried and margins are higher—but shrinking. The goals are to insure predictability and completeness of the orders, delivered undamaged and at a reasonable cost, he says.

"We're looking at how to distribute product for future competitiveness," says McGovern. "We have a couple of teams looking at the situation."

---

tries to warehouses in the United States and Europe," explains Barrell. "Under those conditions, it's hard to integrate the information that's needed to keep product visible and the system flexible."

So what Timberland is doing at the level of physical distribution is moving to a system of consolidated regional warehousing. Timberland now has separate warehouses in a dozen Asian countries, several in the United States and three in Europe.

Under the new system, sources throughout Asia will feed one or two warehouses. The company will also have single continental distribution centers in North America and Europe.

That way, the company will have a better handle on where product is located so that it can quickly and flexibly route and reroute the product to where it is needed.

But centralization isn't the end of the story. "The real watchwords are flexibility and timeliness," says Barrell. "We still want to be able to make direct deliveries to our larger customers."

And timeliness doesn't necessarily mean delivering as quickly as possible. "We want to have the flexibility to control the timing of deliveries so that they arrive when the customer needs them," says Barrell. "Sometimes that means slowing the pipeline down, not speeding it up."

How does Timberland intend to accomplish its logistics goals?

Barrell has developed a three-step approach. First is the articulation of a mission for his distribution organization and making sure that everyone understands it. Timberland's distribution mission is to provide services for the uninterrupted flow of merchandise from the source to the customer over an integrated logistics pipeline.

Next is to define long-term goals to implement that strategy. The key long-term goals are the consolidation of facilities and more—but not total—centralization.

In addition, Timberland intends over the long term to attain greater awareness of customer needs; automate information systems and distribution facilities; design a facilities network; and hire the necessary resources to bring it all about, such as professional management personnel, new facilities and material handling equipment, and re-engineered business systems.

Third is to implement short-term goals—or "quick hits"—as interim measures toward the accomplishment of the long-term actions. "Working on the long-term goals pushes out the quick hits that you need to work on," says Barrell.

In this area, Barrell and his people have re-engineered the physical layout of facilities to optimize work; developed a transportation planning program; and streamlined Timberland's carrier pool.

How far is Timberland to the full implementation of its revamped logistics?

"About halfway," says Barrell. "We're knee-deep in it, soon to be waste-deep."

NORTH AMERICAN BUSINESS INTEGRATION

Once NAFTA appeared to be imminent, U.S. firms began integrating their Canadian operations into North American or global enterprises, without waiting for NAFTA

MAJOR U.S. CORPORATIONS WERE MOVING TO CREATE NORTH AMERICAN BUSINESS STRATEGIES AND STRUCTURES EVEN BEFORE NAFTA WAS APPROVED. IN A RECENT STUDY WE CONDUCTED FOR THE AMERICAS SOCIETY, WE FOUND THAT AN EMERGING NORTH AMERICAN REGIONAL MARKET MADE UP OF CANADA, THE U.S. AND MEXICO, HAS BECOME A CENTREPOINT IN MANY FIRMS' STRATEGIC OUTLOOK.

Stephen Blank, Stephen Krajewski, and Henry S. Yu

STEPHEN BLANK IS A PROFESSOR AT THE LUBIN SCHOOL OF BUSINESS, PACE UNIVERSITY, AND DIRECTOR OF CANADIAN AFFAIRS AT THE AMERICAS SOCIETY IN NEW YORK. HE RECEIVED A B.A. AT DARTMOUTH COLLEGE AND A PH.D. IN GOVERNMENT AT HARVARD

STEPHEN KRAJEWSKI IS A CONSULTANT TO THE CANADIAN AFFAIRS PROGRAM OF THE AMERICAS SOCIETY. HE GRADUATED FROM CLARK UNIVERSITY, AND RECEIVED AN M.A. AT THE UNIVERSITY OF KENTUCKY. HE IS CURRENTLY EMPLOYED BY JOHN SNOW INC. OF BOSTON.

HENRY S. YU GRADUATED FROM THE UNIVERSITY OF WESTERN ONTARIO AND IS CURRENTLY ENROLLED IN THE MBA PROGRAM AT PACE UNIVERSITY.

FUNDING FOR THE SURVEY WAS PROVIDED BY THE ROYAL BANK OF CANADA.

The unifying of these three economies — the emergence of a new North American "economic architecture" — rather than the NAFTA agreement itself is driving this change in strategic perceptions. The prospect of NAFTA was the trigger. Scott Wallinger, Senior Vice President of The Westvaco Corporation, echoed other respondents when he told us, before NAFTA was approved, "Business is so far ahead of politicians on this one that it almost makes the agreement secondary. To many in our industry, NAFTA is a *fait accompli*."

We received completed questionnaires from 34 U.S. *Fortune 500* manufacturing firms. The questionnaires had been directed to U.S. headquarters, and, to supplement earlier surveys of managers in Canadian branch plants,

sought specifically to test headquarters' opinion. We interviewed executives in several of the firms that responded.

CORPORATIONS RATIONALIZING AND INTEGRATING

Fully half of the firms that responded to our survey said they have already adopted a North American focus in their corporate strategy and structure, and 20% more are now considering doing so. A further 17% said that they have not yet moved in this direction, but are likely to soon. Only three of the responding firms have considered and rejected the idea.

This new North American focus has two key dimensions. The first is the integration of Canadian, American and, somewhat more slowly, Mexican business operations into continental operations. The second is the rationalization of production capacity, which has preceded and typically intensified integration.

Efforts to rationalize and integrate American, Canadian and Mexican business operations are moving forward rapidly, and are accompanied by high levels of organizational innovation and experimentation. The main reason given was to meet global competition. In a world characterized by low growth, uncertain profit margins and rapid technological change — an environment in which dozens of companies that were household names for most of a century have ceased to exist — competitive intensity has soared. Central to meeting competitive pressures is the reduction of excess capacity. Firms have to shed redundant capacity if they are to survive in the new global economy. Protected by high tariff walls, many high-cost Canadian branch plants generated large profits. Without protection, and in an increasingly competitive environment, these plants are painful liabilities.

Efforts to enhance quality in design, production, delivery and service drive integration as well. With growing emphasis on customer satisfaction and total quality management, higher levels of integration are necessary to achieve greater control over quality and inventory. One survey respondent commented, "The current recession and greater competition have forced us to reassess our manufacturing capability, reduce costs, shrink production time and, most importantly, to improve the overall quality of our business."

Markets in North America are also changing rapidly. Many have escaped entirely from national borders. Subsidiaries increasingly become operations *in* Canada rather than operations producing *for* Canada. Distinct national markets begin to blur, and operations with what once were national mandates now find themselves competing with other divisions in the firm. Westvaco's Scott Wallinger told us how his company is "... finding more overlap in what we once thought of as separate customer bases."

Markets can sometimes be serviced better now by regional than by national sites. There is usually no reason for a Quebec-based subsidiary of a U.S. firm to supply Canadian buyers in Vancouver. Firms are working out more rational, less expensive sourcing and marketing networks in North America. J. P. Cousins, Vice President of Xerox, told us his firm is beginning to ship products to Canadian customers directly from U.S. production sites, rather than through a system of warehouses in Canada.

As firms restructure on a North American basis, others — suppliers for example — will do so as well. "If our customers are going to organize along North American lines," Bill Etherington, CEO of IBM Canada, told *The Globe and Mail*, "then our company will do the same."

Our research clearly reveals the extent of strategic and structural change underway in a sample of U.S. firms. Most are moving towards some sort of North American-wide strategy and structure. But our discussions with executives in these firms and the case studies we have written suggest strongly that this new focus

Major Goals in Canada for 1995 *(32 respondents)*	No. of Mentions
Increase profitability of Canadian operations	22
Increase market share	22
Increase volume of Canadian operations	20
Integrate Canadian operations into U.S. or North American network	19
Reduce overheads of Canadian operations	12
Integrate operations into global networks	7
Heighten Canadian identity of business	6
Increase lines of business	6
Reduce lines of business	1
Close Canadian operations	0

on North America is not typically the result of a long and gradual evolution. It is not the culmination of a slowly dawning awareness of an emerging continental economy. More commonly, we believe, these firms met a drastically changing and threatening world at the end of the 1980s. Many responded by launching a wide range of initiatives. They slimmed down, closed plants and laid off workers and managers. They put new management systems in place and brought new technologies on line. They reorganized and restructured, globalized and localized. And, as part of all of this, they lurched toward new North American structures as well.

CANADIAN SUBSIDIARIES IN A NEW CORPORATE SYSTEM

Most of the firms that responded to our survey have long-established Canadian operations. We asked them whether there had been significant change in the relationship with their Canadian affiliates in the past five years. The responses were remarkable: 68% reported a significant change in

relationship with their Canadian operations during this period, with the direction of change overwhelmingly toward integration.

This trend is not new and was well underway before the Canada-U.S. free trade agreement was in place, although the trend seems to have accelerated over the past few years.

Despite continued concerns that U.S. firms are abandoning Canada, only two respondents in our study reported that their firms have actually closed down their Canadian operations, whereas three firms have recently established new Canadian headquarters.

We asked respondents what their firms hope to achieve in Canada by 1995 (see table). The three objectives mentioned most frequently were to increase the profitability of Canadian operations, to expand market share in Canada and to increase the volume of Canadian business operations.

Only one of the respondents mentioned that among his firm's goals will be reducing lines of business. None stated closing down Canadian operations as a goal. But

12 companies hope to reduce overheads in Canada, and only half a dozen seek to heighten the Canadian identity of their operations in Canada. More interesting is that 19 companies see, as a goal for Canadian operations, the integration of Canadian operations into either a U.S. or North American production network.

Our survey throws some light on changing levels of autonomy of U.S. subsidiaries operating in Canada. Canadian head offices are much leaner than they were a decade ago. The Canadian office is often now, in York's Professor Isaiah Litvak's words, "... a skeleton of its former self — in terms of staff numbers, professional breadth and resources, and authority." The reason, he observes, is that globally rationalized, specialized and integrated manufacturing and marketing organizations — which firms will require to be successful in the 1990s — rest on centralized global planning, direction and coordination of resources and activities.

Do not assume, however, that while Canadian branch plant head offices are skeletons in terms of staff

Degree of Autonomy Compared to 1988
(33 Respondents)

	Same	Less	More
Sales	26	5	3
Procurement	25	6	2
Marketing Research	25	5	3
Public Affairs	25	5	3
Treasury	24	7	2
Finance	23	8	2
Exporting	23	8	1
Advertising	22	6	4
Development	22	10	1
Management Appointment	22	8	3
Investment (including mergers and acquisitions)	21	10	2
Production Planning	19	12	2
Research	19	12	2

and resources, U.S. headquarters are fat. The axe has swung everywhere, and the ranks of managers and levels of resources in U.S. operations have also been reduced. The media notion that a job lost in Canada is a job saved in the U.S. is simply untrue.

While levels of intra-firm integration and coordination are higher now than ever, the creation of new oganizational structures has not meant that local autonomy has diminished in every function. Most respondents at U.S. headquarters believe that their Canadian operations have retained much the same level of autonomy in most functions since 1988. Others reported that managerial autonomy of Canadian units has decreased on some scales and increased on others.

The survey paints a fairly clear picture. While most respondents reported that the operating autonomy of Canadian subsidiaries remains at the same level as in the past, the trend since 1988 is toward diminished autonomy, particularly in product development functions.

Some firms reported that the autonomy of their Canadian operations has increased in this period of integration, particularly in sales, advertising and market research, where localization has the most value. A larger number of firms reported that Canadian operations have less autonomy, particularly in investment, production planning and R and D.

Less autonomy over production is not surprising, given the trends

described by respondents. Canadian subsidiaries of U.S. companies are no longer standalone entities dedicated to supplying the Canadian market with the entire range of products produced by the U.S. parent. As trade barriers have declined, Canadian operations have been integrated more fully into global, continental and regional production networks. As one Canadian manager remarked to us, "We have lost capacity and product lines, but our Canadian operations have been given the mandate to produce a number of different products for the North American market, a development which has come about largely through our view of a continental market."

AMERICANS CAN LEARN FROM CANADIANS

How firms work out these new organizational arrangements that integrate formerly distinct national systems and define the levels of autonomy for different units will be determined in individual companies by corporate cultures, management style and the sensitivity of people involved. Strong opinions are voiced by Canadian managers in many companies about the impact of these changes in structure and strategy. They complain that it

Intra-firm competition for production mandates is much tougher than ever before. Plant managers throughout the firm — not just in Canada — know they will be scrutinized and constantly forced to justify their existence in the eyes of their parent. One Canadian participant asked rhetorically, "Why do I need to have a plant in Canada if I can manufacture more cheaply in the United States and supply Canada without duties to worry about?"

> "Firms have to shed redundant capacity if they are to survive in the global economy."

is more difficult to stay ahead of global competitors or adequately service local needs when key strategic functions have been removed.

U.S. heavy handedness is never appreciated, and another generation of Canadian managers in U.S. firms stamp their feet in frustration. In a confidential paper prepared for the Americas Society, Barry Burton wrote, "I would like to see the U.S. managers in direct-connect businesses listen to what we have to say rather than assuming their methods for doing business are always right. Contrary to what they may think, Americans can learn from Canadians."

More to the point, another Canadian observed, "Globalization is not equivalent to Americanization."

NORTH AMERICAN FIRMS BEING DRIVEN TO CHANGE

The survey shows that the factors driving change in corporate strategy and structure today are fundamentally different from those that influenced patterns of business in Canada and Mexico only a decade ago. Even in the early 1980s, the operations of U.S. firms in Canada and Mexico were greatly influenced by national regulations on such matters as local equity participation, significant benefits clauses and technology transfer. Foreign firms viewed Canada and Mexico as distinct national markets, and typically sought to produce a wide range of their products in each country.

Today, perceptions of globaliza-

tion, increasing competition and change in competitive advantage are the most powerful factors driving change in North American markets. National issues, political and regulatory factors in particular, are no longer viewed by respondents with the same weight as in the past. The prospect of NAFTA, at the time of our survey, was seen as the most powerful driver of change (4.21 on a 5-point scale of importance), although we think the operative definition of NAFTA here is not a trade agreement as much as an economic community. Globalization received the next highest average ranking (4.03).

In addition to their views on NAFTA, issues of competition and market conditions were seen by the respondents as being important for their future strategy and structure in North America. Firms thought changes in competitive advantage and product development would also be important determinants of their strategy and structure.

The overwhelming importance of the effects of NAFTA and globalization suggests that developments in North America are viewed by many firms as one dimension of wider, global changes in markets and competition. If the prospect of NAFTA drives them to rationalize and reorganize continentally, it is probable that companies are rationalizing and integrating operations in every part of their operations around the globe.

INTRA-FIRM COMPETITION INCREASING

Another important issue is the role of intra-firm trade relations. Much Canada-U.S. trade takes place within firms. This trend has resulted from patterns of foreign direct investment over the past 40 years — U.S. firms investing in manufacturing operations in Canada, and Canadian firms doing likewise in the U.S.

High levels of intra-firm trade tighten the economic links between the two countries. The question then is how intra-firm trade may be affected by the evolving North American scene.

The survey asked whether the level of intra-firm competition for product mandates has increased or decreased in recent years. More than 40% of the respondents said that competition had increased greatly, and almost 20% said that competition has increased some-what. About 14% stated that com-petition remains at the same level. No one reported that intra-firm competition for mandates has declined. These results support the view that internal production markets are as sensitive to global-ization as external markets.

The survey also asked how important internal trade with affiliates in Canada, Mexico and the rest of the world would be in five years. Eighty per cent of the respondents believe that intra-firm trade with their Mexican subsidiaries will become more important, whereas 57% said that intra-firm linkages with the rest of the world will become more important. No one said that either will be less important in five years. Just more than half of the respondents said intra-firm trade with Canada will be more important in five years, and 40% said it will be about the same.

The picture that emerges from these data is not one of a zero-sum game in which intra-firm trade within one segment (U.S.-Mexico) replaces that of another segment (U.S.-Canada). Respondents pro-ject a more rapid growth of intra-firm trade with Mexico, but do not suggest that trade with Canadian subsidiaries will collapse. The key

> "The key here is expectations of rapid economic growth in Mexico, rather than massive relocation of production."

here is expectations of rapid eco-nomic growth in Mexico, rather than the massive relocation of production.

LOOKING FORWARD...

The key findings of our research are clear:

• The erosion of the old sys-tem of U.S. branch plants operat-ing in Canadian and Mexican import substitution economies has accelerated remarkably in the past few years.

• Many firms are moving quickly to assess alternatives for how they will operate in an emerging North American eco-nomic system. These firms have backed into a North American strategy as they struggle with intensified global competition.

Now these experiences need to be monitored, and different approaches evaluated. Those firms that are best able to respond to this emerging North American system will likely have a competi-tive advantage.

• This is not to suggest that economic integration is leading toward the homogenization of taste, markets, rules or business practices in North America. Rather than opening the way to the Americanization of Canada or Mexico, so feared by economic nationalists, integration has real-ly encouraged greater regional differentiation. The need for local responsiveness within this emerging continental system is as great as ever.

• Finally, North American business systems are characterized less by centralized control and allocation of functions and responsibilities than by intensified competition for mandates among units within individual firms. As technology alters the nature of the production process, levels of internal competition will surely increase still further.

A Global Glance at Work and Family

U.S. corporations have been leaders in developing work-family programs.
But our Asian and European neighbors can teach us the benefits of
additional change agents such as unions, agencies and the government.

Bonnie Michaels

Bonnie Michaels is president of Managing Work & Family, Inc., an international work-family consulting firm based in Evanston, Illinois, and co-author of Solving the Work/Family Puzzle.

As we near the 21st century, work and family issues are changing rapidly. Wherever we look, we see more women entering the labor force; single parents working because of economic necessity; and companies responding to the aging work force by addressing such issues as age discrimination, retirement benefits and elder care. All these social trends affect how global workers manage their jobs and personal lives. But where does the United States stand in comparison to other countries' values, policies and programs that address work and family issues simultaneously? What can Americans learn from our Asian and European neighbors?

The United States has led the pack in studying work-family issues. Indeed, the New York-based Families and Work Institute's 1993 Study on the Changing Workforce revealed that 87% of the American work force has some family responsibility that could potentially interfere with a job. The study also showed that employees value the employer who offers assistance such as flexible time, leave programs and dependent-care programs. In fact, many of the employees said that they'd be willing to make substantial trade-offs to receive these services. The study confirms that family-friendly programs also benefit the company because employees are more committed to performing their jobs well, are more loyal to their employers and show more initiative on the job.

But, even though the United States is a leader in studying and initiating corporate work-family programs, I wonder if our culture is family-friendly—especially in this era of downsizing and reengineering. As a work-family consultant, I've interviewed employees working in companies that are well known for their work-family programs and services. Many of their stories indicate that they're expected to work long hours and they're afraid to use programs or ask for flexibility. I also see the need for longer-term planning and a united effort between government and corporations. Even though we're a large country with diverse needs, it seems that the backbone of our nation is being overlooked.

By contrast, some Asian and European governments and social institutions have demonstrated their commitment to the welfare of families because they value the family as an essential institution. For example, Singapore's prime minister, Goh Chok Tong, says, "Our institutions and basic policies are in place to sustain high economic growth. But if we lose our traditional values, our family strength and cohesion, we will lose our vibrancy—and decline. This is the intangible factor in the success of East Asian economies."

Likewise, countries in Europe also look at work-family benefits from a larger perspective. Rebecca Rolfes, a Chicago-based journalist, explained European attitudes during a speech she gave at the 1994 Canadian Conference Board Work-Family Conference: "European social legislation stems from a holistic view of society," she says. European workers don't have and use work-family benefits because their employers are nicer than those in the United States. Rather, European companies recognize that the stress of balancing work and family life have an economic cost that's passed on to all citizens. Of course, these companies welcome enhanced productivity, loyalty and retention, but the main reason many of them assist workers is for the betterment of all. Hence, it would be valuable for U.S. business and government leaders to learn from some of the Asian and European practices and attitudes. If the United States is going to remain competitive for the long haul, we must ensure our workers' future.

However, as U.S. corporations continue to downsize and tighten their budgets, employees face mounting pressures and workloads. Workers still have to manage their personal responsibilities, and they'll do a better job for the corporation if they have the necessary support. Yet many American companies no longer look at work-family benefits from a strategic point of view. A recent study by Stamford, Connecticut-based Towers Perrin indicated that nine of 10 senior executives said that people are their company's most important resource, but when developing strategic priorities, these *people issues* ranked near the bottom.

What's needed to change this mindset? John Naisbitt, author of *Megatrends*, says that change occurs when economic necessity and changing values merge. Researchers already have proven that, in order to recruit and retain productive and motivated employees, there's an economic necessity for companies to provide viable work-family support systems. Faith Wohl, President Clinton's appointed director of Workplace Initiatives, says, "We have to stop diminishing ourselves with pat solutions and cute packaging. The place where work and family intersect is a critical juncture in our society. Those are the two essential elements in any individual's life."

The United States can learn from its global neighbors. At a conference last year in Singapore, representatives from Malaysia, India, Japan, Indonesia, Brunei, Thailand, the Philippines, Korea and Vietnam shared strategies for strengthening the family.

They discussed government policy as a vehicle to assist families. Stella Quah, a family sociologist from Singapore, says that family policies don't change people's behavior. "It merely creates the conditions to facilitate behavioral or attitudinal change," she says.

PHOTO: BONNIE MICHAELS

In Singapore, working women such as the one pictured here are increasingly entering the global work force. The country's government is among several in Asia and Europe that provide generous maternity leaves and child-care subsidies.

Family policies such as flextime, she adds, don't create better families, but they certainly establish the social mechanisms to satisfy family needs.

In Singapore, the Ministry of Community Development has allocated $1 million for assistance in promoting family values. Its 17-member committee strives to help individuals maintain and enhance their family life. Some of the government-sponsored benefits include:

• A government advisory council on family and community life

• Eight weeks' paid maternity leave; four years' unpaid

• Four years' unpaid child-care leave for parents with sick children

• Child-care subsidies of $100 per child

• Elder care

• Government-sponsored family resource centers.

The Australian government has been involved in a variety of initiatives to promote the importance of family-support programs. The premier of New South Wales published a booklet entitled "Valuing the Family." He emphasized the government's commitment to families: "Families are the core unit of society, and my government is focused on strengthening this core unit to create stronger communities." New South Wales also is the first state in Australia to introduce flexible working arrangements for public-sector employees. For example, the government generally provides 12 months of unpaid parental leave, but also provides six to 12 weeks of paid parental leave in the public sector. Moreover, the father is given the right to share unpaid leave with the mother of the child during the first year following birth or adoption.

In Sweden, employees enjoy 38 weeks of paid parental leave, which covers 90% of their paycheck. Through the European Union and European Free Trade Association in Sweden, workers enjoy paid maternity leave because they're considered valued employees with qualifications, training and seniority. Swedes share the belief that it's society's duty to care for its citizens. A directive adopted in late 1992 provides for a minimum of 14 weeks' leave—paid at an amount similar to sickness benefits.

Unions play leading role in work-family issues. As a free-spirited, independent country, we have often rejected mandates. Even the 1993 Family and Medical Leave Act, which allows 12 weeks of unpaid leave, hasn't been fully accepted by many company leaders. But union representatives have been among the leading change agents and have contributed to the support of work-family programs both in the United States and abroad. According to Donna Dolan, a spokeswoman for the New York-based Communication Workers of America (CWA): "U.S. unions are now coming together to address workers' work-family needs." A coalition was formed in July 1994 to address such issues. The CWA and IBEW (International Brotherhood of Electrical Workers) have put $7 million into a subsidy fund to assist employees with child- and elder-care expenses.

Other pilot programs in New York include a spring arts camp during the school recess for working parents' children. In addition, the AFL-CIO established an international labor committee to explore work-family issues and domestic violence, says Dolan.

Another positive example of union involvement is the National Trade Union Congress of Singapore (NTUC), which is a major institution providing for the improvement of the socio-economic status of workers and their families. Since 1973, a Women's Program within the NTUC and several women's union committees have focused on labor contract provisions to assist working parents. As far back as 1977, the NTUC set up child-care services that operate near workers' homes.

More recently, many corporate work-family leaders have emerged. Among them are Fel-Pro Inc., Hewlett Packard Australia, Telecom Australia and Biotech Australia Pty. Ltd. Many of their programs support working families. In 1993, the University of Chicago conducted a study of Fel-Pro's work-family benefits (Fel-Pro is a mid-sized auto parts supplier located in Skokie, Illinois). Bottom-line results showed that family-friendly policies and programs are important in facilitating organizational change, and employees who are supported by their employer are in turn supportive of their employer. "Working at Fel-Pro and receiving their benefits is the best thing that's happened to me," says an employee who's worked at Fel-Pro's factory for 20 years. "I have complete concern for and loyalty to this company."

To recognize positive efforts by the business community, the Australian government and members of the private sector initiated the Corporate Work-Family Awards in 1992. The awards identify and honor corporate champions who are implementing work-family programs. Among the past recipients are Esso, Sydney Water Board and IBM.

European managers also are very aware of the positive effect family-friendly programs have on white-collar women's career development, but work-family benefits for the most part have been legislated.

Currently in the United Kingdom, one in four British employers now provide more than a statutory minimum maternity leave. Abbey National, British Gas, the civil service and the national health service offer up to 52 weeks of leave. Companies such as Marks & Spencer, The Rover Group, Amersham International and HP Bulmer also pay 100% of earnings during maternity leave.

Some European companies have even offered career breaks as an alternative to leaves. In her 1991 study for The Conference Board Europe on the glass ceiling, Rolfes learned that 50% of responding companies use career breaks. The initiative has helped to retain female employees who have children. A good example is Midland Bank in Belgium, which allows employees to take up to five years, in three separate breaks with at least one year of continuous service between breaks, for child care, elder care, long-term sick care or pressing family reasons.

Even though European social legislation has been assisting workers, a long-term approach by corporations is still necessary. "Improved long-range planning [yields and embraces] the kind of family-friendly working environment that attracts skilled workers," says Rolfes.

Trust is equally important to long-term strategic planning. Corporate managers often don't trust workers to determine their own work schedules around their family responsibilities. Yet volumes of research extol the value of flexible

A Look at Work-Force Trends Abroad

- In Singapore, a 1993 government survey showed the number of married women entering the work force had grown from 33% to 44%.
- In Malaysia, females made up 49% of the work force in 1993.
- In Australia, the 1993 census showed that married women represented 59% of employed women.
- European firms have hired more women during the last 10 to 15 years, even though employment figures show that this rise in the number of working women comes in the midst of Europe's worse recession since World War II.
- In Singapore, divorce has increased 50% since 1992.
- In Australia, single families with dependent children represent 9% of all New South Wales families.
- By 2031, the Australian population will be predominantly middle aged or elderly, and the proportion over 80 years old will have increased dramatically.
- In Europe, by the year 2000, there will be more people leaving the work force than joining it.
- In Malaysia, nearly 1 million people are more than 60 years old.

—*BM*

work options. A 1990 study by the Conference Board indicated that 50% of 521 large companies reported that they offered flextime. Yet, in a recent survey of 121 private companies in the Chicago area by researcher Linda Stroh of Loyola University, the statistics were dispelled. Of 64 responding companies, only 14% confirmed they had flextime. Moreover, of the 86% of companies without flextime, 92% said it was unlikely or very unlikely they'd ever adopt it.

However, Sao Paulo, Brazil-based Semco, is an extraordinary example of a company that trusts its employees. Since the company introduced "participative management" programs, in which workers to a great extent take responsibility for managing their own workflow, productivity has increased sevenfold and profits have risen fivefold. Ricardo Semler, the company president, has stated: "At Semco, we treat our employees like adults. We trust them. We don't make our employees ask permission to go to the bathroom or have security guards search them as they leave for the day. We get out of their way and let them do their jobs."

If employees want to have breakfast with their kids or take them to school, Semco allows them to do so. "Flexible working hours demonstrated our belief that we wanted to pay workers for results, not merely their time…and we didn't care how those results were obtained," says Semler.

European companies also value alternative work options. In fact, flextime has been common in Europe, where the workweek already is shorter than in North America. In a 1991 study of European companies and the glass ceiling, Rolfes learned that 50% of responding companies offered flexible hours, 30% offered work at home, and 27% offered job sharing. Fortunately, there are many pockets of change, but without a more universal, coordinated effort of such initiatives, the work-family puzzle will still have missing pieces.

Educational institutions can play a major role in changing values. In Singapore, family values are being taught through civic and moral education programs and through pastoral care and career-guidance programs. Parental education courses are offered throughout Singapore's family resource centers. Marcia Brumit Kropf, director of research at New York-based Catalyst, says that a one-time work-family training experience for senior executives and middle managers won't guarantee change. "Education is an ongoing process. It should include coaching, cultivating commitment and changing habits," says Kropf. The United States, she believes, is at a crossroads. Arlene Johnson, vice president of the Families and Work Institute, concurs: "The model of the learning organization is good for the work-family field," says Johnson. "Change isn't something that gets stamped on an organization. It's a gradual and incremental process in which awareness and action reinforce each other until the norms and beliefs have shifted. Education is the application of that learning in real situations," she says.

What makes it harder now, Johnson adds, is that Americans' expectations have risen. We've raised the bar in what we want to achieve. Progress in the 1980s was a child-care program, then manager training and a wider range of programs. Now, our bar has been raised to issues about the work environment and the nature of work itself. "It's like the tide coming in. It hasn't crested yet. Work and family issues aren't only about programs and policies. They're also about flexible work environments, a trusting and respectful workplace, and looking at the nature of work in human terms," Johnson says.

Culture change will occur faster when all the change agents have a collective vision and it becomes a priority for policymakers as well as work-family leaders.

Change is a gradual and incremental process in which awareness and action reinforce each other until the norms and beliefs have shifted.

Without a long-term, strategic plan, we will continue to see a fragmented, piecemeal approach to work and family issues. Hence, we need to keep in touch with our global neighbors and learn from their successes and failures.

UNICEF summed up the importance to society of ensuring positive family experiences by stating, "Families are the fundamental group in society and the natural environment for the growth and well-being of all its members. Beyond providing natural caring and support, families represent the locus of deepest human experience. Intimacy and passion, identity and selfhood, connection to the past and hope for the future…all arise from this nexus."

Lessons From HR Overseas

Every country does something better than the rest. Integrating these best practices can help HR in the United States increase its effectiveness.

Shari Caudron

Shari Caudron is a contributing editor for Personnel Journal.

We hear a lot these days about "thinking outside the box;" about searching in new places for new ways of solving our companies' problems. It's a useful concept. Our organizations aren't the same as they were 20 years ago, so why should our management practices be?

But when you think of that box, that set of parameters that dictates conventional thinking, what does it look like? Is it your job? Your company? Your industry? To come up with truly innovative solutions, you probably have to search outside the boundaries of all three of these entities. However, there's one more box you may want to consider peeking out of, and that's the United States of America. As Michael Marquardt, professor of global human resources development at George Washington University in Washington, D.C., explains: "American companies think they're the keepers of the best management practices. Consequently, they don't try to learn as much as they can from other places."

Whether U.S. business executives are arrogant or simply myopic is open to debate. What's irrefutable, however, is that there's a lot North American HR professionals can learn from their counterparts in companies overseas.

Granted, there's a lot we do superbly in this country as well. "I think we're considered the best country in the world in the practice of HR development," says Marquardt. Adds Ron Kirchenbauer, vice president of HR for Ericsson, a Swedish telecommunications firm with a U.S. division in Richardson, Texas: "I think the pay-for-performance movement in this country is among the most progressive anywhere." And HR consultants agree that management concepts we've pioneered, such as reengineering and the learning organization, put us on the cutting edge.

Our skill in these areas entice business people from around the world to visit our companies. In fact, many people attribute the success the Japanese have had since World War II to the fact that they came to the United States on study tours, looked at the best management practices American companies had to offer, and then adapted those practices to their own organizations. "They were under no illusion that the Japanese had all the answers." Marquardt explains.

Unfortunately, American managers don't appear quite so eager to learn from their foreign colleagues. "We tend to think U.S. companies are the most dynamic," says Andy Craggs, international practice leader with The Wyatt Co. in San Francisco. "We've got the most research. Everybody has MBAs. We think we've got everything figured out. But in fact, things aren't working very well in the states in a lot of areas, including health care, unemployment, homelessness and

> **Things aren't working out very well in the States in a lot of areas, including health care, unemployment, homelessness and worker uncertainty.**

worker uncertainty. If something isn't working with our system, let's look outside and see what we can learn from others."

Few international HR managers are naive enough to think that just because an HR practice works well in another country it will work just as well here. You can't indiscriminately import a management practice into the states any more than you can casually export one—as many U.S.-based multinationals have discovered, albeit the hard way. You need to take a look at differences in cultural expectations, the legislative environment and labor-force economics when considering whether a practice that works in, say, Germany, would also work in the United States.

Furthermore, a management practice with tremendous upside potential probably also has a downside. Many European companies, for example, provide greater benefits and job security to their employees than we do in the states. But the cost of doing business is higher, the government bureaucracy is overwhelming and companies are slower to respond to marketplace opportunities. Simply put, there are two sides to every coin.

Given these caveats, what can we learn from HR practices in companies outside the United States? How are employees treated differently or better than here in the states? How are the HR functions managed? And are there HR programs in other countries that we have yet to consider?

To learn the answers to these questions, PERSONNEL JOURNAL asked international HR consultants, academics and practitioners what they considered to be the best—or at least better—HR practices in other countries. The wide array of responses indicate that American personnel professionals can indeed learn much from other countries.

Look around the world for ways to involve your work force. So what are some of these better practices? For one, European and Japanese companies do a better job soliciting input on business decisions. "Even though in the United States we claim to be participative, I think we still tend to put all the power in the top executive levels," says Craggs. "There's such a focus on business results that we're forced to make decisions that are tough on employees without looking at all the options. We can learn from companies in Europe, where employee input is sought on nearly every business issue."

In many countries, such as Germany, worker input actually is mandated by law. Any company there with more than 100 employees has to set up a works council, which is made up of employees elected from various parts of the organization. German employers must gain the consent of the works council before they can appoint or dismiss employees, set working hours, introduce overtime or even change prices in the lunchroom. In addition, councils have the right to be consulted on a wide range of planning issues, such as decisions to open new plants or close existing ones. They also are entitled to information on company performance.

U.S. managers might see this as a real pain in the neck, but there's little evidence

that German managers feel constrained by the works councils. "In the end, you have to establish a good working relationship with the councils, and if you do, you have no problems," says Thomas Ranft, personnel director of the London, England branch of Deutsche Bank AG.

Although worker input isn't quite as rigidly mandated in Scandinavian companies, employees there do have a great deal to say about management decisions, particularly those related to compensation, safety

These countries are learning new ideas at a faster pace than I've seen in the U.S. They may surpass us in terms of innovation in the next 10 years.

and capital expenditures, explains Alex Hainey, president of Drake Beam Morin Canada, Inc., who has served on the boards of two Norwegian companies.

And the participative management style of Japanese companies is well documented. Within Asian manufacturing firms in particular, workers are more attuned to business results than they are here. U.S. firms are picking up on the bottom-up communications style engaged in these firms, but Craggs says, "we're still a bit behind the times."

Furthermore, human resources operations tend to be more entrepreneurial in Asian companies (with the exception of Japan) than they are here. The economies in countries such as Hong Kong, Malaysia, Singapore and Thailand are expanding so rapidly that HR managers have to constantly create and innovate just to keep up with their expanding work forces. They create new programs out of necessity. "In terms of compensation and benefits, these countries are assimilating new information and learning new ideas at a much faster pace than I've seen in the United States," says Jacque Vilet, senior international compensation and benefits manager with National Semiconductor in Santa Clara, California. "I predict they

may surpass us in terms of innovation in the next 10 years."

Explains Vilet: "There are companies over there that are doing skill-based pay although they don't call it that. They don't know what skill-based pay is. What they've done is reconfigure their factories to improve the work flow. This has resulted in a team model where a group of employees handles a particular process from start to finish. As a result, managers are realizing they have to change the way they pay people because now employees are doing multiple tasks and they have to learn all these new skills. The key is that they have thought this through themselves."

Human resources professionals in other countries also are more willing to informally share information with one another, whereas HR managers in American companies are often reluctant to ask colleagues about their companies' HR practices, preferring instead to rely on formal market surveys. "We're more close to the vest," says Jack Fitzhenry, human resources director for Cupertino, California-based Apple Computer's Pacific division. Why? Because we like to have lots of data, we're concerned with confidentiality, and we're fearful of violating U.S. antitrust laws, he explains.

"My staff members, whether they're in Canada or Hong Kong, seek information from their colleagues on a regular basis," Fitzhenry says. For example, Apple was looking to hire a general manager for a plant in Hong Kong. The top candidate wanted a car and housing allowance that matched what he was getting at his current position. Apple's HR managers thought the allowances he requested were high, but instead of searching for market surveys to validate the amounts, they called the HR manager at the candidate's existing company and asked about the standard car and housing allowances. Turns out, the candidate was telling the truth. "Just by making a couple of phone calls, we were able to put our minds at ease," says Fitzhenry. "We couldn't do that as easily here."

Continuous learning is an established practice overseas. According to Marquardt, the concept of continuous learning is much more enthusiastically received in companies in Asia and the Middle East than it is in North America. Why? Because in both regions of the world, teaching is considered the most important thing a person can do, much of which has to do with the cultural legacies left by Confucius and Mohammed. Because teaching and learning are regarded so highly, the role of managers is seen as being one of teaching or facilitating; of being someone who helps the people around him or her learn.

For instance, in many Asian corporations—specifically those in Japan—whenever one's subordinates are being trained, the manager is there. "This indicates that I think the learning that's occurring is important," Marquardt says.

Because of this strong emphasis on learning, mentoring roles in companies such as Toyota are taken very seriously. In fact, for a year of two before retirement, managers make a great effort to pass along their experience and wisdom to new people. "They realize the past has some value that we can learn from," he adds, "whereas in the United States we tend to look only toward the future."

In Asian companies, the focus on learning also includes an emphasis on developing international management talent, as opposed to just developing local talent. Management training courses frequently include language training, international diplomacy and etiquette. In other words, it's assumed managers will be working across borders. This is because companies there view the Asia-Pacific as one business region, explains Paul Morris, international consultant with The Wyatt Co. "Companies in the United States might have a regional manager who covers several states," he says, "but there, they're trying to develop managers who are able to do business in all of Southeast Asia or all of Greater China."

The focus on learning in Scandinavian and Nordic companies begins when employees start new jobs. More specifically, Ericsson's Ron Kirchenbauer believes these companies do a more thorough job in helping new employees integrate into the company culture. "In the United States," he says, "we tend to let employees find their own way through the company." In Scandinavia, however, companies help new employees understand their internal customers, their suppliers and where to go for certain kinds of information. "It's more than simply passing out a contact list," Kirchenbauer says. "New employees are taken around, introduced to people and given a thorough understand-

Can You Imagine?

Here's a sampling of some human resources practices in other countries that might sound a little unbelievable to U.S. human resources professionals.

• The concept of an hourly wage doesn't really exist in Mexico. Labor law requires that employees receive full pay 365 days a year.

• In Austria and Brazil, employees with one year of service are automatically given 30 days of paid vacation.

• Some jurisdictions in Canada have legislated pay equity—known in the United States as comparable worth—between male- and female-intensive jobs.

• In Japan, levels of compensation are determined using the objective factors of age, length of service and educational background, rather than skill, ability and performance. Performance doesn't count until after an employee reaches age 45.

• In the United Kingdom, employees are allowed to take up to 40 weeks of maternity leave. Employers are required to provide a government-mandated amount of pay for 18 of those weeks.

• In 87% of large Swedish companies, the head of human resources is on the board of directors.   *—SC*

ing of their role as it relates to everyone else's."

In many parts of the world, training incorporates a greater respect for and acknowledgement of the employees' personal lives. Companies in Africa, the Middle East, Asia and Latin America, for example, regard their employees as whole people, who have needs and interests beyond professional and technical ones.

Take an organization like Hitachi. When Hitachi conducts management training courses, participants are given skills in management techniques just as you would expect. But, according to Marquardt, who co-authored the book, *The Global Learning Organization*, participants might also be taught to create haiku—the unrhymed three-line Japanese poems—to give them a sense of creativity and poetry. They might also review the rules of decorum for Japanese tea ceremonies, in which peaceful, simple living is encouraged. In addition, the courses could include book briefings in which participants are ex-

posed to a fairly diverse group of books in an effort to expand their knowledge of current literature. The point is that an effort is made to develop the whole person.

In many parts of the world, respect for the employee as an individual includes a high regard for the employee's family. Latin American companies in particular are very concerned about family members. "When they hire a person, they're also hiring that person's family," Marquardt says. At Carvajal Inversiones, a printing company located in Cali, Colombia, the family is so important that the company is in the process of developing a kindergarten where it plans to enroll employees' children in an effort to detect talents and teach parents how to help develop those talents. Indirectly, the program is intended to help employees acquire the skills to build stable and solid families.

Sam Bernstein, international consultant with Hewitt Associates, L.L.C., in Lincolnshire, Illinois, confirms that respect for a person's family life is greater outside the United States. "When a European goes on vacation, he or she isn't reachable. There's a clear dividing line between work and family. The same is true of Mexico. The Mexican executive on vacation is spending time with family and doesn't want to be bothered by the office," he says. When an American executive goes on vacation, however, everybody in the office usually has access to that person's phone number. "American companies pay a lot of lip service to the importance of being family-friendly, but it just isn't as natural to our culture," Marquardt says.

How to learn from the practices of other countries. What are HR professionals in the states supposed to make of all this? Primarily, it's food for thought; a way to think outside of that proverbial box and look at ways to learn from the practices of companies in other regions of the world. When deciding how to integrate innovative or better HR practices into your own company, however, you need to start, well, inside your own company.

Applied Materials, Inc., in Santa Clara, California, for example, formed a series of global task forces that are charged with identifying the best HR practices in the company, regardless of where in the world they originate. There's a global compensation task force, a global job-grading task force, and global mobility, benefits and training task forces. The goal, according to Carol Kaplan, manager of global compensation and benefits, is to look at which HR practices can be standardized across the 14 countries in which Applied Materials operates, and which practices need to managed on a local or regional level.

In coming up with recommendations, HR managers from each of the firm's major divisions met for one week during each business quarter in 1994 to brainstorm and share information about successful country-specific practices. By the end of the year, members of the task forces presented their recommendations to company executives.

"By working together as a group, we're able to come up with programs that meet all our needs," she says. "In the United States, we've made a mistake in thinking that because we're U.S.-based, what's good for us is good for everybody around the world. What happens, then, is that we export programs that aren't culturally sound and that ends up creating animosities toward corporate headquarters. It's hard to restore those relationships once they've been broken. By coming together, we're learning from each other, and finding better overall ways to do things."

Apple Computer is also learning to listen to input from its HR professionals located outside U.S. borders, although the process has been slow. According to Fitzhenry, the first step has been for Apple's American HR managers to be sensitive to their counterparts overseas and allow them to implement the kinds of programs that make sense for their cultures, as opposed to "cramming our programs down their throats." Has the company begun to import any successful programs? "Not yet, and shame on us for not doing that," Fitzhenry says. "Right now, we're at the stage of sharing information about our programs; we haven't taken the best of what they do and tried to make it work here. But as Asia, in particular, becomes more and more important to our business, we've got to wake up and understand that there's a lot we can learn from the things they do extremely well."

Of course, the truth of the matter is that HR practices *are* becoming more standardized, and differences, where they exist, just aren't as great as they used to be. Look at the analogous trends under way in many parts of the world relative to flexible benefits, teamwork, flatter management structures, the decline of corporate paternalism and the increasing use of contingent workers. HR professionals are well on their way toward creating their own global village, and the village leaders are those who aren't boxed in by their thinking.

The Right Way to Go Global:

An Interview with Whirlpool CEO David Whitwam

"Being an international company—selling globally, having global brands or operations in different countries—isn't enough."

Regina Fazio Maruca

Everybody is talking about going global, but hardly anyone understands what that means, says David R. Whitwam, the 51-year-old chairman and CEO of the Whirlpool Corporation. According to Whitwam, too many managers are still running their businesses with the same old regional fiefdoms and inadequate ways of satisfying customers. As a result, few would-be global companies have escaped the deadly war of attrition in which cost and quality are the only weapons and ever-declining margins the only prize.

When Whitwam became CEO in 1987, Whirlpool was mired in just such an unwinnable war in the North American major-appliances market. Whitwam, who joined Whirlpool in 1968 and rose through the sales and marketing ranks, was determined to make whatever changes necessary to secure real growth for the future. Whitwam's vision of global opportunity led to Whirlpool's daring $1 billion purchase of N.V. Philips's floundering European appliance business in 1989, a move that catapulted Whirlpool into the number-one position in the worldwide appliance business. Whitwam could have chosen to "fix" Philips through cost-cutting and operating changes. Instead, he followed a more ambitious path: transforming two parochial, margin-driven companies into a unified, consumer-focused organization capable of using its combined talents to achieve breakthrough performance in markets around the world. As a result, the new Whirlpool set the pace for the global appliance industry and its price structure.

Whitwam is the first to admit that the transformation is not complete. He discussed the lessons Whirlpool has learned—

and continues to learn—with HBR associate editor Regina Fazio Maruca at company headquarters in Benton Harbor, Michigan.

HBR: *In 1987, Whirlpool was primarily a North American company. Today it manufactures in 11 countries with facilities in the United States, Europe, and Latin America and markets products in more than 120 locations as diverse as Thailand, Hungary, and Argentina. What's the most crucial lesson you've learned about how a company builds a global competitive advantage?*

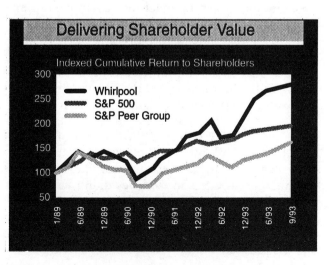

Reprinted with permission from *Harvard Business Review*, March/April 1994, pp. 135-145. © 1994 by the President and Fellows of Harvard College. All rights reserved.

David Whitwam: The only way to gain lasting competitive advantage is to leverage your capabilities around the world so that the company as a whole is greater than the sum of its parts. Being an international company – selling globally, having global brands or operations in different countries – isn't enough.

In fact, most international manufacturers aren't truly global. They're what I call flag planters. They may have acquired or established businesses all over the world, but their regional or national divisions still operate as autonomous entities. In this day and age, you can't run a business that way and expect to gain a long-term competitive advantage.

To me, "competitive advantage" means having the best technologies and processes for designing, manufacturing, selling, and servicing your products at the lowest possible costs. Our vision at Whirlpool is to integrate our geographical businesses wherever possible, so that our most advanced expertise in any given area – whether it's refrigeration technology, financial reporting systems, or distribution strategy – isn't confined to one location or one division. We want to be able to take the best capabilities we have and leverage them in all of our operations worldwide.

In the major-appliances industry, both the size of our products and varying consumer preferences require us to have regional manufacturing centers. But even though the features, dimensions, and configurations of machines like refrigerators, washing machines, and ovens vary from market to market, much of the technology and manufacturing processes involved are similar. In other words, while a company may need plants in Europe, the United States, Latin America, and Asia to make products that meet the special needs of local markets, it's still possible and desirable for those plants to share the best available product technologies and manufacturing processes.

Let me use washing machines as an example. Washing technology is washing technology. But our German products are feature-rich and thus considered to be higher-end. The products that come out of our Italian plants run at lower RPMs and are less costly. Still, the reality is that the insides of the machines don't vary a great deal. Both the German and the Italian washing machines can be standardized and simplified by reducing the number of parts, which is true of any product family. Yet when we bought Philips, the washing machines made in the Italian and German facilities didn't have one screw in common. Today products are being designed to ensure that a wide variety of models can be built on the same basic platform. Our new dryer line has precisely this kind of common platform, and

other product categories are currently being designed in the same way.

But before you can develop common technologies and processes, don't you have to define the new organization's goals?

Absolutely. You must create an organization whose people are adept at exchanging ideas, processes, and systems across borders, people who are absolutely free of the "not-invented-here" syndrome, people who are constantly working together to identify the best global opportunities and the biggest global problems facing the organization. If you're going to ask people to work together in pursuing global ends across organizational and geographic boundaries, you have to give them a vision of what they're striving to achieve, as well as a unifying philosophy to guide their efforts.

That's why we've worked so hard at Whirlpool to define and communicate our vision, objectives, and the market philosophy that represents our unifying focus. Our vision is to be one company worldwide. Our overarching objective is to drive this company to world-class performance in terms of delivering shareholder value, which we define as being in the top 25% of publicly held companies in total returns through a given economic cycle. (See the graph, "Delivering Shareholder Value.")

Our market philosophy suggests that the only way to deliver this value over the long term is by focusing on the customer. Only prolonged, intensive effort to understand and respond to genuine customer needs can lead to the breakthrough products and services that earn long-term customer loyalty. Too many companies implement one improvement program after another but ignore the larger picture, which has to do with establishing enduring relationships between a company and its customers.

"When we bought Philips, the washing machines made in the Italian and German facilities didn't have one screw in common."

Many companies would like to think that if they become "world-class" in cost and quality, they'll win. But it takes more than that.

Why do you think so many international companies aren't managed as global businesses?

Top-level managers often incorrectly assume that since consumers differ from location to location, their businesses can't operate effectively as a unified entity. As a result, they see their industry as a mosaic of specialized businesses, each with its own unique constraints and its own finite opportunities. They look at these "little pictures" when they're creating strategies, and because it's so hard for them to back away from such close-up views, many can't entertain the notion that their industry could evolve into something different over time.

Until the mid-1980s, Whirlpool was no different. When we sat down to plan our future in 1987, it was the first time Whirlpool had ever asked itself what kind of company it wanted to become in the next decade or the next century. This lack of self-scrutiny isn't as surprising as it might sound. Whirlpool was successful, profitable, and reasonably secure in a domestic market that was already eliminating the marginal competitors. The world hadn't broken down our doors the way Japanese automakers had stormed Detroit, for example. If you're a market leader with no imminent catastrophe on the horizon, critical self-examination is more the exception than the rule. But we faced up to that challenge because we could see our future growing more difficult and complicated with each passing year.

How did Whirlpool come to the decision to globalize through this process of self-examination?

We didn't start with the answer that we were going to globalize. We started with the knowledge that if we stuck to the path we were on, the future

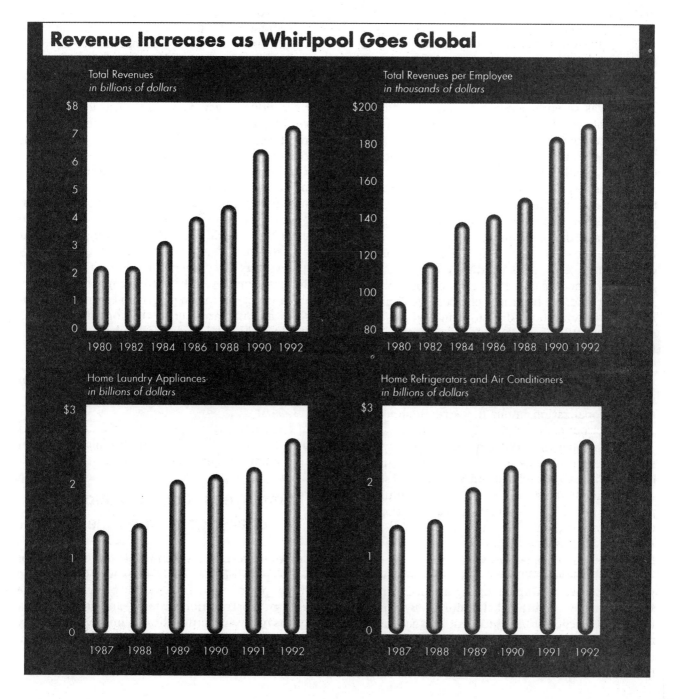

Revenue Increases as Whirlpool Goes Global

Total Revenues
in billions of dollars

Total Revenues per Employee
in thousands of dollars

Home Laundry Appliances
in billions of dollars

Home Refrigerators and Air Conditioners
in billions of dollars

would be neither pleasant nor profitable. Even though we had dramatically lowered costs and improved product quality, our profit margins in North America had been declining because everyone in the industry was pursuing the same course and the local market was mature. The four main players – Whirlpool, General Electric, Maytag, and White Consolidated, which had been acquired by Electrolux – were beating one another up every day.

So we explored our options. We could have restructured the company financially and paid out a lot to our shareholders. We also looked at diversifying the business. If the major-appliances industry didn't offer growth, were there other industries that did? We looked at other kinds of durable products. We looked at horizontal expansion and vertical expansion. And in the process, it became clear to us that the basics of managing our business and its process and product technologies were the same in Europe, North America, Asia, and Latin America. We were already very good at what we did. What we needed was to enter appliance markets in other parts of the world and learn how to satisfy different kinds of customers.

Before 1987, we didn't see the potential power our existing capabilities could give us in the global market because we had been limiting our definition of the appliance market to the United States. Obviously, this also limited our definition of the industry itself and the opportunity it offered. Our eight months of analysis turned up a great deal of evidence that, over time, our industry would become global, whether *we* chose to become global or not. With that said, we had three choices. We could ignore the inevitable – a decision that would have condemned Whirlpool to a slow death. We could wait for globalization to begin and then try to react, which would have put us in a catch-up mode, technologically and organizationally. Or we could control our own destiny and try to shape the very nature of globalization in our industry. In short, we could force our competitors to respond to us.

Before we began making moves on the global stage, Electrolux was out in front of us. It had bought White Consolidated and had acquired several appliance makers in Europe. But Electrolux appeared to be taking advantage of individual opportunities rather than following a coordinated plan. After our Philips acquisition, we also saw General Electric take some opportunistic steps.

Today, however, Whirlpool is the front-runner when it comes to implementing a pan-European strategy and leveraging global resources. By expanding our strategic horizon, not just our geographic reach, we've been able to build a global management capability that provides us with what we feel is a distinct competitive advantage. Clearly, this should enable us to improve returns to our shareholders significantly.

The notion that managers should think "global but act local" isn't a new thought. But it seems to have proven to be a lot easier said than done.

The key is getting your organization – and not just top management – to think globally. Most companies never get to that stage because their leaders haven't understood what they can and cannot do. A CEO can forcibly position his or her organization at the beginning of the path to globalization and help employees take the first step or two. But ultimately, employees must cover the miles with their own feet. CEOs have to create the processes and structures to get the organization going and keep people aimed in the right direction, but they cannot achieve anything requiring sustained effort by edict alone. Organizations have changed radically in recent years. When the chairman walked down the halls in my early years with Whirlpool, you found an office to duck into. According to the old paradigm of hierarchy and discipline, it wasn't his subordinates' place to question his decisions.

Employees today question and challenge all the time. They don't accept things at face value. As a result, a contemporary CEO has to convince employees why transformation is necessary. Then there's the critical step of persuading them that they can perform at what seem to be impossibly high levels. For a company to become a truly global enterprise, employees have to change the way they think and act, taking on progressively more responsibility and initiative until the company behaves globally in all of its parts – without the CEO cracking a whip.

So change at the global level requires more patience than many senior executives seem to have.

In our society, there seems to be an expectation that CEOs should be able fix things in a flash, even if that entails engineering an organizational trans-

"Employees today question and challenge all the time."

formation overnight. When we acquired Philips, for example, Wall Street analysts expected us to ship 500 people over to Europe, plug them into the plants and distribution systems, and give them six months or a year to turn the business around. They expected us to impose the "superior American way" of operating on the European organization.

But you have to remember that we were planning

to build a global enterprise, not a U.S. army of occupation. If you try to gain control of an organization by simply subjugating it to your preconceptions, you can expect to pay for your short-term profits with long-term resistance and resentment. That's why we chose another course. During that first year, I think we had two people from the United States working in Europe, and neither was a senior manager. By the end of the second year, we had maybe half a dozen U.S. managers there – again, none at senior levels. We listened and observed. We worked hard to communicate the company's vision, objectives, and philosophy to the European workforce. Building a shared base of understanding takes time, and we had to learn how to do that in a multilingual, multinational environment. Today we have 15,000 employees in Europe with only 10 from U.S. operations. They all report to European bosses, with the exception of Hank Bowman, executive vice president of Whirlpool Europe.

The hardest part of globalization is avoiding the temptation of trying to build Rome in a day. The purchase contract might state that you own the land. But you don't own the builders; they have to enter into the work contract of their own free will.

It's one thing to get senior managers to buy into globalization. How do you persuade employees throughout the organization?

Very slowly. You can't expect it to happen overnight. Bear in mind that we have many, many employees in our manufacturing plants and offices who have been with us for 25 or 30 years. They didn't sign up to be part of a global experience. Most of our North American employees joined Whirlpool to live in places like Benton Harbor, Michigan, or Clyde, Ohio – not Cassinetta, Italy. And a lot of our Italian colleagues didn't join Philips to work in the United States. In addition, we have a fairly large group of managers around the world, including me, who have acquired all of their experience in very traditional, hierarchical organizations. Suddenly we give them new things to think about and new people to work with. We tell people at all levels that the old way of doing business is too cumbersome.

Changing a company's approach to doing business is a difficult thing to accomplish in the United States, let alone globally. In the beginning, our North American Appliance Group didn't want any part of this new one-company vision. They saw it as a threat. They thought, "Whitwam's running off and spending a billion dollars in Europe, and that's going to take away resources that we need to succeed." In addition, when we first took engineers and manufacturing people from the United States to Europe to go through the plants, they would

spend all their time walking around and saying to themselves, "We do all of these things better at home." The Europeans who toured the U.S. facilities had the same parochial attitude. Neither group spent any time looking at what it could learn from the other.

During the first two years after we acquired the Philips business, we didn't concentrate on immediately improving performance. Instead, we spent a lot of time building trust and creating a common vision of our future. We deliberately encouraged our employees to think like owners so that they would come to believe that it was in their best interest to create a global organization. When we started the process, I told the organization that the only reason we existed as a large publicly held company was to create value for the shareholders. Now, the employee who works on a production line or in an office down the hall doesn't necessarily feel very good about that. Think about all the negative stereotypes of fickle shareholders. I explained that creating value for shareholders was the only way we could hope to create value for all our other stakeholders—employees, the communities we live in, our suppliers, and so on. Seeing the connections among interests is a key part of acquiring the global, one-company mentality we need. People don't see that vision just because you say it.

One of the approaches we're using to help employees feel like owners is to give them more responsibility. We need their heads thinking as well as their hands working. In some of our factories today, there is no supervisor on the floor. Teams made up of hourly workers hire new employees, create production line layouts, decide on production levels, and even make employee termination recommendations. They drive the quality process. That's a real change from how industrial companies have traditionally been managed.

Another approach is our compensation system. Its driving principle is "pay for performance." For example, essentially all of our U.S. employees received stock options in 1991. Some operations have gain-sharing programs, which allow employees to benefit directly from their own productivity and quality improvements. Other programs, including our 401K program, pay people—from top management to those on the factory floor—on the basis of whether or not we achieve corporate return-on-equity (ROE) or return-on-net-asset (RONA) goals. Employees at Whirlpool all understand what ROE and RONA mean, what drives those measurements, and how they're linked to shareholder value.

It's one thing to empower employees and communicate to them the importance of a common vision. But how did you translate that vision into the fabric of the organization—the day-to-day operations?

By helping employees throughout the organization do it for themselves. Six months after we acquired Whirlpool Europe, we brought 150 of our senior managers to Montreux, Switzerland, and we spent a week developing our global vision. What did it mean? What were the implications? The benefits of a week of "feel good" discussion didn't end when the meeting adjourned, because everyone who attended took away an assignment.

We made those 150 people accountable for educating all of our 38,000 people around the world. When going global, you have to communicate to everyone what the company vision is and what the long-term goals are. And then you have to follow through and design processes that force the interaction to continue. Every single employee must believe that there is great value in managing the company in an integrated way. To do that, you have to bring people together on real projects that tackle real problems or that explore opportunities on a cross-border basis.

To that end, managers at Montreux commissioned 15 projects – what we call One-Company Challenges. They ranged from creating a global product-strategy review process to developing a product-creation process worldwide to establishing a talent-pool system for human resources. Each of these challenges had to have a major impact on the realization of the vision. Each person who attended the meeting at Montreux went back home and gathered a team of employees from all levels of the company to work on a given project.

One of the One-Company Challenges was creating a companywide total-quality-management system, which we now call the Whirlpool Excellence System (WES). When we acquired Philips, we suddenly had one organization that focused on ISO-9000, the European total quality system, and another that focused on the U.S. Baldrige approach to quality.

Instead of imposing one approach on the entire organization, we created a cross-cultural team with members from Europe and North America and asked them to examine the best quality programs in the world, including ISO-9000 and Baldrige. The team then developed a global quality system that was appropriate for the new Whirlpool. The result was WES. It was this Euro-American group that then designed all the details of WES, including the training, communications, and deployment programs needed to create a common approach—a common language of quality—for all our operations.

A company needs to have one management process, one understanding of performance requirements. But it takes more than one person to design that management process if it is to be accepted, used, and turned into a competitive advantage. One of the best ways to change an inflexible mind-set is

to expose people to both challenges and the new ideas that can meet those challenges. When they've completed the work at hand, they've also gained a new sense of what is possible and desirable.

Was setting the process of globalization in motion at Montreux all that was required?

No. First, I should stress that we are not "there" yet. Although we've made a lot of progress, we are not yet a truly global organization. It will take more time to become one. Second, I want to make it clear that the art of management is not confined to orchestrating the creation of a bold vision, a great plan, or even one set of actions that causes the organization to face up to the need for change. It must also encompass relentless follow-through, meticulous attention to detail, and the establishment of personal accountability throughout the organization. These are not glamorous functions, perhaps, but like conscience and memory in a human being, they are all that protect good intentions from the distractions of the moment. Without them, the organization cannot maintain interest or momentum, and the initiative— no matter how spectacular the fireworks of the start-up—will fizzle out.

An initiative like globalization doesn't acquire momentum just because it is enormous. You have to push hard to overcome the initial inertia, and then you have to keep pushing so that friction—in the form of fear, uncertainty, and confusion—doesn't stop it in its tracks. We made a good start with the Montreux conference, then brought the same delegates together again the following year, this time in Washington, D.C. There, we studied the implications of WES and developed a whole new set of projects to continue to change company behavior. The Washington delegates were assigned the job of establishing 15 or 20 One-Company Teams to carry out the new projects.

You have to remind everyone over and over again that the new organization and its tenets aren't going to disappear. In addition to annual meetings of our top 150 managers, we have been bringing all development, marketing, and manufacturing leaders together twice a year for global product and technology reviews. We examine our product designs and how consumer needs affect them. Nothing came of it the first year in terms of actual global product creation. But you must expect that. Even if nothing concrete comes out of it, a preliminary session is still creating awareness that building a washing machine in Clyde, Ohio, isn't different from building one in Schorndorf, Germany.

You've made it sound as if an organization can globalize without outside help. Can a collection of regional organiza-

tions transform themselves in such short order without an injection of new skills or perspectives?

Absolutely not. When you change a company as rapidly as we did, you wake up one morning and suddenly realize that you don't have the skills and experience you need, and that includes the CEO. I had never run a multinational company until January 1, 1989, when we bought Philips. I've often said that there's only one thing that wakes me up in the middle of the night. It's not our financial performance or economic issues in general. It's worrying about whether or not we have the right skills and capabilities to pull the strategy off.

Traditionally, Whirlpool executives were homegrown. They came up through the ranks, and their knowledge and experience were limited to North America. Needless to say, we experienced some pain as we tried to match existing skills with emerging global management requirements. There were shortfalls at every level, including my own. In

"If you want to open the door to imagination and innovation, isn't it more useful to think of the 'fabric-care business'?"

some cases, they could be remedied by education and training programs. But some could only be remedied by recruiting from the outside.

It is a simple and inescapable fact that the skills and capabilities required to manage a global company are different from those required for a domestic company. But that's a leap we wanted to make, one that we chose in the interest of the company and its shareholders. And that tends to be a helpful factor when you're negotiating the hard parts: you know you're making these tough changes because you're dramatically increasing the overall opportunity for the company and its employees.

We've moved into a different realm, and there is no turning back. For example, there is no question in my mind that the person who replaces me as CEO and chairman will need experience managing in a foreign environment.

But isn't Whirlpool still planting flags too? For example, you have sales and distribution subsidiaries in Hong Kong, Thailand, and Taiwan, but you have no Asian manufacturing operations.

It may indeed look like flag planting, but that is not our intention. When you enter a new market, your sales organization, your knowledge of the local consumer, and your overall capabilities have to develop to a certain level before your business can hope to become a full-fledged, participating member of the global organization. That is the goal for our Asian business.

In 1988, we began in Asia with what I called the learning phase of the strategy, which resembled flag planting. But the purpose was to build a distribution system in Southeast Asia and to gain an understanding of the consumer. Within the past year, we have opened three regional offices in Asia: an office in Singapore to serve Southeast Asia, an office in Hong Kong to serve Greater China, and an office in Tokyo to serve Japan. We also currently have a design, engineering, and product development center in Singapore for all of Asia, which will help us reach the point at which we can manufacture in our own facilities in Asia. We know when and where these facilities will be established.

Our interim plan is to have a cadre of 80 to 100 people in the Singapore center who can call on Whirlpool resources around the world to shape and direct the plants and the products we produce in Asia. So when we start manufacturing in Asia, it will be as a global company. The beauty of starting a new operation like this one is that you don't have to overcome decades of managing habits that are ineffective when creating a global organization.

You seem to believe that truly global companies can leave their competitors in the dust by scoring breakthroughs in satisfying customers. Given that none of the major players in your industry has been able to pull away from the pack by dramatically slashing costs and improving quality, is this goal a fantasy?

No, it's not a fantasy. Whirlpool, its biggest competitors, and many companies in other industries have been too obsessed with cost and quality at the expense of other variables. You can't achieve a competitive advantage by focusing exclusively on cost and quality. Everybody in this industry is driving down the same cost and quality curve. And let's assume we're all going to become world-class performers. When that occurs, you'll have a handful of companies building great products that will last for 80 years, but no one will make any margins on them. And what then gives one product the edge over another?

Our strategy is based on the premise that world-class cost and quality are merely the ante – the price of being in the game at all. We have to provide a compelling reason other than price for consumers to buy Whirlpool-built products. We can do that only by understanding the consumer better than anyone else does and then translating our understanding into clearly superior product designs, features, and after-sales support. Our goal is for consumers to prefer the Whirlpool brand because it offers greater overall value than competing products. Achieving that goal requires taking a giant step back from our business and rethinking who our customers are and what their needs are. This may not sound earth-shattering, but it is. It means rethinking the very nature of the business.

All of us in this industry have been telling ourselves that we're in "the refrigerator business," "the washing-machine business," or "the range

"Our purpose at Whirlpool is to build a perfect product."

business." None of us saw a great deal of room for product innovation, which is undoubtedly why there hasn't been radical innovation in 30 years, apart from the microwave oven and the trash compactor. If you want to open the door to imagination and innovation, isn't it more useful to think of "the fabric-care business," "the food-preparation business," and "the food-preservation business"?

The starting point isn't the existing product; it's the function consumers buy products to accomplish. When you return to first principles, the design issues dramatically change. The microwave couldn't have been invented by someone who assumed he or she was in the business of designing a range. Such a design breakthrough required seeing that the opportunity is "easier, quicker food preparation," not "a better range."

We are applying these broader definitions in very direct ways. Organizationally, we have created what we call an advanced product development capability to serve markets around the world. Its charter is to look beyond traditional product definitions to the consumer processes for which products of the future will have to provide clear benefits.

Take "the fabric-care business," which we used to call the "washing-machine business." We're now studying consumer behavior from the time people take off their dirty clothes at night until they've been cleaned and ironed and hung in the closet. What are we looking for? The worst part of the process is not the washing and drying. The hard part is when you take your clothes out of the dryer and you have to do something with them – iron, fold, hang them up. Whoever comes up with a product to make this part of the process easier, simpler, or quicker is going to create an incredible market.

In other words, you're redefining what it means to satisfy the customer?

Our purpose at Whirlpool is to build a perfect product. With that as the point of departure, you can indeed take the notion of satisfying the customer to a completely different plane, and that's where breakthroughs become possible. Reaching such a plane means studying consumers' lifestyles to decipher what they might want even if they cannot articulate that desire in terms of a product request. Ten years ago, what consumer would have said he needed a CD player? Yet today records have virtually ceased to exist. Note that a company could have missed this breakthrough by asking the wrong questions of consumers or by narrowly interpreting consumer answers to good questions. In fact, consumers often speak in code. For example, our market research showed that customers wanted "clean refrigerators." Did this mean refrigerators that were easy to clean? No. We figured out that it meant refrigerators should look clean and hide finger marks, which helped us come up with a textured finish.

In rapidly segmenting consumer markets, you have to understand not only the lifestyles that people have today but also the kinds of lifestyles they are going to have five years from now and beyond. Can you tell me what you want your refrigerator to look like in the year 2010? Of course not. So we have to move away from the traditional approach of reacting to what customers say they want.

How do you do that?

One way is to develop close relationships with organizations in related businesses. For example, we have had a close, well-defined contractual relationship with Procter & Gamble in the United States. We have a long-standing relationship with them, exchanging basic information, ideas, and so forth. But now we have a more intense involvement at the development, engineering, and technology levels. We've established a formal partnership, in which one party is not worried about sharing proprietary information with the other.

We also work with Unilever in Brazil. Our engineers work together on product development, because both companies need to understand where the other is going over the long term. Unilever is working with other manufacturers too, because they can't be designing detergents ten years out for washing machines that can't use them.

Finally, we're moving toward a significant consolidation of our suppliers. Instead of working with five steel suppliers, for example, we want to have an important partnership with one or two. We want to have agreements that give us access to supplier technologies so that we can work together on process improvements in all of our plants. That's difficult to do with a broad supplier base.

As well as redefining customer satisfaction, are you redefining who your customers are?

Yes. There are numerous companies and many improvement experts who talk about satisfying internal customers. At Whirlpool, we once did the same, but we currently believe that internal cus-

"Complacency should have no part in any organization."

tomers do not exist. In fact, the only customer is the final consumer.

Companies that believe they have internal customers – that manufacturing is marketing's customer, for example – lose sight of what they're trying to accomplish as an organization. Today we're organized around multifunctional processes that are focused on serving the end user. Take, for instance, the product business teams we've established. They behave completely differently than functions at Whirlpool behaved in the past. We used to make a lot of dumb decisions in manufacturing for the sake of manufacturing. We don't do that nearly as much today. The product business teams are meant to divert the focus from the function to the consumer.

Of course, we have to be careful to prevent any weakening of functional excellence. The job of our vice president of manufacturing for the North American Appliance Group is to drive functional excellence. You have to keep benchmarking single functions even as you're working multifunctionally. It's a tough balance. But it's an ongoing effort.

How does this approach change the relationship between the manufacturer and the retailer?

Until you stop thinking about retailers as customers and start thinking about them as part of the process, you're going to be delivering the wrong kinds of products. For too long, we viewed the retailer as a customer.

Sears, Roebuck & Company is a great example. Until 1947 or so, Sears was our only retailer, and we still do in excess of a billion dollars of business with them. But for too much of our relationship, we treated Sears as a customer. We developed products to sit on their floors in competition with other products that were sitting on their floors. If they said, "I want this washing machine with three whistles and two bells, and I want it to be pink," we gave it to them. Little did we know that the con-

sumer didn't want machines with whistles. Today we don't treat each other as customer/supplier. We see ourselves as partners trying to solve a consumer need.

What is the end of the road? When will you know that Whirlpool has become global?

Strictly speaking, there is no end of the road. Continuous change is the essence of the global market. But there are some milestones I look forward to. For example, I'll know we've arrived as a global company when we have cross-border product business teams – one for washing machines, one for refrigerators, one for ovens, and so on – running all of our operations throughout the world. These teams, which will have functional and brand objectives, will identify the best opportunities and the most important problems to solve and then assess the related trade-offs.

There will also come a day when we'll identify a location where the best skills in a certain product area should be concentrated, and that place will become the development center for that type of product. But here's an important distinction: while we may have only one major design center for a given product, not everyone associated with that product will have to be located there. For example, the development center for refrigeration products may be in Benton Harbor, but we may also have people working for that center in China or Italy. Think about the communication technologies that exist today. People don't need to sit next to each other anymore to work together on the same project. In fact, it's no longer appropriate or effective to design organizations that way. Instead, global competitors will increasingly make use of "virtual teams," as we – and others – are already doing.

Admittedly, we're not an "old hand" at virtual teams yet. But we have used them effectively. For example, we recently developed a super-efficient, chlorofluorocarbon-free refrigerator that won a contest sponsored by a group of U.S. utilities. We used insulation technology from our European business, compressor technology from our Brazilian affiliates, and manufacturing and design expertise from our U.S. operation. If we had still been the kind of company we were in 1987, we couldn't have pulled off this kind of cross-border teamwork.

As we look to the future, perhaps the greatest trap will be our own successes. Success has a way of drawing attention away from the present and future and onto the past. The history of business is littered with companies that were short-term successes. Complacency should have no part in any organization. It is the responsibility of leaders to manage against it.

The Son Also Surprises

Allied with Ford Motor Co. in a Nonclassic *Keiretsu*,
Manufacturer George Loranger Seeks Success in Hungary.

Neil King Jr.

George Loranger races the engine of his Ford Scorpio and screeches onto one of Budapest's busiest streets. Just as quickly, he whips a U-turn and heads the opposite direction.

"That's a taxi-cab move," he explains, shifting into third gear. Speeding through the farmlands west of Hungary's capital, Mr. Loranger flips on his radar detector and makes a quick call to the office to say he's running a little late.

The 47-year-old CEO of Loranger Mfg. Corp. is 4,500 miles from Warren, Pa., the sleepy town where his father founded a parts business in the family basement in 1950. Forty-five years later, the son is definitely not tiptoeing through the business brambles that characterize much of the new Eastern Europe. For four years now, Mr. Loranger has been making a lot of unusual moves—and not just on the highway.

Most likely the boldest move was his 1991 decision to make his family's $50 million plastic-parts company a player in international business. Along the way, Mr. Loranger has wagered almost $7 million on a deal in Hungary and become the proud owner of a 600-acre former Soviet military base. Indeed, it's on that base 50 miles from Budapest, amid grazing sheep and the hulks of airplane hangars, that Loranger Mfg.'s Hungarian factory sits. "The big . . . guys show up and say, 'What's a small fry like you doing here?'" relates Mr. Loranger. "And I say, 'Look, we saw an opportunity and we took it.'"

The opportunity that Mr. Loranger seized was a rare but telling partnership with Ford Motor Co. In an Eastern European version of Japan's *keiretsu* system, when Ford made a manufacturing move into Hungary, Loranger Mfg., an established supplier in the U.S., went along. Mr. Loranger figured that expansion—and continuing to satisfy a key customer—was going to be crucial to his company's growth. Relations between

Ford and Loranger Mfg. in Hungary have been, at times, like some of Eastern Europe's back roads: rough. Nearly everything, from basic negotiations to the prompt delivery of high-quality parts, has taken far longer than either partner had originally hoped. "Go slow and assume nothing" has become the guiding adage for the partnership. But neither company regrets the linkage, and both say it should soon prove profitable. "Of course, there are still ups and downs," concedes Bruce Jacobson, Ford's plant manager in Hungary. "But what we've both come to realize is that the launch period will always be tough, especially in a place as challenging as this."

"Any contract can be broken. The important thing is to know whom you're dealing with."

When Ford first suggested in 1989 that Loranger Mfg. follow the automaker to Europe, George Loranger had already been thinking beyond U.S. borders. Two years earlier he had visited Japan and returned to the U.S. impressed by the cooperation between big manufacturers and their small, local suppliers. So when Ford finally opted to build an ignition-systems plant in Hungary and offered Mr. Loranger a long-term contract to come along, he was primed.

Nevertheless, launching into Hungary demanded new moves and attitudes in a company whose stock in trade had been supplying high-tech plastic parts to a complement of U.S. companies that included Ford, Du Pont, and IBM.

In Hungary, government officials at first were little impressed by overtures from an unknown (to them) such as Loranger. Financing was tight; talent limited. And good factory space was incredibly scarce. Back in the U.S., skepticism ran high in Warren, located about two hours' drive southwest of Buffalo. Some of the firm's 425 employees feared losing their jobs. Others, in management, saw the Hungarian venture as a bottomless pit, sucking in much-needed money from other projects. Even among his business peers, Mr. Loranger received only lukewarm support. "I've had a lot of pats on the back and a lot of that-a-boys," he chuckles. "But I've also had a lot of 'My God, I wouldn't do that.'"

To keep moving ahead while avoiding fatal mistakes, Mr. Loranger has employed the kind of crafty fleet-footedness that frequently eludes firms larger and less agile than his. He deliberately kept simple his initial chats with government officials and other people around Budapest. He took his wife, and often his children, along. He stuck to friendly talk about family—and life in the U.S. and Hungary. "For a small guy especially, relationships are everything," he explains. "Any contract can be broken. The important thing is to know whom you're dealing with."

In the early days, the business was run out of his Budapest apartment, where he and a cadre of employees kept the kitchen table littered with faxes, coffee cups, and piles of contracts. Last year, Mr. Loranger moved to Hungary and now spends nearly 70% of his time overseeing the alliance with Ford. Loranger Mfg. has an office in Budapest and a plush headquarters above its factory in Székesfehérvár, 50 miles from Budapest and minutes from Ford's ignition-systems plant.

Obtaining that factory itself was an adventure. Mr. Loranger found the building on the edge of an army base built by the Soviets and liked the structure immediately. The trouble was that many others also coveted the plant. Mr. Loranger did a little homework and found that the Hungarian government really wanted to sell the whole base, a complex of 150 buildings, acres of weeds, and a few miles of crumbling roads. After eight months of negotiation, a deal was struck. Mr. Loranger got his plant as part of a package, believed to be the first of its kind, which called for Loranger Mfg. and the government to jointly develop the complex as an industrial and education park.

The Soviets were slow to leave the site—but apparently quick to pilfer from it. Toilets, telephone lines, electrical switches, doors, bathtubs, and even half a building disappeared from under the noses of government guards. Mr. Loranger fired the guards. He replaced them with demolition workers, carpenters and plumbers. Restoration began.

Taking on a major property-development project would seem a heavy, potentially crushing burden for a small company entering Eastern Europe. But so far the project does seem to be succeeding. Philips Electronics N.V. and Royal Dutch/Shell Group are breaking ground at the former military base, as are half a dozen other international firms. "Creativity is an absolute requirement for doing business here," states Mr. Loranger. "So is the willingness to take on risk." But the biggest need is for patience. "If I'd had to show quarterly profits, my family would have fired me a long time ago."

Getting his own plant in shape took nearly a year. Equipment leases languished for months. Some machines, once in place, broke down and had to be retooled. Ford then delayed acceptance of the parts Mr. Loranger made, claiming they didn't meet quality standards. Even today, thanks to what Mr. Loranger calls the "European old-boys' club," the cost for raw materials remains so high that he continues to draw on suppliers in the U.S.

Retaining good workers may be Mr. Loranger's biggest current problem. He employs nearly 150 people at Székesfehérvár, and he continues to lose many of the most qualified. The reason: good accountants, technical engineers, and financial experts are in short supply across Eastern Europe; consequently, companies feed off each other.

He is, however, moving to ease the shortage. Along with consultant Donald Corey, a former human-resources director at Loranger, and administrators from Pennsylvania State University, the company is trying to transform the complex's former military barracks into a technical institute for the training of accountants, engineers, and managers. Ford and Shell have expressed interest in supporting the institute. Programs could get underway this spring.

In the meantime, Ford remains Loranger's main customer, accounting for about 90% of sales. But theirs is not the classic *keiretsu* arrangement. Ford has no equity in Loranger's Hungarian operation. And the business bonds between the two companies are bound to loosen as Loranger expands its European customer base. It already supplies parts in Europe directly to General Electric Co. and indirectly to Intel Corp. By 1996, it hopes to have lowered Ford's share of its European sales to 50%.

"A lot of people talk about branching out. Only a few really act."

Peace of mind was what both Loranger and Ford sought from the start. Loranger Mfg. clearly would not have assumed the risk of an overseas venture without a long-term contract from Ford. And for Ford, despite the venture's initial difficulties, the companionship of a trusted supplier has brought comfort.

"It is not easy to set up a place like Hungary and to deal with new people on all sides," says Ford's Mr.

Jacobson. "So it can mean a lot to have a familiar face nearby. . . . This is also part of Ford's larger strategy to reduce [the number of companies in] our supply base and to encourage our core suppliers to grow along with us."

Meanwhile, fine-tuning continues at Loranger's Hungarian plant—and not only to improve its ability to do its own tooling. Loranger has put a premium on individual initiative and plans soon to implement on ownership deal that will give employees 10% of the company. It's truly a foreign idea to many employees in Hungary.

"Our principle is that you can achieve the necessary efficiency only by recognizing the importance of the individual within the organization," explains Istvan Szabo, the quality-control manager in Hungary. "But that concept is still strange here, and few workers are prepared to stick their necks out to change something they believe to be wrong."

More than a year has passed since Loranger Mfg. began producing and assembling parts in Hungary—and five years since Mr. Loranger first contemplated a leap into Europe. Mr. Loranger no longer worries much that the gamble might fail. The Hungarian operation was expected to generate nearly $10 million in sales in 1994—and it hopes to see a profit within two or three years.

"Granted, it hasn't been easy," Mr. Loranger says near the end of another long day. "Will this be a huge success? That remains to be seen. What's clear, though, is that the manufacturing business demands that you have a foot in more than one place. A lot of people talk about branching out. Only a few really act."

Transnational Management Systems: An Emerging Tool for Global Strategic Management

 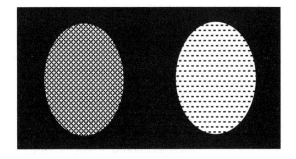

Sean B. Eom

Ph.D., Professor of Management, Southeast Missouri State University

Introduction

One of the most significant business and economic trends of the late 20th century is the stateless corporation. A recent issue of *Business Week* reported (May 14, 1990, cover page) that a new type of company is emerging. Global companies conduct research wherever necessary, develop products in several countries, promote key executives regardless of nationality, and even have shareholders on three continents.

Many global companies are making decisions with little regard to national boundaries. Many heads of the world's largest companies believe that the trend toward statelessness is unmistakable and irreversible due to the following advantages:[9]

(1) *Solving trade problems*—Northern Telecommunication of Canada could win Japanese contracts by establishing manufacturing facilities in the U.S. because Japan favors U.S. over Canadian companies due to the politically sensitive U.S.-Japanese trade gap.

(2) *Avoiding political problems*—A German company, BASF, has moved its cancer immune system research to Cambridge, Massachusetts, U.S. to avoid Germany's stiff environmental regulations concerning animal rights, safety, and a clean environment.

(3) *Sidestepping regulatory hurdles*—Smith-Kline of the U.S. and Britain's Beecham have merged to avoid licensing and regulatory hurdles in the U.S. and Western Europe.

(4) *Winning technology breakthroughs*—Becoming a stateless corporation could mean the company will be better able to scour the globe for leading scientific and product development ideas.

Reprinted with permission from *SAM Advanced Management Journal*, Spring 1994, pp. 22-27. © 1994 by the Society for Advancement of Management, Vinton, VA 24179.

With this changing global environment, a new type of support system, transnational management support systems (TMSS), is emerging. Computer-based management support systems are playing vital roles in the complex decision making process at multinational corporations (MNCs). For example, when Dow Chemical noticed the recent decline in European demand for a certain solvent product, the decision support system at the company responded quickly to suggest the reduced production of the chemical product at a German plant and a shift from the idle production capacity to another chemical product that was imported from the U.S.[9]

The purpose of this paper is to inform academicians and practicing managers of the emergence of transnational management support systems by:

- reviewing prior research on the development and applications of global management support systems;
- suggesting the definition and architecture of TMSS;
- describing unique functional requirements of TMSS in supporting operational, tactical, and strategic decision making processes of MNCs; and
- providing some practical benefits to the practicing managers and pointing out what managers need to know to introduce or improve their organization's TMSS.

The Emergence of Transnational Management Support Systems

In the early 1970s, Decision Support Systems (DSS) focused on helping an individual user in an organization in a single location. In the 1980s, many companies shifted their attention to the application of DSS technology to large-scale organizational and global decision making. For example, General Motors, in association with EDS, developed PLANETS, a modeling system for business planning. The automotive section of GM manages the thousands of products that are manufactured and distributed by several hundred facilities worldwide.[1] The Decision Support Systems of GM supports analysts and managers in making decisions, either independently or simultaneously regarding expansion at existing plants, buying or building new facilities, and the allocation of production volume among existing plants, to mention a few types of decisions. GM has developed the 80 major applications of this Decision Support Systems software, resulting in

over a \$1 billion cost savings and approximately 2% or 3% capital expenditure saving.

The forces unleashed by the telecommunication and microcomputer revolutions over the past decade have brought two significant phenomena: increasing global interdependence and internationalization of business firms. Furthermore, telecommunications are significantly changing the traditional ways of manufacturing, marketing, financing, decision making, and so on. For example, International Aero Engines was established in 1984 as a joint venture of five world leaders in jet engine manufacturing to produce the turbofan engine of the Airbus.[16] The companies are Pratt & Whitney (U.S.), Rolls-Royce (U.K.), MTU (Germany), Fiat Aviazione (Italy), and Aero Engines (Japan). Each of the five shares responsibilities for producing particular engine modules or sections to be assembled as one final product. In the manufacturing process, each location generates large volumes of data such as master parts lists, bills of materials, and parts catalogs. Further, each plant has access to the data generated from other countries. Without the data network, it may not have been possible for five companies in five countries to function as one.

The management of of multinational corporations' decision making must deal with extreme complexities due to the multiplicity of currencies, taxes, languages, and sovereign governments. Decision Support Systems alone are not sufficient to handle such complexities. Effective management of global complexities necessitates the integration of three types of decision technology.

The Definition and Architecture of TMSS. Transnational management support system is an evolving concept for the decision making process of MNCs. TMSS is an integrated system of decision support systems (DSS), expert systems (ES), and executive information systems (EIS), TMSS supports the operational, tactical, and strategic decision making process of MNCS in an attempt to integrate organizational decision making across functional fields, planning horizons (long-, medium-, and short-range) and national boundaries.

The TMSS can be best designed as a network of management support systems (DSS, ES, and EIS that links a set of management support systems (MSS) in the headquarters with a set in each foreign and domestic subsidiary. Management support systems in each subsidiary consist of an array of Executive Information Systems, Expert Systems, and Decision Support Systems. The decision support systems in the TMSS may include individual DSS, group decision support systems, distributed decision making systems, and organizational DSS in each operating country. The functions of Executive Information Systems may be even more important in the management of MNCs. Tracking performances of the consolidated corporation as well as each subsidiary against plans is, indeed, the critical activity of the top management of MNCs.

Unique Functional Requirements of TMSS

Complexities of global decision making require several distinctive functional requirements of TMSS as well as the generic functional requirements of DSS, experts systems, executive information systems in a uni-national environment. Generic functions of DSS, for example, include on-line retrieval, display and manipulation of data (current, historical, internal, and external), inventing decision alternatives, and choosing alternatives based on the computation of the consequences of each possible decision. Several distinctive functional requirements of multinational decision support are classified into two levels: operational and strategic.

Operational Management Support Requirements.
• Requirement #1: Global Data Access. To many global companies, on-line access to corporate data has already become vital for their success in managing numerous overseas subsidiaries. An essential function of TMSS should be to allow corporate managers desktop, on-line access to corporate statistics in order to monitor global operations from headquarters. Global networks of MNCs provide real-time communication links with foreign and domestic subsidiaries through an all-digital system integrating voice, data, video, and video conferencing systems. Many MNCs are progressing toward complete worldwide linkage of corporate data bases in foreign marketing and manufacturing facilities. Texas Instruments' network, for example, allows 76,000 employees to access data bases in 20 data centers around the world. According to the company's senior vice president of information systems [12, p. 49], "Whenever we report our financial data, as soon as someone hits an enter key—wherever they are in the world—that information comes back to a central data base from which we can do our

financial rollups at the general ledger and forecast levels."
• Requirement #2: Global Consolidated Reporting. Numerous accounting and financial reports need to be integrated into a global consolidated report. Consolidating financial statements is a crucial activity for sensitivity analysis of any multinational financial decision making. Thus, TMSS should be able to provide accurate, timely information for planning, controlling, and budgeting. Other reports for internal control include inventory, receivables, sales, cash flow by currency, cash and capital expenditure budgets, and product line income statements for each foreign subsidiary, the parent company, and the consolidated entity.

Tactical/Strategic Management Support Requirements. At tactical or strategic levels, a host of complex management tools are needed to deal with various multinational management issues such as risk management, conflict management among host and home governments, parent companies, and foreign subsidiaries.
• Requirement #3: Providing Effective Means of Communication between the MNC Headquarters and Its Subsidiaries. Strategic planning involves participation from all units of the corporation including headquarters, foreign subsidiaries, regional offices, divisions, and groups. Although theory suggests that global strategic management requires stimulative inputs from planners at functional, business, and corporate levels of each operating country, and that the interactive/iterative flow of the decision making process is extremely important for strategic planning of MNCs as well as domestic corporations, empirical research found no such interactions through a formalized pattern of top-down/bottom-up interactions.[13] For example, Ghetman investigated how MNCs make decisions to restructure their international strategic portfolio or close plants overseas and concluded that "the foreign subsidiaries seem to carry most of the decision making effort for their own plant closures, while for strategic portfolio readjustments during which they change owners, they are not consulted."[7]

To facilitate the organization-wide planning process, TMSS should provide an effective means of communication between the headquarters and its subsidiaries. The advancement in management support systems technology during the last two decades certainly facilitates multinational planning. The technology includes distributed decision making (DDM) systems[15] and four group decision support system alternatives (local area decision network, wide area decision network, decision room, and teleconferencing systems) suggested by DeSanctis and Gallupe.[3] Due to the decreasing cost of computer hardware and software and the acceptance of a worldwide standard, teleconferencing (video conferencing) systems have become a powerful tool for executive meetings, R&D, and many other applications. In the near future, we expect to see more advanced forms of video conferencing systems that are capable of translating voice and characters simultaneously.

• Requirement #4: Providing Planning Risk Management Support. Worldwide integration is characterized as global unification of functional strategies (production, finance, marketing, and R&D) through a network of subsidiaries in which R&D, production, and marketing tasks are centrally allocated and coordinated to achieve global economies of scale.[4,9] Due to the social and political diversity of operating countries, MNCs must adapt their planning to many country-specific factors. To be an effective strategic decision support tool, TMSS must aid this process of finding a proper balance between integrative and adaptive planning methods.

Global Strategic Management Support. Supporting the strategic management process is the core role of TMSS. The strategic planning and control systems at MNCs aim at rationalizing resources more effectively on a global basis

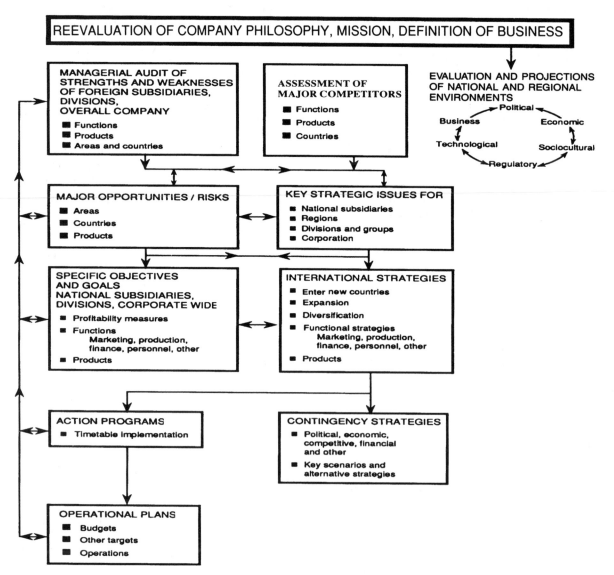

Figure 1. Model for Comprehensive Strategic Planning for Multinational Corporations

to respond to rapid environmental changes, such as increased political and foreign exchange risks and global competition.[5] The strategic planning process begins with evaluating the company's philosophy, mission, and definition of business (Step A). Step B is a realistic and subjective evaluation of the firm's present strengths and weaknesses and an assessment of major competitors. An analysis of major opportunities and risks and the specification of key issues for entire corporate units (Step C) must precede Step D, formulating objectives for each unit of the MNC. The specific objectives are to increase the firm's return on investment by expanding investment in profitable product lines and divesting country and product lines that do not meet the firm's mission and definition of business. The next step is the choice of a strategy among four generic international competitive strategies—global high-share strategies, global niche strategies, national high-shares strategies, and national niche strategies. (For a detail of each strategy, see.[10] Step E is the formulation of various global competitive strategies including new entry, expansion, diversification, and functional strategies, based on specific goals of corporate headquarters and foreign subsidiaries. A subsequent step is the formulation of contingency strategies, action programs, and operational plans (Step F).

One of the objectives of DSS is to support a whole range of decision making processes. In Step A, scanning the international environments (political, economic) was the crucial activity. The economic and technological domains of the external environment have been ranked as the most crucial factors in making strategic decisions by top management of many MNCs in the U.S. and Europe.[9] A recent survey revealed that international environmental scanning activities had been integrated as a part of information systems to regularly monitor a broad range of environmental and foreign risk factors.[14] Many executives reported their frustrations due to the "inability to organize for environmental scanning" and "delay between external developments and interpretation." To satisfy these needs, transnational MSS should be able to effectively collect, analyze, and interpret environmental scanning data to extract meaningful information. Therefore, in Step A, EIS subsystems of the TMSS should be a major element in the top management's MSS.

In Steps B, C, and D, global decision support systems with international teleconferencing systems can increase the effectiveness of these processes. In Step E, corporate goals are converted into global strategies, which can be most effectively supported by the TMSS. In this conversion process from specific objectives to specific strategies, the multiplicity of the economic, political, legal and cultural forces in global environments must be taken into consideration. In addition, management decisions regarding global operations are further complicated by the multiplicity of the environments.

When making any global decision, several global risks must be considered, including political, foreign exchange, and tax risks.

• Requirement #5: Conflict and Political Risk Management Support. As world markets consolidate, the trend will accelerate, raising some critical questions about sovereignty, national interest, and potential conflicts between companies and their own governments. The focus of conflict management in MNCs is not on conflicts among individual managers or executives, or intraorganizational conflicts. Rather, it is on interorganizational conflict among MNCs, host governments, home governments, and multilateral organizations.

As Gladwin and Walter noted, effective conflict management must be a continuous and major element in the line manager's DSS to support the process of scanning, forecasting, design, and choice.[8] In the scanning stage, it is critical to scan, filter, and interpret information concerning the potential emergence and actual character of conflict.[8] In the next stage of forecasting, information gathered in the previous stages is used to predict the potency and demands of various interest groups. After that, alternative sets of means and corresponding effects are invented and evaluated to select a best choice.

The integration of political assessment into global management decision making has been an important subject in all functional areas of multinational business management such as investment and divestment, capital budgeting, plant location, and financing and capital structuring.

In addition to foreign exchange and political risks, tax implications complicate the decision making process. A further complication arises from the combined effects of the various risks. A global decision will involve some or all risks, which may be conflicting. For instance, a decrease in the level of tax risk as a result of a certain decision may result in an increase in the level of other risks.

• Requirement #6: Global Foreign Exchange

Risk Management Support. A mix of freely floating (no government intervention), managed floating, and fixed exchange rates characterizes today's international monetary system. Relative currency values change every day. Consequently, an essential task of management of global corporations is to minimize the potentially negative impact of these fluctuations. There are numerous examples of real-world companies which were forced out of business due to mismanagement of the foreign exchange risks such as the British company Laker Airways. From 1979 to 1982, the company's failure to anticipate and deal with the substantial exchange rate change between the U.S. dollar and British pound resulted in the company's bankruptcy.[17]

The long-run health of an MNC can be best maintained by emphasizing management of economic exposure. This requires integrated efforts involving various functional strategies. TMSS can support the global financing decision process by recommending either a matching strategy or a portfolio approach.[6]

Essential Steps For Designing And Implementing TMSS

Since TMSS is an evolving concept, there are no current examples of the ideal system with all the functional capabilities described here. Managers need to know several essential steps to introduce or improve their organization's TMSS:
1) There are several prerequisites: well-functioning TPS, MIS, individual DSS, and group DSS. If your organization is in the early stage of information technology adoption, any attempt to build TMSS should be avoided.
2) Global telecommunication networks and distributed database management systems (DBMS) are the next level of prerequisites.
3) Once the two levels of prerequisites are met, organizational DSS must be designed and implemented in each unit (headquarters and each foreign subsidiary. Carter et al. [2, p. 4] define organizational DSS as "a DSS that is used by individuals or groups at several workstations in more than one organizational unit who make varied (interrelated but autonomous) decisions using a common set of tools." The practical step-by-step guidance to implementing organizational DSS is clearly discussed in their book.[2]
4) The final stage is building integrated TMSS that consists of a network of individual DSS, group DSS, distributed decision making systems, organizational DSS, expert systems, and EIS.

Practical Benefits of TMSS

TMSS is a viable weapon for improving the effectiveness of global strategic and tactical management processes by:
1) analyzing the multinational, multifunctional, or multibusiness consequences of the decisions;
2) evaluating the trade-offs between long- and short-term effects of a decision that seeks to balance the conflicting goals of long- and short-range planning;
3) facilitating the interactive and iterative flow of the multinational strategic decision making process.

Conclusions

Today's global manager can no longer be the hunch-player with myopic or tunnel vision who used to rely heavily on intuition and judgment. Global managers need global vision. The complexities of global decision making in MNCs requires the large array of decision technologies we have been developing since the early 1970s. The TMSS are the last frontiers of computer-based decision technologies to be conquered as we enter the age of the global village. Multinational decision making presents today's managers with unprecedented challenges that can only be managed properly by this emerging tool, the transnational management support system.

Dr. Eom has published over 25 articles concerning decision support systems and expert systems and serves on the editorial boards of the Journal of Global Information Management *and the* Journal of Financial and Strategic Decisions.

Endnotes
1. Breitman, R. L. and Lucas, J. M., "PLANETS: A Modeling System for Business Planning," *Interfaces*, Vol. 17, 1987, pp. 94–106.
2. Carter, G. M., Murray, M. P., Walker, R. G., Walker, W. E., *Building Organizational Decision Support Systems*, Boston, MA: Academic Press, 1992.
3. DeSanctis, G. and Gallupe, B., "Group Decision Support Systems: A New Frontier," *Data Base*, Vol. 16, No. 2, Winter 1985, pp. 3–10.
4. Doz, Y. L. and Prahalad, C. K., "Patterns of the Strategic Control within Multinational Corporations," *Journal of International Business Studies*, Vol. 15, No. 2, Fall 1984, pp. 55–72.
5. Dymsza, W. A., "Global Strategic Planning: A Model and Recent Developments," *Journal of International Business Studies*, Vol. 15, No. 2, Fall 1984, pp. 169–184.
6. Eom, H. B., Lee, S. M., Snyder, C. A., and Ford, N.

F., "A Multiple Criteria Decision Support System for Global Financial Planning," *Journal of Management Information Systems*, Vol. 4, No. 3, Winter 1987, pp. 94–113.

7. Ghertman, M., "Foreign Subsidiary and Parents' Roles During Strategic Investment and Divestment Decisions," *Journal of International Business Studies*, Vol. 19, No. 1, Spring 1988, pp. 47–67.

8. Gladwin, T. N. and Walter, I., *Multinational Under Fire: Lessons in the Management of Conflict*, New York: John Wiley and Sons, 1980.

9. Holstein, W. J., Reed, S., Kapstein, J., Vogel, T., and Joseph Weber, J., "The Stateless Corporation," *Business Week*, May 14 1990, pp. 98–105.

10. Leontiases, J. C. *Multinational Corporate Strategy*, Lexington, MA: Lexington Books, D. C. Heath and Company, 1985.

11. O'Connell, J. J. and Zimmerman, J. W., "Scanning the International Environment," California Management Review, Vol. 22, No. 2, 1979, pp. 15–23.

12. Pantages, A. "TI's Global Window," *Datamation*, September 1, 1989, pp. 49–52.

13. Pearce II, J. A., Robinson, R. B., Jr., *Strategic Management: Strategy Formulation and Implementation*, Homewood, Ill: Richard D. Irwin, 1985.

14. Preble, J. F., Rau, P. A., Reichel, A., "The Environmental Scanning Practices of U.S. Multinationals in the Late 1980's," *Management International Review*, Vol. 28, No. 4, Fourth Quarter 1988, pp. 4–14.

15. Rathwell, M. A. and Burns, A., "Information Systems Support for Group Planning and Decision Making Activities," *MIS Quarterly*, Vol. 9, No. 3, September 1985, pp. 254–270.

16. Ryerson, W. M., and Pitts, J. C., "A Five-Nation Data Network for Aircraft Manufacturing," *Telecommunications*, October 1989, pp. 45–48.

17. Srinirasulu, S. L., "Currency Denomination of Debt: Lessons From Rolls-Royce and Laker Airways," *Business Horizons*, Vol. 26, September-October 1983, pp. 19–21.

Repatriation: Up, Down or Out?

Global employees can best contribute to a company's bottom line if their return is tied to business strategy.

Charlene Marmer Solomon

Charlene Marmer Solomon is a Los Angeles-based contributing editor for PERSONNEL JOURNAL.

Nina and David Cissell are the lucky ones. For 2 1/2 years, David was business director for the chemical division in Brussels for Monsanto Corporation—a company that takes international human resources planning seriously. Consequently, when the Cissells returned to St. Louis, they were among the first participants in Monsanto's repatriation program.

They attended a repatriation training program in which they learned what they should expect upon re-entry. They were warned about the culture shock of returning home, about how colleagues and friends might be different, about how the office environment might have altered, about how much the expatriate experience had changed them and their three children.

Monsanto's program included an opportunity for the Cissells to showcase their new knowledge in a debriefing session. Cissell invited five people to a meeting and shared with them what it was like to have lived abroad—personally and professionally—and what it was like to return home. Nevertheless, he and his family admit there were times when they still felt as if they were in a timewarp. They returned to familiar surroundings in the United States, but they were quite changed.

Luckily, the Cissells were surrounded by people who took an interest and maintained it as the expats transitioned back into American life. Cissell was promoted to the position of director of finance for the Latin America World area. The vast majority of re-entering expatriates don't experience similar HR planning and repatriation programs to help them.

"Repatriation has been the classic stepchild in the international HR management," says Nancy Adler, professor of organizational behavior and cross-cultural management at McGill University, a noted researcher and author of articles and books, including most recently: *Competitive Frontiers: Women Managers in a Global Economy* (Blackwell Publishers, 1944) and *Strategic Human Resource Management: A Global Perspective,* (published in *Human Resource Management in International Comparison,* deGruyter, 1990).

If any aspect of globalization points out the complexities of international assignments as well as the systemic weakness and lack of planning within the international HR function, it's repatriation. Repatriation is usually overlooked instead of being seen as the final link in an integrated, circular process that connects good selection, cross-cultural preparation, global career management and completion of the international business objective. Indeed, instead of employees coming home to share their global knowledge with others and encourage additional high performers to go the same route, expatriates face an entirely different scenario.

Often when they return home after a stint abroad (during which time they have typically been autonomous, well-compensated and celebrated as a big fish in a little pond), they face an organization that doesn't know what they've done for the past several years, doesn't know how to use their new knowledge and, worse yet, doesn't care. In the worst cases, re-entering employees have to scrounge for jobs, or companies will create stand-by positions which don't use the expat's skills and capabilities and fail to maximize the business investment the company has made. The situation often is exacerbated by downsized and restructured organizations.

Furthermore, the expat has changed dramatically and wants to share his or her experiences. Usually few people are interested. Add to this unrealistic expectations by the expats, their having lost touch with the domestic office's technological and personnel changes, and the enormous family upheaval, and you begin to have an idea of the tremendous challenges awaiting individuals as they re-enter the United States after assignments abroad.

Statistics bring the situation into bold relief: According to the 1994 Global Relocation Trends Survey Report published in January 1995 by the National Foreign Trade Council and global relocation management specialists Windham International, while 75% of the companies surveyed address repatriation (up from 45%), "repatriation services" can range from simply shipping household goods (97%) to homefinding assistance (55%) to career development (33%). The 110 surveyed companies, which employ collectively more than 24,000 expats, said that given the massive 30% increase in the numbers of expatriates going on international assignment, lack of job guarantee is one of the most critical challenges they face.

In research J. Stewart Black and Mark E. Mendenhall cite in their book, *Global Assignments: Successfully Expatriating and Repatriating International Managers* (by Black, Hal B. Gregersen and Mendenhall, published by Jossey-Bass, 1992), 60% to 70% of repatriating employees didn't know what their positions would be before they returned home. Sixty percent said their organizations were vague about repatriation, about their new roles within the company and about their career progression. Moreover, they felt the firms disregarded their difficulties in adjusting back to life in the United States. When American expats found jobs within their companies, 46% had reduced autonomy and authority. And contrary to the reason that many Americans take international assignments—the idea of advancement—only 11% were promoted. Black and Mendenhall found that 77% of Americans actually took jobs at lower levels than their international assignments.

It's no wonder that 10% of expatriates leave their company within a year after returning home and 14% leave between two and three years, according to the Global Relocation Trends Survey Report. These figures aren't only unfortunate, they reveal poor HR planning and a dramatic loss of talent for the business that sent these individuals.

"I don't think people really understand yet that assignments are a process," says Carol Jones, Monsanto's human resources specialist in international assignments. "They pick it up in the middle. They don't think about why they're sending out the person, what will make that person successful, what they're expecting. They don't realize that successful assignments begin with repatriation planning at the time of expatriation."

In other words, rather than looking at the process in fragmented pieces, assignments have a higher chance at success when the practitioners link the elements together from start to finish. According to Adler, you should be able to see how any one part of the process links with others. The elements of the process include: assessment selection, company orientation, cross-cultural training, dual career support, relocation/move assistance, in-country orientation and support, development, re-entry planning and assistance, repatriation and reintegration.

Understanding international assignments as a process, and realizing that planning helps its success, is critical for human resources professionals. "Clearly the caliber of human resources planning that's done by a company really shows up in the international assignment area," says Eric Campbell, director of global human resources for Avon Products, Inc. "In a company that does excellent HR planning, these types of situations [poor repatriation] don't arise as much. Even though individuals may not be high potentials, if they're considered strong enough for international assignments, the groups that sent them in the first place will be held accountable for their repatriation."

On the other hand, he says, if you're a company that doesn't have an effective HR planning system, these people going on international assignment are essentially taking a leap of faith.

As organizations move into the international arena, human resources staffs will become more adept at recognizing their company's global expansion objectives and plan international assignments more thoroughly. Only then will HR be able to develop company structures and policies that truly support each aspect of an international assignment. Some firms—large and small— are already doing that.

HR planning is key. Monsanto's repatriation program is a model of HR planning. It was created with the idea that all the pieces of the expatriate process work together. The $7.9 billion agricultural, chemical and pharmaceutical company has 30,000 employees with approximately 50 expatriates and 35 international employees working in the United States. International human resources managers get involved in predeparture assessment, cross-cultural counseling, performance management (see *Personnel Journal,* October 1994 issue for details) and other administrative aspects of the international assignment.

One of the strongest features of Monsanto's program is that employees and

Repatriation has been the classic stepchild in international HR management.

Nancy J. Adler
McGill University

their sending and receiving managers develop an agreement about their understanding of the assignment and how it fits into the company's business objectives. The focus is on why they're sending the assignee to do the job. This not only assures they have the same understanding, but also ensures that they've done serious thinking about the global assignment.

John Amato and Carol Jones, responsible for international assignments, developed the company's repatriation program in the fall of 1992. "We did it because the attrition rate was high," says Jones. "People felt they went out and were expecting career advancement and utilization of their knowledge. When that didn't happen, they would feel dissatisfied."

Now, says Amato, manager of human resources for international assignments, the repatriation piece creates significant movement toward globalization.

"This isn't touchy-feely stuff," he says. "We spent a lot of money to send this person out. By saying, 'Let's tap into them, let's give them a chance to tell others what they've learned,' the organization learns, and they feel valued. They know we appreciate their value, and the company sees a return on investment."

Expatriates who have international experience know the company values their expertise. They meet with cross-cultural trainers during debriefings and showcase their experience with their American peers, subordinates and superiors. "Because folks here know there's a resource they can tap into, it creates opportunities for that person to infuse knowledge back into the domestic organization," says Amato. "That gets you back to the employee's expectations and results in retention. It results in a circle." For example, he says expectation management is to create a clear understanding on the part of

Repatriation Planning Checklist

BY CHARLENE MARMER SOLOMON

Repatriation presents one of the most complex sets of issues facing international human resources managers today. Successful re-entry means that the employee reaps career and personal payoffs for the overseas experience, and that the company enriches its organization through the addition of the international competencies of its repatriated employees. Repatriation difficulties vary by company, by job type and by industry. High attrition rates at re-entry, poor integration of repatriated employees, lack of appropriate positions, downsized organizations and dissatisfied repatriated employees and families are some of the most frequently cited problems.

Although there's no easy, one-size-fits-all set of answers to the challenges of re-entry, there are guidelines that corporations can follow to positively facilitate the process. The following checklist targets: senior management involvement; expectation management; comprehensive career planning; selection and development processes that ensure that the expatriate acquires new capabilities; upgraded change management systems; and interventions to address the losses that repatriates experience.

Career Issues

Prior to departure

❏ Involve international human resources at corporate strategic levels when planning for international activities
❏ Clearly establish the need for the international assignment with input from home and host locations
❏ Utilize research-based selection processes to make certain that the employee and family are suitable and able to succeed abroad
❏ Provide cross-cultural and language training to increase effectiveness and adaptation overseas
❏ Offer career spouse counseling and assistance during assignment
❏ Outline a clear job description for the expatriate's position
❏ Communicate realistic expectations

about re-entry to employee at the time the position is offered
❏ Design career tracking and pathing systems that recognize and reward returning employees
❏ Establish expat developmental plans that include international competencies
❏ Link performance appraisals directly to developmental plans with home and host evaluators measuring performance
❏ Adapt performance appraisals to recognize the cultural demands of the assignment
❏ Feed performance appraisals into a larger internal human resource communication vehicle
❏ Appoint home and host *mentors* who are held accountable to track and support the employee during the assignment, and to identify potential positions at re-entry
❏ Send job postings to the expatriate while abroad
❏ Prior to return (one year to six months) arrange a networking visit to home office to establish viability with line and human resources managers
❏ Repeat networking visit three months prior to return if necessary
❏ Assist employee with polishing resume writing and interviewing skills
❏ Circulate resume to all potential hiring units
❏ Establish fallback position if no job is available
❏ Arrange for employee to maintain visibility through regular business trips home and through contact with visiting home-country personnel
❏ Create communication links to employee via E-mail, newsletters, copies of important memos and relevant publications
❏ Enable family members to stay in touch with changes at home through news publications
❏ Encourage employee and family to return *home* for home leave.

At Re-entry

❏ Arrange an event to welcome and recognize the employee and family, either formally or informally
❏ Establish support to facilitate family reintegration
❏ Offer repatriation counseling or work-

shops to ease adjustment
❏ Assist spouse with job counseling, resume writing and interviewing techniques
❏ Provide educational counseling for kids
❏ Provide employee with a thorough debriefing with a facilitator to identify new knowledge, insights and skills, forums to showcase new competencies, and activities that utilize competencies
❏ Offer international outplacement to employee and re-entry counseling to entire family if no positions are possible
❏ Arrange a post-assignment interview with expatriate and spouse to review their view of the assignment and address any repatriation issues.

Financial Planning and Related Activities

❏ Coordinate with home and host offices prior to repatriation to identify repatriation date
❏ Run cost projection with anticipated repatriation date to determine the most cost-effective time frame for departure
❏ Arrange pre-repatriation home country house hunting/school enrollment trip to allow for re-occupying/securing home country housing and registering dependent children for school.
❏ Arrange for shipment of personal goods.
❏ Identify dates for temporary living in home and host countries.
❏ Arrange tax exit interview for employee with tax service provider to determine need for tax clearance/final host country tax return to leave the country.
❏ Provide tax service provider with year-to-date compensation data for tax clearance/return processing.
❏ Process any relocation payment.
❏ Process return incentive payment.
❏ Process payroll documents to remove employee from expatriate status and review need for actual withholding payments for remainder of year with tax service provider.
❏ Provide HR generalist in new location with necessary personnel files.

Source: Bennett & Associates and Price Waterhouse LLP

the employee about the kind of job they're coming home to. Says Amato: "When you say to an employee, 'we value you and we expect the assignment to develop you. This is a career path move,' that means one thing." On the other hand, if supervisors are clear that the move is a project or technology transfer, expectations of the re-entry job is more likely to be in line with the company's future plans for these employees.

Monsanto's repatriation program focuses on more than just business—it attends to the family's re-entry. Sometimes the difficulty with repatriating has more to do with personal adjustment than with work-related matters. But, the personal matters affect the business.

Which is why Monsanto offers repatriating employees a way to work through personal difficulties. Approximately three months after their return, expats like David Cissell meet for about three hours at work with several colleagues of their choice. The *debriefing segment* is a conversation aided by a facilitator who has an outline to help the expatriate cover all the important aspects of the repatriation. Says Cissell, "It sounds silly, but it's such a hectic time in the family's life you don't have time to sit down and take stock of what's happening. You're going through the move, transitioning into a new job, a new house, the children may be going to a new school. This is a kind of oasis," he says, "a time to talk and to put your feelings on the table. The counselor (who is a consultant) leads you through and helps you understand what you're experiencing."

The debriefing segment serves several purposes: to allow the employee to share important experiences, to enlighten managers, colleagues and friends about his or her expertise and to share information so that others within the organization can use some of the global knowledge.

Cissell was moving into his current position. He invited his new boss (Monsanto's vice president of Latin America) as well as other colleagues and a friend. "It was pretty powerful," he says. Cissell talked about the business environment and how he saw European culture impacting that. "My boss had not lived internationally, and although he had an appreciation for cultural changes and things that go on as you move people around the world, he said that he had not really thought through some of it." That conversation really helped open up his eyes.

"We're trying to get the expatriates to be the shining stars out there to radiate their light," says Amato. The debriefing helps others who travel overseas and teaches them how to get more knowledge while they're out there. "In that way, repatriation builds on itself."

Returning assignees need to know the next step. One of the most important questions that anyone can ask an expat is, "What is the next assignment going to be?"—the one after the international assignment, says Avon's Campbell. "The problem is that often the assigning manager doesn't pay attention to what the person is going to be doing next."

The issue becomes particularly important during these days of reengineering and downsizing because often the job this person left has been cut as part of cost-reduction maneuvers. Even though organizations have more difficulty planning far ahead, if companies carefully monitored their expats, they could better prepare for their return.

"Everybody blames this process [poor repatriation] on ineffective career pathing and career planning, which companies have a hard time doing because we're in such a changing environment," says Michael Schell, president of New York-based Windham International. "We can't even tell people who are in the U.S. that if they finish a particular assignment, they'll have a specific job, let alone people who are going on assignment and who will be out of sight."

It's too difficult to do. Therefore, what becomes very important is to watch the performance of the person while on assignment. Then, when there are openings they're qualified for, the employee can be moved into those positions. "That monitoring of career progress doesn't usually take place effectively when people are on expatriate assignment," says Schell. "Therefore, we don't know how well they succeed; how much they fall, or what they can do for us when they come home."

In this complex system, there's a strong relationship between a successful assignment, adequate performance management and good repatriation. Effective HR planning that includes accurate performance evaluation (by someone who understands the assignment and its specific limitations) is one of the underlying requirements for a successful assignment

> ## It's such a hectic time in your family's life you don't sit down and take stock of what's happening.
>
> *David L. Cissell*
> *Monsanto Corporation*

and reintegration into the organization. In addition, employees feel they're being considered and aren't being forgotten while out of the country.

And, companies don't have to be large to have successful expatriate programs. Coherent, Inc., a $200 million Santa Clara, California-based company that makes scientific and medical lasers, has an innovative approach to repatriation. The company has 1,500 employees overall and about 400 in the medical division, with sales and service offices in the United Kingdom, France, Germany, Japan and Hong Kong. With only six expatriates and one third-country national (TCN) in the medical division, the department had been handling expatriates on a case-by-case basis until 1994, when they began formalizing their policies.

The company's inventive programs brings people back to the United States on a short-term project before they're repatriated. Employees who are ready to come back to the United States return for a couple of months to do projects that they're very qualified to do. Then, they go back to their host country to wrap things up and then come back full time.

"It allows them to get to know the area, to spend some real time back here instead of just a five-day house-hunting trip, and allows them to get reacquainted with people in the office, the lifestyle and the work style, she says. They're even doing it with a third-country national.

Coherent, Inc. factors in one other critical component—maintaining close contact with the expats. "It's not like they're gone and forgotten," says Chan. They come back on a regular basis a couple of times a year as well as for the annual sales meeting. In addition, during quarterly sales meetings, directors talk about these employees. Their work is visible and talked about.

There are two crucial parts underlying their repatriation policy, says Chan. First, "These people are super-duper employees. Their expertise is needed here, so they're an excellent resource for a project when they're asked to come back and work here." Secondly, when they spend time here, their faces become more familiar to the rest of the employees and it makes the transition into their new role easier when they return."

Chan believes that expatriate assignments are attractive to employees not only because the assignments themselves are good, but because expats know they will be repatriated well. Because excellent employees are sent on international assignment, typically there are jobs awaiting their return.

Coherent, like Monsanto, has strategies in place to make the repatriation process go more smoothly. Furthermore, they only send their best people.

Whether the company is large or small, this is a fundamental contribution to good repatriation. Says Richard P. Randazzo, Asea Brown Boveri, Inc. (ABB's) senior vice president of human resources of the America's region, "The first step to successful repatriation is don't send anybody anyplace that you're not willing to take back. Ninety-nine percent of the repatriation problem—if you have a problem—is caused by sending somebody someplace that you're looking to get rid of."

If they're good, says Randazzo, the sending organization generally starts to make noise about getting them back even before their global assignment is completed. Wherever that next assignment comes, the knowledge they've acquired on their expatriate job is valued. ABB, the $30 billion transnational giant with more than 220,000 employees around the world, designates the sponsoring manager with the responsibility of finding a new position for the international assignee (although it usually falls to the local HR manager). The process starts about six months prior to the conclusion of the expatriate project. First, as the succession-planning process occurs each year, they devote time to talking about expats—who is out, who is coming back and when. In some cases, the individual will send resumes to a select group of HR managers that may have an opportunity for a person with those skills. Or, Randazzo may know of opportunities.

"The rule is that good performers always will find opportunity within the company," says Randazzo. "If somebody is very good, invariably they'll come back in good shape."

Personal difficulties also affect business adjustments. Even if employees do well in business, some of their trouble readjusting may come from family difficulties. Part of their difficulty in readjusting may be because they've been disconnected from domestic headquarters and left out-of-touch. Consequently, they don't know what to expect upon return.

Intel, the $8 billion-plus computer chip maker located in Santa Clara, California, with almost 30,000 employees, makes a strong effort to keep expats involved in the organization throughout the international assignment. Employees in the company's sites around the world keep in touch frequently via phone, E-mail and video conferencing. They do this as part of their ongoing work assignment, whether they're in California or in Europe. In an effort to keep employees and their families informed—and aware of Intel's business agenda, the company created several books detailing various aspects of the expatriation experience, including information about considering an assignment (for the family as well as employees) and a tool kit for managers regarding selection and preparation. One important component deals with repatriation.

The book details the cycle of *re-entry shock* and why re-entry may be difficult. It raises questions that people may not think of on their own, such as the letdown that occurs upon return and the lifestyle/benefits that will change when they go home. It prepares them for feeling alienated and distanced from their friends and colleagues, and addresses the family issues such as children who might have a difficult time fitting in when they go back to school.

"The repatriation piece is probably the most often overlooked part of the assignment," says Sharon Richards, intercultural training program manager, who created the expatriate books and is instrumental in the company's training programs. However thorough the repatriation booklets, Intel's re-entry process begins well before repatriation. "We believe in training because you need to set realistic expectations for the employee and the family. You're going to have a better shot at success." Intel had a large number of people on a project in Ireland. Before their return, the company conducted a *road show*. They gathered people and had a day-long training session about taxes, relocation, shipping goods. Half the day was spent talking about what it would be like to return home.

One key area that Richards believes is often overlooked is the culture shock expats experience during re-entry. To

> # We help expats identify two or three key things they want to communicate with others.
>
> *Sharon Richards*
> *Intel Corporation*

facilitate the adaptation process, it's critical for expats to know that repatriation is likely to be difficult. "They think, `My friends are there. It shouldn't be any problem at all.' In fact, they're likely to have the initial sense of euphoria they did when they went on assignment, and to enjoy all that they missed when they were gone, but then they will also make comparisons in reverse. They've grown and changed, and they go through an adjustment period similar to the one they experienced when they first went on assignment."

Another important component is putting the assignment into perspective. People are so full with what they want to tell others, that it's overwhelming. They don't anticipate that friends and co-workers may not be interested in their adventures, and may in fact be envious when they try to recap them. "We help expats identify two or three key important things they want to communicate with others," says Richards. "Then, we suggest that they be sensitive to other people. Before launching into a story, ask what has changed in their life and what occurred while the expatriate was gone."

In order to take advantage of the international experience—and to continue to acknowledge the expat's knowledge—Richards has repatriated employees participate in predeparture training and culture-specific training whenever possible. Not only do the expats enjoy it, but their words of wisdom help the prospective international assignee.

Job security brings expatriates full circle. Beyond the crucial personal aspects of repatriation, Richards acknowledges that having a job upon return is probably one of the most important factors to a successful return. At Intel, she says, they're careful to move people only when they have a specific reason— such as training, a project or a special assignment. Although there are no job guarantees, they

make efforts to use the experience of international assignees as much as possible. In addition, because HR planning works in tandem with the business objectives, expats are monitored and performance is managed and appraised.

Indeed, not all organizations today, however, are able to be as sure as they once were about having a job awaiting an employee's return. "There are so many double-edged swords," says Noel A. Kreicker, president and founder of International Orientation Resources. International HR is aware and committed to resolving and supporting the repatriation issues as well as creating supportive programs and clarifying policies. However, in many cases, HR's hands are tied because corpo-

rations are still so busy sorting themselves out. Usually, it's the people who are repatriating who have been forgotten. Not only does HR face the task of helping to prepare and maintain the individual on international assignment, it plays an important role in bringing the employee back to the United States and helping the company to capitalize on its investment. "It's one of the most difficult realities now," he says. But no matter how challenging, there are organizations, large and small, that are meeting it. In companies like Monsanto, Intel, Coherent and ABB, people who are selected well, monitored carefully and shown that the company recognizes and values them, feel rewarded, recognized and will continue to make contributions when they return.

Off and running in Vietnam

With the trade embargo lifted, companies such as Unisys are scurrying to get in on the ground floor.

Andrea Knox

Inquirer *Staff Writer*

In August, when it was clear that it was only a matter of time until the United States would lift its 19-year embargo on trade with Vietnam, Roger Stone paid a call on Vietnam's Ministry of Science, Technology and Communication.

Stone, Unisys Corp.'s general manager for Southeast Asia, was with a colleague from Japan's Mitsui Corp., which has been trading in Vietnam for nearly a century.

The ministry was trying to set guidelines for modernizing Vietnam's computer and telephone systems, but was painfully aware that the country's long isolation meant that few Vietnamese knew much, if anything, about state-of-the art technology.

So Stone made an offer: At no charge to the Vietnamese for its services, Unisys would help the government prepare its information-technology strategy.

Over the following six months, Unisys brought 14 experts to Hanoi for varying lengths of time to work with the ministers. The result was a framework, called IT (for Information Technology) 2000, to guide the country's decision-making in everything from telecommunications standards to technical education.

Now the plan is complete, and various government ministries are beginning to make decisions about computer systems, telephone networks and technical educa-

tion. And Unisys, in the person of recently appointed Vietnam general manager Maureen Flanagan, is on hand in Hanoi to explain the functions and features of different kinds of hardware, software and networks.

Soon, the government will ask for bids on several computer systems to be installed this year. Unisys expects to win at least one of the contracts, Flanagan said last week in a telephone interview from Hanoi.

Such are the stirrings of commercial activity in Vietnam, less than a month after President Clinton's Feb. 3 lifting of the embargo. Although U.S. companies are now free to resume a full range of trade and investment activities, results in terms of sales and investments will still be some time in coming.

Despite Vietnam's poverty and lack of development, more than a few companies want to get in on the ground floor of what they expect will be yet another Asian success story.

Most are providers of basic economic building blocks, consulting services or high-demand consumer products. Locally, they include:

- DuPont Co., which expects to begin selling its Londax rice herbicide this year. The company has been working since last year to obtain sales permits and will open a sales office in Ho Chi Minh City—formerly Saigon—within the next few months. Heading the office is Vietnamese-born Khiet Trankiem, who has been with DuPont for

about 20 years after joining the company in the United States.

- K-Tron International Inc., a Cherry Hill manufacturer of industrial feeders and mixers, whose customers include some European cement manufacturers that are major players in the global cement business. Those companies are now seeking footholds in Vietnam, and K-Tron expects to be there with them, says chief executive officer Marcel O. Rohr.

- SmithKline Beecham, which has been supplying Vietnam with the Amoxil antibiotic, Engerix B hepatitis B vaccine and Tagamet anti-ulcer drugs since the Bush administration lifted restrictions on humanitarian supplies in April 1992. SmithKline recently hired an expatriate Vietnamese to begin setting up a sales organization.

- Hillier Group, a Princeton architectural firm, which has teamed with Gannon Cos., a St. Louis construction company, to explore the possibility of putting up office buildings and resort hotels, as well as Western-style residential complexes for businesspeople with families on long-term assignment in Vietnam. The venture has opened an office, identified promising sites and is holding discussions with potential investors.

- Zippo Manufacturing Co., of Bradford, Pa., which would like to sell

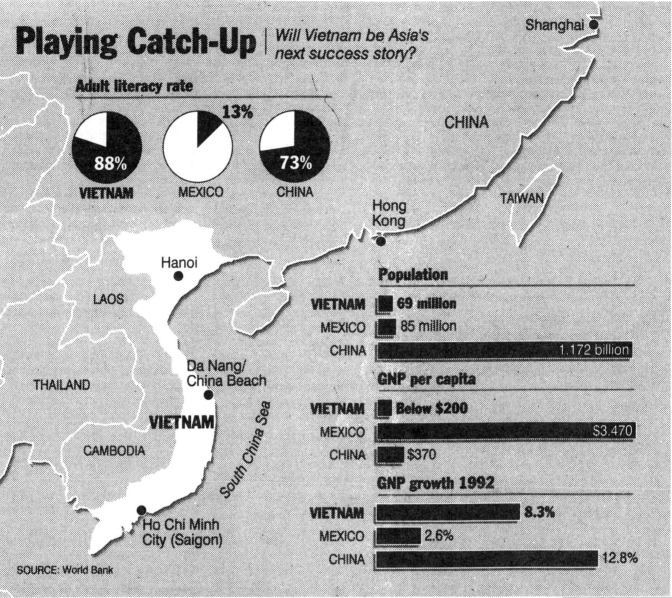

Playing Catch-Up | *Will Vietnam be Asia's next success story?*

Adult literacy rate

88% VIETNAM — 13% MEXICO — 73% CHINA

Shanghai

CHINA

TAIWAN

Hong Kong

Hanoi

LAOS

THAILAND

Da Nang/ China Beach

VIETNAM

South China Sea

CAMBODIA

Ho Chi Minh City (Saigon)

SOURCE: World Bank

Population

VIETNAM	69 million
MEXICO	85 million
CHINA	1.172 billion

GNP per capita

VIETNAM	Below $200
MEXICO	$3,470
CHINA	$370

GNP growth 1992

VIETNAM	8.3%
MEXICO	2.6%
CHINA	12.8%

The Philadelphia Inquirer / ROGER HASLER

genuine Zippos in Vietnam to replace the counterfeits now sold there. While some real Zippos have reached the country through a Hong Kong distributor, sales have been "nothing to write home about," says James A. Baldo, vice president of sales and marketing. Baldo plans a trip to Vietnam in August to set up stronger sales channels · in the country.

• Scott Paper Co., whose products can occasionally be found in Vietnam, thanks to distributors in Thailand and other Asian countries. Scott has begun a search for Vietnamese distributors.

Unisys and Vietnam, in particular, seem made for each other because of

Unisys' expertise in telecommunications, banking, government and airlines.

"The correlation between our strengths and the demands of this market is very close," says Stone, who spoke by telephone from Hanoi. "The development of banking and government infrastructure is at the top of the Vietnam government's list. And the telephone company will get as much of the available government funds as almost any other entity in Vietnam."

Vietnam will buy its computer and telephone equipment—like its roads, bridges, cement factories and power plants—largely with loans and grants from the world's developed nations, which pledged $1.87 billion to Vietnam in November. Additional commitments of at least that amount are expected in

each of the next three years, according to Stone.

The Vietnamese government has earmarked about $130 million of the first year's financing for computerization projects, including technology training and computerized management systems for the tax and treasury departments, Stone says.

The state of Vietnam's computerization roughly parallels that of its roads—only 12 percent paved—and indicates both the opportunities and the difficulties created by the country's lack of development.

While government agencies own a few personal computers, they are all stand-alone devices with no way of sharing information, says Flanagan, who came to Vietnam a year ago for Digital Equip-

239

ment Corp. and joined Unisys just last week.

With no obsolete mainframes to worry about, and no installed jumble of incompatible personal computers, the country is free to adopt the most advanced technology from the outset, Stone says.

On the other hand, managers and even computer professionals are still struggling to understand state-of-the-art computer systems, says Flanagan.

At times, she despaired of ever making a sale, Flanagan says. "They didn't understand the cost, the procurement process, how to define a system or what a system would do for the country or a ministry."

Architect Hank Abernathy of Hillier Group first saw Vietnam from the deck of a Navy destroyer in 1968. Like many visitors, both then and now, he was captivated by a beauty that even war couldn't conceal.

Three months ago, Abernathy saw those beaches from land for the first time and found they had lost none of their charm. Which was just as well, because he was there prospecting locations for the resort hotels he hopes he will design

and that the Gannon Cos. will build.

At least one, they hope, will be at China Beach, near Danang, famous during the Vietnam War as a rest and recreation area for GIs.

"It's just a beautiful beach," says Gannon senior vice president Stephen Hayes, who manned a river patrol boat in Vietnam during the war and is a childhood friend of Abernathy's.

It's not clear when any of Gannon's construction projects—hotels, office buildings, or compounds for Western business people—might come to fruition. The company is talking with "a major U.S. hotel chain" about the resort hotel idea and is "quite far along" in finding investors for at least one residential compound, Hayes says.

In the meantime, Gannon hopes to get Americans to China Beach by other means. The company plans to offer tours to Vietnam starting this summer, including visits to Danang and China Beach—a special draw, he hopes, for vets who remember it from the war.

In fact, for many Americans, the lure of Vietnam seems to be personal as much as commercial. Their conversations

about Vietnam frequently take on an emotional quality quite foreign to most business discussions.

Some had a feeling for Vietnam deeply imprinted on them during the war. Abernathy says publicity about his involvement in Vietnam has attracted inquiries about commercial possibilities from a number of vets. But, he says, "maybe it's more that they want a way to go back for a visit. . . . There's a part of us we've not been able to let go of."

Others, like Unisys' Stone, didn't need the war to develop a special attachment for the country. "Hanoi, especially, is very seductive," he says. "The people are very charming." All 14 members of the project team that Unisys brought to the country want to return, he says.

"There was something about Vietnam that caught their attention and imagination. It generates a strong feeling that makes you want to contribute in something like an altruistic way. I got caught up in this, too. There is something more than just commercial interest. There's a sense of being part of something that, if done right, could be fantastic."

Credits/ Acknowledgments

Cover design by Charles Vitelli

1. The Nature of International Business

Facing overview—Ford Motor Company photo.

2. The International Environment

Facing overview—New York Stock Exchange photo.

3. Foreign Environment

Facing overview—United Nations photo by Derek Lovejoy.

4. How Management Deals with Environmental Forces

Facing overview—Liaison Agency photo, NY.

ANNUAL EDITIONS ARTICLE REVIEW FORM

■ NAME: _____ DATE: _____

■ TITLE AND NUMBER OF ARTICLE: _____

■ BRIEFLY STATE THE MAIN IDEA OF THIS ARTICLE: _____

_____

_____

_____

_____

■ LIST THREE IMPORTANT FACTS THAT THE AUTHOR USES TO SUPPORT THE MAIN IDEA:

_____

_____

_____

_____

_____

_____

■ WHAT INFORMATION OR IDEAS DISCUSSED IN THIS ARTICLE ARE ALSO DISCUSSED IN YOUR
TEXTBOOK OR OTHER READING YOU HAVE DONE? LIST THE TEXTBOOK CHAPTERS AND PAGE
NUMBERS:

_____

_____

_____

_____

_____

_____

■ LIST ANY EXAMPLES OF BIAS OR FAULTY REASONING THAT YOU FOUND IN THE ARTICLE:

_____

_____

_____

_____

■ LIST ANY NEW TERMS/CONCEPTS THAT WERE DISCUSSED IN THE ARTICLE AND WRITE A
SHORT DEFINITION:

_____

_____

_____

_____

_____

*Your instructor may require you to use this Annual Editions Article Review Form in any number of ways:
for articles that are assigned, for extra credit, as a tool to assist in developing assigned papers, or simply
for your own reference. Even if it is not required, we encourage you to photocopy and use this page;
you'll find that reflecting on the articles will greatly enhance the information from your text.

ANNUAL EDITIONS:
INTERNATIONAL BUSINESS 96/97
Article Rating Form

Here is an opportunity for you to have direct input into the next revision of this volume. We would like you to rate each of the 46 articles listed below, using the following scale:

1. **Excellent: should definitely be retained**
2. **Above average: should probably be retained**
3. **Below average: should probably be deleted**
4. **Poor: should definitely be deleted**

Your ratings will play a vital part in the next revision. So please mail this prepaid form to us just as soon as you complete it.
Thanks for your help!

Annual Editions revisions depend on two major opinion sources: one is our Advisory Board, listed in the front of this volume, which works with us in scanning the thousands of articles published in the public press each year; the other is you—the person actually using the book. Please help us and the users of the next edition by completing the prepaid article rating form on this page and returning it to us. Thank you.

Rating	Article	Rating	Article
	1. Global Growth Is on a Tear		26. The Harmonization of Standards in the European Union and the Impact on U.S. Business
	2. The Challenge Grows Thornier		
	3. The New Power in Asia		
	4. Second Thoughts on Going Global		27. Industrial Sea Change: How Changes in Keiretsu Are Opening the Japanese Market
	5. Capital and the Division of Production: Global at Last?		
	6. International Trade and Investment		28. The New Sexenio
	7. From GATT to WTO: The Institutionalization of World Trade		29. A Note on International Market Leaders and Networks of Strategic Technology Partnering
	8. Hemispheric Prospects: NAFTA Changes the Game		
	9. Toward Greater International Stability and Cooperation		30. Global Retailing 2000
			31. Planning for International Trade Show Participation: A Practitioner's Perspective
	10. Global Financial Markets in 2020		
	11. Financing Trade with Latin America		32. Forming International Sales Pacts
	12. European Monetary Reform: Pitfalls of Central Planning		33. Export Channel Design: The Use of Foreign Distributors and Agents
	13. Gradualism and Chinese Financial Reforms		34. Moving Mountains to Market: Reflections on Restructuring the Russian Economy
	14. Putting Global Logic First		35. Yes, You *Can* Win in Eastern Europe
	15. Latin America Heats Up		36. A Framework for Risk Management
	16. Asian Infrastructure: The Biggest Bet on Earth		37. Negotiating the Honeyed Knife-Edge
			38. Timberland's New Spin on Global Logistics
	17. India: Behind the Hype		
	18. Ethics in the Trenches		39. North American Business Integration
	19. Cultural Awareness: An Essential Element of Doing Business Abroad		40. A Global Glance at Work and Family
			41. Lessons from HR Overseas
	20. American Involvement in Vietnam, Part II: Prospects for U.S. Business in a New Era		42. The Right Way to Go Global: An Interview with Whirlpool CEO David Whitwam
	21. Political Risk Analysis in North American Multinationals: An Empirical Review and Assessment		
			43. The Son Also Surprises
			44. Transnational Management Systems: An Emerging Tool for Global Strategic Management
	22. Group of 7 Defines Policies about Telecommunications		
	23. What GATT Means to Small Business		45. Repatriation: Up, Down, or Out?
	24. High-Tech Jobs All over the Map		46. Off and Running in Vietnam
	25. Role of Labor, Environmental, and Human Rights Groups in Trade: Is There a New Protectionist Cabal?		

(Continued on next page)

ABOUT YOU

Name_____ Date_____

Are you a teacher? ☐   Or student? ☐

Your School Name _____

Department _____

Address _____

City _____ State _____ Zip _____

School Telephone # _____

YOUR COMMENTS ARE IMPORTANT TO US!

Please fill in the following information:

For which course did you use this book? _____

Did you use a text with this Annual Edition?   ☐ yes   ☐ no

The title of the text? _____

What are your general reactions to the Annual Editions concept?

Have you read any particular articles recently that you think should be included in the next edition?

Are there any articles you feel should be replaced in the next edition? Why?

Are there other areas that you feel would utilize an Annual Edition?

May we contact you for editorial input?

May we quote you from above?